Presenting Your Data
with **SPSS** Explained

Presenting Your Data with SPSS Explained provides you with all the information you need to conduct small-scale analysis of research projects using SPSS and present your results appropriately in a report. Quantitative data can be collected in the form of a questionnaire, survey or experimental study. This book focuses on presenting your data clearly, in the form of tables and graphs, along with creating basic summary statistics. *Presenting Your Data with SPSS Explained* uses an example survey that is explained step by step throughout the book. This allows readers to follow the procedures and easily apply each step in the process to their own research and findings.

No prior knowledge of statistics or SPSS is assumed and everything in the book is carefully explained in a helpful and user-friendly way using worked examples. This book is the perfect companion for students from a range of disciplines including psychology, business, communication, education, health, humanities, marketing and nursing – many of whom are unaware that this extremely helpful program is available at their institution for their use.

Perry Hinton is a social psychologist at the University of Warwick. He has taught the use of SPSS to a wide range of students from disciplines including communication and media, education, linguistics, nursing, psychology and social work. He is joint author of *SPSS Explained*, also published by Routledge. His own research is on interpersonal perception and he has written three books on the topic.

Isabella McMurray is a developmental psychologist at the University of Bedfordshire. She has taught SPSS to students in psychology, applied social studies and nursing and is joint author of *SPSS Explained*, also published by Routledge. Isabella undertakes consultancy, training and research with local authorities and charities, including working with social workers, probation services, parenting programmes, education and road safety teams.

Presenting Your Data with SPSS Explained

PERRY R. HINTON AND ISABELLA McMURRAY

Routledge
Taylor & Francis Group

LONDON AND NEW YORK

First published 2017
by Routledge
2 Park Square, Milton Park, Abingdon, Oxon OX14 4RN

and by Routledge
711 Third Avenue, New York, NY 10017

Routledge is an imprint of the Taylor & Francis Group, an informa business

British Library Cataloguing in Publication Data
A catalogue record for this book is available from the British Library

Library of Congress Cataloging in Publication Data
A catalog record for this book has been requested

ISBN: 978-1-138-91659-3 (hbk)
ISBN: 978-1-138-91660-9 (pbk)
ISBN: 978-1-315-68952-4 (ebk)

Typeset in Berkeley and Stone Sans
by Florence Production, Stoodleigh, Devon, UK

Printed and bound in Great Britain by Bell and Bain Ltd, Glasgow

To Anna, Anthony and Emma

To Vicky, Lizzie, Joe, Molly and James

Contents

Preface   *ix*
Acknowledgements   *xi*

CHAPTER 1   INTRODUCTION   **1**
THE EXAMPLE STUDY USED THROUGHOUT THE BOOK   3
THE BOOK OUTLINE   4

CHAPTER 2   UNDERTAKING A RESEARCH PROJECT   **9**
THE RESEARCH PROCESS   10
STAGE 1: THE PURPOSE OF THE RESEARCH   11
STAGE 2: SETTING UP THE STUDY   14
STAGE 3: CARRYING OUT THE RESEARCH AND COLLECTING
    THE DATA   29
STAGE 4: MAKING SENSE OF THE DATA   30
STAGE 5 PRESENTING THE RESEARCH FINDINGS   32

CHAPTER 3   WHAT ARE YOU MEASURING IN YOUR RESEARCH?   **37**
DESCRIBING YOUR RESULTS   39
LEVELS OF MEASUREMENT: NOMINAL, SCALE AND ORDINAL
    DATA   39
CONSTRUCTING NOMINAL, SCALE OR ORDINAL OUTCOME
    MEASURES   48
CODING YOUR DATA FOR INPUT INTO SPSS   55
THE SPARCOTE STUDY   56

CHAPTER 4   ENTERING DATA INTO SPSS   **69**
A FIRST LOOK AT SPSS   70
SETTING UP THE SPSS DATASET (YOUR RESULTS SPREADSHEET)   73

ENTERING THE DATA INTO SPSS   84
EDITING THE DATASET   87
TRANSFERRING THE RESULTS FROM OTHER SOFTWARE INTO SPSS   89
A FINAL CHECK OF YOUR DATASET   106

CHAPTER 5   **A FIRST LOOK AT THE RESULTS**   **107**
OPENING AN SPSS DATA FILE   107
THE IBM SPSS STATISTICS VIEWER   109
DESCRIPTIVE STATISTICS FOR EACH VARIABLE   110
THE FREQUENCIES COMMAND   111
A FIRST DESCRIPTION OF THE SPARCOTE STUDY RESULTS   124
DESCRIBING THE RESULTS OF A SINGLE VARIABLE   150

CHAPTER 6   **CREATING TABLES**   **151**
CREATING TABLES IN SPSS   152
CROSSTABULATING DATA   152
THE CROSSTABS COMMAND   154
INTRODUCTION TO CUSTOM TABLES   169

CHAPTER 7   **CREATING GRAPHS**   **199**
CHOOSING A CHART   200
USING CHART BUILDER   209
CREATE GRAPH – GENERATING GRAPHS FROM OUTPUT TABLES   233

CHAPTER 8   **EDITING TABLES AND GRAPHS FOR PRESENTATION**   **243**
EDITING A TABLE – PIVOT TABLE   243
EDITING A CHART – CHART EDITOR   268
EXPORTING TABLES AND GRAPHS TO OTHER APPLICATIONS   303

CHAPTER 9   **AN INTRODUCTION TO STATISTICAL TESTS IN SPSS**   **307**
WHY PERFORM A STATISTICAL TEST?   309
UNDERTAKING STATISTICAL TESTS WITH SPSS   312
LOOKING FOR RELATIONSHIPS BETWEEN VARIABLES   312
THE CHI-SQUARE TEST OF AN ASSOCIATION BETWEEN CATEGORICAL
   VARIABLES   314
THE PEARSON TEST OF A LINEAR RELATIONSHIP BETWEEN SCALE
   VARIABLES   319
THE t TEST FOR COMPARING TWO CATEGORIES ON A SCALE
   MEASURE   325

Glossary   *331*
Index   *341*

Preface

IBM SPSS is an easy-to-use software package for data analysis. It can perform all sorts of analysis from a simple adding up of results to extremely complex statistical procedures. SPSS may be a package that you have heard of but not necessarily something that you have thought about using before. The very idea of conducting statistical analyses might seem rather complicated and not something that you have been taught in depth in your studies. However, SPSS has the capability of producing straightforward summary statistics for describing a set of data (such as totals, percentages or averages) alongside its more complex analyses. Users can choose exactly what they want to do. It also has an excellent facility to quickly and easily generate a range of clear and attractive graphs (such as pie charts, bar charts or line graphs) and tables in which to present your findings. It also allows you to edit and organise these graphs and tables so they are displayed exactly as you wish. While a number of other programs allow you to produce tables and graphs, these often do not have the flexibility of SPSS. SPSS is available in most universities on a site-wide licence, for all staff and students to use in their academic work and so for students undertaking a research project or dissertation their institution will usually be able to supply a licensed copy for their personal use.

We have between us many years' experience as teachers of research methods and data analysis to students in the disciplines of psychology, media, social studies, education studies, health and communication studies and have worked as supervisors of students' own small-scale research projects as part of their undergraduate or postgraduate studies. We have seen how often students open SPSS with trepidation and then very quickly start to navigate around the commands to produce professional-looking graphs and tables that they include in their reports. Furthermore, our experience as researchers working alongside organisations has shown us that often organisations just want a concise summary of the findings from small-scale research rather than a more detailed in-depth statistical analysis. Therefore this book is ideal for someone doing a small-scale piece of research. We have seen over the years the rise in sophisticated online survey packages such 'Survey Monkey' and 'Qualtrics' in student research, which provide the user with an opportunity to access participants who may be hard to reach with face-to-face surveys. These online survey programs allow you to save the survey data in an SPSS format for ease of transfer to, and analysis by, SPSS. However, we know that the step from producing the data to actually creating tables and graphs of the results can be difficult without assistance and so a suitable textbook can be a great help in supporting your own data analysis. However, many SPSS books assume that students are already undertaking a detailed programme of research methods and data analysis training and therefore it can be a challenge to know exactly what to do for students who have had much less – or little – research training prior to their project work. This book does not assume that the reader has had such training. The above was the impetus for writing this book.

When writing this book our students were at the forefront of our minds. We have drawn on the discussions we have had with our students, when acting as their project supervisor, to guide the explanations in the book. We questioned how our students go through the process of conducting research and what questions they have asked their supervisor. We also understand the value of practical examples in helping to explain the various stages of data analysis and the production of tables and graphs. Therefore, throughout the book, we have selected a range of examples to illustrate the points being made. Also we follow a single example throughout the book, of a small-scale survey, undertaken in a (fictional) university called Sparcote University, from the original research idea through to producing a variety of tables and graphs using SPSS to describe the results. We believe that you will be able to relate our examples to your research project to guide your data analysis for presentation.

Acknowledgements

We are particularly grateful to IBM SPSS for allowing us to join their IBM SPSS Academic Authors Program and providing us with the latest version of SPSS. We would like to thank our friends and former colleagues Charlotte Brownlow and Bob Cozens; it was with Charlotte and Bob 17 years ago that we started discussing how we could use the questions that our students asked us about SPSS to produce a book that would be helpful for their work. Together we produced *SPSS Explained* (first edition 2004, second edition 2014), also published by Routledge, which was directed at social science students, particularly in psychology, often undertaking detailed experimental analysis.

Introduction

3 THE EXAMPLE
STUDY USED
THROUGHOUT THE
BOOK

4 THE BOOK OUTLINE

Chapter aim: To introduce SPSS, our example survey and an outline of the book

SPSS is an excellent software package for statistical analysis, that can be easily used to produce simple statistical summarises of data (such as totals and means) or, for those who wish to, undertake complex statistical modelling. Its windows interface means that it is quite intuitive to use regardless of what you want to do. SPSS is commonly available at universities where the licence allows both staff and students to have a personal copy of the software to use with their academic research data. SPSS is particularly popular in the social sciences, but is used by staff and students in a variety of departments in universities, for research in marketing, health, education and the media (to name but a few) and outside universities for data analysis by a wide range of different organisations. The accessibility and ease of use of SPSS means that it can do a lot more than complex statistics. Numerical data can be beautifully presented visually in graphs and tables. With SPSS, you can create graphs and tables at a click of the button and effectively present numerical information, which can easily be transferred to word-processing software for a written report or presentation software for an oral presentation.

You may be about to start a research project at university, examining feedback from a group of people, undertaking some form of product evaluation or wanting to make sense of some published data from an organisation such as a government office. Whatever you are doing, you will have an overall aim for your study that is examined through a research question or hypothesis. Using SPSS, you will be able to summarise the research data in the form of tables and graphs so that you can make sense of the numbers that you have collected, and the reader of your report will gain an insight into what the numbers mean in relation to your aim, question or hypothesis.

SPSS is an easy-to-use program, employing familiar features, such as windows, toolbars and menus. The data you wish to analyse is entered into a spreadsheet similar in format to other spreadsheet programs such as Microsoft Excel. However, it allows you to label your data, giving you the option to display either the actual numbers or the labels in the window. Rather than viewing only lists of numbers in your spreadsheet, where appropriate you can see the data in terms of meaningful words. For example, in the example data below we can see, in the first column, the gender of each of the participants who took part in the survey, with each row showing the responses of a different participant to the survey questions.

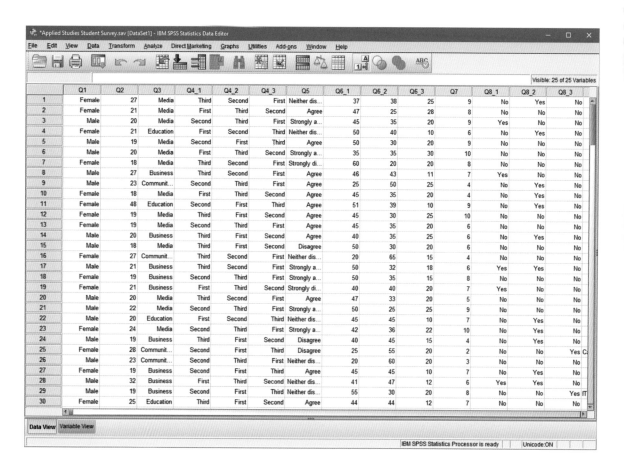

SPSS is made up of drop-down menus, commands and options that enable you to generate tables and graphs (as well as undertaking different statistical analyses). We will go through these step by step and explain the different outputs that can be produced. For example, in the following screenshots, we see that there is a drop-down menu called **Graphs** and the first option is a command called **Chart Builder**. When explaining an SPSS procedure we will highlight the SPSS instructions in bold.

When this is clicked, a **Chart Builder** window appears and by selecting a chart or graph, and dragging and dropping the data into place, you can easily produce the chart that you want. Even after you have created the chart, you can still change any of the features of it through the simple editing process, before saving it to use in your report.

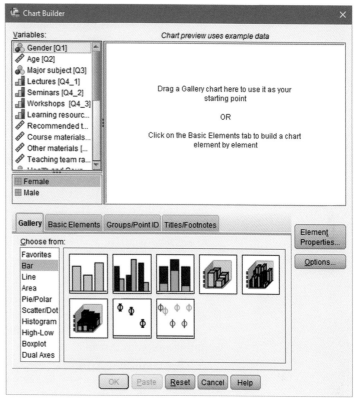

THE EXAMPLE STUDY USED THROUGHOUT THE BOOK

We believe that when learning anything new it is helpful to follow an example that you can relate to your own work. There are number of different examples of small-scale research that are used to describe the different features of SPSS throughout the book, drawing on the different types of research that you might yourself undertake. We follow a step-by-step process of demonstrating each feature of SPSS using our examples but these procedures can be followed using your own data. We shall also describe one example in detail throughout the book, which we have called the Sparcote Study, that we will employ to illustrate the different research concepts, numerical and statistical terms. Also, this will involve describing a survey in detail, explaining how it is constructed, carried out and how the data is input into SPSS and analysed to produce professional-looking tables and graphs to summarise the research findings.

The Sparcote Study

The example we have chosen is of a small-scale piece of descriptive research undertaken in a (fictional) university. Sparcote University is a small campus university on the edge of the city of Sparcote. One year ago the university took in its first cohort of students in the new Department of Applied Studies. At the end of the first year the department wants to review the success of the programme. As part of the review, two of the staff members are undertaking a small research study with the aim of finding out about the students' experiences during their first year in the new Department of Applied Studies. This is the Sparcote Study that we will be referring to throughout the book.

THE BOOK OUTLINE

The chapters are set out so that the reader can work through the book either prior to collecting data or after their data collection has been completed. The chapters will take you through the different types of data that you have collected and explain how to summarise and present them using SPSS. We describe the types of table and graph you can use with different sorts of data and the different SPSS commands you can use to produce them. The book is designed so that you can dip into any chapter to find the procedure you are interested in, as well as following through the chapters to see how we have analysed the data in our examples.

Chapter 2

Chapter 2 introduces you to the process of doing a research study starting with the very important issue of deciding what your research is all about. When considering your research aim(s) and your specific question(s) you will need to think about the purpose of your research: to explore 'new territory', describe a particular situation or test a prediction. When you know what you want to research, and why, the next thing to think about is how to carry it out. While there are a number of different research methods (such as interviews, experiments or surveys), this book focuses on analysing the results of those methods where the research data is collected in the form of numbers rather than spoken or written text. Research questions such as *how many? how much? how long?* all produce numeric data in the results. If the research involves people (asking people to participate in the study to generate the results) then this requires a consideration of who and how many people to ask (called 'sampling') and how to treat them (referred to as 'research ethics'). Once data has been collected, you need to describe and summarise it for communicating to others, usually in the form of a written report. It is at this stage of the research process that SPSS can be extremely helpful, as we explain throughout the book. This chapter also provides an overview of the basic terms used in summarising your data.

Chapter 3

This chapter explains that not all numbers collected in research are the same. Sometimes we collect numbers as names, such as the number on the shirts of the members of a sports team. The numbers do not have any other meaning – we don't expect the player with a 4 on his shirt to be twice as good as the player with a number 2! At other times we use numbers to put things in order, such as listing a person's preference for three different drinks into first, second and third. Finally, we use numbers as precise scores, such as the time it takes a person to run 100 metres or a measure of how tall they are. We explain about these different types of number, called 'outcome measures', so that you can decide what types of data you are collecting in your own research. This is important for preparing your results for analysis, such as entering them into SPSS. We also explain about 'coding', that is, providing a label to explain what a particular number refers to when numbers are used as names, such as the label 'goalkeeper' for the shirt number 1 in a sports team. Particularly with surveys, coding is a very important stage in preparing the data for analysis. In this chapter, we use the example of our Sparcote Study – where a survey has been produced – to explain how to code a range of different types of question. Once the data has been coded, it can be input into SPSS in the form of a spreadsheet (just like Excel) for analysis, as explained in the next chapter.

Chapter 4

Chapter 4 introduces you to SPSS. We explain each of the windows that open up when you run SPSS. SPSS stores the data in the form of a spreadsheet, with the results stored in columns called 'variables', with each row referring to the data from a single participant. Before you can enter your data into SPSS, you can tell it what each of the different 'variables' refers to so that you can give labels to the numbers you are inputting. We explain step by step, using the example from the Sparcote Study, how to set up SPSS and enter the data for your study, so that it is ready for analysis. However, many research projects collect their data electronically (such as when using software to run an experiment) or online (such as when using an online survey program), so the chapter also details how to import your research data from other applications into SPSS. We then explain how you can check that the data has been properly imported. We give examples of how you can edit the labels and correct any problems with importing the data from another program. Finally, the data will be stored in SPSS, ready for analysis.

Chapter 5

This chapter describes how simple it is in SPSS to produce a set of summary results of your data in the form of a table or a graph using a single command, **Frequencies**. For a researcher, the first thing they usually wish to do is to display a set of the basic findings from their research, such as how many people answered each particular response in a survey. Using a number of different examples, including a summary of the different responses in the Sparcote Study, this chapter shows how easy it is to produce summary statistics for different types of data just by using the SPSS **Frequencies** command. The procedure for using the **Frequencies** command is described clearly with screenshots illustrating each step of the straightforward process. Using this one command, a chart of the data can be produced alongside a summary table simply by clicking a button or selecting the appropriate box. For many researchers, this may be all that is required to describe the key results of their study. However, in later chapters, we explain how more sophisticated tables and graphs can be produced and how these basic tables and graphs can be edited to exactly what is required.

Chapter 6

This chapter explains how to produce a range of different tables in SPSS. Researchers often want to combine two variables (such as 'gender' and 'favourite colour') in one table rather than displaying each variable as a separate table. While the **Frequencies** command can display a table for 'gender' (showing how many men and women took part in the study) and for 'favourite colour' (showing how many participants preferred each of the colour choices), combining the two in a table – called a crosstabulation – allows the colour choices of the men and women to be displayed side by side, allowing their choices to be compared. We show how to perform crosstabulations in SPSS using the **Crosstabs** command. This chapter shows the researcher how to recode their data (such as 'age') into groups (such as 'age groups') so that it is suitable for a crosstabulation. The chapter also discusses how to produce tables with percentages as well as, or instead of, counts. The final section focuses on the **Custom Tables** command. **Custom Tables** is a flexible and complex table producing feature in SPSS. However, it has an intuitive and user-friendly interface, so that, once the basics of its instructions are mastered, then some very professional tables can be produced, allowing the researcher to present their data in exactly the form that is required.

Chapter 7

SPSS has an excellent graph drawing feature called **Chart Builder**. While generally it is quite intuitive in operation, there are one or two instructions that appear to be hidden or secret (for example, to produce a specific type of graph you have to click on a small cross on the screen). This chapter will explain how to use **Chart Builder**. This command allows the researcher to create a basic graph using a drag-and-drop method similar to using the Chart Wizard in Microsoft Excel. Examples of producing the most popular charts used in research (pie chart, bar chart, line graph and scatterplot) will be given, so that the reader can follow the example for the particular graph she wishes to produce. Once the basics of **Chart Builder** have been mastered, the user can then produce a wide range of charts and graphs to best illustrate their data. The **Chart Builder** command also includes options of how to add titles and change exactly what is displayed (such as totals, percentages or means). Finally, SPSS has an excellent feature that allows a graph to be drawn from the data in a table that has already been produced, called **Create Graph**. Even if a chart was not selected when the table was created, it is possible to simply click on the table in the output file and, using **Create Graph**, produce the appropriate graph such as a pie chart, bar chart or line graph. This is explained step by step in this chapter, using a number of different examples.

Chapter 8

This chapter explains how SPSS tables and graphs can be edited, providing a range of different examples of the sort of editing that you can undertake. Some other data analysis programs do allow you to create tables and graphs but, once produced, they cannot be changed. Everything that SPSS produces, such as tables and graphs, are all stored an output file. This file can be saved at any time and the output viewed again whenever it is needed. However, an excellent feature of the output file is that it can be edited at any time to change a table, produce a chart or reorganise a graph. The editing tools **Pivot Table**, **Chart Editor** and **Create Graph** (explained in the previous chapter) are extremely flexible with numerous features. We explain a number of the key options in this chapter. New headings can be added to tables and graphs and labels can be changed to exactly what is wanted for a research report. The size and format of the axes on a graph can be changed. Users can look at their output file at any time when using SPSS. SPSS allows the whole of the output file to be saved, but it also allows different parts of it to be saved separately, such as a single graph or table, in different formats (as a jpg or a pdf file). Many researchers wish to produce high-quality tables and graphs for publication and we will explain how to produce pdfs to achieve this outcome. It will also be explained how tables and graphs can be transferred from SPSS to other applications, so that a table or graph can be inserted into a report exactly as the researcher wishes.

Chapter 9

The final chapter introduces the reader to inferential statistics and gives a brief introduction to some different statistical tests that you might want to use in SPSS. In many research studies, the aim is to explore or describe a particular situation or event. We might want to know how many 8-year-olds in a class can ride a bike, which television soap is most popular with teenagers or how satisfied patients are with their medical care. In each case, the data can be collected and descriptive statistics (counts, percentages, averages) are used to answer the questions (such as 24 out of the 30 children, or 80%, can ride a bicycle). However, in other research, data is collected to test a prediction (or hypothesis). In this case, the data is analysed to make a decision whether the prediction is supported or not. Inferential statistics are used to make this decision. This chapter will introduce the reader to statistical testing in SPSS. The reason why inferential statistics are undertaken is explained. A brief introduction to 'probability', 'p values' and 'significance' is given. Statistical tests for comparison and correlation will be explained and examples of chi-square, t test and correlation will be given, to show that statistical tests can be undertaken quite easily and the interpretation of them is relatively simple. These statistics can be used in conjunction with graphs and tables to illustrate what has been found.

Glossary

We also include a glossary of the key terms and concepts used throughout this book. These glossary descriptions will also be included in the margin when a term is first used in the book.

Accompanying website

This book comes with a companion website featuring supplementary resources for students and teachers of SPSS. Please go to www.routledge.com/cw/hinton for more details.

> This chapter has given you an overview of the book. In Chapter 2, we go on to explain the research process because the tables and graphs you want to produce depend on the questions that you want your research to answer.

Undertaking a research project

2

10 THE RESEARCH PROCESS

11 STAGE 1: THE PURPOSE OF THE RESEARCH

14 STAGE 2: SETTING UP THE STUDY

29 STAGE 3: CARRYING OUT THE RESEARCH AND COLLECTING THE DATA

30 STAGE 4: MAKING SENSE OF THE DATA

32 STAGE 5: PRESENTING THE RESEARCH FINDINGS

Chapter aim: To explain the process of doing research

In all areas of academic study, we undertake some form of research. We do this because we want to find things out – we want to gain new information and further insight into the topic under investigation. However, we need to consider exactly what we want to achieve by the research. What are the questions that we wish to be answered by undertaking the research? When we are clear on what we want to find out we can select an appropriate research method and decide how we will collect the data. In some disciplines, research may be characterised by conducting complex experiments using technological equipment in laboratories, yet in other subject areas it might involve the analysis of the words used in a Shakespeare play or the observations recorded from a business meeting. Whatever method we use, research is all about undertaking a careful investigation that systematically produces new information relevant to the topic under study and, if done properly, meets the aims and objectives of the research and provides answers to the questions being asked. Different subject areas will develop different research methods in order to collect the most appropriate data. The research data is analysed and presented in different formats such as words, graphs and tables to describe what was found out in a report – providing an account of what was done, why and what was achieved. This is important as it means that other people can check the work, making sure that the researchers have not made mistakes, ignored crucial factors or misinterpreted the information. It also means that, if the work is done well, other researchers can read the report and share the findings that have been produced – which can then influence their own research work. Collectively, individual pieces of research can combine to create a complex understanding of the subject area under study.

In most academic disciplines in universities and colleges, students will be required to undertake research as part of a small-scale project or dissertation, under supervision. This serves two purposes. First, it provides a way of demonstrating the research skills learnt in the course of study – a little like practising driving a car with a driving instructor. If a student does well in this work, the professors can be confident that the person has the skills to engage in further independent research in the subject – just like a driving test examiner passes the candidate as competent to drive on her own. Second, it gives the student experience of undertaking research that they might find very rewarding in the discovery of new information. Just like having your own car, it can take you to some very interesting places.

THE RESEARCH PROCESS

Doing your own piece of research can be both exciting and challenging. As a new researcher it can be difficult to know how to conduct a piece of research: what method or methods should you use? Who should you ask (if you are undertaking a study with people)? How will you access your participants? Then, when you have collected some data, what is the best way to summarise your findings in a format that is easy for the reader of your report to understand? The aim of this book is to give you an overview of collecting numeric data, guidance on how to enter the data you collected into SPSS and then present the findings in the form of tables and graphs. However, all of these will be determined in part by what you want to know.

Stages of the research process

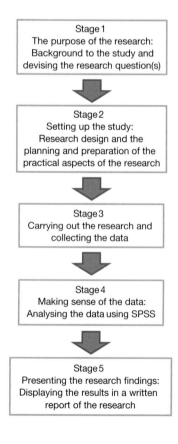

The first stage of the research process is to define what it is that you want to know, what is the aim of your research study? What are your research questions? In the second stage, you need to design a study that answers the research questions you have proposed. Are you undertaking exploratory, descriptive or confirmatory research? What is the most appropriate research method to use? The third stage is to collect the information required to answer your research questions, using the method you have chosen. Then, when you have collected the data, in the fourth stage, you need to make sense of the data you have collected by conducting some form of analysis of the data. This is the stage where SPSS is extremely useful. Finally, in the fifth stage, you need to present your findings in a clear manner so that your audience can understand what you did and what you found.

STAGE 1: THE PURPOSE OF THE RESEARCH

What is the point of doing the research? What is the aim of the research? Once you are clear on the purpose of your research, you need to develop a research question or a number of research questions before any kind research is carried out. Nothing matters more than your research question(s) and at all stages of the research process, you need to keep referring back to it (or them) to make sure that you are on track.

What is the purpose of your research?

You may have an interesting idea of what you want to investigate. Is it something that others would be interested knowing about? Do you want to explore an idea or problem from a different perspective? You will need to have some knowledge of the area under investigation and read around the topic – to find out what others have done – before you can come up with a research question. Furthermore, you will need to consider your level of competency and what resources you have to conduct the study so that it is achievable in the time frame and budget. Start off thinking about what are the underlying reasons for doing your research – the purpose of your study. It may be that you want to explore new ground on a topic where there is limited information available. You might wish to describe a topic or situation that has not been analysed in detail before. Alternatively, you might be interested in testing a prediction about some event or aspect of human behaviour. You need to think carefully about your research question and what you actually want to find out.

Exploratory research

There are many cases where the knowledge of a topic is very limited so you need to first undertake some **exploratory research**. The research question or questions do not have any specific preconceptions or predictions about what answers to expect from the research, but aims to explore what is going on in a specific situation. For example, a local council has to decide what to do with a disused fire station in the centre of town. It decides to undertake a research study to find out what the townspeople would like to do with it. The researchers do not make any predictions about what will be found but simply want to explore what ideas people have. They decide to ask passers-by outside the old fire station on a Saturday (as this is the busiest time of the week in the town – so there are a lot of people around – and it will include people who

exploratory research
The research question or questions do not have any specific preconceptions or predictions about what answers to expect from the research, but aims to explore what is going on in a specific situation.

may be at work during the weekdays). They received a variety of suggestions, from a community centre and swimming pool through to a philosophy centre, a hedge maze and a children's petting zoo. They record all the suggestions and present them in order of popularity to the council. For the council, the research has supplied some information about the townspeople's preferences for what to do with the old building – something they knew nothing about before the study. They might use these results in their decision-making or in designing further studies on the topic.

Descriptive research

descriptive research
Research that sets out to describe the situation under investigation.

Another type of research that often builds on exploratory research is called **descriptive research**. This type of research sets out to describe the situation under investigation, which could involve using data drawn from a range of secondary sources or through data collected with a survey, interviews or other research method. Descriptive research often provides a 'snapshot' of a situation at a particular time or a series of 'snapshots' at different times. For example, a nursing manager wants to know how much time the nurses in a hospital spend on a range of different activities throughout their working week. The researchers, with a good knowledge of the nurses' work, construct a standard set of activities (such as caring for patients, administration, meetings) that the nurses undertake during a normal day, including a catch-all 'other' category for anything that cannot be included in the main categories. Each nurse is provided with a daily record sheet to fill in during a specific number of shifts. At the end of the test period, the researchers use the data collected to describe the balance of these activities carried out by the nurses in the different sections of the hospital. The research report provides the nursing manager with some useful data describing the activities carried out by the nurses. This report may be used by the manager to demonstrate that the hospital is running smoothly and successfully. However, the descriptive research may show interesting findings that might be followed up by further research. For example, the manager may want to investigate why the nurses in one section of the hospital are spending nearly twice as much time on administration than nurses in the other sections of the hospital.

Confirmatory research

confirmatory research
The aim of this type of research is to confirm (or otherwise) a prediction (also called a hypothesis) made at the beginning of the study.

prediction
A testable statement or hypothesis.

hypothesis
A predicted relationship between variables. For example: 'As the attendance at safety workshops increases so the number of accidents at work will decrease' or 'Experienced drivers make fewer driving errors than drivers who have recently passed the driving test'.

The third example of research is **confirmatory research** also known in some disciplines as causal research. This type of research, rather than exploring or describing a research topic, contains within it a specific **prediction** or testable statement (usually called a **hypothesis**). The researchers seek to establish causal links between outcomes that they measure and specific factors that they manipulate. For example, a new drug has been developed for a particular illness. The prediction is that the drug will help people with the illness. Now confirmatory research requires a lot of planning and organisation to make sure that any effects found are due to the specific factor being manipulated (the new drug) and not to other extraneous factors. This is why confirmatory research, often in the form of experiments or trials, is set up in a particular way to maximise the control over the events taking place. In a second example, a road safety team predict that putting up a 'slow down' road traffic sign will result in a reduction of traffic speeds on a busy road. After a controlled study, they are able to confirm the effectiveness of the sign.

Background to the research study

Before you start your study, you need to examine what is already known about the topic under investigation. This can involve reading the research literature (published in academic journals) and evaluating how you own research idea fits into the current knowledge of the topic. This helps to clarify and refine your research question(s) and choose the research methods that are appropriate to use in this field of study. It may be that your background reading includes a review of the theories that have tried to explain the topic you are interested in or an account of other research studies that have been conducted on the same topic. You might evaluate previous findings relating to the topic of interest or find out what information is already held by an organisation about it. Your background review of the literature will provide you with good foundational knowledge of the topic under investigation, for your own research study.

The research question(s)

Now that you have identified a topic that you would like to investigate and have explored the background to your study, you can narrow your focus down to one or more research questions that can be investigated to achieve the purpose of the research. We are going to illustrate this with our example of the Sparcote Study.

The Sparcote Study – stage 1

At Sparcote University, it is coming to the end of the academic year. The academic staff have just finished teaching the first year of students in the new Department of Applied Studies. They have decided that they would like to find out about the student experience during this first year of study in the department at Sparcote.

This is quite a broad aim, but can be expressed in the following question:

- What has been the experience of the applied studies students during their first year at Sparcote University?

The research team decide that they would like to investigate some more specific research questions, focusing on the students' major subject, gender and age. So they decide to collect some demographic information which will allow them to compare different students within the applied studies student body. While they want to know about the overall student experience, they are particularly interested in whether there are any differences in the experiences of the student taking the four different major subjects (business, community health, education and media) within the applied studies programme. There are no specific predictions being made so this is not confirmatory research but *descriptive research*.

Therefore the staff came up with the following research question:

- Are there differences between the experiences of the students on the four applied studies subject majors during their first year of study?

At times, there is not a clear distinction between exploratory and descriptive research but, typically, exploratory research involves an investigation where very little is known and it may not even be clear what research method to use, so is often undertaken to guide or plan further work. Descriptive research seeks to describe the characteristics of a situation or specific group (or groups) of people under investigation to provide a summary account – or 'snapshot' of what is happening.

From their background knowledge, the researchers know that the university administration collects data on a range of demographic factors and undertakes regular research on equal opportunities within the university; for example, they are currently undertaking a university-wide detailed study of ethnicity within the student experience. The applied studies research team decide that they do not want to copy what the wider university is already doing – particularly as their study is on such a small scale. While their focus is on the different subject majors, they do decide to record details of gender and age in their research. As they are aware that in the department as a whole there are more or less equal numbers of female and male students and (although many students are aged between 18–21) there is a mix of ages of the students in the department too, with Sparcote University well known for recruiting mature students. By recording these factors, they can also examine whether differences in the student experience in applied studies can be linked to these factors.

They produced the following additional research questions:

▓ Are there differences in the first year student exerience between male and female applied studies students?

▓ Are there differences in the first year student experience between younger and older applied studies students?

If the research team does find any differences in the student experience between the major subjects, gender or age, this will require further investigation. Having constructed their research questions, the researchers now consider how they are going to go about finding answers to these questions, by choosing a specific research method.

STAGE 2: SETTING UP THE STUDY

The second stage of the research process is designing the research project and preparing the practical aspects of the research. Any research project must be carefully designed so that it can provide answers to the research questions (rather than being off topic). Undertaking research is like going on a car ride, where the answers to the research questions are the goal of the journey. You wouldn't get into a car without having a clue of where you are going. You also must plan the route you are going to take. As well as selecting a research method (the route map) you also need to sort out the practical aspects of the research. To use our analogy again, you might want to find out if the traffic is very busy before you leave for your journey and you will need to make sure that your car has enough fuel. If you don't have a good plan about where you want to go, and how you want to get there, you might end up driving round and round in circles. So, once you have decided on your research destination (your research question), you need to design a plan of how you are going to get to your destination (answer your research question) by selecting a research method and working out the practical details of employing it for your study.

Choosing your research method

Different research questions are often linked to different research methods due to the underlying assumptions within the research. The choice of the research method is often linked to a philosophical approach to research: for example, undertaking an experiment to determine a cause and effect relationship assumes that there are causal relationships to be found! We are not going to discuss the philosophical debate between approaches but instead provide a very brief overview of some of the main qualitative and quantitative methods that you might use in a small-scale research study. As this is a book about SPSS, we will be concerned with analysing quantitative research data.

There are philosophical assumptions about the nature of reality underlying the two fundamental approaches to research, **positivism** and **interpretivism**. Positivism is the approach that predominates in the sciences and assumes that knowledge is based on our experiences of our senses, and can be measured with value-free **quantitative** measures (such as structured observations and experiments) that would result in the same data if used by different researchers. In contrast interpretivists (constructivists), seeking the meaning of actions and events, would argue that there can be multiple 'realities' and that they are very subjective in nature and require **qualitative** research methods to explore individuals' unique experiences. They also highlight the important role of the researcher and the researcher's understandings in the research process.

Qualitative methods

Qualitative research seeks to tease out key 'qualities' of the topic under investigation in the research data collected. For example, in a series of interviews with workers in a company, researchers analyse the recorded interviews tagging the different identifiable topics and use this information to draw out key themes within the interviews, one being that the management do not listen to workers' concerns despite the managers saying that they do. Qualitative methods of collecting data generally use either behaviour-based methods or language-based methods. Behaviour-based methods are ways in which you can physically observe a particular behaviour. For example, observing the reactions of a particular child when his mother leaves the room, the researcher might describe the behaviour of the child as crying and crawling towards the door. Researchers can also analyse photographs, video and television programmes to examine how they convey specific ideas of, for example, masculinity or femininity to the viewer. Language-based methods include analysing oral language, such as interviews, focus groups or speeches or written language such as diaries, blogs or public documents, such as newspapers or government legislation. Qualitative research often seeks to examine 'depth' not 'breadth'. In case study research, a lot of detailed information is collected, often to provide an understanding of how a particular individual or organisation has acted and interpreted events around them. However, the results of this research may not be generalisable to other people or organisations. As we shall see later, quantitative research, unlike qualitative research, is often more about 'breadth' rather than 'depth' – in seeking to produce results about groups of people rather than specific individuals.

positivism
The approach that historically has predominated in the sciences and assumes that knowledge is based on the experiences of our senses and can be measured with value-free quantitative measures (such as observations and experiments).

interpretivism
An opposing philosophical perspective to positivism that suggests that there is not one objective truth but instead that knowledge itself is of a subjective nature.

quantitative
Pertaining to 'quantities'. Quantitative research is undertaken where numerical outcomes (quantities) are produced to answer research questions.

qualitative
Pertaining to 'qualities'. Qualitative research is about obtaining insight into a situation or position; it seeks to produce a depth of understanding or explores the subjective interpretation of events (rather than breadth typical of quantitative methods).

variables

Variables are something that are not fixed but that can change or vary. There would be no point in quantitative researchers studying situations, activities or behaviour that remains constant. Indeed, the aim of the research is to study factors that vary and seek to find explanations for why they vary. This is why quantitative research is all about the study of the relationship between variables, such as gender, age or time of day, and other variables, or outcome measures, such as the performance on a task or the responses to certain questions in a survey.

independent variable

A variable chosen by the researcher, who selects the categories of the variable to study, which is predicted to influence the dependent variable (an outcome measure).

dependent variable

The variable measured by the researcher and predicted to be influenced by (that is, depend on) the independent variable. A dependent variable is an outcome measure.

Quantitative methods

Quantitative research is about measuring 'quantities' (in terms of numbers) to answer the research questions. These quantities might be examinations marks, times to solve a puzzle, people's income, the number of errors made on a task and so forth. For example, an ice-cream vendor might want to know how many ice creams are sold at different times of the year, so keeps monthly records of sales. Here, the researcher is choosing to measure one factor that varies (the ice-cream sales) in terms of another factor that varies (month of the year). Not surprisingly, we call these factors **variables**. For descriptive research, the researcher might report the total number of sales for each of the different months of the year and this provides a useful record of what has happened, which can be used for future planning (such as ordering in new supplies).

In quantitative research, individual results are usually combined together to give a result for a particular group or category of a variable. For example, in evaluating a company website the researchers are more interested in the general view of a group of 'visitors to the website' rather any one specific individual and so report results such as 78% of the website visitors (who completed a survey) found the website easy to use. Quantitative research is therefore often viewed as about 'breadth' rather than 'depth'.

In confirmatory research, researchers wish to test predictions (which they have made in advance of carrying out the study) such as 'the novice drivers will make more driving errors than the experienced drivers.' In this study, the researchers are looking at the variable of 'driving experience' selecting two groups or categories within it: 'experienced' and 'novice'. Ten experienced drivers and 10 novice drivers take part in a study of the number of driving errors made on a test circuit. The results are reported in terms of the groups, such as that the average number of driving errors was 5.3 for the experienced drivers and 7.2 for the novice drivers. In this case, the variable 'driver experience' is called the **independent variable**, as it is independently chosen by the researcher and not measured, and 'the number of driving errors' is called the **dependent variable** as this variable is measured and assumed to 'depend' on the independent variable, that is, it is assumed that the number of errors will depend on the level of driving experience. Statistical comparisons can be made between the driving errors of the two groups to see if the prediction is supported, as explained in Chapter 9.

The advantages and disadvantages of popular quantitative methods are detailed below:

- ■ **Surveys** – A systematically constructed set of questions to find out about an individual's thoughts, feelings, knowledge or behaviours.
  - – Advantage: Can be administered face to face or online; can be administered to a large number of people in a short space of time.
  - – Disadvantage: The answer choices offered to the participants might not reflect how they actually feel or think.

- ■ **Correlational designs** – A procedure in which the relationship between values on two variables is examined, such as the relationship between school attendance and pupil achievement.
  - – Advantage: Can use large data sets from secondary sources.
  - – Disadvantage: Correlations do not indicate causality.

■ **Experiments** – A method to test a prediction (a theory or hypothesis) under controlled conditions. An independent variable (or variables) is manipulated and the effect is measured on a dependent variable (or variables), such as examining the effect of text size on reading performance, in a computer controlled laboratory study.

– Advantage: Used to establish cause and effect.

– Disadvantage: Requires careful control to make sure other variables are not affecting the results. This can be difficult to achieve.

■ **Structured observations** – A systematic observation technique, where the researchers record events according to a predetermined coding system, such as recording parent–child interactions in a parent and baby group.

– Advantage: Different observers can use the same observation scheme producing reliable observations.

– Disadvantage: Meaningful behaviour may be missed if it is not included in the observation scheme; participants may act differently when they know they are being observed.

■ **Quantitative content analysis** – Aspects of a text are systematically recorded and quantified, for example, measuring the column centimetres reporting sports news in a newspaper. A text can be a newspaper or a magazine or a picture or a video.

– Advantage: Can reliably measure content using a standardised procedure within and across texts; it does not have the issues of dealing with human participants.

– Disadvantage: The content categories are determined by the researcher and may not be the key categories employed by the producer or reader; measuring content quantitatively does not interrogate the meaning of that content.

The quantitative research that you undertake may involve people but it does not have to – secondary research, literature research or analysing videos, pieces of art or magazines can also be used as different methods of investigation. For example, a researcher interested in perfume advertising in men's and women's magazines might count up the number of perfume adverts in the current issue of the top five best-selling men's magazines and compare the total with the number of perfume adverts in the top five best-selling women's magazines. Secondary data can come from a variety of different sources. It can be collected from data that is held internally within an organisation that you may be working with, such as databases that contain information about customers, financial statements or sales reports. Alternatively, secondary data can come from external sources that have been created, recorded or generated outside of the organisation that the researcher works with. This data can include government statistics, published journals, books or from the internet.

Most researchers use the term 'survey' and 'questionnaire' interchangeably. Where people do make a distinction is in arguing that 'survey' is the process of asking lots of people to give a response (or responses) to a particular task, and a 'questionnaire' is the set of questions that they are asked to complete but not necessarily. In this book, we shall adopt the former approach (treating the terms synonymously) but use the term 'survey' throughout.

frequency
Another name for 'count', indicating the number in a particular category.

sampling
Researchers want to use the results of their studies to make claims about populations but (normally) they can only test a sample rather than the whole population. Therefore, they engage in sampling; that is, undertake a process to select their samples to represent the populations under investigation.

ethics
All researchers should behave morally in carrying out their research. In particular, when using human participants, they should make sure that they do not inadvertently cause any harm. Academic research, whether carried out by students or academic staff, is scrutinised by ethics committees, which may require changes before the research is allowed to proceed.

instructions
In any research study involving human participants, they need to be given precise details of what to do – written or verbal instructions – in their role as participant.

population
A complete set of items or events. In statistics, this usually refers to the complete set of participants or scores we are interested in, from which we have drawn a sample.

Mixed methods

Although we have given examples of different quantitative and qualitative methods, there is not always a clear cut distinction. When conducting an observation, you may want to just write down a description of a piece of behaviour (qualitative) or you may have a structured observation schedule in which you can note an exact number (or the **frequency**) of occurrences of a particular behaviour (quantitative). These two types of observation may also be combined in some way in the research. Similarly, research into professional practice might involve in-depth interviews with a small number of selected professionals about their work but it also may contain observations of their practice and a survey of a number of their professional colleagues. You may want to use a mixture of methods when conducting research to try and draw on the advantages of each method and also reduce the disadvantages.

Planning your study

While research in many fields does not require human participants (such as examining changing rainfall patterns in Scotland), research in the human and social sciences involves asking people to take part as participants in the research and undertake certain activities to generate the research data. Where human participants are employed in research there are certain key issues to consider before asking them to take part in the study:

- Deciding who to select? This is a question of **sampling**.

- Making sure that participants taking part in the study do not come to any harm. This is a question of research **ethics**.

- Ensuring that the participants know what to do in the study and are willing to do it. This is a question of providing clear and informative **instructions**.

All three of these issues are considered next.

Sampling: The people you are interested in

Researchers usually want to know about a group of people but for reasons of cost, time and other resource limitations are unable to test them all. We refer to the complete set of people or things that the research is interested in as a **population**. For example, a researcher wants to find out what family doctors think about a piece of new government legislation. Now, there are thousands of doctors in the country and it is impossible to test them all, so a small group or **sample** has to be selected for the research to represent the population. The problem is then: Which sample to select? If the sample only comprised doctors who support the government then the research might show them to be favourable to the legislation in spite of the fact that most doctors are against it. Here the sampling has biased the results.

In some cases, researchers are not very worried about sampling bias – they just want to collect information from whoever they can get. For example, a researcher would like to collect some information about a store's customers and testing the first 100 people who walk in the store will give them some information about them (when currently they have none). As a piece of exploratory research, this information might be useful to guide more detailed research later. In other cases, it is crucial to select the sample carefully (as the first 100 customers in the store might be a highly specific sample of early-morning commuters and not typical of the 'general' customer). For example, an experimenter looking at the effect of a new teaching method compared to the old method on children's mathematics performance would not want a sample of high ability children following one method and a sample of the lower ability children following the other method, as any results could be unrelated to the teaching method and due to a biased selection of the samples. In this case, any differences and could be unrelated and due to the teaching method but simply due to the children's intelligence. The researcher would want to make sure in advance that the children following the two methods did not differ in their intelligence (or age or another possibly biasing factor).

The way the sample is selected – the sampling strategy – will be related to the research question and the method of data collection. At a very basic level, the sample has to be directly related to the question under investigation. For example if you are trying to find out about how young adults spend their leisure time, you would need to conduct research with young adults (and not young children or older adults). If you were interested in knowing how satisfied people were with their purchase of a new piece of technology, your sample should be made up of participants who had bought that piece of new technology. It is remarkable how often the sample is not from the target population. A **purposeful sampling** strategy is to intentionally select participants who are specific to the aims or research question.

You may have a limited amount of time and do not require a carefully selected sample to represent a specific population; in this case, **opportunity sampling** or **convenience sampling** can be the quickest and simplest sampling method to use. In this sampling strategy, a sample is drawn on the basis of opportunity – you just select the people who are available to be tested, on the basis that anyone will do: for example, in a supermarket, asking anyone willing to stop to give their opinion on a new soft drink you give them to try. Within a **snowballing sampling** method, existing participants ask their friends and contacts to take part in a study, such as via social media, and those participants might go on to ask their friends and other social contacts with the same interests. For example, if you were interested in finding out about the therapeutic benefit of adults doing crochet, you might ask the organiser of a crochet club to send an online link to other acquaintances whom they know who share their enthusiasm for this hobby. In this way, the initial small sample snowballs to a larger sample.

If you are undertaking confirmatory research, such as an experiment, in order to generalise your findings from your sample to a larger population, you will need to select a sample of people who are representative of a larger population. This could be achieved by **stratified sampling**, which is seeking to make sure that the sample has the same groupings within it as the population. For example, if there is an equal number of men and women in the population then the sample is selected to have equal numbers of men and women in it, too. Other important factors, such as age, experience, health might all be included in the stratification if they are viewed as relevant factors. However, the most common way in which researchers try to select an unbiased sample from a population is through **random sampling**, where every person in the population has an equal chance of being picked. Like a lottery where

sample
A subset of a set of items, usually a group of participants that are all members of a larger group (or population).

purposeful sampling
This is a sampling method that relies on the judgement of the researcher for the selection of the sample. While this is clearly not going to produce a random or representative sample, it can be very useful in certain circumstances. For example, a researcher exploring the treatment of workers in a company may choose certain people who he believes to be particularly of interest (such as those who are viewed by the researcher as potentially vulnerable to exploitation or discrimination).

opportunity sampling
Another name for convenience sampling. The members of a sample are selected from a population simply on the basis that there is an opportunity to select them, rather than selecting sample members randomly or representatively.

convenience sampling
A method of choosing a sample for research where the participants are selected from the people who happen to be available at the time, rather than seeking a representative or random sample.

snowballing sampling
Selecting a sample where one participant leads to the recruitment of further participants by her connections associated to the topic of the research.

stratified sampling

One way of selecting a representative sample from a population is to match key strata within the sample. For example, the population of people who visited a dentist's surgery in the last year included 50% male and 50% female, and 40% under 18 years, 35% between 18 and 64 years and 25% of 65 years and older. The population is, in this example, stratified by gender and age. A researcher selecting a sample of patients for a research project may choose to use stratified sample selection, by making sure that the sample contains the same proportions of male and female patients and the same proportions of the different age groups as in the population.

random sampling

To avoid bias in sample selection, a researcher may engage in random sampling, in which each member of a sample is randomly selected from a larger group (or population).

numbers are randomly chosen 'out of the hat', researchers randomly select their sample, such as randomly picking 100 names from a doctor's surgery patient list of thousands of people, who are then asked to take part in the research. The assumption is that, with the selection left to chance, no deliberate biases are included in the sample choice.

Ethics

Ethics are sets of values or moral principles that guide our behaviour. Research studies carried out in universities by any student or staff member have to be reviewed by a supervisor and/or an ethics committee to ensure that the researcher has considered any ethical issues inherent in their project and explained how any ethical issues will be dealt with. Some disciplines also have an ethical code of practice that you are expected to adhere to and these can be useful as a frame of reference of what to include in your study. Unethical research should not be carried out and, in most disciplines, a failure to follow ethical guidelines may result in sanctions such as not being awarded a degree or the loss of one's job.

Here we provide a summary of the key things to consider in research ethics:

■ *Not to cause harm.* The fundamental purpose of research ethics is to protect the prospective participants from any harm. Participants should be respected at all times and be in the same emotional and physical state at the end of the study as they were at the start of the study. If you are going to do or ask something that might make someone feel uncomfortable, you need to think about whether this is really needed or question how could you mitigate against making someone feel uncomfortable. One idea is to provide information to support services after the study has ended in a debriefing of each participant. It is also important that the researcher themselves should not be harmed when conducting research. For example, it might not be safe for a researcher to collect data late at night in a certain part of town. The researcher must conduct research that is at the level of their own competency and follow the guidance of their supervisors, showing respect for their discipline of study or the organisation they work for.

■ *Informed consent.* Participants need to be provided with enough information so they can make an informed decision of whether they want to take part in the research, which should be in a written format. There should be a balance between enough information and too much information for the participant to make an informed decision on whether they consent to take part in the study. Like the terms and conditions displayed with various products, too much information (or technical jargon) might lead participants to get bored and then not to read it all! Participants, if they choose to take part in the study, should know clearly what to expect, and certainly not feel at any time as if they have been misled.

■ *Anonymity and confidentiality.* You need to let your participants know that their participation in your study and that the information that they give you will remain confidential and not be shared beyond the researchers. For example, if you are undertaking a study in a workplace then you need to think carefully about the questions that you might ask your participants. Answering questions about the workplace could have adverse effects on the participants, for example in the question: Do you like your boss? Participants may not wish to answer this question honestly, for obvious reasons, if they believe that their answer may be seen by the boss. One way of dealing with this issue is to ensure that your participants are aware that the data they individually provide remains confidential. A way of doing this is to allocate participant numbers that are used through the research process, so that no names are included in the research information. Also, participants must be assured that their anonymity would be preserved and that taking part in the study would not have repercussions for their future. In writing up the results of your study, you must ensure that, despite being anonymous, individual participants cannot be identified in other ways, for example, by a specific characteristic that other members of the sample do not have.

■ *Right to withdraw.* Participants should be made aware that they have the right to withdraw at any time and remove their data from the study. Before they take part, they should be provided with information on the process of how to withdraw. It is quite possible that a person will agree to take part in a study but then change her mind in the middle. She needs to be aware that she can stop and remove herself from the study at any time and that it is perfectly acceptable for her to do this.

The issue of potential harm is particularly of concern with vulnerable groups (such as children, patients or prisoners). Research on these groups often requires detailed ethical scrutiny via formal ethics committees that check the value of the research, the competency of the researchers and that proper informed consent will be given by the participants or their responsible legally defined representatives (such as parents or next-of-kin).

Information and instructions

Participants not only need to be aware of their 'rights' in a research study, they also need to know what to do in order to carry out their role properly. While we may all now be familiar with simple surveys (as they seem to pop up all over the place in the modern world!), taking part in research is likely to be something unfamiliar to many participants, so they need to be given clear instructions as to what they will be asked to do in the study. A researcher needs to provide the potential participants with enough clear information so that they can make an informed decision whether to take part in the study (and so give their informed consent if they agree to take part). For example, the information has to provide answers to the following questions that a participant might have: What is the study about? How long will it take? What will it require me to do? In some studies, researchers want the participants to give a quick answer to a series of questions (in a survey for example) – often asking for the first thing that comes to mind – and not spend a long time deliberating, whereas in others (such as an experiment on problem-solving), they want the participants to be as accurate as they can and take as long as they need on the task. The instructions need to make these aspects of the study clear. It may be important, in certain surveys for example, for the participant to answer every question, so the instructions might include a statement at the end of the study asking the participants to check that they have answered all the questions. The instructions need to be written with clarity so that there is no room for misinterpretation. You may wish to check that the participants do not interpret your instructions differently from how you interpret them. People try to make sense of even the oddest experiences (and taking part in research may appear odd). Straightforward and clear instructions are less likely to be ambiguous.

Creating the research study

Now that you have a clear idea of the background to your study, have constructed a research question or questions and have selected your research method, you need to sit down and work out the practicalities of carrying out the actual study. This is often done in the form of a research proposal. All the details of the research are included so that a reader knows exactly what the researcher intends to do. In many universities, the preparation of a research proposal is required as this is the document that goes before the ethics committee who decide if the piece of research can be carried out or not. Also when researchers are seeking financial support to carry out their research, they are often required to submit their research proposal to the funding body that then chooses who to support on their evaluation of these proposals.

Putting together a research proposal

A research proposal is the overall plan of the study. The proposal details to the reader why your study is important and how you propose to conduct it. It normally contains the following information:

- *Title.* A concise title to give an indication of what the research will be about.

- *Introduction.* A short summary of the background to the study such as the previous literature and the rationale for doing the study.

- *Research question(s).* Exactly what you are trying to find out or the hypotheses you want to test.

- *Research methods.* The specific details of what your research will involve, including the method you will employ, such as which qualitative or quantitative research method you will use, the procedure you will follow (such as a description of the survey or experiment(s) you will be undertaking) and, if you are going to involve participants, what your sample will be and how they will be selected.

- A *timeframe* for the stages of the research detailing when the data will be collected and analysed and the final report completed.

- You may include *how you will be analysing the data* you collect.

- In many cases, the researchers are required to include a detailed *costing* of the resource requirements of the piece of research.

The Sparcote Study – stage 2

The researchers at Sparcote now need to decide what method that they want to use to answer their four research questions. They look at the advantages and disadvantages of each of the methods and ask themselves.

- ▨ Is there any other source of information (such as university data) available that could answer the research questions?
  - *No, not about the applied studies students first-year experience*

- ▨ Is there a hypothesis (or hypotheses) that is (are) being tested?
  - *There are no specific predictions about differences between majors, gender or age but these will be examined to see if any differences emerge in the data that can be followed up in later investigations*

- ▨ Does the research seek a breadth of information or a depth of information?
  - *The researchers want to gain a broad 'snapshot' of the students' first-year experience from as many students as possible*

outcome measures
In all quantitative research, data is collected to answer research questions. However, these data are obtained by using outcome measures: recording category frequencies, such as how many people select each of a set of choices in a survey, or scores on a performance measure, such as the number of correct answers in a test. The researcher devises the appropriate outcome measure (or measures) to obtain data relevant to the research question(s).

Data held by the university might be able to provide information such as attendance and grades but not about their experience on the applied studies programme. The researchers know that they want the views of all (or most) of the students in the department, rather than undertaking a few in-depth discussions with a small number of students and so it is decided to to carry out a survey. The research team believe that this should provide a breadth of information from a large number of students in a short time. Also, it does not require a lot of resources and can be funded within the department. The survey is organised by the first-year tutor who has some knowledge of survey design and construction.

Once a survey has been decided on, the next thing to do is to turn the Sparcote research questions into survey questions that can provide appropriate answers to the research questions. Let's unpick the research questions and break them down into smaller manageable chunks to produce **outcome measures**. (Outcome measures are explained in Chapter 3.)

See Chapter 3

The four research questions are again:

- ▨ What has been the experience of the applied studies students during their first year at Sparcote University?

- ▨ Are there differences between the experiences of the students on the four applied studies subject majors during their first year of study?

- ▨ Are there differences in the first year student experience between male and female applied studies students?

- ▨ Are there differences in the first year student experience between younger and older applied studies students?

The first question is quite broad so needs to be broken down into specific key examples of the student experience. The researchers decide to ask a few questions about the students' academic experience during the year, a few questions about their non-academic university experience and use of university facilities and, finally, measures of overall satisfaction. The last three questions relate to demographic information (students' major subject, gender and age), so a demographic section will begin the survey asking for this information, which can then be used to examine the student experience of the groups identified by these demographic factors. Therefore, the researchers decided that the survey will include four sections to give a clear structure to the survey:

Section 1: Demographics

Section 2: Academic Experience

Section 3: Non-Academic Experience

Section 4: Overall Satisfaction

They now need to ensure that they have questions that are related to each section, which, in turn, will be able to answer the research questions without there being too many questions (which could lead to the students becoming bored and not likely to answer correctly). The three questions of Section 1 are fairly clear, as they simply ask for the relevant demographic information. The researchers choose four questions for Section 2 and four questions for Section 3, which they believe are central to the student experience. Finally, they select three questions about the students' overall satisfaction with the year: Their satisfaction with their academic life, their social life and their personal development during the year. The survey is given an appropriate title: 'The Applied Studies Student Survey'.

The final task is to construct an information and instruction sheet for the survey. This needs to provide the following information:

- A clear statement of the purpose of the survey and why the person is being asked to complete it.

- How long it will take to complete.

- That the survey is voluntary.

- That answers are confidential and the data is aggregated.

- Contact details for any questions, concerns or if the participant wanted to withdraw.

- Specific details of who is responsible for the survey.

The complete Applied Studies Student Survey is shown on the following pages.

✓

The Applied Studies Student Survey has been designed by us (pretending to be the researchers!) to illustrate a number of aspects of quantitative research and how different types of response can be analysed by SPSS. For example, we have employed a range of different question types in the study, probably more than is typical, specifically for illustrative purposes. We will be showing, in Chapter 3, the different ways of creating quantitative research measures (such as scores on a test or answers in a questionnaire or survey) and this survey comprises many of these different types of response. However, we are also aware that we have had to make certain decisions for illustrative purposes as well, such as keeping some questions simple and the survey short. For example, we could have asked many more questions to gain a detailed knowledge of the student experience but chose these ones as a good subset for illustration. We are also aware that other researchers might construct the questions in different ways. Generally speaking, however, we believe that the survey follows best practice.

We are assuming that the researchers at Sparcote have knowledge and experience of designing surveys. You may need to read further about writing a survey.

The Applied Studies Student Survey

In the Department of Applied Studies at Sparcote University we are always interested to know about your experiences whilst at university. We would be grateful if you could complete the following short survey about your first year of study with us.

We value your views, and would like to know more about your experiences to see 'what works' and what aspects of your university experience we can develop.

This survey should only take about five minutes of your time to complete.

Your participation is voluntary and you can withdraw from the study at any time. The information you provide will be confidential and only aggregated data will be reported.

By completing this survey you are consenting to take part.

If you have any questions or concerns about the survey please contact Susan Green, the First Year Tutor, by telephone on extension 286, or by email via skgreen@sparcote.uni.

Thank you.
Susan Green and Robert Jones
Department of Applied Studies, Sparcote University
Email: skgreen@sparcote.uni, bobjones@sparcote.uni

The Applied Studies Student Survey

Section 1: About you

1. What is your gender? Please tick.   Female ☐   Male ☐

2. Please enter your age in years

3. Which subject is your Major?

  Business ☐   Community Health ☐   Education ☐   Media ☐

Section 2: About your academic experience

4. Rank the following modes of study in terms of your preferred learning experience. (Give a value of 1 to your favourite, 2 to your next favourite and 3 to your least favourite)

    Lectures

    Seminars (small group discussions)

    Workshops (small group practical activity sessions)

5. Please state your level of disagreement or agreement with the following statement:
"The learning resources (teaching rooms, library, IT facilities) are appropriate to support my course."

Strongly disagree	Disagree	Neither disagree nor agree	Agree	Strongly agree
☐	☐	☐	☐	☐

6. Please give an estimate of your relative use of the following three resources for your studies. Place a percentage figure against each resource so that the total of the three figures adds up to 100%:

    The recommended textbooks   %

    Materials provided on the course website (lecture notes, seminar materials, readings)   %

    Other materials not provided by the course team   %

    100 %

The Applied Studies Student Survey

7. Please rate the teaching team on your course on the following 10 point scale in terms of their overall teaching quality (1-low quality, 10-high quality). Consider both how well they present the teaching material (clarity and ease of *understanding*) and engage with student performance (*helpfulness* of responses to student questions and their feedback on student work).

1	2	3	4	5	6	7	8	9	10
☐	☐	☐	☐	☐	☐	☐	☐	☐	☐

Section 3: About your non-academic experience

8. Please indicate if you have used the following University student support services during the last year (tick as appropriate)

The Health and Counselling Centre (doctor, dentist, nurse, counsellor)	☐
The Student Advice Centre (for advice on issues such as finance, accommodation)	☐
Other	☐

If you have ticked 'Other', please specify:

....

9. Which of the following campus social spaces have you spent time with your peers in during this last academic year? (tick as many as appropriate)

The Student Eatery	☐
The Wholefood Café	☐
The Hub	☐
Racquets Retreat	☐
The Media Munch	☐

10. How often have you used the Sparcote Sports and Fitness Centre during the last year? (Please select the category that best represents your usage.)

Often	(once per week or more often)	☐
Regularly	(more than once per month)	☐
Occasionally	(a few times each Semester)	☐
Rarely	(one or twice during the year)	☐
Never		☐

The Applied Studies Student Survey

11. Please give the number of hours of paid work have you have undertaken on average per week during the last academic year? (Please estimate the figure to the nearest whole number. If you have not worked please put zero.)

Hours [   ]

Section 4: Your overall view of your first year at Sparcote University

12. Overall, on the basis of your experience in the last year, please tick your satisfaction with:

	Very unsatisfied	Unsatisfied	Neither unsatisfied nor satisfied	Satisfied	Very satisfied
Your academic life at Sparcote	☐	☐	☐	☐	☐
Your social life at Sparcote	☐	☐	☐	☐	☐
Your personal development over the last year	☐	☐	☐	☐	☐

Thank you for your participation in this survey.

Many surveys are carried out using online survey computer programs. The Applied Studies Student Survey can easily be run online. However, a key consideration is the convenience and ease of completion for the participants. While running a survey online has its advantages, such as the data being automatically stored for each participant, the researchers need to make sure that the participants have access to an input device with which to complete the survey (such as a smartphone, tablet or computer). This is not always convenient for all participants, so a paper-and-pen version of a survey, which might appear old fashioned in this digital age, can also have distinct advantages over online presentation. In the case of the Applied Studies Student Survey, the researchers know that the students have a final class at the end of the academic year, providing them with information about their second-year studies. Allocating 10 minutes at the end of this session, to fill in the survey, means that most students will be available if they wish to complete it. Handing out copies of the survey to be completed at the end of the session means that the researchers are available to answer any questions about the survey immediately and also the response rate is likely to be significantly higher than if all the students were sent an online link to click on to complete the survey.

Piloting the study

Once you have designed your experiment, produced an observation schedule or constructed your survey it is a good idea to pilot the study. Piloting the research is a complete run-through of study with a pilot participant. The pilot participant is often a helpful 'real' participant willing to go through the study with you (but whose data is not normally used to contribute to the final results). Undertaking this 'test run' often brings out issues that need to be resolved, such as the instructions being unclear or ambiguous – so need to be rewritten – or the fact that the study takes much longer than expected. In this case, the procedure might be altered or the instructions changed to make it clear how long the study really takes. Piloting your study will give you a good idea of what works and if there are any areas that need further developing – before you start running the study 'live'. Testing one or two pilot participants can really help to make sure that the study works as it is expected to work.

STAGE 3: CARRYING OUT THE RESEARCH AND COLLECTING THE DATA

A lot of work has been undertaken by a researcher in order to get to the point at which the research can be carried out. The research has been planned, designed and constructed in order to seek answers to the research questions. The selection of participants has been decided, with the appropriate sampling strategy. Where necessary, the research proposal has successfully passed through the required approval processes, such as an ethics committee and, in many cases, organisational approval (such that the research does not bring the organisation in disrepute) by following departmental or professional guidelines. In some cases, there may be quite a detailed process of participant recruitment for the study. There are also practical issues to deal with in terms of setting up the research material and considering all the things that might occur during data collection. For example, do the participants know how to get to the research location and have they been booked into timeslots so that they do not have to wait? If you are going to observe someone in their workplace (such as a teacher giving a class), have you left enough time to get there on time? If you are giving out paper-and-pen surveys, do you have enough pens to go around for all participants to complete the survey? If people agree to come and participate in your study, you need to ensure that the room and any equipment are ready *before* they are due to arrive.

Often things may not go as planned. Traffic delays may mean that some participants are unable to arrive for testing, laboratory or computer equipment may break down temporarily and participants are unable to complete their tasks. Sometimes people don't turn up as expected. In the case of a survey, there may be only 10 rather than the hoped for 100 completed surveys during the period the survey is online. (Indeed, a 10% response rate is not unusual for an online survey.) To some extent, all of these issues have to be considered in advance and some degree of planning to deal with them put into place. For example, if a two-week period is allocated for data collection, is there a further two-week period available in the future that can be used for further data collection if the first period is inadequate? The key point here is that the data collection may work precisely as planned but may not, so the research should be undertaken well in advance of any planned presentation of the data in terms of a report deadline or a conference presentation.

The Sparcote Study – stage 3

As was noted above, the Sparcote researchers chose to give their survey out in the final class of the year where they were expecting all the students to attend to discuss their second-year studies. As the survey only takes about five minutes to complete, this was undertaken at the end of the class. As a result all the students were given a copy of the survey to fill in concurrently, producing the data from a large number of students all at the same time. In this way, the researchers were able to get 183 completed surveys out of a student cohort of 195 (with twelve students not completing it for various reasons – mostly that they were absent from that class), an exceptionally high response rate for a survey. (Had the survey been put online and the students emailed with a link to follow for the completion of the survey, we would expect the completion rate to be considerably lower.)

STAGE 4: MAKING SENSE OF THE DATA

Why we need statistics

statistics
A characteristic of a sample, such as the total or the sample mean. More generally, statistic and statistics are used to describe techniques for summarising and analysing numerical data.

As we have explained earlier, the point of collecting data in a research study is to answer a research question or questions. However, when you have completed the study the resultant data can often look like a large and overwhelming spreadsheet of numbers and you may not yet be able to say what conclusions you can draw from the information gathered in relation to your research question or aim. Therefore you need to do something with the data to start to make it easier to understand – and provide answers to the research questions. Remember that quantitative research is usually about groups rather than individuals, so we need to find a way to sum up the results of a group of participants rather than listing out all their individual results. This is where **statistics** come in.

Descriptive statistics: to summarise the findings

The word statistics sounds more complex than it actually is. Statistics need not be complicated. In reporting information about the participants who took part in the study we do not provide detailed descriptions of each person but report relevant details about groups such as there were 74 women and 69 men in the study. A **total** – simply adding up the number in a group or category – is a statistic. The first thing we need to do with our data is to provide a summary of the findings. To do this we use **descriptive statistics**, like the total or the average (or **mean**), to provide clear descriptions of our findings, often in the form of a table, along with **illustrative statistics** such as charts and graphs. We will be explaining which descriptive statistics to use with which type of data in Chapter 3 and explaining how to create tables and graphs with SPSS in subsequent chapters.

When we present a report of our research to other people, we do not list every single result we found, such as the individual responses of every woman who liked the website under investigation. We summarise this information, such as saying that '61 out of the 74 women in the study liked the website.' When we present a report of our research, it includes the results in summary form, with the findings expressed in terms of descriptive statistics. If a reader of a research report wants to find out who took part in the study, then the statistical description of the demographic information provides this information, such as the number of people, their ages and gender. The characteristics of the sample of people under investigation are presented at an appropriate level of detail to understand the study. Listing out each person and all the information about them would be far too detailed, but describing the sample in vague general terms such as 'quite a few people took part in this study' or 'there were some men and women in this study' would also prove unhelpful. This is why specific numerical information is used to describe the participants: 'There were 143 participants in this study, 74 women and 69 men'. These numbers, 143 (the number of people who took part in the study), 74 (the number of women in the study) and 69 (the number of men in the study), are called descriptive statistics, and are presented as summary descriptions of the participant groups in the study. Remember that research is undertaken to answer research questions, therefore descriptive statistics are presented for data relevant to those questions. If gender is relevant to the study, then descriptive statistics of gender are reported, if hair colour is not relevant to the research questions, then details of the participants hair colour would not be collected or reported.

Inferential statistics: to test predictions

More detailed data analysis can be undertaken where research results are compared and correlated with each other using statistical techniques, called **inferential statistics**; such as a *t* **test** to test a prediction about the difference in the performance of two groups of participants (such as novice and experienced drivers) on a particular test (such as their performance on a driving simulator). This book is mostly concerned with presenting descriptive and illustrative statistics, although we do briefly consider inferential statistics in Chapter 9. (Readers who wish to use SPSS to perform complex inferential statistics are referred to our companion text: Hinton, McMurray and Brownlow, 2014, *SPSS Explained.*)

total
The 'total' is a statistic – it describes a characteristic of the sample, fundamentally – how many there are.

descriptive statistics
Usually, researchers wish to describe and summarise their research data to report the findings of a study. Descriptive statistics such as frequency counts, totals, percentages, the mean and standard deviation enable a researcher to summarise a dataset.

mean
A measure of the 'average' score in a set of data. The mean is found by adding up all the scores and dividing by the number of scores.

illustrative statistics
Illustrative statistics are the visual representation of data, often in the form of a chart or a graph. It may be easier to understand a graphical representation of data than the same information in the form of a table or written description.

See Chapter 3

inferential statistics
Statistics that can be used to make inferences about the data collected from samples to wider groups or populations: Whether, on the basis of probability, data showing a difference in samples can be used to infer a difference in populations or not.

t **test**
A statistical test to examine the difference in means obtained from two samples, to see if the difference in the samples can be generalised to the populations under investigation.

See Chapter 9

The Sparcote Study – stage 4

The Sparcote Study involves a survey with 12 questions, with the first three questions providing demographic information on the groups of interest to the researchers (gender, age and subject major). The remainder of the questions concern the students' experiences in the university during their first year. The researchers want to describe what the students have responded to each of these questions, so in most cases, they wish to summarise the data so that it can be clearly presented in a report, in the form of a table or a graph, to illustrate the student view of their experience. They also want to explore the results in terms of the demographic groupings, to see if there are any indications of different experiences between them. Explanations of how to describe the results of the Applied Studies Student Survey using SPSS will be given throughout the rest of this book. In exploring the results of the different types of questions used in this survey, readers will be able to see how to present different types of numeric data (employed across a range of quantitative methods and not just surveys).

STAGE 5: PRESENTING THE RESEARCH FINDINGS

The final stage of research is to report the findings. There is no point in undertaking research unless it is communicated to other people. In the case of the Sparcote Study, the research has been undertaken to describe the student experience, and will be communicated to the departmental members and the university, which could be either in the form of a report or in a PowerPoint presentation (or both). If any issues are identified from the results of the study, then the academic team can examine these issues further or change their practice to improve the student experience. This is why verbal reports in the form of conference presentations and written reports in terms of academic papers (such as dissertations or publications in academic journals) are so important in the development of knowledge. One piece of research can stimulate further research; contradictions between the results of two studies can be examined and a body of knowledge developed around a particular area of study. From this work theories are constructed, developed and challenged. Thus, the community of researchers in a field of study are able to do so much more than an isolated researcher working on their own.

replicate
The findings of a single research study, however well carried out and analysed, may still be subject to chance effects. Repeating the study to see if the same findings reoccur is a way of demonstrating that the effect did not arise by chance. If the same results do reoccur in further studies, it provides further support that the findings are not 'one-off' or chance effects. The ability to replicate (repeat) a finding is a crucial aspect of knowledge development in a field of study.

Research reports need to be clearly organised in a manner that is both easy to follow and detailed enough for the study to be repeated by other researchers if they wish to do so. The ability to **replicate** a finding is a crucial aspect of knowledge development. Research reports are normally structured according to a particular format and style, so student dissertations in a particular discipline in a university department will be required to follow the specific dissertation guidelines of their subject. Academic journals will require researchers to structure their reports according to the requirements of that journal. While these are specific to the department, journal and subject – and so have to be learnt and followed – certain general points can be made. The writer of the report also needs to have the reader in mind when they write their report. A report for a general readership may require a different level of explanation compared to one for specialists in the field. Reports need to be clear and readable, with enough detail for the reader to understand what was done and what was found. However, they should not be overlong and verbose.

Also, most importantly, the results of the research need to be presented precisely and unambiguously.

There are three ways of presenting results in the form of numeric data in a report:

- In the main body of the text in a narrative form.

- Separately as a table.

- In a chart or a graph.

Presenting results in text form

When presenting your findings, you will usually include some form of narrative account of the numerical data. This may be reporting what you have found or explaining what this information means in relation to your research questions and background reading. In many cases, it is adequate to present a simple result in text form, for example: '74 (52%) of the participants were women and 69 (48%) were men.' It is unlikely that presenting this information in a table or graph would add to the understanding of the reader. However, with more complex results, a table and graph can provide a clear – and more easily understood – summary of the findings.

Tables

Tables allow you to present numerical data in a format that is clear and organised. The information in a table presents a summary of the data you have collected. The advantage of a table is that it often takes up only a small amount of space on the page, which allows the results to be easily inspected by eye to make comparisons and contrasts between the values. When the data can be summarised in only one or two numbers, as in the gender example above, drawing a table may not add to the clarity of the presentation. However, when there is more information, simply describing it in a text description can be confusing, whereas presenting it in a table can make the results very clear; for example, the following information from a traffic study is clearly displayed in table format as the first table in a report.

Table 1: Traffic counts on North Street

| | | Traffic direction | | |
		Into town	Out of town	Total
Time of day	8-9am	1798	128	1926
	11-12noon	476	362	838
	2-3pm	324	521	845
	5-6pm	216	1587	1803
	Total	2814	2598	5412

It is easy to observe in the table that the volume of traffic along North Street is greatest going into town between 8 and 9 am, and leaving town between 5 to 6 pm (which is likely to be due to commuter traffic). The table provides a clear, easy-to-read summary of the findings. Now the writer can simply point out, in the text, the key findings in the table (such as the times of high traffic volumes) without having to describe every result in words.

See Chapters 5 and 6

In this book, we will be explaining in Chapters 5 and 6 three different methods for producing tables in SPSS:

- The **Frequencies** command (simple tables of counts or totals and percentages).

- The **Crosstabs** command (a crosstabulation, like the table above, combining two or more variables in the one table, which in this case combines, or crosstabulates, the 'time of day' with the 'traffic direction' in or out of town).

- The **Custom Tables** command (a flexible table creation module that allows all sorts of complex tables to be created).

Graphs or charts

Graphs (or charts) can be powerful illustrative tools. Indeed, just over a century ago a newspaper editor stated: 'Use a picture. It's worth a thousand words.' This can be said for the presentation of numbers. Graphical representations of the results are referred to as illustrative statistics – such as a chart of a person's weight loss over a period of months. Indeed, graphs are very useful in showing trends, patterns and relationships in the results that are visually immediate and easier to appreciate than when the data is described in text or presented in a table. For example, in Figure 1 of the traffic study report, it can clearly be seen that cars are the most frequent vehicle on the road.

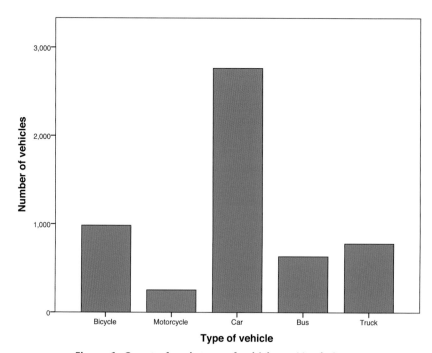

Figure 1: Count of each type of vehicle on North Street

We will explain how to produce graphs, such as pie and bar charts and line graphs using SPSS in Chapters 5 and 7 and how to edit them in Chapter 8, to produce the graphs that illustrate your findings clearly for your reader.

See Chapters 5, 7 and 8

The Sparcote Study – stage 5

We will be explaining the different ways the results from the Applied Studies Student Survey can be presented in tables and graphs – using SPSS – throughout the rest of the book.

Now that we have explained the research process, we will describe the types of tables and graphs with which to present your data, using SPSS. However, as we explain in the next chapter, this depends very much on the type of data that you have collected.

What are you measuring in your research?

3

39 DESCRIBING YOUR RESULTS

39 LEVELS OF MEASUREMENT: NOMINAL, SCALE AND ORDINAL DATA

48 CONSTRUCTING NOMINAL, SCALE OR ORDINAL OUTCOME MEASURES

55 CODING YOUR DATA FOR INPUT INTO SPSS

56 THE SPARCOTE STUDY

Chapter aim: To examine different types of numeric outcome measures

As discussed in Chapter 2, there are a number of methods that we could use to answer our research questions that produce numerical data. An experiment, an observation, secondary data and surveys all produce numerical data. Essentially, in this type of research – quantitative research – in order to answer the research questions we are measuring 'number' outcomes. For example, you want to know how many people prefer coffee rather than tea in your office. You go to each member of staff and ask them if they prefer coffee, tea or have no preference (or don't drink either of them). You then count up the number of people in each group. To get the information you want – to answer your question – you count the number of people. This is your outcome measure – you are measuring how many people there are in each category: You are measuring the 'frequency of responses'. Researchers measure an outcome that will provide an answer to a research question. Doctors examining how young babies are thriving will often measure their weight, teachers assessing how well their students are doing will give them a test that is measured as a score – such as the number of correct answers – and researchers in a large food company will ask a panel of consumers in a product test to put a number of different types of pizza in an order of their preference. The baby's weight, the test score and the consumer order of preference are all outcome measures. The outcome measures are chosen and then used in the research to answer the research questions. If 21 people in the office preferred coffee rather than tea, four preferred tea and two had no preference, then you might proceed with the suggestion that you jointly buy a coffee machine to supplement the kettle you already have. The babies' weights, the test scores and the consumer preferences all provide information for the researchers.

In many cases, researchers want to find out about issues that are fairly simple to measure. To measure a baby's weight we can use a set of scales, to measure how long it takes a person to run 100 metres we can use a clock (a stopwatch), to measure

operationalisation

Redefining a concept so that it can be studied. Concepts such as intelligence or happiness are often difficult to define. However, in order to study such ideas, researchers operationalise them in terms of measurable outcomes. For example, 'intelligence' has been studied by operationalising the term as 'the quality measured by an intelligence quotient (IQ) test'; 'happiness' may be defined in terms of the responses to certain items in a questionnaire. It is important to specify in a research report how such terms have been operationalised so that other researchers are aware of how the concept has been defined.

the temperature at different times of the year we can check a thermometer. However, for lots of things we are interested in there are no handy measuring devices – there is no intelligence-o-meter or happiness-o-meter that we can test people with. Researchers construct measuring devices – in the form of a set of tasks or questions – that they hope produce outcomes relevant to the issue under study. This is called **operationalisation** – producing a 'device' to measure the concept under study. This is often quite tricky as some concepts are quite difficult to successfully operationalise. The most famous of these is the intelligence quotient or IQ test, which comprises a series of questions (involving different tasks), with the overall score used as a measure of the child's intelligence. Originally IQ tests were used to see if children were lagging behind their peers in their development, but they have often been used, controversially, for a range of other purposes. Indeed, many psychologists have questioned whether IQ tests are actually measuring 'intelligence' in a meaningful way. There are a number of aspects of life that researchers are interested in that are not easily measured, such as a person's level of happiness or, to take a more mundane example, a person's satisfaction with a new washing machine. In these cases, the solution is simply to ask the people a question or set of questions and then give a numerical value to the answers in order to measure them. One of the most popular outcome measures, or set of outcome measures, is the questionnaire or the survey. These are formal ways of essentially asking people for information relevant to the research question. The questions 'Are you happy today?' or 'Are you satisfied with your new washing machine?', asking for a yes-or-no response, are often viewed as rather uninformative, so a more complex set of questions are constructed, such as asking a person about their happiness in their personal life, their working life and their social life and then using the answers to give a more detailed picture of their level of happiness. Also, a researcher might try and refine the outcome measure so that it does not simply produce a yes-or-no answer to a 'satisfaction' question but a more subtle one such as asking a person to choose between a set of answers such as: very unsatisfied, unsatisfied, neither unsatisfied nor satisfied, satisfied, very satisfied. There are lots of instances where surveys are used to measure outcomes to answer research questions such as 'What do customers think about our new website?', 'Did the new parents find the parenting classes helpful?', 'Do the students find the online seminars useful?', 'Are the staff happy with their working environment?'

SPSS is a very flexible program and can analyse a wide range of numeric outcome measures. Indeed, it will do all of the hard work of counting up the results, providing summaries in the form of tables and graphs and performing any of the comparisons you are likely to want to do. You just to tell it what you want it to do – and we will be explaining the instructions for SPSS in the subsequent chapters. However, first you must input your data into SPSS for analysis. When doing this, it is crucial that you tell SPSS what type of outcome measures you have in your research.

There are three key types of outcome measure with numerical data: nominal, scale and ordinal. These are often referred to as **levels of measurement**. The outcome of any quantitative research will be measured according to one of these three levels of measurement. In any piece of research, there may be a number of different outcomes measured at different levels. For example, in a survey some questions will result in a yes-or-no answer (nominal) whereas others might ask for a score or a value such as a person's age (scale) and others might ask for the degree of agreement or disagreement (ordinal). In the following section, we will explain the differences

levels of measurement

(also known as *level of data*). Not all data is produced by using numbers in the same way. Sometimes we associate numbers with categories (nominal), we place items in an order (ordinal), or we use a measuring scale with equal intervals (scale or interval scale).

between the three levels of measurement, so that you can tell SPSS what type of measurement you have for your own research data.

DESCRIBING YOUR RESULTS

Quantitative research is about measurement, but when we have undertaken the measurements and collected the data, we then wish to summarise the findings, that is, describe what we have found. Just as there are different types of measurement, there are also different ways of describing the results – and these are linked to the type of measurement you have undertaken. In this chapter, as well as describing the different levels of measurement, we shall also explain the ways you can describe your data depending on what type of data it is.

LEVELS OF MEASUREMENT: NOMINAL, SCALE AND ORDINAL DATA

The reason why it is called quantitative research is that we are measuring 'quantities', that is, the research measures specific numeric outcomes to answer research questions. However, these outcomes will be measured according to one of three types – or levels – of measurement.

Nominal data

The first type of outcome measurement is called **nominal**, which essentially means that you are using numbers as category labels (as nominal means 'name'). These numbers are arbitrary in that they do not have any mathematical significance. For example, players in sports teams often have numbers on their shirts. Traditionally, in some sports, the number 1 is on the goalkeeper's shirt, but this does not mean that the goalkeeper is the best (or the worse player) in the team or that the player wearing the number 2 shirt is twice as good! The numbers are identification codes. Recently in an English Premier League football match the goalkeeper had the number 44 on his shirt. This simply indicated his arbitrarily chosen squad number. Using numbers as codes can be very useful. When deciding to dispose of a plastic drinks bottle in the recycling we have to choose which box to put it in (see the figure). Notice that these boxes are coded by a colour (so red has been arbitrarily chosen for plastic) and they have even written labels, too. The red box has 'plastic' helpfully written on it. We could also number the boxes 1 to 4, which creates a third way of coding them! We therefore select Box 4 – the red one with 'plastic' written on it – to put our plastic bottle into. In research, people often use numbers as codes as this makes the data easier to input and analyse, and a computer program like SPSS is set up to deal with both numerical codes and the associated written labels for the data.

nominal
Nominal refers to the term 'name'. In research terms, nominal data is data collected in named categories for a variable, such as the variable 'home location' with the categories 'north', 'midlands', 'south'. A person gives the location of his home by selecting one of these three categories.

Box 1   Box 2   Box 3   Box 4

Research studies often collect nominal data. For example, many questions ask the participant to choose a category from a number of different choices in their answer. These questions produce nominal data. There could simply be a two category choice, such as yes-or-no for the question *Do you like watching football?* Similarly the choice of either 'female' or 'male' might be offered as a question in a different study when asking a person to give their gender. In a third study, there might be a number of categories to choose from, such as the answers to the question: *Which one do you prefer the most: apple, orange, pear, or banana?* The response simply tells us that there is one more person in the chosen category. From the examples above, we can look at a response in a category and say: This person does not like watching football, this person is a female and this person likes pears more than the other fruits. At the end of the survey, adding up the total number of responses in each category (their frequency) provides the overall results of these questions, such as 84 people like watching football and 36 do not, that there were 62 females and 54 males who took part in the survey or that 42 people prefer apples, 55 prefer oranges, 26 prefer pears, and 32 prefer bananas. We might want to express these frequencies (counts or totals) as percentages, so in the first example, 70% of the people in the survey like to watch football (as 84 out of 120 chose the yes category) and 30% do not like to watch football (36 out of 120).

When we have nominal data to analyse with SPSS we give the different categories a numeric code, such as 0 for 'no' (to the question *Do you like watching football?*) and '1' for yes. It does not matter which numbers we choose (so we could have chosen anything, such as the numbers 22 and 136) but it is better to be simple and consistent in our choice of number codes. For example, we might give a numeric code of 1 to the category 'female' and 2 for 'male' in the responses to the gender question; and give the codes 1 to 'apples', 2 to 'oranges', 3 to 'pears' and 4 to 'bananas'. In the examples, we have simply coded the categories using numbers, starting from 1, in the order we have listed the categories in the survey. This numeric **coding** helps researchers to input their data into SPSS and also helps SPSS to analyse it. However, we also tell SPSS what the numerical codes refer to, such as the number 3 indicates a choice of 'pears'. SPSS is able to use the written labels in the tables and graphs it produces so that it will helpfully display the label 'pears' rather than the numeric code '3' in its output.

coding

In research using categorical variables, responses are placed in a category (such as 'day' or 'night'). These labels are given a numeric code (such as 1 for 'day' and 2 for 'night') so that they can be analysed by statistical software. Coding is the process of allocating codes to categorical responses in a study.

Descriptive statistics: Describing nominal data

The total or frequency

In the gender example above, 116 people took part in the study, so 116 is the total number of people in the study. The 'total' is a statistic – how many there are. You have worked out this statistic by doing something mathematical – you have 'added up' the number of people. You have also added up the number of women, which gives a total for the women of 62, and added up the number of men, which gives a total for the men of 54. Now, it is reassuring to check that the total for the women (62) and the total for the men (54) add up to the overall total (116). In some cases, you might find that the totals for men and women do not add up to the overall total. You might find that some people have forgotten (or chosen not to) tick a box in response to the 'gender' question. You might have, say, 62 women and 54 men but

118 people in total in your study. In this case, we would report this as 62 women, 54 men and two **missing values**. Calculating the 'total' can be a very useful statistic to describe your results. Researchers also refer to totals as 'counts', 'frequencies' or even 'frequency counts': because, to produce a total, we must 'count' up the number; and the total of, say, the women tells us how 'frequent' women are in the study. When there are more than two categories, the counts are usually shown most clearly in a **frequency table**, such as the one given here:

Fruit choice	Frequency
Apples	42
Oranges	55
Pears	26
Bananas	32
Total	155

Percentages

A second statistic, linked to counts, is a **percentage**. In a sample of 116 people, where 62 are women and 54 are men, we can work out the percentage of women and men in the sample. The percentage of women is calculated by dividing the total number of women (62) by the total for the whole sample (116) and multiplying by 100. This tells us that 53% of the people in the study are women (or if we want to be more accurate 53.45%). We also can work out that 47% of the participants are men (or 46.55% to be more accurate). The percentage of men plus the percentage of women adds up to 100%. Adding percentages to the frequency table allows a reader to compare the percentages as well as the frequency counts, as in the fruit example:

Fruit choice	Frequency	Percent
Apples	42	27
Oranges	55	35
Pears	26	17
Bananas	32	21
Total	155	100

We can also calculate a **valid percentage**, which refers to the percentage of answers in a category in terms of the actual answers received. Here is the table of frequencies with percentage and valid percentage when everyone answers the question (percent and valid percent are the same):

Fruit choice	Frequency	Percent	Valid Percent
Apples	42	27	27
Oranges	55	35	36
Pears	26	17	17
Bananas	32	21	21
Total	155	100	100

missing values
A missing value indicates that a person did not answer a question.

frequency table
A table listing out the frequencies of the different categories of a variable (or variables), often used to show the results of a research study.

percentage
A proportion of a whole, expressed out of a total of 100. To turn a frequency or count into a percentage for a category, the category count is divided by the total for all the categories and multiplied by 100.

valid percentage
In any study, there a possibility that there will be missing data, for various reasons. For example, a participant in a survey may miss a question or choose not to answer it. In analysing the data, it is important to know both the number of valid responses (where a result was present) and the number of missing responses. The valid percent is the number of valid responses in a category divided by the total number of valid responses, and then multiplied by 100.

For details on how to produce frequency tables in SPSS, please see Chapter 5

cumulative percentage
When data are allocated to categories, the frequency values in each category can be converted to their percentage of the total. The percentage values of the categories can be can be added together to produce a cumulative percentage for the categories chosen. When all categories are selected the cumulative percentage will be 100%.

mode
The most frequently occurring category or score in a set of data.

scale
A measurement scale with equal intervals (like centimetres on a tape measure), and the data collected by using it.

Sometimes in a research study participants do not give an answer (they might miss a question by mistake or refuse to answer). For example, if five people in the fruit preference study did not give an answer, then there are only 150 valid answers in a total of 155 participants, and the frequency table might look like this:

Fruit choice	Frequency	Percent	Valid Percent
Apples	42	27	28
Oranges	53	34	35
Pears	25	16	17
Bananas	30	19	20
Valid Total	150	97	100
Missing	5	3	
Total	155	100	

In this situation, the researchers might wish to report 'of those people who gave a preference, 35% preferred oranges.' Notice that here the valid percentage is the reported percentage value.

There is another type of percentage that can be reported – **cumulative percentage**. Let us assume once again that everyone answered the fruit choice question. We can produce the following:

Fruit choice	Frequency	Percent	Valid Percent	Cumulative Percent
Apples	42	27	27	27
Oranges	55	35	35	63
Pears	26	17	17	79
Bananas	32	21	21	100
Total	155	100	100	

The final column shows the cumulative percentage, adding up the percentages of each of the categories up to that point. We see that 27% preferred apples, and 63% preferred apples or oranges and so on.

The most popular value or category: The mode

Sometimes, with nominal data, it is useful to highlight the most popular category chosen. In the fruits example (above), we can see that the most popular choice is oranges – which was selected by 55 people as their preferred fruit. The most popular value or most popular category in a set of results is referred to as the **mode**.

(Interval) scale data

The next data type, **scale** is one we are all familiar with, as a wide range of measuring devices, such as clocks, thermometers, tape measures and speedometers, for example, all measure scale data. The key aspects of scale data are that, first, it has equal intervals on the measurement scale and, second, it is 'continuous'. A tape measure has equal intervals as the distance between the centimetre marks is the always the same: it does not matter if I examine the distance between four and five centimetres or 66 and 67 centimetres, this interval will always be the same (i.e. one centimetre). Also, the scale is continuous, in that there are no gaps or 'jumps' in the scale. We might choose to round up a measurement to the nearest centimetre, so we might say something that is more than four centimetres is nearly five centimetres (when we don't need to be too accurate), but if we choose to be more accurate we can report the measurement more precisely as, say, 4.82 centimetres, as the scale is continuous. When we measure a person's height, weight, age, or even the time it takes them to run 100 metres, the answer we produce is scale data. With this research data, each result is a point on a (continuous) scale. For example, the answers to the following questions produce scale data: *How old are you?* or *What temperature do you set for the central heating in your family home?* Here, age and temperature are measured on continuous measures of equal intervals. A year is always the same length, so a person who is 24 years old is one year older than a 23-year-old, which is the same interval (one year) as that between a 37-year-old and a 38-year-old person. Degrees on a temperature scale are always the same size as well.[1]

Descriptive statistics with scale data

A 'middle' position: The average or the mean

We could count up the frequency of each different response on a scale but, unlike nominal data, these results will not be in a set of fixed categories that we have set up in advance. If we have 30 adults in a study we might get 30 different ages, so each of the different ages will have a frequency of 1 – which is not a very interesting or informative description of the participants' ages. That is why, with data from an interval scale, we look for a central or middle value – sometimes referred to as a **measure of central tendency** – to represent the set of results. Rather than listing out 30 different ages we can calculate and report that the average age of our participants is, say, 24 years (or 24.54 years depending on how accurate we wish to report the results). The technical term for this statistic is called the mean (which is simply another way of saying 'average'). We add up all the participants' ages and divide by the number of them (30) to find the mean age.

The mean is the most commonly used statistic to describe (interval) scale data, and in many cases it is a very good way of expressing a 'middle' position in the data

measure of central tendency
In describing a set of results from a single variable, researchers often wish to summarise the data by presenting a typical or 'middle' value to represent the results. There are different ways of calculating a 'middle' position or measure of central tendency. The mean is the most popular for scale data, but the median and the mode may also be chosen.

---

1 Some interval scales, such as distance or speed also have a meaningful (non-arbitrary) zero point. This means that zero literally means no distance or no speed. These types of interval scale are called ratio scales. Not all interval scales are ratio scales. Consider the Celsius temperature scale. Here 0°C does not mean 'no temperature' and the zero is arbitrarily chosen as the freezing point of water. Temperature can be measured on other interval scales, such as the Fahrenheit scale, with a different value chosen for zero (0°C = 32°F). With ratio scales such as distance and speed we can refer to ratios like or 'a third' or 'twice', such as *This stick at 10 centimetres is a third the length of that one at 30 centimetres* or *That car travelling at 40 mph is going twice as fast as that one at 20 mph*. With the Celsius or Fahrenheit temperature scales, it is not possible to say one temperature is a third or twice another temperature. However, most of the time in research we do not need to worry about whether an interval scale is ratio or not – as we normally do the same analysis with either. SPSS, for example, just needs to know that the measurement is on an interval scale and does not need to be told whether the scale is ratio or not.

– or central tendency. It gives a good indication of what a typical result looks like. Consider the following 12 scores measured on a scale: 6, 8, 5, 7, 5, 6, 6, 4, 5, 3, 7, 4. The mean of 5.5 is a good 'middle' score and describes the results very well. The scores cluster very nicely around this value with the scores spreading out symmetrically about it, with fewer scores as the values get lower or higher. We can see this by listing the scores in order: 3, 4, 4, 5, 5, 5, 6, 6, 6, 7, 7, 8. This is what researchers normally find when measuring along a scale – the scores will normally cluster around a 'middle' position and this is the mean value. This is normally much better than the mode as a description of a 'middle' score in the results for scale data. In this case, there are two modes, 5 and 6 (both numbers occurring three times in the results). The mode is not a very stable measure of central tendency as a few slightly different results (such as one result of 6 changed to a 7) and the mode could suddenly changes quite radically (now 7 is a mode, along with 5, and 6 is not). A slight change and the mean will remain more or less the same. A 6 changing to a 7 only increases the mean to 5.58.

However, on occasion, the mean might not be a very good measure of central tendency, particularly when one or more extreme results occur. Consider the following example. A group of five male friends decide to test their 100 metres running times. The results (in seconds) are 28, 25, 27, 14 and 26 seconds. This gives a mean time to run the 100 metres of 24 seconds, which is not a very good description of their 'typical' times – being faster than four out of five of them can run. The presence of the very good runner at 14 seconds (although nowhere near Olympic standard) is an extreme score compared to the others, who are all running the 100 metres between 25 and 28 seconds. An alternative to the mean as a measure of central tendency, a 'middle' position, is the **median**. To find the median, we list the scores from lowest to highest and count along to the middle position and take that score as the median. In this case, the scores in order are 14, 25, 26, 27, 28. The middle score is the third one, so the median value is 26. Here, 26 seconds looks a more reasonable measure of the 'typical' man's running times for the 100 metres, compared to the mean of 24 seconds. If there had been an even number of scores we would

median

If we order a set of data from lowest to highest, the median is the point that divides the scores into two, with half the scores below and half above the median.

✓

There may be a situation where there is no 'middle' position in the data, when the results obviously do not form a single cluster, the mean might not be the best description of a 'typical' score, as there is not one. For example, if the scores in a test were 19, 1, 4, 17, 18, 3, 1, the mean is 9, which does not really represent a typical score at all. In this case, there are two clusters of scores, a low group (1, 1, 3, 4) and a high group (17, 18, 19). Not surprisingly, none of our 'middle' position descriptive statistics works very well (mean = 9, median = 4, and the mode is 1!). In this case, this might be something to note – the fact that there are two clusters might be really interesting. It may be that the participants are making a categorical judgement – either giving a 'low' score (giving a value of 1, 1, 3 or 4) or a 'high' score (17, 18, 19) and not using the measure as a scale at all.

We can always choose to convert data from an interval scale to nominal if we want to. For example, we could recode the above data in SPSS so that the actual scores are converted to the categories of 'low' and 'high'. Now the response data are no longer scale but nominal, with a count of 4 in the 'low' category and a count of 3 in the 'high' category. (See Chapter 6 on how to do this.)

take the two scores around the middle point and find their average for the median. However, results from scale data often cluster symmetrically around a central position – the mean – so that most of the time calculating the mean gives a very good and stable description of a 'middle' score – which is why the mean is the descriptive statistic usually calculated with scale data.

The standard deviation: How spread out are your numbers?

The mean is usually a good summary statistic for the 'typical' or 'middle' score with a set of scale data, however, it is also good to know if the results in the data are clustered tightly around the mean or if they are more spread out. The set of scores 5, 6, 4 have a mean of 5 and the set of scores 7, 3, 5 also has a mean of 5, yet the first set are clustered more closely around the mean compared to the second set. Even though they have the same mean there is a difference in their 'spread'. To describe this second aspect of our results – how spread out they are – we calculate a second descriptive statistic. Just as we have three possible ways of describing a 'middle' position (mean, median and mode) there are a number of different ways of describing the spread of a set of results. The first statistic is called the **range**. We calculate the range by subtracting the smallest score from the largest. In our first set of results, the range is 2 (6 – 4) and in our second set the range is 4 (7 – 3). Even though the two sets of results have the same mean, the second is more spread out as it has a range twice that of the first. A more complex way of describing the spread of the results is the statistic called the **standard deviation**. This is a little more complicated calculation, but essentially every score is compared to the mean and an 'average' (or standard) distance – or deviation – is calculated. For the first set of results the mean is 5 and the standard deviation is 1 and for the second set of results, the mean is 5 and the standard deviation is 2. Notice that these two statistics (mean and standard deviation) sum up the two sets of results very well – they both have the same 'middle' score but the second is more spread out than the first. In this example, there are only three results in each set but the mean and standard deviation can be used to summarise any number of results. Instead of 3 scores, we could have 300 or 3000 and still be able to describe them by these two useful statistics: the mean and standard deviation. We can use SPSS to calculate the descriptive statistics for any amount of data.

range
The difference between the lowest score and the highest score in a set of results.

standard deviation
A measure of the standard ('average') difference (deviation) of a score from the mean in a set of scores.

Ordinal data

Ordinal data is the third type, or level, of data. Ordinal measurement is often viewed as somewhere between nominal and scale. It does comprise a set of categories (like nominal data) but also has an order to the categories (like scale data). Consider the rating system for hotels. We expect a five-star hotel to be the best and the one-star hotel to be the most basic in the system. A one-star hotel might be good, but we expect a two-star hotel to be better – with more facilities. The rating system puts hotels in a rank order, which people find useful in deciding in which hotel to stay. However, two hotels might be quite different even with the same star rating. One three-star hotel might not be that much better than a very good two-star hotel whereas another three-star hotel is nearly as good as a four-star hotel. Therefore, the hotel star-rating system is not necessarily measured on a scale with equal intervals.

ordinal

Ordinal comes from the word 'order'. In research, when items are ordered or people are asked to make rating or ranking judgements, it cannot be assumed that they are making these judgements using a measurement scale of equal intervals, so the data are referred as ordinal rather than scale.

categorical data

Data can be measured at different levels: nominal, ordinal or scale. Nominal and ordinal data are recorded by a response being allocated to a category, so the term 'categorical data' is used to refer to either nominal data or ordinal data or both.

We have left ordinal to last as ordinal is the most tricky to work with. Consider this question: *Do you like this new flavour ice cream?* We could set up two response categories, 'yes' or 'no'. This is clearly nominal. However, researchers often want a bit more subtlety in the answers, so we could set up more than two categories, such as these five categories: 'I really don't like it', 'I don't like it', 'It is ok', 'I like it' and 'I really like it'. Notice that now we have an order of responses. We assume that someone who selects the category 'I like it' likes the flavour more than a person who selects 'It is ok', and less than a person who selects 'I really like it'. These categories are arranged in an order of liking. This is why the data is called **ordinal**. Now, there is no special way to analyse ordinal data so we have to decide whether to treat the data in the same way as nominal data or in the same way as scale data. The answer is unambiguous. Mathematically, ordinal data is just the same as nominal data: They both involve a choice of categories, so we work out frequencies and percentages. They are both referred to as **categorical data**. We do not work out means and standard deviations because the responses are not measured on an interval scale. The different participants may not see the interval between 'It is ok' and 'I like it' as the same as the interval between 'I like it' and 'I really like it'; and it certainly is not a continuous scale. Therefore, the simple rule is to analyse ordinal data in the same way as nominal data.

Descriptive statistics with ordinal data

Ordinal data is usually described in the same way as nominal data, in terms of frequencies and percentages. Consider the ice cream example above. The ice cream company ask 64 participants to blind test two new ice-cream flavours, breadfruit and avocado. Each participant gives an opinion of the flavour on the five-point ordinal scale described above. The results for breadfruit flavour ice cream are shown in the frequency table below.

	Rating of the Breadfruit flavour icecream					
	I really don't like it	I don't like it	It is OK	I like it	I really like it	Total
Frequency	3	6	14	22	19	64
Percent	5%	9%	22%	34%	30%	100%

We can see that 64% of the participants either liked it (34%) or liked it a lot (30%) and only 14% didn't like it (9%) or really didn't like it (5%). With the avocado flavour we get the following table of frequencies:

	Rating of the Avocado flavour icecream					
	I really don't like it	I don't like it	It is OK	I like it	I really like it	Total
Frequency	21	19	2	8	14	64
Percent	33%	30%	3%	13%	22%	100%

Here, the majority of people do not like it (30%) or really do not like it (33%) totalling (63%) but there are another group of people (35%) – around one-third of the sample – who like it (13%) or really like it (22%).

As in this example, just like nominal data, frequencies, percentages and cumulative percentages can all be used to describe and summarise ordinal data in research. The mode can also be used with ordinal data, however, with an ordinal scale it is the pattern of frequencies and percentages that is often the most useful to describe the data.

There are some occasions when you would treat ordinal data as scale. Consider the following situation, with the same question as above: *Do you like this new flavour of ice cream?* The participants are asked to make a choice from 1 ('I really don't like it') to 5 ('I really like it'), so they can choose one of the following: 1, 2, 3, 4 or 5. This type of response is often called a **rating scale**. This seems to indicate that it is a 'scale' so we can work out means and standard deviations. Unfortunately, this is not true mathematically. Notice that it is simply an ordered set of five categories just like the ones in the previous example. The only difference is that we have used the numbers 1–5 as the codes rather than written labels of 'I really don't like' and so on. The participants might use the numbers very differently to each other. One participant who really likes the flavour might only give it a 4 whereas someone who only likes it a little might also give it a 4. Unlike age or distance, the numbers might not be used in a standard way across the different participants. There is no such thing as a standardised ice cream-flavour-o-meter. To be safe – that is not make a mathematical error of working out meaningless statistics – researchers are often told that the 'rule' is that ordinal data should always be treated in the same way as nominal data – as we have stated in the previous section – *do not work out means and standard deviations; only work out frequencies and percentages* – and that is that!

Well, no. Some researchers argue that, even though it is ordinal data, treating it as scale in certain circumstances can be very useful. In a well-organised study of ice cream tasting, 100 participants rate each flavour on the five-point rating scale, described above. When we look at the table of frequencies, we see the following.

		Rating of the ice cream flavours				
		1	2	3	4	5
Flavour A	Count	20	30	26	16	8
Flavour B	Count	4	12	27	32	25

It is clear to some extent that Flavour B is liked more than Flavour A, but it is not really obvious in this table, in that you have to look closely at the pattern to make sense of these values. Adding percentages will not change anything as, with 100 participants, these figures are also the percentages for each of the categories. However, some researchers argue that it does look as though the participants are using the category codes 1 to 5 like a 1 to 5 scale. There also seems to be a general clustering around a

rating scale
Human participants are often asked in research to make a rating on a rating scale, such as a teacher asked to judge the politeness of the children in the class on a 1 to 10 scale. Rating scales often provide a way of measuring a difficult to define concept, such as politeness. The data from a rating scale should normally be treated as ordinal as the raters may not be using it like an interval scale. However, in a number of subject areas, researcher do (for various reasons) choose to treat rating data as if it were measured on an interval scale.

'middle' value for each flavour, so it looks as though a mean value might be a sensible summary of participants' choices. For these practical reasons, some researchers treat a rating scale like this as actual interval scale – and to the horror of the purists – work out mean values. If we use the mean values to summarise the findings we get the following:

Flavour A   Mean = 2.62
Flavour B   Mean = 3.62   (with very similar standard deviations)

These figures make it very easy to see that Flavour B is preferred over Flavour A and for many researchers this is a much clearer way of displaying the results than simply presenting frequency counts and percentages. Indeed, they might argue that they know what they are doing with their numbers and, for them, this is a more useful way of presenting the data.

We would advise you to use caution when you do this. First, look to see if this is typical practice in your field of study (in some fields of study, everyone does it and, in others, it is frowned on). Second, check to see whether treating the ordinal data as if it is from an interval scale is reasonable. It is not reasonable if the data clusters into two or three groups such as half the people really disliking the ice-cream flavour and the other half really liking the flavour. In this case, the mean (a neutral position) is meaningless – it is not a good summary of what you found – so better to stick with the frequency counts. However, if the evidence indicates that treating the data as a scale would be practically useful (and remember they are your numbers so you can do what you like with them as long as it makes sense!) then proceed with caution to calculate means – but don't be surprised if you get some people telling you that you should not be doing it. In this book, we will indicate where we have treated ordinal data as scale and why.

Therefore, which descriptive statistics you use with your ordinal data will depend on how you view that data. If you are not sure, then treat it as nominal and only work out frequency counts and percentages. However, if you are confident that treating the data as scale is appropriate for your research, then you may choose to calculate means and standard deviations.

One compromise with ordinal data is that rather than calculating the mean as the 'middle' point in the data, often with ordinal data researchers will choose to calculate the median, as it is not subject to the same assumptions about the data. Researchers look at their data and for various reasons (such as the presence of extreme scores, the data does not appear to cluster around a middle point) may decide that the median is a better description of a 'middle' position than the mean.

CONSTRUCTING NOMINAL, SCALE OR ORDINAL OUTCOME MEASURES

As we have said, all quantitative research involves measuring something in order to collect numbers to use to answer the research question or questions. In this section we are going to examine a number of different ways in which we can ask participants to provide information relevant to the research questions. Essentially, we will be looking at how you can construct the appropriate 'measuring devices' for your research.

Nominal measures

Often in research, there is a requirement to collect categorical data. If the research involves people, demographic details of these people are collected, such as their gender, age, occupation and so on. Many of these measures – such as gender or occupation – involve presenting a number of options from which the participant is asked to choose one or more of them. These options are unique independent categories, such as male or female, or non-overlapping age categories. Sometimes the researcher asks the participants to select only one answer (i.e. male or female) or tells that they can select more than one option, as in a question about drinks where the participants ticks all the types of drink that they regularly consumer from a range of options such as coffee, tea, chocolate, cola and lemonade.

One benefit of these types of question is that they don't take long for the participant to answer; they can read the question and quickly select the answer that is best suited to them. They also make good 'screener' questions – questions that ensure that the respondent is suitable to take part in the research, for example, if you were exploring the views of people who had borrowed a book from a library, you would need to ensure that the participants have taken a book out of the library first.

A multiple choice question requiring a single answer

There are many instances where researchers wish to find out which of a fixed number of categories a participant in their study belongs to, for example, a person selecting where they live in a town from a list of the six districts of the town. A key point about this type of question is that the different categories are mutually exclusive (that is, the respondent cannot belong to more than one category). In the following example from a travel survey, participants are asked about where they would like to visit.

Which one of these cities would you like to visit most?

Dublin   ☐
Paris   ☐
Berlin   ☐
Rome   ☐
Vienna   ☐

In this instance, the participant must choose only one answer, therefore responding to one category negates the membership of the other categories (an equal first choice is not allowed). A simple way to turn this data into numbers is to provide a numeric code which SPSS can use for its analysis. One way to do this is to allocate the number 1 for the first choice 'Dublin', 2 for the second choice 'Paris', 3 for 'Berlin', 4 for 'Rome' and 5 for 'Vienna'. Typically, when there are a range of categories researchers simply code the first category as 1, the second as 2 and so on.

When participants are asked a question or given a statement and they are only given two different choices (such as female or male or yes or no), this is known as a **dichotomous response**. An example of a dichotomous choice is shown below:

Have you drunk any coffee so far today?

Yes   ☐
No   ☐

dichotomous response
In certain research situations (such as a particular question in a survey), a participant has to make a choice between only two options (such as yes or no): This is a dichotomous response.

With a choice of two categories, researchers will often numerically code them as 1 and 2 following the same logic as with multiple categories so, for example, 'female' might be coded as 1 and 'male' as 2. Sometimes, however, researchers choose to code a yes-or-no question with the code 1 for 'yes' and '0' (zero) for 'no'. The reason they do this is that if you add up all the numbers then (as the zeros don't count) the answer will be the total number of 'yes' responses.

A problem with dichotomous questions is that there may be other options that the participant would prefer. Essentially, it is a **forced choice** and many yes-or-no questions seek to get the participant to make a decision one way or the other. Sometimes the participant may not wish to give a straightforward yes or no response, as it does not properly reflect their view. Researchers, aware of this, will often include an additional option such as 'sometimes' or 'don't know' or 'not relevant', for example in the following question:

forced choice
In some research situations, participants are required to make a choice from the available options (such as yes or no) rather than being given an option *not* to make a specific choice (which is possible when categories such as 'sometimes' or 'maybe' are included in the choices).

Do you approve of the recent changes to the government regulations on childcare?

Yes   ☐
No   ☐
I don't know ☐

In this case, as we now have more than two categories it is common to simply code them from 1 upwards, as in 1 for 'yes', 2 for 'no' and 3 for 'I don't know'. As long as you are consistent in your coding, SPSS will be able to analyse the data successfully.

A multiple choice question allowing for multiple answers

It is also possible to set up nominal measures where there is a choice of independent categories but the participant can choose more than one category. Consider the following example of a question on healthy eating:

Which of the following vegetables have you eaten since Monday? (tick as many as appropriate)

Carrots   ☐
Beans   ☐
Peas   ☐
Sweetcorn   ☐
Cauliflower   ☐

The participant can tick any or all of the choices depending on her answer, so a person who has eaten carrots and peas will tick two boxes. Essentially, this one question is the equivalent of five separate yes-or-no questions:

Question 1: Have you eaten carrots since Monday?   Yes ☐   No ☐
Question 2: Have you eaten beans since Monday?   Yes ☐   No ☐
Question 3: Have you eaten peas since Monday?   Yes ☐   No ☐
Question 4: Have you eaten sweetcorn since Monday?   Yes ☐   No ☐
Question 5: Have you eaten cauliflower since Monday? Yes ☐   No ☐

As you can see the orginal version of the question is shorter and neater, but it has to be appreciated that it is still made up of five separate **items**, or components of the question and each item requires a response (the box either to be left blank or to be ticked). When analysing multiple choice questions with multiple answers, we need to use different numeric coding than when using multiple choice questions which only require a single answer. The way this is done is to record a response for each item, so, in this example, five responses have to be recorded. One way of numerically coding the responses is to give the code of 1 for a 'tick' and 0 for 'no tick' in each box (as it is really a set of yes-or-no questions). For a participant who ticked only carrots and peas, the data would be numerically coded as 1, 0, 1, 0, 0.

item
A part or whole of a question in a survey.

Scale measures

Continuous interval scales

Many studies ask for data that is measured on a continuous, interval scale. For example, measurements based on 'how fast', 'how long (in time)', 'how long (in distance)', 'how accurate', 'how many' can all be measured on a scale. Examples of scales are height, or weight or age. Many experiments time how long it takes a human participant to perform a task. This might be a task that takes quite a while such as driving a car around a circuit, measured in minutes and seconds, or the time to recognise a word on a computer screen, which might be measured in milliseconds. Any study that uses an outcome that can be measured on a measuring device such a clock or a tape measure will be measuring the data on a continuous interval scale.

As the results from such a measurement are already numbers they do not need to be coded for SPSS but can be input directly, so a task that is completed by a participant in 1 minute 30 seconds can be input into SPSS as 1.50 (if the results are input in minutes) or 90 (if the results are input in seconds).

Discrete interval scales

In many research studies, the outcome measure is a scale but may not be continuous. Time is a continuous scale as there are no gaps in the scale and you can make measurements between the intervals, so 4.6 minutes or 3.25 seconds are measurable – you just need an accurate enough timer. Discrete interval scales are interval scales that are not continuous but have a distinct 'gap' between each scale point, such as the number of children in a family where there can be one child, two children, or three children (and so on) but not 1.4 of a child or 3.6 children. Many outcome measures are discrete interval scales, for example, the number of correct answers on a test, the number of errors on a task: indeed, most of the how-many-type questions that are asked in research. Normally, researchers simply treat these data as scale – as the measurement is on an interval scale. There are two provisos here. First, if the scale is very short, such as a measurement of errors where the maximum number of errors possible is five, then it is not as 'scale-like' as a longer scale (such as marks out of 100), and a 'scale' of five points could be viewed as simply five categories and not a scale at all. Second, certain complex statistical tests assume that the data is measured on a continuous scale, so if you are undertaking an inferential statistical test it is worth checking the assumptions to see if it is appropriate to use with your data (see Chapter 9). Most researchers are happy to calculate means and standard deviations with discrete interval scales, as we know from the mean number of children per family, often presented in the media, as the familiar 2.4 children. SPSS is also happy to analyse discrete interval scales, indeed if you select your measure as being scale SPSS doesn't make a distinction between discrete and continuous scales.

See Chapter 9

Ordinal measures

rank order
When a set of data is ordered from lowest to highest, the rank of a score is its position in this order.

There are occasions in research where participants are asked to **rank order** a set of items, such as: *Please put into order of importance these qualities in terms of a seeking a potential partner.* Then a list of items is presented such as: good sense of humour, honest, physically attractive, hard working, intelligent, good income earner. Each participant is essentially being asked to create a table of the items, like a 'league' table. The researchers then combine the results to create a combined 'league' table for all the participants. If, for example, 'honest' is put first 68% of the time (more than any other characteristic) then this can be seen as the most important quality for the participants and is put top of the overall table. While the positions in the table appear to be like a scale (first, second, third and so on), the intervals between the positions are not fixed. Two people may have put 'honest' first and 'good sense of humour' second; however, the first participant might view honesty as considerably more important than a good sense of humour but the second participant sees it only slightly more important. Despite giving the same order of the items, the interval between them is different for the two participants. Thus, the final order is not an interval scale but simply an ordered set of items, so rank ordering is an ordinal measure and the data is usually treated as categorical rather than scale.

A second form of ordinal outcome measure, which is extremely common in research, is a rating scale. This can be a very confusing term as a rating scale may not be a 'scale' such as an interval scale at all! Rating scales can be used to attempt to measure aspects of human experience not easily measured by other means, so are very popular with researchers. For example, to find out how much pain a person is suffering, a patient might be asked to give a rating of his level of pain on a scale from from 0 ('no pain') through to 10 ('severe pain'). The problem with this type of 'scale' is that the researchers cannot be sure how the different patients are using the scale: is one person's rating of 6 the same as another person's rating of 6? Does one person give a rating of 4 to a particular level of pain but another person gives it a rating of 7? Rating scales can be of different lengths, so a person might be asked to give their level of happiness (from 'very unhappy' to 'very happy') on a five-point scale or on a 100-point scale. As we saw earlier, some researchers argue that the data measured by these scales should be treated as ordinal so the results should be analysed categorically (in terms of frequencies and percentages). Yet other researchers argue that the scales can be treated as 'scale-like' and much more information is gained from the data by treating it as scale data (and working out means and standard deviations).

A variant of the rating scale is called the **semantic differential**, which involves placing two polar adjectives (opposite terms) at the end of a scale and asking the participant to choose a point between them, for example:

Cold ☐ ☐ ☐ ☐ ☐ ☐ ☐ Warm

The participant ticks the box representing their position. Notice that there is a seven-point scale in this example. Different researchers include different numbers of choices here. One alternative is to simply ask the participants tick a point on a line and the distance from the low end is measured to give the results, as in the following example:

Bad ———————————————————— Good

The data may then be treated as scale, but it should be appreciated that it is really ordinal.

Measuring outcomes on a Likert-type scale

One way to broaden out the range of answers to a dichotomous question is to create a **Likert-type scale** (named after its inventor, psychologist Rensis Likert). These are symmetrical scales offering a range of choices, between the two ends of the scale. Often researchers will present the participants with a statement such as 'I am currently happy in my work' to which the participants either disagrees or agrees. But rather than simply providing the two choice (dichotomous) response options, this is extended out to a wider number (commonly five or seven choices) so that the response options are now, for example:

Strongly disagree	Disagree	Neither disagree nor agree	Agree	Strongly agree
☐	☐	☐	☐	☐

semantic differential
This is a rating scale employed in research where a point has to be chosen between two opposing adjectives, such as good–bad, or happy–sad. These semantic differential scales are often used to gauge a person's attitudes or feelings about a particular action, activity or situation.

Likert-type scale
A measuring scale in which participants are asked to indicate their level of disagreement or agreement to a particular statement on, typically, a 5- or 7-point scale (from strongly disagree to strongly agree), named after psychologist Rensis Likert.

It is usual to have a middle, 'neutral', position where participants can respond 'neither disagree nor agree'. There is some debate about the efficacy of having a middle choice and an odd number of options, with some researchers choosing an even number of options so that participants are forced to express some degree of preference for 'disagree' or 'agree'.

A popular form of research is to have whole sections of a questionnaire (or indeed a whole questionnaire) comprising statements all requiring a response on the same format Likert-type scale. These responses in combination are viewed as providing an insight into the person's views and feelings about a particular topic. So a range of questions might be asked about a person's workplace, their views about relationships, their exercise activity (or lack of it), and so forth.

The reason why Likert-type scales are viewed as ordinal rather than scale is because, again, one cannot be sure that the scale is being used by the participants in the same way and that they are treating the scale as having equal intervals. Some people might simply tick 'strongly agree' whenever they agree (to any extent) but other participants might be reluctant to tick 'strongly agree' and only tick 'agree' even for statements they are in complete agreement with. Again, as we have noted above, some researchers do however argue that their data is scale-like so rather than treating a Likert-type scale as ordinal (and hence categorical), they do give a numeric value for each of the five points of a scale (from 1 for 'strongly disagree' to 5 'strongly agree') which they treat as scale responses and then work out means and standard deviations for data measured by these numbers. In these cases, researchers also sometimes combine the responses of a number of questions together to arrive at an overall score for the section of the questionnaire. For example, if participants were asked four questions all related to their exercise activity, an overall score might provide a good indication of how active they were. For example, if a person answered 'agree' (a value of 4) to all four questions, each asking about a different type of activity, then their overall score would be calculated as 16 for the exercise section of the questionnaire.

Text measures

On some occasions, quantitative researchers may want to know more details than simply the occurrence of an event or the degree to which a participant has an attitude or performs a behaviour. At these times, they will ask an open ended question which gives the participant the chance to write a statement in their own words. One of the most popular reasons for doing this is when the research offers the participant a range of options but is concerned that they may not have been comprehensive in their list of choices. For example, in the following question the researcher has added an 'other' category to their choices, with a space for the participant to give a written answer:

Which doctor did you see on your last visit to the surgery?

Dr Khan   ☐
Dr Lee   ☐
Dr Jones   ☐
Dr Martinez   ☐
Other   ☐
If other, please specify . . . .

The researcher can then count up the frequency of each additional category given by the respondents. For example, Dr Khan was ticked by 42 participants, 36 ticked Dr Lee, 37 ticked Dr Jones, 46 ticked Dr Martinez, and five people ticked 'Other'. The written responses were 'Dr Morley', 'Dr Morley', 'I don't remember', 'Dr Morley', 'Dr Artem'. The researchers can choose how they might code and record these 'other' results. For example, if Dr Khan is coded as 1, Dr Lee as 2, Dr Jones as 3, and Dr Martinez as 4, then Dr Morley can be added as another option with a code of 5, with three responses, and Dr Artem added with a code of 6 with one response. The response of 'I don't remember' can be input as a missing value.

CODING YOUR DATA FOR INPUT INTO SPSS

The results of a research study have to be input into SPSS in the form of a spreadsheet. This means that all the results have to be input as numbers or numeric codes. As we have seen, this is fine for scale data as these responses are already in numeric form – they are measurements along a scale. However, with nominal or ordinal data (categorical data), the responses have to be given number codes that are then input into SPSS, such as the number 1 for a tick in the 'female' box and a number 2 for a tick in the 'male' box for a question on gender. It is a good idea to document the particular choice of number codes so that you do not make a mistake in inputting your results. Also, if the codes are all written down then more than one person can input the data (using the designated codes) without making errors – as everyone is using the same codes. This document is often referred to as a **codebook** (even though it might simply be a single sheet of paper). You might already have undertaken surveys, either using paper-and-pen or completed online and never heard of the word 'codebook' before. If you have undertaken a very short paper-and-pen survey you may have added up the different responses without bothering to make a codebook. Alternatively, online survey programs automatically create a codebook for you – but do not specifically tell you that they are doing it. A 'codebook' is not an actual book, in the same way an Excel 'workbook' is not a book. A codebook is a summary table of all of your outcome measures and the decisions you have made as to what to name them, what types of numbers you are collecting and the numeric codes and written labels you have chosen for them.

codebook
In any one particular research study, there may be a number of categorical variables that require coding for analysis. Writing down the codes for each variable in a single document – called a codebook – avoids potential mistakes of different researchers using different codes in recording and analysing the results.

Most online survey programs allow you to change the names and labels for the questions and also change the codes if you want to. One reason why you might want to check which codes the online survey program has given you is that if you want to export the results spreadsheet to SPSS (and the online survey program lets you save your data as an SPSS .sav file; see Chapter 4) then you might want to make sure that the codes are the ones that you want. Don't worry if you don't bother to do this, as you can always change this information after it has been transferred to SPSS, if you wish.

See Chapter 4

In the following section, we will be describing a range of different outcome measures that can be used in research in the example of the different question types in the Sparcote Study. This survey was constructed so that it illustrates a range of different question types, which you may choose for your own survey (if that is the research tool you choose to use). Also we show how the data from the research can be coded (when necessary), the construction of a codebook, and how the data can be recorded to input the results into SPSS.

THE SPARCOTE STUDY

The Sparcote researchers decided to construct a survey to answer their research questions about the student experience of their first year in the Department of Applied Studies at Sparcote University. They constructed a short, five-minute survey of 12 questions, divided into sections to evaluate each of the important aspects of the student experience.

Section 1 of the Applied Studies Student Survey

The first section is there to collect relevant demographic information about the students: gender, age and subject major.

Question 1

The first question on gender is a multiple choice question requiring a single answer. As only a single answer is required, this question is made up of only a single item. This question is collecting nominal data so will need to be coded. A numeric code has to be chosen for the ticks in the 'female' and 'male' boxes. A simple choice of number codes is 1 for 'female' and 2 for 'male'.

What is your gender? Please tick.   Female ☐   Male ☐

See Chapter 4

We can give the question a short unique name such as 'Q1' which we are going to use to refer to it in SPSS. SPSS uses names and labels to refer to items (see Chapter 4 on inputting data into SPSS). We can choose any written label we want for the item but 'Gender' is an obvious choice for this question. SPSS has no restrictions on an item label so we could use the whole question as the label if we wished.

Question 2

This question produces scale data, as age is measured on an interval scale. As an age response (such as 21 years) is already in numeric form (the answer is a number) the results do not need to be coded.

Please enter your age in years ☐

We only need to choose a name for the question, and, to be consistent with our names, we give the name 'Q2' to Question 2 and give the question the label 'Age'.

Question 3

This is a multiple choice (single answer) question, just like Question 1, so the data type is nominal, but here there are four choices, so a straightforward choice of codes is 1 for 'Business', 2 for 'Community Health', 3 for 'Education' and 4 for 'Media'.

Which subject is your major?

Business ☐   Community Health ☐   Education ☐   Media ☐

This is a single answer question, so is a single item. We give the question the name 'Q3' to Question 3 and the label of 'Major subject'.

Section 2 of the Applied Studies Student Survey

The second section of the survey is there to measure outcomes concerning the students' academic experience. While they are all focused on different aspects of the students' academic experience, the four questions in this section all illustrate different types of question format that can be used in a survey.

Question 4

This question requires the participant to rank order, in terms of their preferences, three items: lectures, seminars and workshops. The data collected in this case is ordinal. As it is made up of three items, all requiring an answer, all three responses need to be coded.

Rank the following modes of study in terms of your preferred learning experience. (Give a value of 1 to your favourite, 2 to your next favourite and 3 to your least favourite)

Lectures   ☐

Seminars (small group discussions)   ☐

Workshops (small group practical activity sessions)   ☐

We choose to name the first item 'Q4_1' to indicate it is the first part of Question 4, with the label 'Lectures', and the other items 'Q4_2' (with the label 'Seminars') and 'Q4_3' (with the label 'Workshops') respectively. In this question, the participants have already been told to give the numeric codes (1, 2 and 3) so the coding is already done. To show that these codes indicate a rank position, written labels are chosen for each of the codes as follows: 1 is given the label 'First', 2 'Second' and 3 'Third'. The same codes and labels are used for all three items.

Question 5

Question 5 is a five-point Likert scale question about the learning resources available for the students. It requires a single response so the question is also a single item.

Please state your level of disagreement or agreement with the following statement: 'The learning resources (teaching rooms, library, IT facilities) are appropriate to support my course.'

Strongly disagree	Disagree	Neither disagree nor agree	Agree	Strongly agree
☐	☐	☐	☐	☐

constant sum
A technique used to determine the relative contribution of elements to a 'whole' or specific total in research (such as a survey), where it is required that the values given to the elements must always add up to the same amount. For example, a person could be asked to give the number of hours per day they worked (by allocating a specific number of hours to the category 'work'), slept ('sleep') and did other things ('the rest of my time'). However, every participant is required to make sure that the total number of hours adds up to the constant sum of 24 hours.

We give the question the name 'Q5' with the label 'Learning resources'. We have ordinal data here. (Some people might choose to treat a Likert scale as scale data but here we are sticking to ordinal, making no assumptions about it being on an interval scale.) As the participant ticks a box, we have to code these boxes to create numeric values for analysis. A simple coding system is to give the 'worse' or 'lowest' value 1 and then 2 for the next, 3 for the next and so on. Here we can give the numeric code of 1 for a 'strongly disagree' response, 2 for 'disagree', 3 for 'neither disagree nor agree', 4 for 'agree' and 5 for 'strongly agree'.

Question 6

This question type is referred to as a **constant sum** question. In a constant sum question, the participant portions a total amount into various categories. Here, the students are being asked to portion out 100 (as a percentage) into the relative use of three items: recommended textbooks, course materials and other materials.

Please give an estimate of your relative use of the following three resources for your studies. Place a percentage figure against each resource so that the total of the three figures adds up to 100%:

The recommended textbooks   ☐ %

Materials provided on the course website
(lecture notes, seminar materials, readings)   ☐ %

Other materials not provided by the course team   ☐ %

     100%

We name the first item 'Q6_1', with the label 'Recommended textbooks', the second item as 'Q6_2' with the label 'Course materials' and the third item as 'Q6_3' with the label 'Other materials'. This is the first tricky question for trying to decide what type of data we have. We are asking people give a percentage (which is normally treated as scale data), but we are asking then to make a judgement (which we would often treat as ordinal data – as they may not be using the scale in the same way). In practical terms, treating each percentage point as a different category is excessive, with 100 separate categories to list and not necessarily very informative. Also with 100 points, the data will result in being scale-like, so (we have decided that) the Sparcote researchers choose to treat the data as scale. This will also allow them simply to summarise the findings in terms of means. There are three items in the question and three answers to record for every participant in Question 6, so we record the three percentages given, without requiring any coding as scale data is already in numeric form.

Question 7

Question 7 is a 10-point rating scale. Teaching quality is quite a difficult concept to define and yet simply asking people to rate it is quite possible. While two scales could have been used, one for 'understanding' and one for 'helpfulness', the students have been asked for an overall judgement.

Please rate the teaching team on your course on the following 10-point scale in terms of their overall teaching quality (1 – low quality, 10 – high quality). Consider both how well they present the teaching material (clarity and ease of *understanding*) and engage with student performance (*helpfulness* of responses to student questions and their feedback on student work).

1	2	3	4	5	6	7	8	9	10
☐	☐	☐	☐	☐	☐	☐	☐	☐	☐

This question requires a single response so is a single item, and is given the name 'Q7' with the label 'Teaching team rating'. As this is a rating scale, the type of data is ordinal. However, the researchers for practical reasons would like to treat the data as scale. They make the assumption that the points on the rating scale are being treated as equal intervals and the overall ratings are from a scale measurement. (It is worth looking at the results later to see if these assumptions are reasonable – see the discussion on this issue above.) As the data is assumed to be scale, the numbers on the rating scale (1 to 10) are assumed to be actual numbers on a scale (rather than simply codes), so they are treated as scale values that do not require coding.

Section 3 of the Applied Studies Student Survey

Section 3 of the survey contains questions about the students' experience linked to the university but not about their academic experiences, so concern their use of the university facilities and the amount of paid work they do alongside their studies.

Question 8

Question 8 is a multiple choice question that also allows for multiple answers, so results in nominal data. This means that the students might tick all or none of the choices available. As there are three choices, plus a supplementary 'other' text response, this question has four items to it.

Please indicate if you have used the following university student support services during the last year (tick as appropriate)

The Health and Counselling centre (doctor, dentist, nurse, counsellor)	☐
The Student Advice Centre (for advice on issues such as finance, accommodation)	☐
Other	☐

If you have ticked 'Other', please specify . . . .

The first item, named 'Q8_1' with the label 'Health and Counselling centre', requires the box to be left unticked for a no answer, and ticked for a yes answer. As this is nominal data, a simple code is to give the value 0 (zero) with the label 'No' and 1 with the label 'Yes' for the two possible answers. The second item, 'Q8_2' with the label 'Student Advice Centre' is the same, so is nominal with the same coding.

The third item, 'Q8_3' with the label 'Other student support service', is nominal too and has the same coding. Now, participants can write in the name of an additional student support service in item four, which we can name 'Q8_4' with the label 'Other student support service used'. Written words are not numbers, so are not called 'numeric', but are referred to as a 'string', meaning a string of letters, by SPSS. As these can also be considered 'names' the data is nominal. So, Q8_4 is a special type of response – text not numbers – that we record as a string of letters. However, we can later look at these answers and examine how to analyse them (see Chapter 5).

See Chapter 5

Question 9

Question 9, like question 8, is a multiple choice – multiple answer question. Students can tick any of the five 'social spaces', so there are five items in Question 9, all of the same format.

Which of the following campus social spaces have you spent time with your peers in during this last academic year? (tick as many as appropriate)

The Student Eatery	☐
The Wholefood Café	☐
The Hub	☐
Racquets Retreat	☐
The Media Munch	☐

Some researchers would include an additional option with Question 9, a sixth choice at the bottom labelled 'None of the above'. This guarantees that the participant has read and has ticked something on the question, even if they have visited none of the social spaces. In this case, the Sparcote researchers believed that this was not necessary for their participants.

We name and label them as follows: 'Q9_1' with the label 'The Student Eatery', 'Q9_2' with the label 'The Wholefood Café', 'Q9_3' with the label 'The Hub', 'Q9_4' with the label 'Racquets Retreat', 'Q9_5' with the label 'The Media Munch'. Each item is nominal and given a code of 0 (for unticked) and a label of 'No' and 1 (for ticked) with a label of 'Yes'.

Question 10

Question 10, about the use of the Sports and Fitness Centre, asks for a response on an ordered scale, but the researchers are not making any claim for the data produced being scale, so are happy to treat the data as ordinal.

How often have you used the Sparcote Sports and Fitness Centre during the last year? (Please select the category that best represents your usage.)

Often	(once per week or more often)	☐
Regularly	(more than once per month)	☐
Occasionally	(a few times each semester)	☐
Rarely	(one or twice during the year)	☐
Never		☐

This question is a single-item question, asking for a response on an ordinal scale. We name the item 'Q10' with a label 'Use of the sports and fitness centre'. We code such a scale with the lowest code (1) for the 'worst' end of the scale, so 1 is the code for the label 'Never', and we code up from there: 2 for 'Rarely', 3 for 'Occasionally', 4 for 'Regularly', and 5 for 'Often'.

Question 11

The final question in section 3 requires a response on a standard measuring scale (time in hours), so is measured on an interval scale, and the data produced is scale.

Please give the number of hours of paid work have you have undertaken on average per week during the last academic year? (Please estimate the figure to the nearest whole number. If you have not worked please put zero.)

Hours [   ]

Question 11 is a straightforward single item question. We give the name 'Q11' with the label 'Paid work per week' and simply record the actual number of hours given by the participants.

Section 4 of the Applied Studies Student Survey

The final section of the survey presents the students with three Likert scales, asking them to rate their satisfaction with three aspects of their life during the last year. In this question, the Likert categories range from 'very unsatisfied' to 'very satisfied' and the data is assumed to be ordinal.

Question 12

Overall, on the basis of your experience in the last year, please tick your satisfaction with:

	Very unsatisfied	Unsatisfied	Neither unsatisfied or satisfied	Satisfied	Very satisfied
Your academic life at Sparcote	☐	☐	☐	☐	☐
Your social life at Sparcote	☐	☐	☐	☐	☐
Your personal development over the last year	☐	☐	☐	☐	☐

Question 12 is made up of three items, each a separate Likert scale. We will name and label these items as follows: 'Q12_1' with label 'Satisfaction with academic life', 'Q12_2' with 'Satisfaction with social life', and 'Q12_3' with 'Satisfaction with personal development'. These are ordinal measurement scales. Each item is coded with 1 as 'Very unsatisfied' through to 5 as 'Very satisfied'.

The codebook of the Applied Studies Student Survey

We can now use this information to construct the codebook for the Sparcote Study, shown in the following table.

Question	Name	Label	Type of Measure	Numeric codes or values	Labels for the values
1	Q1	Gender	Nominal	1 2	Female Male
2	Q2	Age	Scale	(actual value)	
3	Q3	Major	Nominal	1 2 3 4	Business Community Health Education Media
4	Q4_1	Lectures	Ordinal	1 2 3	First Second Third
	Q4_2	Seminars	Ordinal	1 2 3	First Second Third
	Q4_3	Workshops	Ordinal	1 2 3	First Second Third
5	Q5	Learning resources	Ordinal	1 2 3 4 5	Strongly disagree Disagree Neither disagree nor agree Agree Strongly agree
6	Q6_1	Recommended textbooks	Scale	(actual value)	
	Q6_2	Course materials	Scale	(actual value)	
	Q6_3	Other materials	Scale	(actual value)	
7	Q7	Teaching team rating	Scale	(actual value)	
8	Q8_1	Health and Counselling Centre	Nominal	0 1	No Yes
	Q8_2	Student Advice Centre	Nominal	0 1	No Yes
	Q8_3	Other student support service	Nominal	0 1	No Yes
	Q8_4	Other student support service used	String (of letters)	(input the actual words)	
9	Q9_1	The Student Eatery	Nominal	0 1	No Yes
	Q9_2	The Wholefood Cafe	Nominal	0 1	No Yes
	Q9_3	The Hub	Nominal	0 1	No Yes
	Q9_4	Racquets Retreat	Nominal	0 1	No Yes
	Q9_5	The Media Munch	Nominal	0 1	No Yes
10	Q10	Use of the Sports and Fitness Centre	Ordinal	1 2 3 4 5	Never Rarely Occasionally Regularly Often
11	Q11	Paid work per week	Scale	(actual value)	
12	Q12_1	Satisfaction with academic life	Ordinal	1 2 3 4 5	Very unsatisfied Unsatisfied Neither unsatisfied nor satisfied Satisfied Very satisfied
	Q12_2	Satisfaction with social life	Ordinal	1 2 3 4 5	Very unsatisfied Unsatisfied Neither unsatisfied nor satisfied Satisfied Very satisfied
	Q12_3	Satisfaction with personal development	Ordinal	1 2 3 4 5	Very unsatisfied Unsatisfied Neither unsatisfied nor satisfied Satisfied Very satisfied

Notice that there are 12 questions in the survey, but 25 separate items listed in the codebook. The advantage of producing a codebook is that now anyone involved in the research can refer to it to make sure they are correctly inputting any data into SPSS (or Excel or any other program) and they are doing it in the same way as the other members of the research team. You may not choose to do this if you are using an online survey program, which produces this automatically for you. However, knowing what a codebook does means that you can go into the online survey program and make sure that it codes your survey as you want it to – and change the codes and labels it has allocated to your items to ones you prefer.

Scoring the completed Applied Studies Student Surveys

As well as automatically creating a codebook for a survey, many online programs will automatically score the completed surveys – that is, allocate a set of codes and labels to the completed surveys – and store the results in a results spreadsheet, which can be exported to SPSS. If you have administered a questionnaire or survey by hand, then you will need to score the completed surveys and input the results into a spreadsheet that can be typed into a spreadsheet program such as Excel or SPSS.

Here is an example of the scoring of the results of a single participant in the Sparcote Study.

	Scoring the survey

The Applied Studies Student Survey

Section 1: About you

1. What is your gender? Please tick.   Female ☑   Male ☐

    Scoring: 1

2. Please enter your age in years   `23`

    Scoring: 23

3. Which subject is your Major?

    Business ☐   Community Health ☐   Education ☑   Media ☐

    Scoring: 3

Section 2: About your academic experience

4. Rank the following modes of study in terms of your preferred learning experience. (Give a value of 1 to your favourite, 2 to your next favourite and 3 to your least favourite)

    Lectures   `1`   **Scoring: 1**

    Seminars (small group discussions)   `3`   **Scoring: 3**

    Workshops (small group practical activity sessions)   `2`   **Scoring: 2**

5. Please state your level of disagreement or agreement with the following statement:
    "The learning resources (teaching rooms, library, IT facilities) are appropriate to support my course."

Strongly disagree	Disagree	Neither disagree nor agree	Agree	Strongly agree
☐	☑	☐	☐	☐

    Scoring: 2

6. Please give an estimate of your relative use of the following three resources for your studies. Place a percentage figure against each resource so that the total of the three figures adds up to 100%:

    The recommended textbooks

    `48` %   **Scoring: 48**

    Materials provided on the course website
    (lecture notes, seminar materials, readings)

    `45` %   **Scoring: 45**

    Other materials not provided by the course team

    `7` %   **Scoring: 7**

    `100` %

The Applied Studies Student Survey

		Scoring the survey

7. Please rate the teaching team on your course on the following 10 point scale in terms of their overall teaching quality (1-low quality, 10-high quality). Consider both how well they present the teaching material (clarity and ease of *understanding*) and engage with student performance (*helpfulness* of responses to student questions and their feedback on student work).

1	2	3	4	5	6	7	8	9	10
☐	☐	☐	☐	☐	☑	☐	☐	☐	☐

6

Section 3: About your non-academic experience

8. Please indicate if you have used the following University student support services during the last year (tick as appropriate)

The Health and Counselling Centre (doctor, dentist, nurse, counsellor)   ☐   **0**

The Student Advice Centre (for advice on issues such as finance, accommodation)   ☐   **0**

Other   ☑   **1**

If you have ticked 'Other', please specify:

.... *computing service* ...... ⟶

9. Which of the following campus social spaces have you spent time with your peers in during this last academic year? (tick as many as appropriate)

The Student Eatery   ☐   **0**

The Wholefood Café   ☐   **0**

The Hub   ☑   **1**

Racquets Retreat   ☐   **0**

The Media Munch   ☑   **1**

10. How often have you used the Sparcote Sports and Fitness Centre during the last year? (Please select the category that best represents your usage.)

Often   (once per week or more often)   ☐

Regularly   (more than once per month)   ☐

Occasionally   (a few times each Semester)   ☐   **2**

Rarely   (one or twice during the year)   ☑

Never   ☐

		Scoring the survey

The Applied Studies Student Survey

11. Please give the number of hours of paid work have you have undertaken on average per week during the last academic year? (Please estimate the figure to the nearest whole number. If you have not worked please put zero.)

Hours **12**

12

Section 4: Your overall view of your first year at Sparcote University

12. Overall, on the basis of your experience in the last year, please tick your satisfaction with:

	Very unsatisfied	Unsatisfied	Neither unsatisfied nor satisfied	Satisfied	Very satisfied	
Your academic life at Sparcote	☐	☐	☑	☐	☐	3
Your social life at Sparcote	☐	☐	☑	☐	☐	3
Your personal development over the last year	☐	☐	☐	☑	☐	4

Thank you for your participation in this survey.

You can see the responses that this particular student gave in the Sparcote survey. On the right is a column in which the results of the survey are recorded by the researchers according to the coding listed in the codebook. Sometimes you will find a paper survey with such a column on the right-hand side of the page with the heading 'For Office Use Only', where the researchers have designed the survey to include this column for the scoring the survey in the production of the printed surveys.

Once all the surveys are coded and scored, the results can be typed into a spreadsheet program such as Excel, or directly into SPSS.

In the next chapter, we explain how to input the data into SPSS if you type it in by hand. We also explain how to input the data into SPSS if it has been created automatically by an online survey program, or other computer research tool. SPSS has the flexibility that it can import data saved in a range of formats.

Entering data into SPSS

70 A FIRST LOOK AT SPSS

73 SETTING UP THE SPSS DATASET (YOUR RESULTS SPREADSHEET)

84 ENTERING THE DATA INTO SPSS

87 EDITING THE DATASET

89 TRANSFERRING THE RESULTS FROM OTHER SOFTWARE INTO SPSS

106 A FINAL CHECK OF YOUR DATASET

Chapter aim: To show how to input or import your data into SPSS

At this point in the book, we are now assuming that you have carried out your data collection.

You may have undertaken an observation and have a tally of behaviours or occurrences. If you have carried out a survey with pen and paper, you now have a stack of completed surveys sitting on your desk, or you may have undertaken an online survey or experiment and have the data saved from an online software package. The hard work of carrying out the research – the third stage – is complete. The important next stage of analysing the results and presenting the findings now needs to be conducted to produce a clear account of what you have found out, with the explanation of how this helps to answer the research questions you set out at the beginning of the study.

To start the fourth stage of the research process, the data needs to be input into SPSS for analysis. If you have undertaken a computerised research study or an online survey, all the results will have been coded and stored by the software. Most online survey programs have a facility to present a number of basic graphs and tables of your results. However, they are aware of their limitations, so allow you to save the data as a spreadsheet for further analysis by specialist programs such as SPSS. SPSS stores data in the form of an SPSS data file with the suffix .sav. A number of online survey programs will allow you to export your data directly to SPSS in the form of an SPSS .sav file, if you have the right sort of licence for the survey program. (A number of universities, or university departments, pay for these licences for their staff and students to use such programs.) If you can do this, then you can simply open the saved .sav file containing your data by SPSS. We explain how to do this later in this chapter. If your survey program does not allow you to export the data as an SPSS .sav file, it might allow you to export your data as an Excel .xlsx file or a comma separated values .csv file (or both). The really nice thing about SPSS is that it can read Excel and .csv files too. You can open the saved .xlsx or .csv by Excel and analyse the data in Excel if you wish, but SPSS has much greater flexibility and optionality in creating tables, graphs and in performing statistical analyses. There are also many computer software packages that can save the results of experiments in Excel format. If you have your results in an Excel file, don't worry because SPSS can open an Excel spreadsheet too, for SPSS analysis. What we are going to do now in the following sections is to start to use SPSS. In the first section, we will be looking at typing your results into SPSS yourself. The second section will look at importing an SPSS .sav from another program (such as an online survey program), the subsequent section will show how SPSS can import data from an Excel file and, finally, we will examine how to import a .csv file into SPSS.

A FIRST LOOK AT SPSS

SPSS can initially appear quite daunting as a computer program, yet just because it can do lots of complicated things does not mean that you will want to do them. Consider Microsoft Word; it is a clever program and can do lots of complicated things. However, we use Word every day – in fact, we are using it to write this book – and everyone else in the universities in which we work uses it too. Most people (including us) only use a small set of the commands in Word. In fact, we are sure there are lots of things you can do in Word that most people (including us!) have never found out how to do, as we have not needed to. We have learnt the things we need to know in Word to write an essay, write a book, or whatever we want to do. When we occasionally need to do something more complex, we will learn a little bit more. IBM SPSS is like Microsoft Word in this way. It is an amazingly clever program – and is used by lots of people in universities. It is fairly easy to pick up how to do the things you want, particularly as it has a familiar menus-and-windows-style interface that anyone who has used Word or Excel will recognise. When you first start SPSS the following window appears.

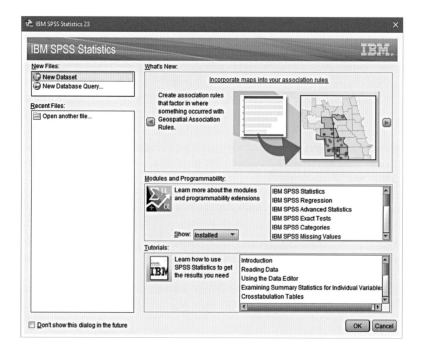

We want to type in our results. We do this by creating a new spreadsheet. SPSS calls the results spreadsheet a **dataset**, so we must select **New Dataset**. Notice that it is highlighted in yellow when we click on it with the mouse.

dataset
A collection (or set) of data, usually comprising all the results of a particular study.

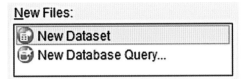

Data View
The Data View window in the SPSS Data Editor presents a spreadsheet style format for entering the data.

■ Click **OK** to continue.

A window appears headed by the title **IBM SPSS Statistics Data Editor**. This is where you will provide SPSS with all the information about your results, type in the data and perform your analysis. If you look at the bottom left of the screen, you see the tab **Data View** highlighted in yellow and the screen shows a blank spreadsheet (looking similar to Excel when you open that up). We shall now, like SPSS, call this spreadsheet the dataset. We will type our results into SPSS to create our dataset.

Variable View
The Variable View window within the SPSS Data Editor is where the characteristics of the variables are assigned.

Notice that at the bottom of the screen is a tab labelled **Variable View**. **Variable View** is the place where we tell SPSS what the numbers mean in our results spreadsheet – the coding. If you click on the **Variable View** tab the following screen appears.

labels

Variables are often given short names for the convenience of researchers. However, they can also be given more meaningful labels that can be used in reports. SPSS allows variables to have both a name and a label.

name

SPSS uses a short name to refer a variable (although it can be up to 64 characters). It must start with a letter and have no spaces (that is why we use underscore in our names, such as 'Q8_1'). A label can be longer and have spaces in it. If a label has been given for a variable then SPSS uses that in the output tables and graphs; otherwise it uses the name.

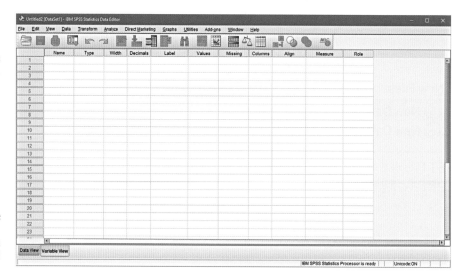

There are a number of things you can tell SPSS about each of your variables, such as giving them a **name** and a **label**, describing the coding in the **Values** sections and listing the type of the responses in the **Measure** box. We can often leave the default for a number of these and change others when appropriate. You can flip between the two screens by clicking on the **Data View** and **Variable View** tabs. Finally, if you minimise the **IBM SPSS Statistics Data Editor**, you find another window behind it called the **IBM SPSS Statistics Viewer**.

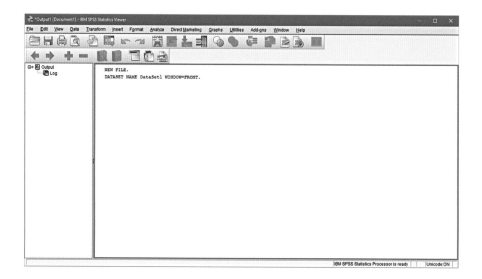

Here, SPSS keeps a record of what you have done. This screen has two adjacent windows. In the right-hand window, it will show all your tables and graphs and you can save everything you have done and copy anything you want to other programs

– such as a Word file of your research report. The left-hand window is the **Output Navigator**, which displays the output in an outline view. At the moment it simply tells us that we are setting up a new file, a dataset (or spreadsheet) that it gives the default name DataSet1. We, of course, will choose a name for our dataset when we save it.

We can at any time switch between the **IBM SPSS Statistics Data Editor** and the **IBM SPSS Statistics Viewer** by clicking the **Window** drop-down menu and selecting the window that you want.

SETTING UP THE SPSS DATASET (YOUR RESULTS SPREADSHEET)

There are two key rules in typing in your results into a SPSS dataset.

First rule: The results from a single participant are all on a single *row* of the spreadsheet. The row can be as long as you like but the results from a single person must not be split into more than one row. SPSS helpfully labels the rows so you type in the data for the first participant in row 1, the second participant in row 2 and so on.

Second rule: A *column* shows the results of an item or variable (see Chapter 3) for all of the participants. For example, the column where you typed in the age for the first participant will always be the same column where you type the age for all the other participants.

At the start the columns are all labelled 'var' which means 'variable' but we will change these to give sensible headings to the columns. SPSS refers to your items as variables.

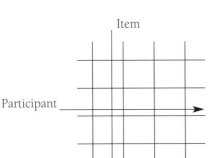

Item

Participant

As we saw in Chapter 3 with the survey in the Sparcote Study, some questions, such as a person's gender, will only be one item (or variable) – as the question requires only a single answer – so will only require one column in the dataset. Other questions, such as the use of the different social spaces, will be more than one item or variable. In fact, it requires five variables as we have to record separately whether the participant had been to each one of the five cafés or not. In order to properly record the results, we will need to specify the number of SPSS variables that each question requires. This will be shown below.

Output Navigator
An SPSS navigation and editing system in an outline view in the left-hand column of the output window. This enables the user to hide or show output or to move items within the output screen.

In the Sparcote Study, we saw in Chapter 3 that even though there were 12 questions in the survey, there were actually 25 items in the survey – that is, we had to record 25 items of information from each participant. This is because some questions asked for more than one answer, so were multi-item questions. We now have to consider the survey as a 25-item survey rather than a 12-question survey.

For an explanation of items and question types, see Chapter 3

Introduction to data entry

Before we enter any data in SPSS, we need to set up the coding for the dataset; that is, tell SPSS all about our coding and provide labels for our questions and responses so that when SPSS undertakes any analysis, it can use the more meaningful labels (rather than the numeric codes) in the tables and graphs it creates. As noted above, the dataset will be shown in the **Data View** screen of the **IBM SPSS Statistics Data Editor**. This is the spreadsheet into which we type in the results of the study. The **Variable View** screen is where we type in all the coding information for each of the variables so that, for example, SPSS knows that the number code of 1 in the gender variable is linked to the label 'female' and 2 refers to 'male'. The first variable (column) in the dataset in the **Data View** screen is described in the first row of the **Variable View** screen. So the column variables in the **Data View** screen are transposed into rows in the **Variable View** screen. A row in the **Variable View** screen describes the details of one variable, including its coding and labels and also what type of data has been collected for this variable – nominal, ordinal or scale.

Setting up the SPSS dataset (using the Sparcote Study)

We are going to use the example of the Sparcote Study to show how to enter the data into SPSS. If you are undertaking a fairly simple study, such as comparing two groups on a particular measure – such as two groups of schoolchildren on a reading test or conducting a structured observation of particular behaviour – you may not have much data to input into SPSS. The advantage of explaining how to input the data from the Applied Studies Student Survey in the Sparcote Study is that it involves a number of different types of variable and different types of measurement. For this reason, we are going to work our way through the survey, sorting out the coding in the **Variable View** screen first, so that we can later enter the data into the **Data View** screen.

The first question in the Applied Studies Student Survey of the Sparcote Study asks the respondent to tick their gender:

What is your gender? Please tick.   Female ☐   Male ☐

See Chapter 3

The problem is how you put the answers to this question (a tick in a box) as an entry in a dataset. The solution is to provide a number code or label for the possible answers (female or male). By coding the answers into numerical form the results can be stored in the best way to analyse them. As we saw in Chapter 3, a simple way of coding this 'gender' question is to give the first possible answer (Female) the number code of '1' and a participant who ticks the Female box will have the code 1 placed in the dataset, and a code of '2' for the second answer category 'Male'. As this is the first item in the survey, the results will be stored in the first column of the **Data View** screen. We now display the **Variable View** screen to define this variable in the first row.

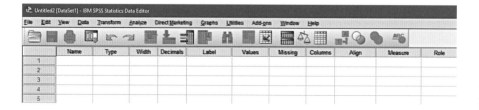

We can change different aspects of the way SPSS displays the 'gender' results. We are going to input the following:

- **Name.** We can input something meaningful like 'Question1' or 'gender'. This is only a short name to head up the column in the dataset (to replace 'var') and SPSS places a restriction on what characters you can use here. However, when you display the tables and graphs in the **IBM SPSS Statistics Viewer**, SPSS uses the **Label** (see below), which allows for more detailed names. We have chosen to give short a name to the variables in the Sparcote Study, so have named this first variable 'Q1'.

- **Type.** This is set by default to 'numeric', which means we will be inputting a number. As we will be entering numerical data most of the time we will leave it as the default. You can also set how many decimal places you would like. The default is two decimal places.

- **Label.** The 'Label' is the information that SPSS uses when displaying any analysis about a variable (such as in a table or a graph), so we can change this to something sensible like 'Participant gender' or 'Student's gender'. There are almost no restrictions on this so you can more or less put what you like here. You could even list the complete question, if you wanted to. We are going to simply use 'Gender' as the label for this variable.

- **Values.** Now this is a key piece of information for all variables that have a nominal or ordinal level level of data. This is where we type in the codes and what they mean. SPSS refers to the **Value Labels** as the labels associated with each code for the variable. Here, we tell SPSS that the code or value '1' has the label 'Female' and '2' has the label 'Male'. If we click on the right of the **Values** box a new **Value Labels** window appears.

Value Label

The categories of a nominal or an ordinal variable are given numeric codes (such as 1 for men and 2 for women) so that the data collected on these categories can be analysed by statistical software (such as SPSS). However, these numeric codes are not informative about the category itself, so SPSS allows a value label to be included with the numeric code to identify the category, for example, the value label 'men' for the numeric code 1 and the value label 'women' for the numeric code 2. Then when SPSS displays the results of the study, it uses the (meaningful) value labels rather than the numeric codes to label the results.

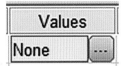

Now we type '1' into the **Value** box, and 'Female' into the Label box, then click **Add**. We now see in the lower box the following: 1.00 = "Female". We then type '2' in the **Value** box and 'Male' in the **Label** box and click **Add** to produce the following:

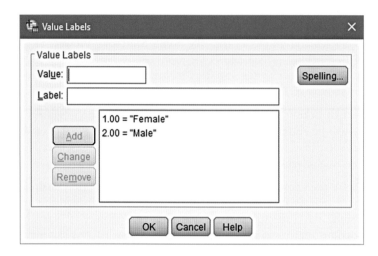

We then click **OK**. Now SPSS knows that when we type in a '1' or a '2' in the first column of the dataset this refers to a female or a male participant respectively.

See Chapter 3

■ **Measure**. When we click on the right of the **Measure** box a drop-down menu appears with three choices: nominal, ordinal and scale. These different types of data measurement were explained in Chapter 3. The numbers 1 and 2 are simply numeric values or codes for the two different categories (female and male), so we select Nominal as the measure here.

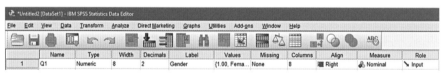

SPSS uses the following icons to indicate the measure of a variable.

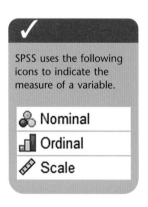

Notice that SPSS has filled in all the other cells for us, for this row, giving us the default values. In many cases, researchers are happy with these values. However, they can be changed if you wish to do so. For example, we do not want two decimal places for gender (the default values), displaying the data as 1.00 and 2.00. So we set the decimal places to 0, as described below.

Setting the decimal places
SPSS sets the number of decimal places to display in the spreadsheet as 2 in the **Decimals** column in **Variable View** (which is why SPSS displays the number as 2.00 for a male in **Data View** if you don't change it).

Again, we can leave this if we want to, but if we want to display only the number '2' as a whole number (without the decimal points) in the dataset, so we can change the decimal places to '0' – which we have done by clicking on **Decimals** and clicking on the down arrow on the right of the box to decrease the value to zero. (This does not affect any calculation by SPSS, which are always done accurately to as many decimal places as it requires.) As none of our results involves decimal places, we are going to set **Decimals** to 0 for all our variables.

Now that the first question has been coded, we can set up the coding for Question 2. In the Applied Studies Student Survey, Question 2 asks the student to give their age (in years) – which only requires a single answer for each participant, so is a single variable in SPSS. We set up the information about Question 2 (age) in the **Variable View** screen as follows:

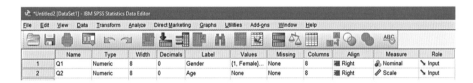

We give a **Name** of 'Q2' (to be consistent in our naming), a **Label** of 'Age' (which is nice and clear). Notice that we have not entered anything in **Values** and that under **Measure** we have selected Scale (as age is measured on a scale). We do not need to specify codes or labels as age is already a meaningful number, as we will be typing the actual age into the dataset. We have also set **Decimals** to 0 again (as we are only asking for age in years).

Question 3 is also a single item question, as it asks the students to indicate their major subject, which only requires a single variable in SPSS. We choose the **Name** as 'Q3' and the **Label** of 'Major subject'. We set up the **Value Labels** for the codes for the four major subjects in order (1= 'Business', 2 = 'Community Health', 3 = 'Education', 4 = 'Media') and set the **Measure** to Nominal.

	Name	Type	Width	Decimals	Label	Values	Missing	Columns	Align	Measure	Role
1	Q1	Numeric	8	0	Gender	{1, Female}...	None	8	Right	Nominal	Input
2	Q2	Numeric	8	0	Age	None	None	8	Right	Scale	Input
3	Q3	Numeric	8	0	Major subject	{1, Busines...	None	8	Right	Nominal	Input

That is the coding of the first section of the survey described to SPSS.

Saving the dataset as you go

It is important to save the data as you input it. Even though we have not typed any of the results into the dataset yet, we want to save the coding that we have done so far.

■ Click on the **File** drop-down menu.

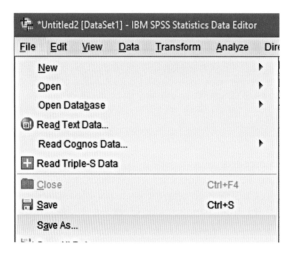

■ Click on **Save As**.

■ The **Save Data As** box appears. Select where you want to save the data (the dataset) and give it a name. We will call ours 'Applied Studies Student Survey'.

Notice that the data is stored as the SPSS file type '.sav', so the data of the Sparcote Study will be saved in the file called 'Applied Studies Student Survey.sav'. It will also have the SPSS dataset icon next to it in the file list.

It is a good idea to save your work regularly. As with other applications, you can now just click on the save icon on the menu bar.

Opening an SPSS data file

If you have already saved your dataset and closed down SPSS, when you wish to continue using SPSS you can open the saved file. When you start SPSS it will display the **Recent Files** list showing the recently used SPSS data files (with the .sav file extension). If the file you wish to open is on that list, you can click on it to open it.

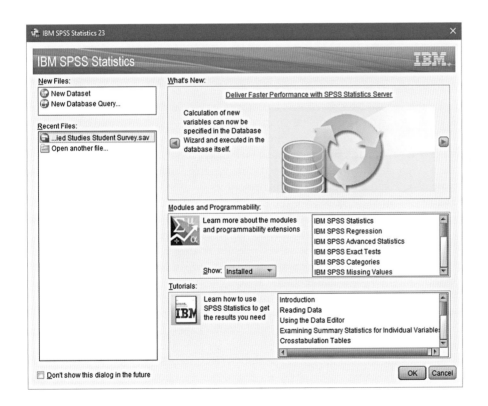

However, if the data file you wish to open is not on that list, then you can double click on **Open another file** and then a **dialog box** will open up and you can find the .sav file on your computer.

dialog box
A type of window in SPSS in which options can be selected, choices made and information input, in order to carry out a command.

Back to setting up the dataset

We now input the coding for the second section of the survey. Question 4 is a slightly more difficult question to set up as we have three separate answers for this question – so we need three variables for this question. We can **Name** the first variable 'Q4_1' with the **Label** 'Lectures' (we could choose other names and labels but these are clear and simple); the second variable is given the **Name** 'Q4_2' with the **Label** 'Seminars'; and the third variable has the **Name** 'Q4_3' with the **Label** 'Workshops'. We set **Value Label** for the codes for each variable as follow: 1 = 'First', 2 = 'Second' and 3 = 'Third'. As we have asked the participants to put these in order of preference, the **Measure** for these variables is Ordinal.

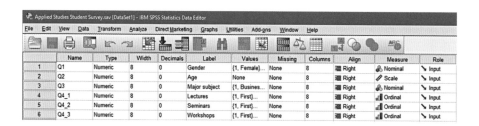

Notice that, as we have saved the dataset, the header at the top of the window has the name of the dataset 'Applied Studies Student Survey.sav' displayed.

Question 5, presented a statement about the learning resources to which the participant gave their level of agreement on a Likert scale. It only asks for one answer so is a single item and SPSS only needs one variable for this question. We give it a **Name** of 'Q5' and a **Label** of 'Learning resources'. The answers range from 'Strongly disagree' to 'Strongly agree', we therefore assign **Values** as follows: 1 = 'Strongly disagree', 2 = 'Disagree', 3 = 'Neither disagree or agree', 4 = 'Agree' and 5 = 'Strongly agree'. These are ordered judgements so the **Measure** is set to Ordinal.

Question 6 of the Sparcote survey asks for relative use of three different study materials, which requires three separate answers so we have to use three variables for this question. We **Name** them as 'Q6_1', 'Q6_2', 'Q6_3', with **Labels** of 'Recommended textbooks', 'Course materials' and Other materials', respectively. Notice that as we have asked the participants to give a percentage value (which is already a number) we do not need to specify **Value Labels**. As discussed in Chapter 3, the choice of measure for these three items is set as Scale for all three variables.

The last question in the second section of the survey is Question 7, which asked about the participant's rating of the quality of the teaching team. With one answer required, we only need one SPSS variable. We call the **Name** 'Q7' and the **Label** 'Teaching team rating'. This question uses a 10-point rating scale, from 1 to 10, and the participant ticks a box at the point they decide. It was decided to treat this ordinal scale as an interval scale (see Chapter 3), so we do not need to input any value labels and we set the **Measure** to Scale.

See Chapter 3

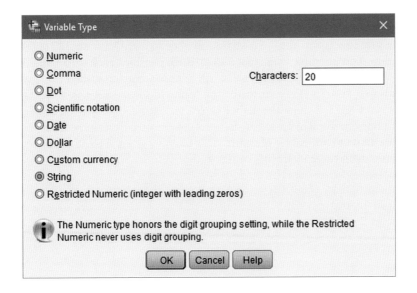

	Name	Type	Width	Decimals	Label	Values	Missing	Columns	Align	Measure	Role
1	Q1	Numeric	8	0	Gender	{1, Female}...	None	8	⬛ Right	🔵 Nominal	↘ Input
2	Q2	Numeric	8	0	Age	None	None	8	⬛ Right	📏 Scale	↘ Input
3	Q3	Numeric	8	0	Major subject	{1, Busines...	None	8	⬛ Right	🔵 Nominal	↘ Input
4	Q4_1	Numeric	8	0	Lectures	{1, First}...	None	8	⬛ Right	📊 Ordinal	↘ Input
5	Q4_2	Numeric	8	0	Seminars	{1, First}...	None	8	⬛ Right	📊 Ordinal	↘ Input
6	Q4_3	Numeric	8	0	Workshops	{1, First}...	None	8	⬛ Right	📊 Ordinal	↘ Input
7	Q5	Numeric	8	0	Learning resour...	{1, Strongly ...	None	8	⬛ Right	📊 Ordinal	↘ Input
8	Q6_1	Numeric	8	0	Recommended ...	None	None	8	⬛ Right	📏 Scale	↘ Input
9	Q6_2	Numeric	8	0	Course materials	None	None	8	⬛ Right	📏 Scale	↘ Input
10	Q6_3	Numeric	8	0	Other materials	None	None	8	⬛ Right	📏 Scale	↘ Input
11	Q7	Numeric	8	0	Teaching team ...	None	None	8	⬛ Right	📏 Scale	↘ Input

Section 3 of the survey starts with Question 8, which asked students to indicate their use of different university support services. Students could give up to four answers so we must have four variables for this question, which we **Name** as 'Q8_1', 'Q8_2', 'Q8_3', 'Q8_4'. We give Q8_1 a **Label** of 'Health and Counselling centre' and, in this case, a tick in the box indicates 'Yes' (the service has been used) and a blank indicates a 'No', so Q8_1 is given the following **Value Labels**:1 = 'Yes' and 0 = 'No'. Q8_2 is given the **Label** 'Student Advice Centre' and, in the same way, has **Value Labels** of 1 = 'Yes' and 0 = 'No'. Q8_3 is labelled 'Other student support service' and, in the same way, has **Value Labels** of 1 = 'Yes' and 0 = 'No'. Q8_1, Q8_2 and Q8_3 are all set as Nominal in **Measure**. Now if a participant has ticked 'Other' in Q8_3 they are then asked to specify the service used.

This final item in the question is given the name of Q8_4, with the **Label** 'Other student support service used'. The response to Q8_4 is a written answer and can be anything the participant chooses to write so we do not give a number code for this text but simply type in what they have written. For Q8_4 we set **Type** to String (as it is a 'string' of letters rather than a number), which automatically sets **Measure** to nominal. We also set **Characters** to 20 because this is enough characters for the different responses.

We can (if we wish) increase the size of the **Width** and **Columns** so more of the text is shown on the screen in the SPSS **Data View** window. We have set these values to 20. As we are inputting text we set **Align** to Left (rather than the default of Right which is the correct alignment for numbers).

Question 9 asks about the participant's use of five social spaces at the university. There might be as many as five answers (five ticks), so a separate variable must be set up for each of the five items, with **Name** 'Q9_1', 'Q9_2', 'Q9_3', 'Q9_4', 'Q9_5' and the **Value Labels** 1 = 'Yes' (ticked) and 0 = 'No' (unticked). Q9_1 has **Label** 'The Student Eatery', Q9_2 has **Label** 'The Wholefood Café', Q9_3 has **Label** 'The Hub', Q9_4 has **Label** 'Racquets Retreat', and Q9_5 has **Label** 'The Media Munch'. The variables Q9_1 to Q9_5 are all set as nominal in **Measure**.

Question 10 on the use of the Sports and Fitness Centre, asked for only one answer, so we only need one variable here. It is given the **Name** 'Q10' with a **Label** as 'Use of the Sports and Fitness Centre' and **Value Labels** 1 = 'Never', 2 = 'Rarely', 3 = 'Occasionally', 4 = 'Regularly', 5 = 'Often'. We set the **Measure** as Ordinal. Notice that we are being consistent in our coding, in that we start with a lowest number, the code 1, for the lowest or 'negative' or 'worst' end of the Ordinal scale.

The final question in Section 3 asks for a single answer, the number of hours of paid work per week. We can **Name** this as 'Q11', and give a **Label** of 'Paid work per week'. As the participant gives a number (number of hours worked per week) we do not need to input any **Values** and the **Measure** is set to Scale.

11	Q7	Numeric	8	0	Teaching team ...	None	None	8	Right	Scale	Input
12	Q8_1	Numeric	8	0	Health and Cou...	{0, No}...	None	8	Right	Nominal	Input
13	Q8_2	Numeric	8	0	Student Advice ...	{0, No}...	None	8	Right	Nominal	Input
14	Q8_3	Numeric	8	0	Other student s...	{0, No}...	None	8	Right	Nominal	Input
15	Q8_4	String	20	0	Other student s...	None	None	20	Left	Nominal	Input
16	Q9_1	Numeric	8	0	The Student Ea...	{0, No}...	None	8	Right	Nominal	Input
17	Q9_2	Numeric	8	0	The Wholefood ...	{0, No}...	None	8	Right	Nominal	Input
18	Q9_3	Numeric	8	0	The Hub	{0, No}...	None	8	Right	Nominal	Input
19	Q9_4	Numeric	8	0	Racquets Retreat	{0, No}...	None	8	Right	Nominal	Input
20	Q9_5	Numeric	8	0	The Media Munch	{0, No}...	None	8	Right	Nominal	Input
21	Q10	Numeric	8	0	Use of the Spor...	{1, Never}...	None	8	Right	Ordinal	Input
22	Q11	Numeric	8	0	Paid work per ...	None	None	8	Right	Scale	Input

We are now up to the final section of the survey, Question 12, on student satisfaction. This has three items so we set up three variables, each with **Value Labels** of 1 = 'Very unsatisfied', 2 = 'Unsatisfied', 3 = 'Neither unsatisfied nor satisfied', 4 = 'Satisfied', and 5 = 'Very satisfied'. The **Name** of the variables is set to 'Q12_1', 'Q12_2' and 'Q12_3' and the **Label** is set to 'Satisfaction with academic life', 'Satisfaction with social life' and 'Satisfaction with personal development' respectively. These are all set to ordinal for **Measure**. This has now given SPSS all the information it requires about the 25 variables in the study.

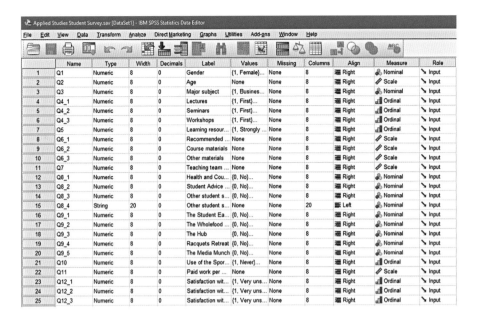

SPSS is now ready for the results to be input into the dataset. To do this, we switch from **Variable View** to **Data View** to show the empty dataset. However, now each column is headed by the name of each variable and SPSS has all the coding information stored.

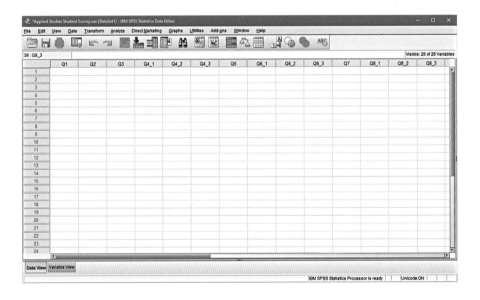

ENTERING THE DATA INTO SPSS

We are now in a position to enter the results of the participants into the dataset. Selecting a completed survey from the top of our pile we can transfer the results into the first row of the dataset. This first participant has ticked female for Question 1, so a 1 is typed in the first row and first column headed Q1. Her age is given as 27 so 27 is typed in the same row but in column 2 under the heading Q2. This student ticked Media for major subject, so 4 is input in column 3, headed Q3. For Question 4 she put workshops first, seminars second and lectures third, so in the column headed Q4_1, the Lectures column, a 3 is input; under Q4_2, the column for Seminars, a 2 is input and a 1 is input for Q4_3 for Workshops. We type in the rest of this participant's results in the further columns along the first row of the dataset.

	Q1	Q2	Q3	Q4_1	Q4_2	Q4_3	Q5	Q6_1	Q6_2	Q6_3	Q7	Q8_1	Q8_2	Q8_3
1	1	27	4	3	2	1	3	37	38	25	9	0	1	0

We then input the results for the rest of the students, one row at a time, making sure that we input the data in the correct column. Finally, we have all the data input in the dataset (making sure that we do not forget to save it as we go). If we look down one of the columns, such as column 2 containing the student ages, we can see whether the data has been input correctly in that all the values can be seen as appropriately showing ages. (It is a good idea to scan down the columns to check for any input errors – it is easy to spot if 222 has been input by mistake instead of 22 for a participant's age, for instance).

	Q1	Q2	Q3	Q4_1	Q4_2	Q4_3	Q5	Q6_1	Q6_2	Q6_3	Q7	Q8_1	Q8_2	Q8_3
1	1	27	4	3	2	1	3	37	38	25	9	0	1	0
2	1	21	4	1	3	2	4	47	25	28	8	0	0	0
3	2	20	4	2	3	1	5	45	35	20	9	1	0	0
4	1	21	3	1	2	3	3	50	40	10	6	0	1	0
5	2	19	4	2	1	3	4	50	30	20	9	0	0	0
6	2	20	4	1	3	2	5	35	35	30	10	0	0	0
7	1	18	4	3	2	1	1	60	20	20	8	0	0	0
8	2	27	1	3	2	1	4	46	43	11	7	1	0	0
9	2	23	2	2	3	1	4	25	50	25	4	0	1	0
10	1	18	4	1	3	2	4	45	35	20	4	0	1	0
11	1	48	3	2	1	3	4	51	39	10	9	0	1	0
12	1	19	4	3	1	2	4	45	30	25	10	0	0	0
13	1	19	4	2	3	1	4	45	35	20	6	0	0	0
14	2	20	1	3	1	2	4	40	35	25	6	0	1	0
15	2	18	4	3	1	2	2	50	30	20	6	0	0	0
16	1	27	2	3	2	1	3	20	65	15	4	0	0	0
17	2	21	1	3	2	1	5	50	32	18	6	1	1	0
18	1	19	1	2	3	1	5	50	35	15	8	0	0	0
19	1	21	1	1	3	2	1	40	40	20	7	1	0	0
20	2	20	4	3	2	1	4	47	33	20	5	0	0	0
21	2	22	4	2	3	1	5	50	25	25	9	0	0	0
22	2	20	3	1	2	3	3	45	45	10	7	0	1	0
23	1	24	4	2	3	1	5	42	36	22	10	0	1	0
24	2	19	1	3	1	2	2	40	45	15	4	0	1	0
25	1	28	2	2	1	3	2	25	55	20	2	0	0	1 C
26	2	23	2	2	3	1	3	20	60	20	3	0	0	0
27	1	19	1	2	1	3	4	45	45	10	7	0	1	0
28	2	32	1	1	3	2	3	41	47	12	6	1	1	0
29	2	19	1	2	1	3	3	55	30	20	8	0	0	1 m
30	1	25	3	3	1	2	4	44	44	12	7	0	0	0

✓

Save the data regularly as you type it in
Don't forget to save the data at the end of your data entry. Click on the **File** drop-down menu and select **Save** (to save the data in the same location) or **Save As** (if you want to save the file with a new name).

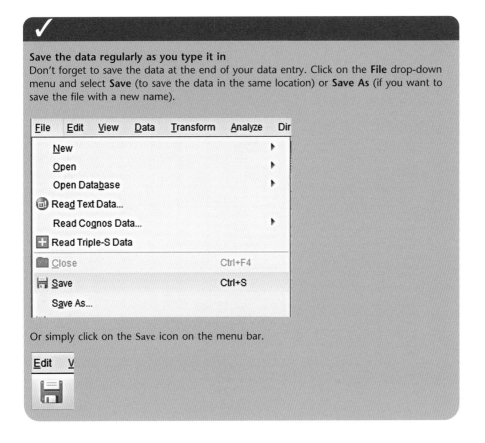

Or simply click on the Save icon on the menu bar.

Viewing value labels

In the **Data View** window, if you hover the mouse over the title of a column (such as over Q3), SPSS then displays the label for that variable.

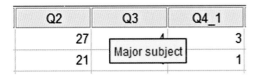

Also, there is an icon on the meu bar – this allows you to show the **Value Labels** rather than the numeric codes.

When you click on this icon, you then see that the dataset is displayed with the **Value Labels** shown rather than the numeric codes.

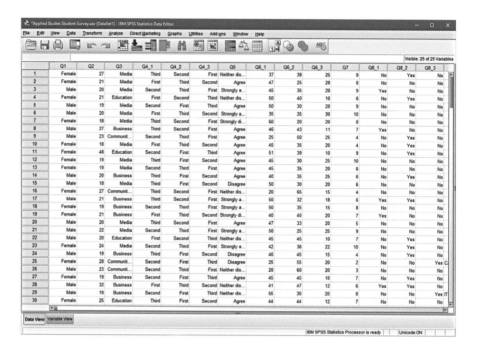

Rather than seeing a list of '1's and '2's in Q1 (Gender), you now see a column of 'Female' and 'Male' labels for the participants. Toggling the **Value Labels** icon switches between the two views of the data showing either the numeric codes or the value labels.

Missing values

Sometimes there will be missing data in a set of research results. A participant might only do a part of the task required of them, or miss out one or more questions in a survey. There are many reasons why there might be missing values in a dataset, from people deliberately choosing not to answer a question through to another participant inadvertently skipping over a question by mistake. In some cases, the researcher might remove the participant's results from the dataset if there is little to analyse and they note this fact in their report. However, in many cases, the participant has only missed out one question in a survey and provided valuable data in the rest of their answers. SPSS has a facility for dealing with missing data in the dataset. When you discover that there is missing data for a variable in SPSS, you can set up a special code to tell SPSS when the data for a certain participant is missing. Normally, when the variables are set up in **Variable View** the default for the **Missing** option is set to **No missing values**. However, at any time you can open up the **Variable View** window and change the missing values option for any variable, so that you can specify when there is a missing value. When the **Missing** box is clicked against a variable in **Variable View** the following dialog box appears. If we have no missing values in the results at all we click the **No missing values** radio button, then **OK**. However, we can also specify a code for a missing value. (We can even specify more than one code to identify different types of missing value if they arise.) Normally we give a value that makes it clear that the result is obviously missing. If we use a distinct code, say 99, for a missing value it is obvious when we look down the spreadsheet what this means. We select **Discrete missing values** and type 99 here. If we do this for the gender variable, then, when we encounter a missing value in a survey (a person has not ticked their gender), we type 99 instead of 1 or 2 in the gender column to tell SPSS that the gender result is missing. When you analyse your data using SPSS it will tell you the number of missing values in the tables it displays.

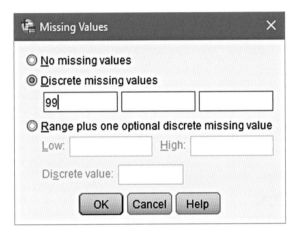

EDITING THE DATASET

The SPSS dataset is very easy to edit. If you spot an incorrect value, you can simply click on that value and change it in the **Data View** screen. If you want to add a new variable, one way to do this is to right click on the header of the variable to the right of where you want the new variable to go. A menu appears as shown below.

Select **Insert Variable** and a new column will appear in the dataset. You will need to set up the details of the variable in the **Variable View** screen, and then input the data in the **Data View** screen.

You can easily add new cases (data for new participants) to the end of the dataset by simply typing them in. However, if you wish to add a new case to a specific place in the dataset, then you can right click on the row number after the place where you wish the new case to go and the following menu appears. Select **Insert Cases** and a new row is inserted at that point for the new case to be added.

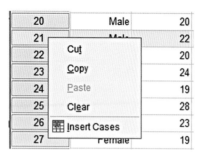

Editing can be also done using the **Edit** drop-down menu. Make sure you are at the position in the dataset where you want the edit to go and then, from the **Edit** menu, you can select one of the options, such as **Insert Variable** or **Insert Cases**. Notice that the **Edit** menu also allows you to navigate around the dataset. This is particularly useful for people with very large datasets and they want to check a particular participant's results (a case) or a variable, which they can do by selecting the commands **Go to Case** and **Go to Variable**.

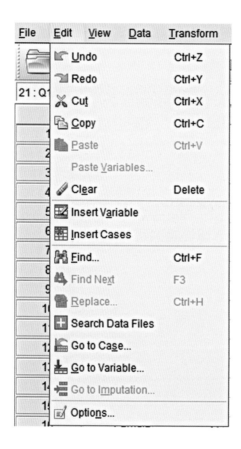

Now all the data has been typed in (and saved!) we are ready to analyse the results of the research study.

TRANSFERRING THE RESULTS FROM OTHER SOFTWARE INTO SPSS

If you have undertaken your research using computer software, such as software to run an experiment or an online survey program, the option to save your data in a particular file format will very much depend on the software itself and the licence you have. If the online survey program has a licence supplied by your university or department, you may be able to use this facility of the program, so that you can directly save the data in the form of an SPSS dataset (a .sav file). If not, you may still have the option to save the data as an Excel .xlsx file or a comma separate values (.csv) file. If the program or the licence does not let you save the data, the majority of online software programs will allow you to view each participant's results on the screen individually, which, although a laborious process, can be displayed on screen and then copied into SPSS. You may also be able to save each result individually as pdfs or maybe print them out (if there no other solution) and then type in the results by hand as described above. However, most software will usually allow you to save your data electronically in one of the formats mentioned.

For illustrative purposes, we are now going to assume that the Sparcote Study was undertaken with an online survey package and produced the same data. Below we are going to show how the data from the online survey program can be imported into SPSS as a .sav, a .xlsx and a .csv file.

✓

Question numbering/naming in online surveys

Online survey programs will usually name questions automatically and sequentially. However, instructions and headings are often also referred to as 'questions' as well, with the text being input into a 'descriptive text question'. So it is quite possible that the instructions for your online survey will be referred to as 'question' 1 – and given a name such as 'Q1' in the survey. When typing your questions into an online survey if you replace one question in the middle of your survey by a different one then the new question will not be given the same question name and will be given the next question number in the sequence. For example, if you have input 10 questions already and then decide that you want to change question 7, it will be given the next number in the sequence (question 11 rather than question 7). However, most online survey programs allow you to rename the questions if you wish to make sure that the names are the ones that you want. In the Sparcote online survey, we have changed the heading and question names. For example, the instructions were given the name 'Q1' automatically by the program. We changed this name to 'Instructions'. The heading of Section 1 was given the name 'Q2'. We changed this name to 'S1Head'. The first proper question in the Sparcote survey (asking for the participant's gender) was automatically given the name 'Q3' by the online survey program and we changed this name to 'Q1'. We carefully checked the names given by the program to the questions and changed the names so that the question names were the same as those listed in the codebook in Chapter 3, e.g. 'Q1' for Question 1, 'Q2' for question 2 and so on. You can also change the names once in they have been moved to SPSS if you wish to.

Working with a SPSS .sav file saved from an online survey program

A number of programs will allow you to save your data as an SPSS data file (with the file extension .sav). This is often referred to as 'exporting' the data from online survey programs. We used an online survey program to run our Sparcote Applied Studies Student Survey. It is important that you get to know your survey program so that you are aware of how it stores the results and the codes it uses for the different answers. The automatic coding does not always produce the codes you prefer for SPSS. You can often check and recode the data into the codes you want in the online survey program. For example, it might code a yes-or-no question with the codes 1 and 0, or 1 and 2. If you want to use the codes 1 and 0 then it is often possible to instruct the program to allocate these codes. However, do not worry if you have not checked these things as you can always make the changes in SPSS after opening up the exported file. Even if you do not know how the online survey program has stored your results, in the SPSS file you can always 'clean up' the results to produce the codes you want in SPSS later. We explain how to do this below.

In the Sparcote Study we exported the online survey results to an SPSS data file called 'Applied Studies Student Survey.sav'. Now we can open the new .sav file by double clicking on it (to open SPSS) or open SPSS first and then find our saved .sav file and open it as described above.

Cleaning up your imported SPSS dataset

When you open up your online survey results in SPSS, you will notice that there are additional variables in addition to those generated by your research data. In the **Data View** screen, you will have to scroll to the right until you see your first question.

In the **Variable View** screen, we can check how the data has been coded by the online survey program.

	Name	Type	Width	Decimals	Label	Values	Missing	Columns	Align	Measure	Role
1	V1	String	20	0	ResponseID	None	None	15	Left	Nominal	Input
2	V2	String	20	0	ResponseSet	None	None	15	Left	Nominal	Input
3	V3	String	2000	0	Name	None	None	15	Left	Nominal	Input
4	V4	String	2000	0	ExternalDataRe...	None	None	15	Left	Nominal	Input
5	V5	String	2000	0	Email	None	None	15	Left	Nominal	Input
6	V6	String	2000	0	IPAddress	None	None	15	Left	Nominal	Input
7	V7	String	2000	0	Status	None	None	15	Left	Nominal	Input
8	V8	Date	20	0	StartDate	None	None	5	Right	Scale	Input
9	V9	Date	20	0	EndDate	None	None	5	Right	Scale	Input
10	V10	Numeric	1	0	Finished	None	None	5	Right	Scale	Input
11	Intro	Numeric	8	0	The Applied St...	None	None	5	Right	Scale	Input
12	S1_Head	Numeric	8	0	Section 1: Abo...	None	None	5	Right	Scale	Input
13	Q1	Numeric	8	0	What is your g...	{1, Female}...	None	5	Right	Scale	Input
14	Q2	String	2000	0	Please give you...	None	None	15	Left	Nominal	Input
15	Q3	Numeric	8	0	Which subject i...	{1, Busines...	None	5	Right	Scale	Input
16	S2_Head	Numeric	8	0	Section2: Abou...	None	None	5	Right	Scale	Input
17	Q4_1	Numeric	8	2	Rank the followi...	None	None	5	Right	Scale	Input
18	Q4_2	Numeric	8	2	Rank the followi...	None	None	5	Right	Scale	Input
19	Q4_3	Numeric	8	2	Rank the followi...	None	None	5	Right	Scale	Input
20	Q5	Numeric	8	0	Please state yo...	{1, Strongly ...	None	5	Right	Scale	Input

The first thing to note is that there are a lot more variables than there are items in the survey. At the beginning of the survey are a number of extra variables added by the online survey to give extra information about the participant – at what time and which day they responded and their IP address. In our example above, you can see that Q1, our first question, is the 13th variable in the list rather than the first – so the online survey program has added 12 extra variables. There may also be a number of variables at the end of the survey giving details of the participant's location (for example, three extra variables). You might find these useful for checking where and when the survey was filled in (and in some cases to check that people did not do it more than once). However, we are only interested in keeping the variables created by the survey questions. We are not interested in these other variables, so we will delete these from the SPSS file in our example. We also delete any other extra variables within the dataset. Some online survey programs also regard the section headings and titles as text variables. In our survey, we had headings to each of the four sections. If we find a text variable for each of these sections, which we do not want to keep in the dataset, we can delete these as well.

To delete a variable in the **Variable View** window, click with the mouse on the number in the first column corresponding to that variable then that row is highlighted in yellow. If we right click with the mouse, a menu appears. If we click in the **Clear** option, then that variable is cleared from the SPSS data.

In the Sparcote Study, when the survey was created online, the items (or variables) were coded with the same names as those described in the codebook in Chapter 3. Check that your question numbering in your online survey matches your codebook.

	Name	Type	Width	Decimals	Label	Values	Missing	Columns	Align	Measure	Role
1	V1	String	20	0	ResponseID	None	None	15	Left	Nominal	Input
2	Copy		20	0	ResponseSet	None	None	15	Left	Nominal	Input
3	Paste		2000	0	Name	None	None	15	Left	Nominal	Input
4	Clear		2000	0	ExternalDataRe...	None	None	15	Left	Nominal	Input
5	Insert Variable		2000	0	Email	None	None	15	Left	Nominal	Input
6	Paste Variables...		2000	0	IPAddress	None	None	15	Left	Nominal	Input
7	Descriptive Statistics		2000	0	Status	None	None	15	Left	Nominal	Input
8			20	0	StartDate	None	None	5	Right	Scale	Input

We can clear a selection of variables by left clicking on the first variable to clear them then holding down **Ctrl** and selecting the other variables. We deleted the extra variables at the beginning of the survey, the text variables for our headings and the extra variables at the end of the survey. Now the dataset has only variables associated with the questions in the survey.

We have not quite finished 'cleaning up' our SPSS file imported from the online survey program, as we need to check that all the coding, such as the names, labels and values are correct. Check each variable **Name** and **Label**. If you are not happy with the variable names then you can alter them to suit what you prefer. Also, online programs often export the whole question as the **Label**. For example, it creates the **Label** 'What is your gender? Please tick.' for Question 1 (Q1) and 'Please enter your age in years' for Question 2 (Q2). You might be happy with these labels or wish to change them. We are changing these labels to simply 'Gender' and 'Age' for Q1 and Q2, and we have changed the other labels to the ones given in the earlier data entry section of this chapter. We might reduce the **Width** of our string variables as sometimes an online survey allocates very large numbers to string variable widths – but the **Width** values can be left, if you wish. We also decided to display the results in the dataset as whole numbers so we can change all the **Decimals** settings for the numeric variables to zero.

Check all the other details of the variables in the **Variable View** screen. It is a good idea to check the **Values** for each of the variables to make sure that the **Value Labels** are correct. Also, one of the key things to check is that the **Measure** is correctly set to scale, ordinal or nominal for each of your variables. Remember from Chapter 3 there may be a decision to make as to whether a variable is scale or ordinal so check that the survey program's choice of **Measure** is what you want. If it is not then you can change it in SPSS now.

See Chapter 3

Recoding data for a variable

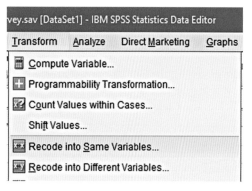

Now switch back to the **Data View** screen and inspect the data. It is a good idea to toggle the **Value Labels** icon to see if both the data and the labels are correct. If you notice that instead of zeros in one variable these are replaced by dots, this means that the online survey program has interpreted the unticked boxes as missing values rather than as boxes deliberately left unticked. For example, for our variables Q9_1 (The Student Eatery) to Q9_5 (The Media Munch) the results should be coded as 1 (the participant ticked the box) or 0 (the participant did not tick the box). However, the online survey program has correctly coded the ticks as 1 but has miscoded the unticked responses as missing values (which is shown as a dot in the SPSS dataset). To change this we:

■ Click on **Transform**.

■ Select **Recode into the Same Variables** from the drop-down menu. We choose the variable(s) we wish to recode by selecting the variables from the list and clicking on the arrow between the boxes to send them to the **Numeric Variables** box.

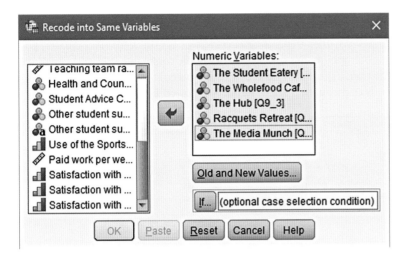

- We then click on the **Old and New Values** button.

- We click on the **Value** button under **Old Value** and put a '1' in the **Value** box and a '1' in the **Value** box under **New Value**.

- We then click **Add**.

- We then click on the **System-missing** button under **Old Value** and put a '0' in the **Value** box under **New Value**.

- We then click **Add**, followed by **Continue**.

- Finally, we click **OK** in the **Recode into Same Variables** window.

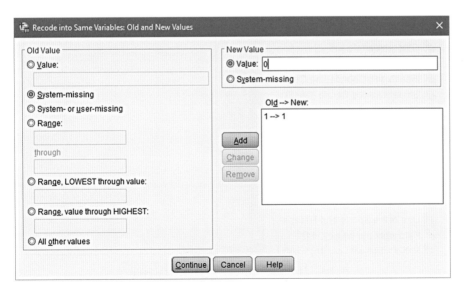

When we now look at the variables Q9_1 to Q9_5 they have a 1 for a ticked response and a 0 for an unticked response – which is what we want.

Checking the coding

If you are not sure whether the coding is correct or not in your SPSS dataset, you can check the coding by using the SPSS **Codebook** command. We will check the coding for Question 1 (gender) in the Sparcote Study.

In the **Analyze** menu, you select **Reports** followed by **Codebook**.

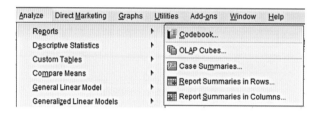

The following dialog box appears:

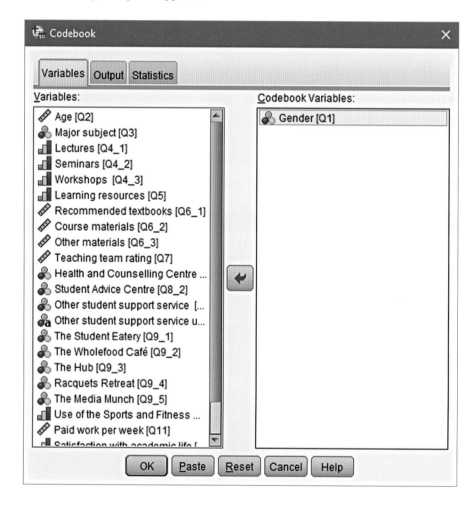

In the left-hand box are all your variables. You can send one or more (or all) of the variables to the right-hand box to display the coding for that variable. We are going to check the coding for Question 1 about gender as an example.

▇ We send 'Gender (Q1)' to the right-hand box and click **OK**. SPSS displays the following table showing the coding for this question.

Q1

		Value	Count	Percent
Standard Attributes	Position	1		
	Label	Gender		
	Type	Numeric		
	Format	F8		
	Measurement	Nominal		
	Role	Input		
Valid Values	1	Female	94	51.4%
	2	Male	89	48.6%

This gives us all the details of the coding for this variable. Notice that it is correctly specified as nominal with the code 1 for 'Female' and 2 for 'Male'. It also displays the summary of the data for this variable. Having imported the data from an online program we can check all the variables if we wish and check that we have the correct codes or labels. If not, we can change them in SPSS.

When you are finally happy with the dataset do not forget to save it.

Working with an Excel file saved from other software

Some research software and online survey programs may not let you save the data in SPSS .sav format, but will still let you export the data as an Excel file. SPSS can read in a spreadsheet written in Excel and use it as an SPSS dataset. Some programs record the research data in an Excel file for data analysis. You can do some analysis in Excel, however SPSS has a wider range of analyses that you can undertake. SPSS also allows more complex editing of tables and graphs than Excel. Data exported to an Excel file can be imported into SPSS and the dataset created. We will follow the example of the Sparcote study data saved in an Excel file called 'Applied Studies Student Survey.xlsx' and show how it can be imported into SPSS.

The first thing to note is that SPSS expects the Excel file to have a basic structure. It expects the spreadsheet to look like the SPSS **Data View** spreadsheet. First, it expects the results from each participant to be on only a single row. Second, the columns are all aligned so that the responses to one variable (or item) form a column in the spreadsheet, just like SPSS variables. Also it expects that where a response has been coded (such as '1' for female and '2' for male) the numeric codes '1' and '2' have been put in the spreadsheet to indicate the participants' gender and not the words 'female' and 'male'. SPSS can import text responses (which it identifies as string variables) as well, but if there is a numeric code then it should be used in the spreadsheet. Finally, a popular convention (which SPSS is able to deal with) is that the first row of the Excel spreadsheet has column headings – the variable names.

The data from the first participant is in the second row. If this is the case then SPSS, when importing the data, can pick up the column headers and use them appropriately as the SPSS variable names. This is the format that many online survey programs will use when they export the data as an Excel file. The following shows the Sparcote Study data in an Excel file that SPSS can import.

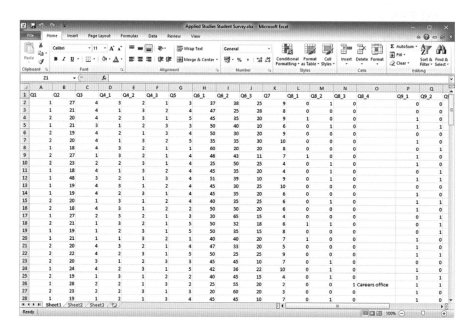

Once you have exported the Excel file from the survey program (or other software), you may wish to open it up in Excel to check that it looks correct (as we have done here). If there are two rows of headings then you should delete one – usually the first as the second normally has the helpful column headings. You will also see quite a few extra columns along with the responses to your questions, included by the survey program to provide more information about the participants, such at what time and which day they responded and their IP address. You can delete these now or leave them to be deleted when the file is imported into SPSS.

You can now import the Excel file into SPSS. Open SPSS and then from the **File** drop-down menu select **Open** and then from the submenu select **Data**. Click on the **Files of type** option and scroll down to **Excel (*.xls, *.xlsx, *.xlsm)**.

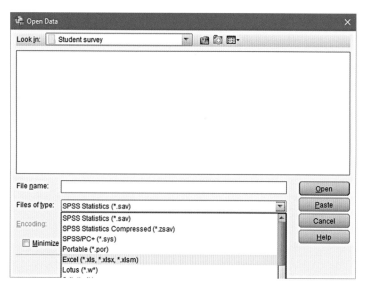

Then select your Excel file from its location on the computer.

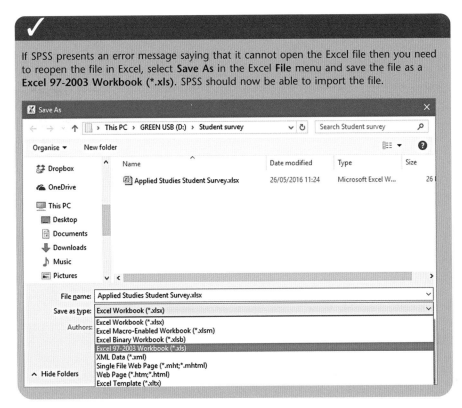

If SPSS presents an error message saying that it cannot open the Excel file then you need to reopen the file in Excel, select **Save As** in the Excel **File** menu and save the file as a **Excel 97-2003 Workbook (*.xls)**. SPSS should now be able to import the file.

SPSS will then show the following dialog box.

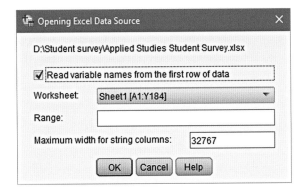

Notice that the **Read variable names from the first row of data** is ticked. As our Excel file does have the variable names in the first row, ticking this box will allow SPSS to transfer the names on the first row into the variable names in SPSS. The **Worksheet** box allows us to select the worksheet we would like to work with and shows the range of data in the spreadsheet. We leave the **Range** box empty as we are not selecting a range. Finally, we might change the **Maximum width for string columns** to a smaller number, as in the Sparcote survey a figure of 100 is ample for the text-based questions.

SPSS will then open up the Excel file in the **Data View** window. The first thing to do is to save the datset as an SPSS .sav file. The next thing to do is to clean up the dataset.

Cleaning up your imported Excel spreadsheet to make your SPSS dataset

First, in the **Data View** screen, delete the variables (columns) that you do not want by right clicking on the variable name and selecting **Clear**. (Online survey programs will often include additional variables which you can delete. We illustrate how to do this in the previous section on importing a .sav file from an online survey.) Now switch to the **Variable View** screen. You will find that you need to type in the coding information for the variables, as an Excel file only normally stores the variable name with the data and no other details of the coding. Check that each **Name** is what you want. You will have to type in a **Label** for each of the variables and add all of the numeric codes and **Value Labels** in the **Values** box. Make sure that you check each of the **Measure** values for the variables as these might need to be changed. When you are happy that all the coding information is correct in the **Variable View** screen, switch back to the **Data View** screen and toggle the **Value Labels** icon and check that all the data and the labels look correct.

If the data does not look correct and you wish to **Recode** any of the data, then follow the procedure described in the previous section. Also, to check that all is correct with the coding and the data, you may wish to use the **Codebook** command to check the coding. (This is also explained above.) Finally, do not forget to save the dataset after all the changes.

Working with a .csv (comma separated values) file in SPSS

If you have exported your results spreadsheet from an online survey program or other software in the form of a .csv (comma separated values) file, a type of text file, then SPSS can still import the file to create an SPSS dataset. Scroll down the list of **Files of type** in the SPSS **Open Data** window. In order to import the .csv file you need to select **Text (*txt, *dat, *.csv, *tab)**.

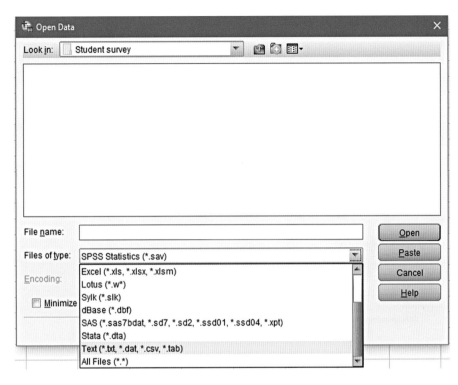

You can then select the .csv file from the location on the computer where it is stored.
Our file is called 'Applied Studies Student Survey.csv'.

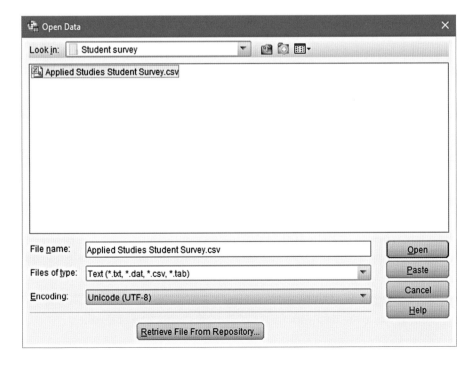

■ Click **Open** and a new **Text Import Wizard** appears.

While there are a number of dialog boxes in the **Text Import Wizard**, the default answers are usually the ones to accept. This is **Step 1 of 6** different dialog boxes which will pop up. It asks first **Does your text match a predefined format?** The default response is **No**. Leave this as it is.

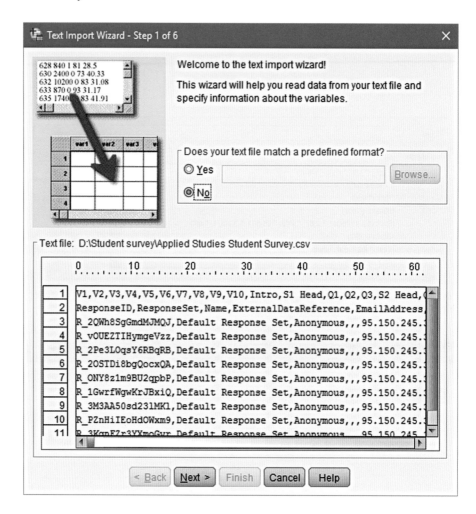

■ Click **Next**.

The next dialog box **Step 2 of 6** asks first: **How are your variables arranged?** Leave this response as **Delimited** as this means that the results are separated by a delimiter such as a comma. Second, it asks **Are variable names included at the top of your file?**

■ Change this to **Yes**, by clicking the **Yes** radio button (as survey programs will normally save the data with the variable names at the top of the file).

■ Click **Next** to continue.

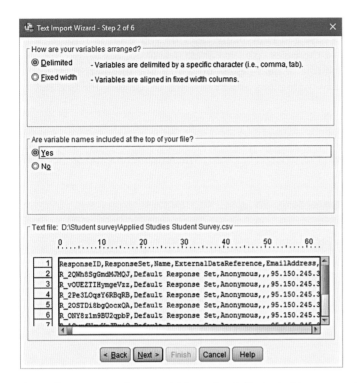

As we have arranged our variables to be delimited, this appears in the header of the next dialog box **Delimited Step 3 of 6**.

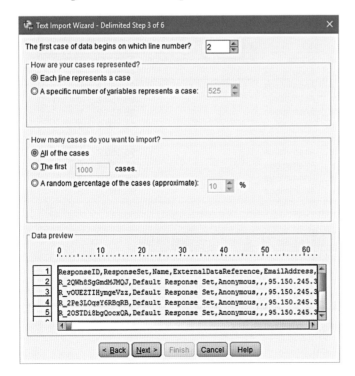

This dialog box asks **How are your cases represented?** with the default answer **Each line represents a case** and **How many cases do you want to import?** with the default answer **All of the cases**. We leave these default options as they are. We also check that **The first line of data begins on which line number?** is set to the default of 2. (Online survey programs usually save the headings in the first row of a .csv file.)

■ We accept these default answers and click on **Next** to continue.

■ The **Delimited Step 4 of 6** dialog box asks **Which delimiters appear between variables?**

■ We untick **Space** and **Semicolon**, and leave the **Comma** box as ticked – as commas are the delimiters in the .csv file.

■ We set the **What is the text qualifier?** to **Double quote**.

■ We then click on **Next** to continue.

The following window might appear. This message does not indicate there is a problem and is related to SPSS assigning variable names. This message can be ignored.

■ Click **OK**.

In the next dialog box, **Step 5 of 6**, SPSS tells you how it decides on the data format of the values. We leave these values as the default ones.

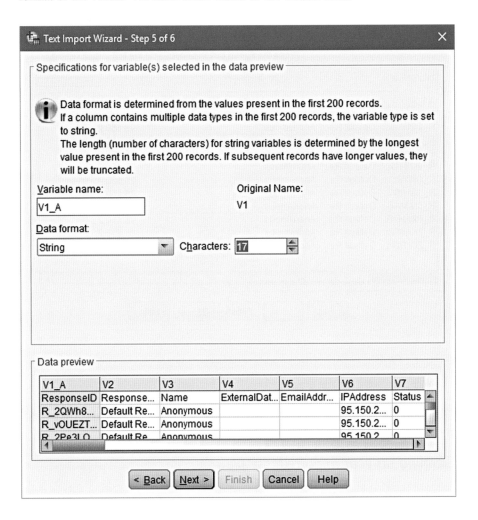

■   Click **Next** to continue.

The final dialog box, **Step 6 of 6**, appears. We accept the default choices.

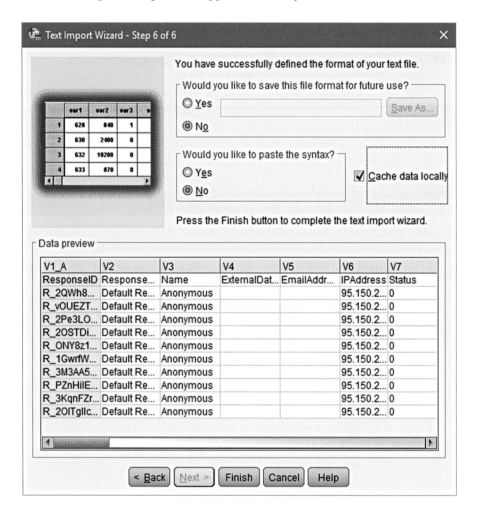

■   Click **Finish**.

You then see how the data has been imported into SPSS.

The dataset will now be displayed in the **Data View** window of the **IBM SPSS Statistics Data Editor**.

Cleaning up your imported .csv file

You will see that at the beginning of the .csv file, if you are importing survey data, that there are a number of extra variables at the beginning of the dataset added by the online survey program to give extra information about the participant – at what time and which day they responded and their IP address. There may also be a number of extra variables at the end of the survey giving details of the participant's location.

You might find these useful for checking where and when the survey was filled in (and, in some cases, to check that people did not do it more than once). However, we are only interested in keeping the variables to do with the survey questions. We are not interested in these other variables in our example, so will delete these from the SPSS file. Some online survey programs also regard the section headings and titles as text variables. In our survey, we had headings to each of the four sections. If we find a text variable for each of these sections, we can delete these as well.

We now switch to the **Variable View** screen. You will find that you need to type in additional information for the variables. Check that each **Name** is you want – and, if not, you can change these. Also you will note that the variable **Type** is set to **String** for the variables (as they have been read from a text file). You need to change these to **Numeric** by clicking to the right of the **Type** box for that variable.

You can delete the columns that you do not want in the SPSS dataset by right clicking on the column name and selecting **Clear**. This is explained in detail in the section on importing a .sav file.

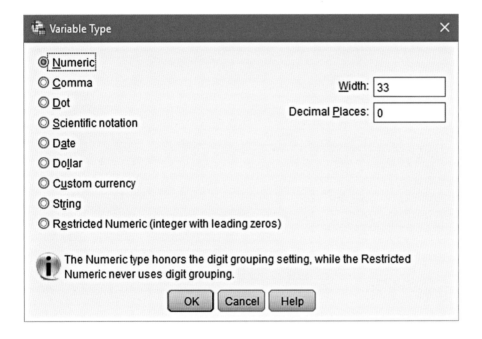

You may choose to reduce the **Width** and the **Column** values to make the variables easier to view in the **Data View** window. You will have to type a **Label** for each of the variables and add all of the **Value Labels**. Make sure that you check each of the **Measure** values for the variables as these will need to be changed, as they will all be set to Nominal (as the data was read from a text file). When you are happy that all the information is correct in the **Variable View** screen, switch back to the **Data View** screen and toggle the **Value Labels** icon and check that all the data and the labels look correct.

If you need to recode any of the data as it is not correctly coded then you can use the **Recode** command (described above). Also you can check the coding by using the **Codebook** command (also described above). Finally, do not forget to save the dataset after all the changes.

A FINAL CHECK OF YOUR DATASET

However you have entered your data into SPSS, there is always the possibility of making a mistake in typing data into any program and SPSS is no different. Also, in importing data from other programs there may be differences in the coding that you have missed. So it is always a good idea to 'eyeball' your dataset (looking up and down the columns) in the **Data View** window just to check that the numbers look correct. The **Codebook** command is also reassuring as it usually highlights any mistakes, such as a value typed in incorrectly or a coding that you wish to change.

When you are satisfied that your dataset is complete, you are now ready to undertake your analyses and produce the tables and graphs for your report. In Chapter 5, we discuss how to produce tables and graphs using the **Frequencies** command.

A first look at
the results

107 OPENING AN SPSS
DATA FILE

109 THE IBM SPSS
STATISTICS
VIEWER

110 DESCRIPTIVE
STATISTICS FOR
EACH VARIABLE

111 THE FREQUENCIES
COMMAND

124 A FIRST
DESCRIPTION OF
THE SPARCOTE
STUDY RESULTS

150 DESCRIBING THE
RESULTS OF A
SINGLE VARIABLE

Chapter aim: To demonstrate how to summarise your results data in SPSS

At this point in the research process, the study has been designed, the data has been collected and has been entered or transferred into SPSS. Now, this is where all the features of SPSS can be used to make the hard work of data analysis very easy. This chapter explains how to produce a description of your results after having input all of your data into SPSS. You know that you want to answer your research question or questions but the first step is to take a look at your results. Initially, it is helpful to summarise the **demographic** information about the sample of people who took part in your study. This is the characteristics of the sample such as their gender or age. Also, it is useful to get an overview of how your participants have responded to each individual question or task. As we have discussed in previous chapters, there are a range of summary statistics such as frequency counts, percentages, means and standard deviations that you can use to summarise your data. The type of summary statistic you present depends on the type of data you have collected: the level of measurement of the responses – nominal, ordinal or scale. This chapter explains how to present a summary of your results using the SPSS **Frequencies** command.

demographic
In research involving human participants, the relevant characteristics of the sample are called the demographics. Details of these characteristics (often age, gender and other qualities, such as relevant group membership) and their frequency are included in the research report

OPENING AN SPSS DATA FILE

When you start SPSS it will display the **Recent Files** list showing the recently used SPSS data files (with the .sav file extension). If the file you wish to open is on that list you can click on it to open it.

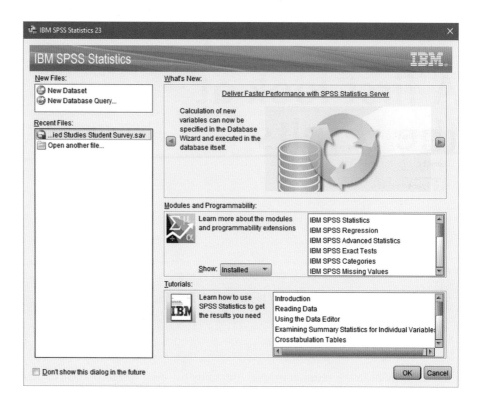

However, if the data file you wish to open is not on that list, then you can double click on **Open another file** and then a dialog box will open up and you can find the file on your computer.

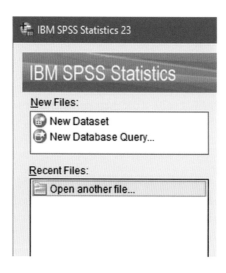

We called our survey 'Applied Studies Student Survey.sav' and therefore we open this file.

When you are in the SPSS program you can also open a data file by clicking on the **Open** icon on the menu bar and then locating the data file in the folder that you have saved it in.

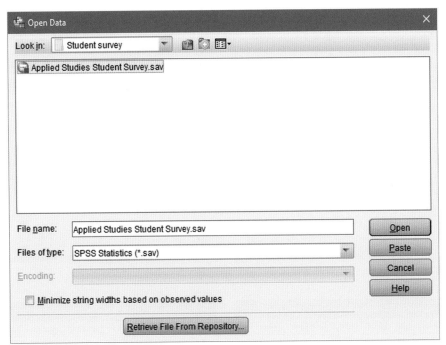

THE IBM SPSS STATISTICS VIEWER

Whenever you open SPSS, the **IBM SPSS Statistics Data Editor** window opens. In this window, you can switch between **Data View** and **Variable View** windows to look at your data as well as the coding set up. However, you will notice that there is another window opened behind the **Data Editor** window. This is the **IBM SPSS Statistics Viewer** window. This viewer shows the output that has been generated through the SPSS procedures. Whenever you produce any tables or graphs, they will be shown in this window along with any other output or messages from SPSS. For example, when you open a dataset the **IBM SPSS Statistics Viewer** window will display some information beginning 'GET'. You will see that it then lists the name of the file that it has opened.

```
GET
FILE='D:\Student survey\Applied Studies Student
Survey.sav'.
DATASET NAME DataSet1 WINDOW=FRONT.
```

There will be a number of other occasions when SPSS messages appear in the **IBM SPSS Statistics Viewer**. As a general rule of thumb, these messages are just for information – and sometimes may appear rather incomprehensible! However, essentially it is presenting this information in the SPSS 'syntax language', describing what it has done, such as opened a file or created a table. Some people learn this language and can program SPSS to do complex things with it. However, for most users, the windows-based instructions are easy to use and adequate for most needs. You can either leave these messages in the **IBM SPSS Statistics Viewer** or you can click on them and delete them. Essentially the **IBM SPSS Statistics Viewer** displays all of the tables and graphs you produce. This information can be saved at any time as an output file (with the file extension .spv) and opened and viewed again in SPSS when required. Alternatively, information in the **IBM SPSS Statistics Viewer** can be copied and pasted into other programs, such as Microsoft Word.

DESCRIPTIVE STATISTICS FOR EACH VARIABLE

When you first open your dataset you will see your dataset in the **Data View** window in the form of a spreadsheet (columns and rows of numbers). In the **Data View** screen, when you hover the mouse over the title of a column, the label for the variable is displayed in a yellow box. In the example of the Sparcote Study data, holding the mouse over 'Q1' displays the **Label** of 'Gender'. By looking down this column, we can see that there are a lot of 1s and 2s, which are the numeric codes assigned to the males and females in this sample. Remember that you can also click the **Value Labels** icon on the toolbar to view the value labels instead of the numeric codes.

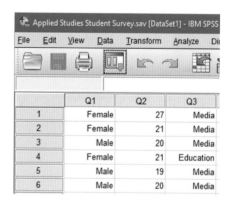

See Chapters 3 and 4

As we discussed in Chapters 3 and 4, SPSS classifies the data as nominal, ordinal and scale in the **Measure** option in the **Variable View** screen. There are general rules of thumb for the best way to describe data for each type measure and we will go through these with you. The **Frequencies** command in SPSS is an excellent general purpose command for presenting a summary description of any type of data. You can decide within this command what sort of descriptive statistics you would like displayed (such as frequency count, mean, median, mode, range, standard deviation and so on), whether you would like a table of the frequencies for your results, and also whether you would like SPSS to display a chart (a bar chart, a pie chart or a histogram) for your data. Some people find that the **Frequencies** command provides them with all the information they need for their report.

THE FREQUENCIES COMMAND

There are a number of methods of producing summary statistics in SPSS. The **Analyze** drop-down menu provides a wide range of choices for you to be able to undertake a variety of statistical analyses and the **Frequencies** command can be found within this menu.

The option **Descriptive Statistics** enables you to carry out different analyses that summarise your data, generating a range of tables and graphs.

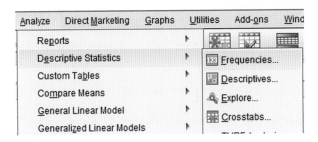

We are going to specifically explore the use of **Analyze**, **Descriptive Statistics**, then **Frequencies** to show you how to produce a table of frequency counts and percentages and also how to generate means and standard deviations in SPSS. We are going to use a number of examples to show how you might use this command with your own data, and then use it to summarise the Sparcote Study data. The decision on which statistical table to produce is based on whether the data collected for the variable is nominal, scale or ordinal.

Our example here is of a research study about a group of 76 10-year-old children and we will look at three variables to illustrate how you can produce appropriate summary information for nominal data, scale data and ordinal data.

File Edit View Data Transform Analyze Dir

	Occupation	Puzzle	Sportiness
1	3	19	2
2	4	23	4
3	6	30	3
4	4	23	1
5	1	22	4
6	6	24	5
7	6	24	1
8	2	22	3
9	6	26	2
10	2	28	1

Describing nominal data

The **Display frequency tables** box is ticked as a default. It is important to leave this ticked if you want to produce a table of frequencies.

We are going to examine an example of nominal data and how we can describe it using SPSS. A group of 76 10-year-old children were asked to select their favourite future occupation from a list of six different choices: doctor, scientist, teacher, veterinarian (vet), athlete and musician. There are multiple categories and the children are asked to select one single category, their favourite occupation. Thus, the data collected is nominal. We are going to produce a table of frequencies to show the number of times the different occupations were chosen as the favourite occupation by this sample of children.

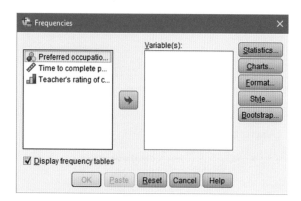

■ Open the dataset in SPSS and select the **Analyze** drop-down menu.

■ Now select **Descriptive Statistics** followed by **Frequencies**.

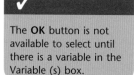

The **OK** button is not available to select until there is a variable in the Variable (s) box.

A **Frequencies** dialog box pops up on your screen. You will notice that on the left-hand side are all of the variables in the dataset, an arrow button in the middle of the window and a **Variable(s)** box on the right-hand side.

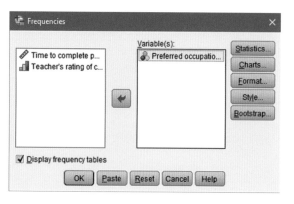

■ You need to send the variable(s) you are interested in from the variable list on the left to the **Variable(s)** box on the right-hand side. This can be achieved by clicking on the variable, in this case 'Preferred occupation' and then clicking on the arrow button between the variables list and the **Variable(s)** box to send the variable across for analysis.

■ Other commands in SPSS produce dialog boxes of a similar format.

■ Your variable then appears in the **Variable(s)** box.

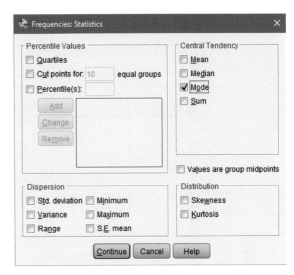

■ Select the **Statistics** option. We can see that there are a number of descriptive statistics that we can ask SPSS to display. As this is nominal data, we do not want the mean (or most of the other choices) and these are left blank with nominal data. We have only ticked the mode option – to show the most popular category – then selected the **Continue** button.

As well as producing tables, the **Frequencies** command also enables you to produce some useful charts.

■ Select the **Charts** button and you will see four options of **Chart Type**.

■ As we want to see how each preferred occupation is as a portion (or share) of all of the occupation choices, we have selected **Pie charts**. (We could have chosen a bar chart instead of a pie chart to display these data. Chapter 7 explains when you might choose one or the other chart.)

■ **Chart Values** shows the frequencies or the percentage values in the chart. We select **Frequencies** to show the actual number of children selecting each occupation. This is the place where you would select **Percentages** if you wanted to show the percentage values. (Also, as **Display frequency tables** is ticked we will see the percentages with the frequencies in the displayed frequency table.)

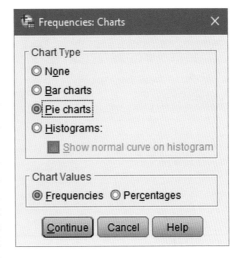

■ Select **Continue**, and then **OK** in the **Frequencies** dialog box.

For details of different types of charts and graphs, see Chapter 7

SPSS generates two tables and a graph. The first table is the **Statistics** table, which shows that all 76 children have given their preferred occupation and there are no missing values. It also shows that the most often occurring choice – the mode – is the occupation that has been assigned a numerical code of 4, which is the fourth occupation category.

Statistics

Preferred occupation

N	Valid	76
	Missing	0
Mode		4

By looking at the following table, **Preferred occupation**, we can see that the fourth occupation – 'Vet' – is indeed the occupation that has the highest frequency in the Frequency column with 19 children choosing this option. The next column shows the percentage of children who have selected each occupation with 25.0% of the children selecting the occupation 'Vet'. The next highest frequency is 16 children (21.1%) wanting to be a 'Musician', then 14 (18.4%) for 'Doctor', 12 (15.8%) for 'Athlete', 10 (13.2%) for 'Scientist' and five (6.6%) children saying that their preferred future occupation was 'Teacher', which was the lowest frequency preferred occupation.

Preferred occupation

		Frequency	Percent	Valid Percent	Cumulative Percent
Valid	Doctor	14	18.4	18.4	18.4
	Scientist	10	13.2	13.2	31.6
	Teacher	5	6.6	6.6	38.2
	Vet	19	25.0	25.0	63.2
	Athlete	12	15.8	15.8	78.9
	Musician	16	21.1	21.1	100.0
	Total	76	100.0	100.0	

The **Preferred occupation** table also shows the **Valid Percent**. In this instance, this column is exactly the same as the **Percent** column (as there are no missing values). The final column of the table is the **Cumulative Percent** column. This provides a running total of the valid percent values. In the table above, 31.6% of the children have stated that they would like to be either a 'Doctor' or a 'Scientist'.

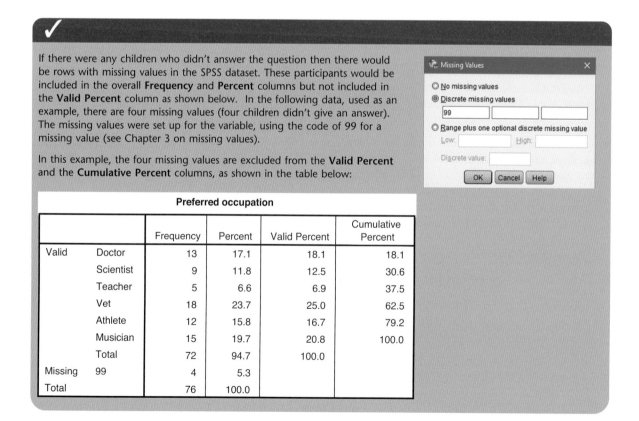

If there were any children who didn't answer the question then there would be rows with missing values in the SPSS dataset. These participants would be included in the overall **Frequency** and **Percent** columns but not included in the **Valid Percent** column as shown below. In the following data, used as an example, there are four missing values (four children didn't give an answer). The missing values were set up for the variable, using the code of 99 for a missing value (see Chapter 3 on missing values).

In this example, the four missing values are excluded from the **Valid Percent** and the **Cumulative Percent** columns, as shown in the table below:

Preferred occupation

		Frequency	Percent	Valid Percent	Cumulative Percent
Valid	Doctor	13	17.1	18.1	18.1
	Scientist	9	11.8	12.5	30.6
	Teacher	5	6.6	6.9	37.5
	Vet	18	23.7	25.0	62.5
	Athlete	12	15.8	16.7	79.2
	Musician	15	19.7	20.8	100.0
	Total	72	94.7	100.0	
Missing	99	4	5.3		
Total		76	100.0		

A pie chart was selected along with the frequency table in the **Frequencies** command. This is displayed in the **IBM SPSS Statistics Viewer**, and shown below.

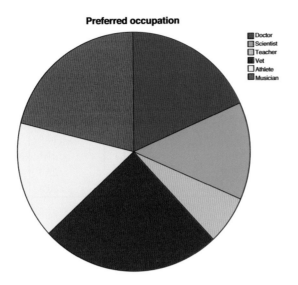

Preferred occupation

- Doctor
- Scientist
- Teacher
- Vet
- Athlete
- Musician

For details of which charts to choose for what type of data, see Chapter 7. For editing graphs, see Chapter 8

This is the basic SPSS output for a pie chart – the chart is divided into the different coloured slices with a key to the colour codes and a heading of the variable label (with the slices ordered clockwise in terms of the category numeric codes). This chart can be copied and pasted into a report, but you may choose to edit it first, which could be to add a title or to display the frequency counts or percentages on each slice.

The Format option – sorting the data into frequency order

In the **Frequencies** command, the **Format** option can be used to present the data in ascending (or descending) order of frequency. The frequencies can be ordered from lowest to highest by selecting the **Ascending counts** radio option in the **Format** option, as in this example.

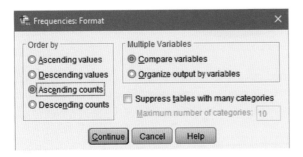

The categories in the frequency table are now displayed in ascending order in the **IBM SPSS Statistics Viewer**: from Teacher with the smallest frequency of five to Vet with the largest frequency of 19.

Preferred occupation

		Frequency	Percent	Valid Percent	Cumulative Percent
Valid	Teacher	5	6.6	6.6	6.6
	Scientist	10	13.2	13.2	19.7
	Athlete	12	15.8	15.8	35.5
	Doctor	14	18.4	18.4	53.9
	Musician	16	21.1	21.1	75.0
	Vet	19	25.0	25.0	100.0
	Total	76	100.0	100.0	

Format also orders the data for the chart as well, in frequency order. The pie chart is ordered clockwise in terms of the size of the slices from smallest to largest. This is referred to as a sorted pie chart, as shown below.

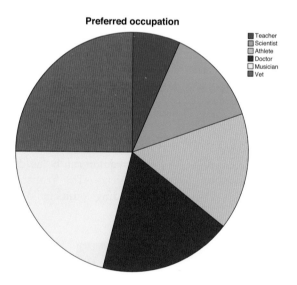

Preferred occupation

Teacher
Scientist
Athlete
Doctor
Musician
Vet

See Chapter 8 for details on changing colours in charts

Notice how the colours are allocated clockwise starting from blue (first), so the sorted pie charted has the slices coloured differently to the unsorted pie chart. A sorted pie chart is often preferred as it is easier to see the relative sizes of the slices than with the unsorted chart.

Describing scale data

The group of 76 10-year-old children were asked to complete a small wooden puzzle as quickly as they could. The times (measured in seconds) are recorded. A timer (such as a digital stopwatch) produces data along an interval scale, so the **Measure** of the children's times to complete the puzzle is Scale. With scale data, the most commonly chosen descriptive statistics are the mean and standard deviation (see Chapter 3). We use the **Frequencies** command to produce these statistics.

See Chapter 3

- Select the **Analyze** drop-down menu.

- Now select **Descriptive Statistics** followed by **Frequencies**.

- In the **Frequencies** dialog box, send the variable 'Time to complete puzzle' to the **Variable(s)** box.

- Select the **Statistics** button. This time, as it is scale data, we would like to know more details than simply the mode to summarise the findings. We shall select the following: the minimum and maximum values and the mean, median, mode and standard deviation (Std. deviation) to illustrate some of the statistics you can display.

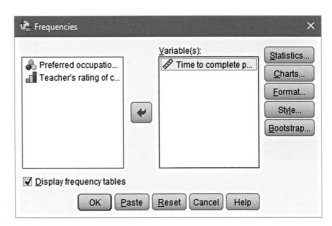

- Click on the **Continue** button to close the **Statistics** dialog box.

- Select the **Charts** button and then the option to produce a histogram.

Histograms are explained in Chapter 7

- Select **Continue** and then **OK**.

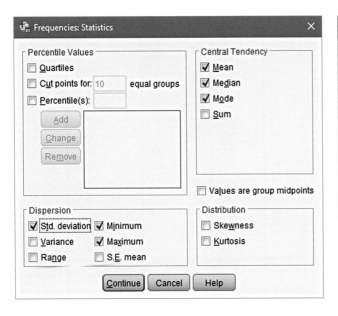

SPSS generates two tables. The **Statistics** table includes all of the information for the statistics that we selected. We can see that there are no missing values. The quickest time that the children completed the puzzle was 10 seconds and the longest was 31 seconds. We can see that the mean, median and mode values are almost identical (the mean being 22.03), so it is clear the 'central tendency' – or 'typical' time - to complete the puzzle is about the 22 seconds mark.

If we take one standard deviation below the mean (22.03 – 4.34 = 17.69) and one standard deviation above the mean (22.03 + 4.34 = 26.37), then the majority of the scores lie between 17.69 seconds and 26.37 seconds.

Statistics

Time to complete puzzle (in seconds)

N	Valid	76
	Missing	0
Mean		22.03
Median		22.00
Mode		22
Std. Deviation		4.342
Minimum		10
Maximum		31

The **Time to complete puzzle (in seconds)** table shows the frequencies of each time to solve the puzzle (how many children solved the puzzle at each different time). We can see that the frequencies get higher as the seconds increase towards 22 seconds and then reduce thereafter.

Time to complete puzzle (in seconds)

		Frequency	Percent	Valid Percent	Cumulative Percent
Valid	10	1	1.3	1.3	1.3
	11	1	1.3	1.3	2.6
	13	1	1.3	1.3	3.9
	14	1	1.3	1.3	5.3
	16	2	2.6	2.6	7.9
	17	4	5.3	5.3	13.2
	18	4	5.3	5.3	18.4
	19	6	7.9	7.9	26.3
	20	7	9.2	9.2	35.5
	21	7	9.2	9.2	44.7
	22	8	10.5	10.5	55.3
	23	7	9.2	9.2	64.5
	24	6	7.9	7.9	72.4
	25	5	6.6	6.6	78.9
	26	4	5.3	5.3	84.2
	27	3	3.9	3.9	88.2
	28	3	3.9	3.9	92.1
	29	3	3.9	3.9	96.1
	30	2	2.6	2.6	98.7
	31	1	1.3	1.3	100.0
	Total	76	100.0	100.0	

This table shows why a frequency table is not usually produced for scale data. As a participant can theoretically produce a result at any point on the scale, the frequency table is usually large and therefore is not a good summary of what has been found. With scale data, the frequency values are clearer when shown in a histogram. Histograms show the distribution of frequencies for scale data and the pattern of frequencies looks easier to see as a histogram in comparison to a frequency table.

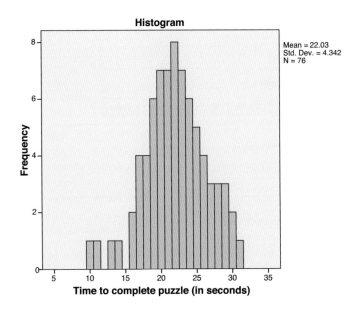

The histogram shows that the results are clustered around a central position and they are also (more or less) symmetrical around this middle position. If a distribution is completely symmetrical the mean, median and mode values will be the same. The distribution above is very symmetrical, with the mean (22.03) median (22.00) and mode (22.00) all very much the same.

Please see Chapter 7 for more details on histograms

Describing ordinal data

A teacher is asked to rate 76 10-year-old children on their degree of 'sportiness' on a five-point Likert scale: 'very unsporty', 'unsporty', 'neither unsporty nor sporty', 'sporty' and 'very sporty'. This is an ordinal scale as the teacher is ordering the children by their perceived sportiness. It is not assumed to be an interval scale. We will again use the **Frequencies** command to produce the descriptive statistics for these data. As this is ordinal data, we will produce a frequency table and a bar chart. (Chapter 7 explains which charts to choose with which data.)

Please see Chapter 7 for which chart to select

- Select the **Analyze** drop-down menu.

- Now select **Descriptive Statistics** followed by **Frequencies.**

- In the **Frequencies** dialog box send the variable 'Teacher's rating of child's sportiness' to the **Variable(s)** box.

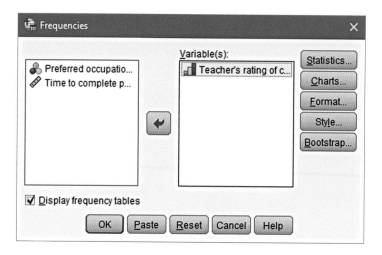

In this example, we are not going to select any statistics from the **Statistics** option.

■ Select the **Charts** button and then the **Bar charts** option.

■ Select **Continue** and then **OK**.

We could have also selected a pie chart here. Please see Chapter 7 for more details on creating graphs

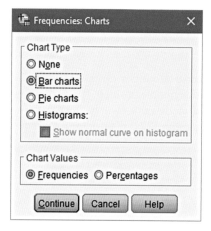

The first table produced by SPSS simply tells us that there are 76 valid results with no missing data.

Statistics

Teacher's rating of child's sportiness

N	Valid	76
	Missing	0

The second table presents a list of the frequency counts for each of the categories. Notice from the cumulative percent column that 40.8% of the children are 'very unsporty' or 'unsporty'. We can also work out from the figures that 53.9% of the children are 'sporty' or 'very sporty', so there seems to be two groups of children in the teacher's rating – the unsporty group (40.8%) and the sporty group (53.9%), with only a small group of children in the middle of the rating scale (5.3%).

Teacher's rating of child's sportiness

		Frequency	Percent	Valid Percent	Cumulative Percent
Valid	Very unsporty	18	23.7	23.7	23.7
	Unsporty	13	17.1	17.1	40.8
	Neither unsporty nor sporty	4	5.3	5.3	46.1
	Sporty	22	28.9	28.9	75.0
	Very sporty	19	25.0	25.0	100.0
	Total	76	100.0	100.0	

Bar charts clearly illustrate the differences between the distinct categories. By looking at the bar chart below we can see that the teacher rated more of the children as 'sporty' than 'unsporty' and the lowest frequency of the children were in the 'neither unsporty nor sporty' category.

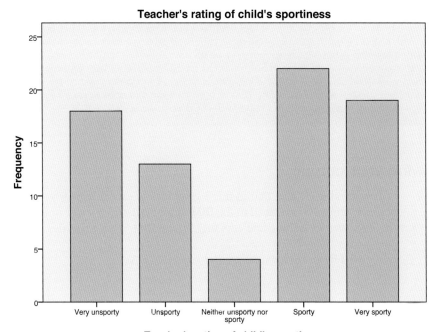

Teacher's rating of child's sportiness

✓

You can sort the order of the bars in a bar chart by selecting the **Format** option in the **Frequencies** command and choose the option for **Ascending counts** for the bars to been ordered in terms of increasing frequency.

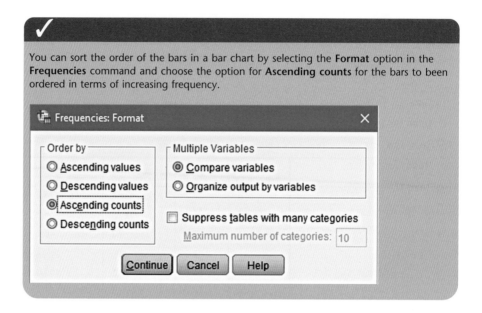

✓

SPSS does allow you to calculate means with ordinal data (if you really want to!). In the **Statistics** option, we could ask for a mean to be displayed. The **Statistics** table then shows that the mean rating of a child's sportiness as 3.14, which is in the middle of the rating scale and might give the impression that the children were generally neither unsporty nor sporty. However, if we look at the **Teacher's rating of child's sportiness** table, we can see that the teacher rated the children at the two ends of the ratings and the mean doesn't really give a good representation of the findings – it does not indicate a 'typical' child's rating. The SPSS **Frequencies** command allows us to calculate the mean with ordinal data – but SPSS is not advising whether we should or not here. Now, as we have discussed earlier, the mean is not viewed as the appropriate statistics for ordinal data, unless we can be convinced that a rating scale is acting as an interval scale. Some researchers do choose to treat ordinal data as scale data but you need to assure yourself that this is an acceptable choice to make in the field of research you are in.

See Chapter 7 for details of how to produce other bar charts

Saving your output

Once you have produced some output it is a good idea to save it regularly. You can save all of the information contained in the **IBM SPSS Statistics Viewer** (for looking at again in SPSS later for editing and copying). In the **IBM SPSS Statistics Viewer**:

■ Click on the **File** drop-down menu and select **Save As**.

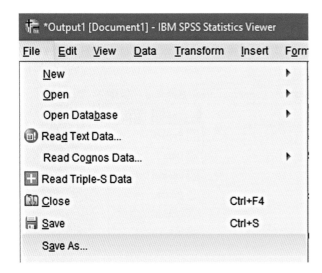

You can then choose where to save your output from SPSS as a file. Notice that the name of the saved file will have a file extension of .spv. SPSS offers you a default name for the file ('Output1.spv') but you will normally give the file a more meaningful name. We have decided to call the Sparcote Study output 'Applied Studies Student Survey.spv'.

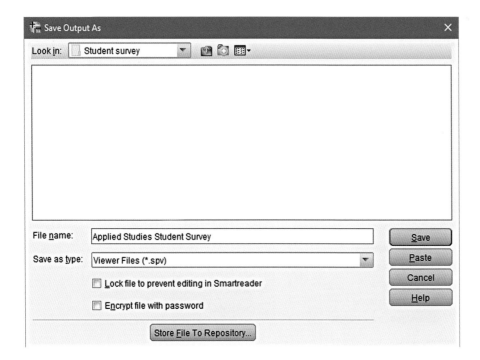

■ Type in the title and click **Save**.

Now, if you want to look at this output again you can open it up in SPSS.

An alternative way to open an SPSS output file is to double click on the file (with file extension .spv) and SPSS will open with this output displayed in the **IBM SPSS Statistics Viewer**.

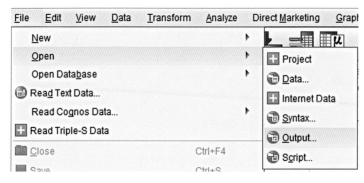

See Chapter 3

As described in Chapter 3, you now have an output file in which your tables and graphs are stored, along with your dataset in another file. These are two separate files and should be saved separately. When you save them you will be able to distinguish the difference between them, as the dataset is saved as a .sav file while the output file ends with a .spv extension. You can switch between the two files at the task bar at the bottom of your screen when in SPSS.

A FIRST DESCRIPTION OF THE SPARCOTE STUDY RESULTS

The Sparcote Study has been designed to highlight a range of different response types that you might have in a survey. We are going to go through each question and response type and show how you could present an initial summary of your findings using the **Frequencies** command. Therefore, each procedure starts with:

■ Select the **Analyze** drop-down menu.

■ Then **Descriptive Statistics** and then **Frequencies**.

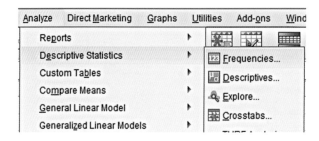

Question 1 – Multiple choice (single answer) – Nominal

The first variable is 'Gender'. As the responses are nominal data, we are going to produce a table that shows the frequency of males and females in our sample. We have chosen not to produce any addition statistics under the **Statistics** options. We have also chosen not to produce a chart under the **Charts** option. With only two categories for gender, a simple frequency table is adequate for displaying a summary of the gender data.

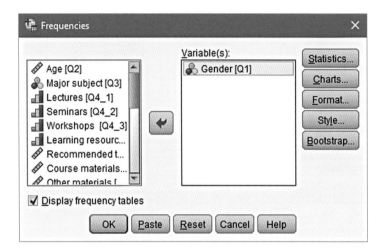

- 'Gender' is sent to the **Variable(s)** box.

- Click **OK**.

The first table is the **Statistics** table. It shows two figures, the number of participants who answered this question and how many participants did not answer this question. We can see that all 183 participants in the sample answered this question and none of the participants missed this question.

Statistics

Gender

N	Valid	183
	Missing	0

You might not want to put every table SPSS produces into your report. For tables with only a few numbers in it, it can be clearer to simply write the figures in the text of your report rather than present these numbers in a table.

The second table shows that 94 (51.4%) female students and 89 (48.6%) male students answered the survey.

Gender

		Frequency	Percent	Valid Percent	Cumulative Percent
Valid	Female	94	51.4	51.4	51.4
	Male	89	48.6	48.6	100.0
	Total	183	100.0	100.0	

We can see that overall there are more or less equal numbers of women and men students in the first cohort in the Department of Applied Studies.

Question 2 – Scale

The second question in the Sparcote Study is the students' age, which is measured on an interval scale.

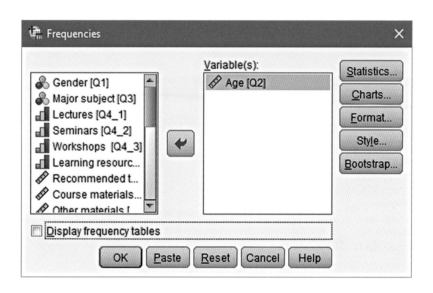

■ Notice that the **Display frequency tables** box has been unticked here. This will mean that the frequency table showing the frequencies for each individual age will not be produced. With scale data, a frequency table can be very large and uninformative (as we saw in the above example of the children's puzzle-solving times).

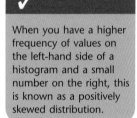

When you have a higher frequency of values on the left-hand side of a histogram and a small number on the right, this is known as a positively skewed distribution.

■ Instead, we have selected the **Statistics** button and we would like to find the minimum and maximum values, and the mean, median, mode and standard deviation values as these provide a more useful summary of the ages. Click on **Continue**.

■ In the **Charts** option, we have selected **Histograms**, then clicked **Continue** and **OK**.

SPSS produces a **Statistics** table, which shows that the students who completed the Applied Studies Student Survey were aged between 18 years old and 48 years old with a range of 30 years. The most frequent age of the students was 19 years old as shown by the mode, with the median age as 21 years old. The mean age is 22.32 years with a standard deviation of 4.892.

The **Histogram** also shows the Mean = 22.32 and Std. Dev = 4.892 noted on the right hand side of the chart.

Statistics

Age

N	Valid	183
	Missing	0
Mean		22.32
Median		21.00
Mode		19
Std. Deviation		4.892
Minimum		18
Maximum		48

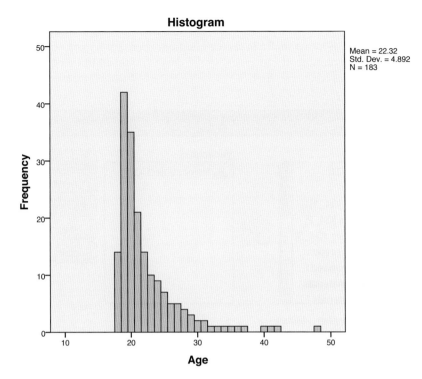

Histogram

Mean = 22.32
Std. Dev. = 4.892
N = 183

skew
When scale data is plotted on a frequency distribution, it can be observed whether the distribution is symmetrical about a 'middle' position or not. If the distribution is not symmetrical, it is said to be 'skewed'.

positive skew
When a frequency distribution is plotted in a histogram, it can be seen whether the distribution is symmetrical or not. Often the pattern of data looks like a hill or a bell shape with the most frequent scores in the centre and the frequencies tailing off in both directions. However, if most of the scores pile to the left of the distribution with a long tail to the right then the distribution is said to be positively skewed

negative skew
When a frequency distribution is plotted in a histogram, it can be seen whether the distribution is symmetrical or not. Often the pattern of data looks like a hill or a bell shape with the most frequent scores in the centre and the frequencies tailing off in both directions. However, if the most of the scores pile to the right of the distribution with a long tail to the left then the distribution is said to be negatively skewed

Looking at this histogram confirms that the highest frequency of students (the mode) is at 19 years old. This pattern of frequencies is not symmetrical (unlike the histogram of the children's puzzle-solving times above). As the students are not normally admitted to Sparcote University under the age of 17 or 18, we can see that there are no students under 18 years old at the end of their first year of study. However, we can see, from the range of students admitted, that there a number of students in their 20s, 30s and 40s with the oldest student 48 years old. The distribution of the frequencies of student ages shows a clustering around 19–21 years with the ages 'tailing' off as age increases. This distribution is not symmetrical but shows **skew**. It is referred to as a **positive skew** as the long tail is to the right of the main cluster. (If the tail had been on the left of the cluster it would have been called a **negative skew**.) With a positive skew, we see that the mean value is higher than the median and the mode. This is because scores far from the 'middle' position tend to have a strong influence on the mean and 'pull' it further up the scale. In this case, the mean (of 22.32 years) is over one year older than the median value of 21.00 years). With a distribution like this, some researchers will present the median as well as (or instead of) the mean as the measure of 'central tendency' for these data.

Question 3 – Multiple choice (single answer) – Nominal

'Major subject' is also a multiple choice question where participants choose a single answer from a number of categories, so the data is nominal. In this question, there are four options to choose from.

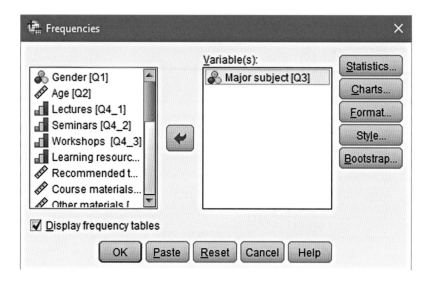

- We will also select the **Charts** option and choose **Bar charts**.
- We then click on **Continue** and **OK**.

By looking at the output of this procedure, we can see that again there are no missing values (we have not shown the first output table here). We can examine the frequency table displayed in the **SPSS IBM SPSS Statistics Viewer**.

Major subject

		Frequency	Percent	Valid Percent	Cumulative Percent
Valid	Business	59	32.2	32.2	32.2
	Community Health	33	18.0	18.0	50.3
	Education	45	24.6	24.6	74.9
	Media	46	25.1	25.1	100.0
	Total	183	100.0	100.0	

The **Major subject** table shows that the major subject with the most students was business with 59 (nearly one-third of the students in the department with 32.2%) and the fewest were in community health with 33 (only 18%). Education and media each had just about one-quarter of students in the year studying them: 45 (24.6%), 46 (25.1%).

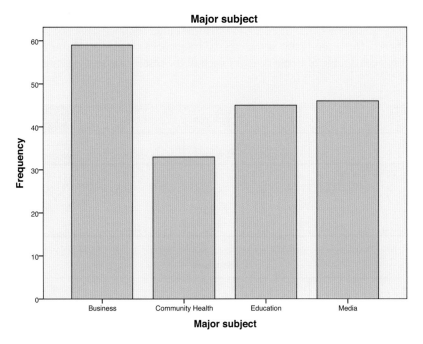

These results provide some useful information about the student demographics and are a good start to looking at the results but they do not provide all the information. We would like to know how many men and women there are in each major subject area and how the ages are distributed across the major subjects, too. This shows that further analysis is necessary to produce this information.

> *To produce tables that combine questions together such as 'Gender' and 'Major subject', see Chapter 6*

Question 4 – Rank ordering of three items – Ordinal

Question 4 is made up of three items (or in SPSS terms, three variables), with the students ordering 'lectures', seminars' and 'workshops' into their order of preference. We decide to display them all together so send all three variables to the **Variable(s)** box for analysis. This is a rank order question, so the data is ordinal.

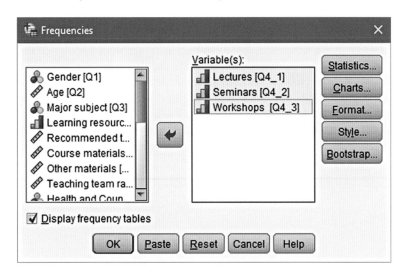

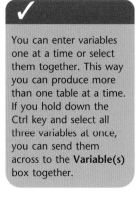

> You can enter variables one at a time or select them together. This way you can produce more than one table at a time. If you hold down the Ctrl key and select all three variables at once, you can send them across to the **Variable(s)** box together.

We will not change the **Statistics** options or select any charts from the **Charts** option. The first table shows that there are no missing values (and we have not shown this table here). The second table is the table of frequencies. However, in this case, SPSS has displayed a table of frequencies for each of the three variables separately, shown below.

Lectures

		Frequency	Percent	Valid Percent	Cumulative Percent
Valid	First	58	31.7	31.7	31.7
	Second	64	35.0	35.0	66.7
	Third	61	33.3	33.3	100.0
	Total	183	100.0	100.0	

Seminars

		Frequency	Percent	Valid Percent	Cumulative Percent
Valid	First	59	32.2	32.2	32.2
	Second	65	35.5	35.5	67.8
	Third	59	32.2	32.2	100.0
	Total	183	100.0	100.0	

Workshops

		Frequency	Percent	Valid Percent	Cumulative Percent
Valid	First	67	36.6	36.6	36.6
	Second	56	30.6	30.6	67.2
	Third	60	32.8	32.8	100.0
	Total	183	100.0	100.0	

To produce a table that combines questions together such as major subject and modes of study, see Chapter 6

Notice that, overall, there is not much difference in the ordering – 58 students have put lectures first with lectures ranked as second being the most popular choice (64). Fifty nine students put seminars first, with second the most popular choice (65). Workshops are chosen in first place by 67 students, which is the most popular choice for workshops. While this does not show any general tendency for any particular preference, we would like to know now whether these choices differ between the different major subjects, which will require further analysis. It might be that there are very different preferences dependent of the major subject being studied. (We will follow this up in Chapter 6.)

Question 5 – Likert scale – Ordinal

This question on the learning resources is a typical Likert scale question, where the students were asked for their level of agreement with a statement about the appropriateness of the learning resources.

- We have not asked for any statistics in the **Statistics** option, but have chosen a bar chart from the **Charts** option.

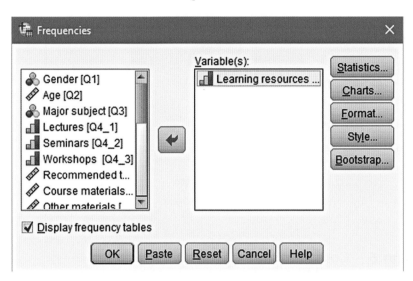

The first table shows that there are no missing values (and we have not shown this table here). The second table shows the pattern of frequencies across the different categories of the Likert scale.

Learning resources

		Frequency	Percent	Valid Percent	Cumulative Percent
Valid	Strongly disagree	18	9.8	9.8	9.8
	Disagree	29	15.8	15.8	25.7
	Neither disagree nor agree	46	25.1	25.1	50.8
	Agree	54	29.5	29.5	80.3
	Strongly agree	36	19.7	19.7	100.0
	Total	183	100.0	100.0	

We can see that 25.7% of the students 'strongly disagree' or 'disagree' with the statement, indicating that they do not view the learning resources as appropriate. While a further 25.1% have chosen the 'neither disagree nor agree' category, 49.2% have chosen 'agree' or 'strongly agree'. These results are worth breaking down by major subject to see if the students viewing the learning resources as inappropriate are located in one or more specific subject area. The bar chart illustrates these frequency values across the different categories.

✓

SPSS allows you to calculate means with ordinal data even though it is often regarded as inappropriate (see Chapter 3). However, some researchers do treat Likert scale data as if it is measured on an interval scale and present mean values. In the **Statistics** option, we could ask for a mean to be displayed for these data. In this case, the mean of 3.33 looks like a reasonable summary of a 'middle' position, as this lies between the 'neither disagree nor agree' value of 3 and the 'agree' value of 4. Even though this is an ordinal scale, there is some evidence from the distribution that the students may be using it in a similar way to an interval scale. However, with this question, this is not an assumption that the Sparcote researchers decide to make.

See Chapter 3

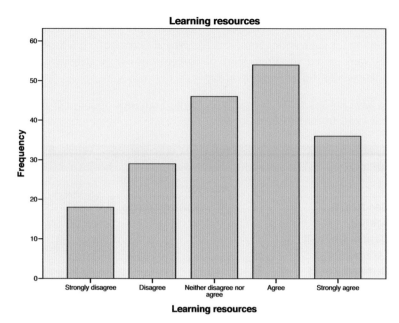

The chart shows that the results follow a 'hill-like' pattern with the mode being the agree category (chosen by 54 students).

Question 6 – Constant sum – Scale

Question 6 is a constant sum question involving three items: recommended textbooks, course materials and other materials. The students have been asked to choose in percentage terms their relative use of these items, with the sum being 100. While it could be argued that this data is not scale, the Sparcote researchers have argued that this is the best way to treat it (see Chapter 3). We would like to analyse all three variables at the same time, so we have sent them across together to the **Variable(s)** box.

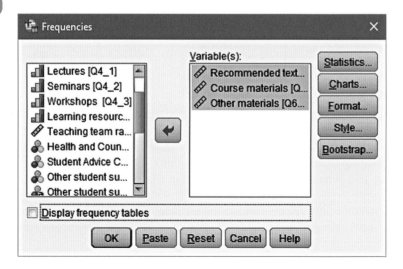

■ We have asked for means and standard deviations in the **Statistics** option, and unticked **Display frequency tables** in the **Frequencies** dialog box. The **Charts** option has not been chosen so no chart will be generated.

Only one table is displayed by SPSS. The top two rows of the table simply indicate that there are no missing values:

Statistics

		Recommended textbooks	Course materials	Other materials
N	Valid	183	183	183
	Missing	0	0	0
Mean		40.19	43.27	16.56
Std. Deviation		9.066	10.145	6.354

Notice that SPSS has displayed the three means and standard deviations in the same table. We can see than the 'Recommended textbooks' (40.19) and the 'Course materials' (43.27) are both selected by the students as being used for over 40% of the time on average, with 'Other materials' only used 16.56% of the time on average. The combination of 'Recommended textbooks' and 'Course materials' account for 84.46% of relative use of these three types of material used by the students.

Question 7 – Rating scale – Scale

Even though Question 7 is a rating scale asking the students to rate the quality of their teaching team, the Sparcote researchers decided to treat it as an interval scale, so are interested in presenting the means and standard deviations for these data.

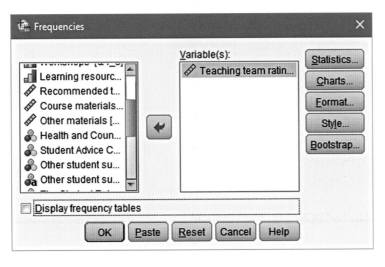

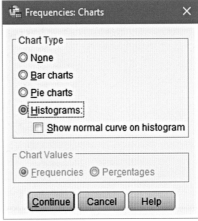

■ In this case, the mean and standard deviation were selected in the **Statistics** option, a histogram was selected in the **Charts** option, and the **Display frequency tables** was unticked in the **Frequencies** dialog box.

Only one table is displayed by SPSS. The top two rows shows that there are no missing values.

The mean for the teacher rating is 6.68. This can be viewed as a positive opinion of the overall teaching quality in the department as it is a score of nearly 7 out of 10. However, the researchers are interested to see how this breaks down across the different subject majors and gender. This will

See Chapter 7

be examined in Chapter 7.

SPSS also displays the histogram that was selected in the **Charts** option.

Statistics

Teaching team rating

N	Valid	183
	Missing	0
Mean		6.68
Std. Deviation		1.955

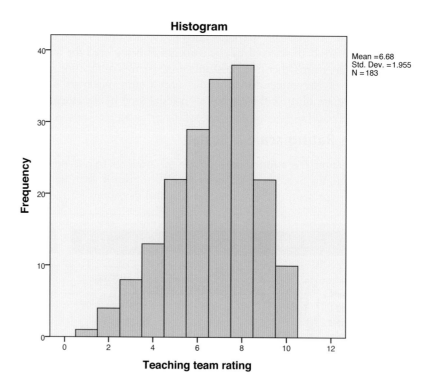

Notice that the data does show a clustering around a 'middle' position and the distribution is reasonably symmetrical, so the histogram does not undermine the choice of the data as scale. (The researchers might feel that they do have some justification to their decision to treat the data as measured on an interval scale – see

Decisions on measuring are discussed in Chapter 3

Chapter 3.)

Question 8 – Multiple choice (multiple answer) – Nominal

Question 8 has an interesting feature in that it asks if the students have used two key university services, the Health and Counselling Centre and the Student Advice Centre, but also asks if they have used any other service and, if so, to name it. This means that the question comprises four items, so we select all four variables and send them to the **Variable(s)** box in the **Frequencies** command.

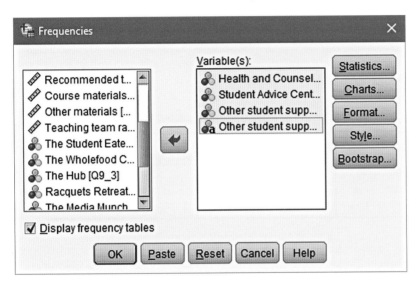

■ We have not selected any **Statistics** or **Chart** options for this question so we just press **OK**.

The first table simply indicates that there are no missing values in any of the variables.

Statistics

		Health and Counselling Centre	Student Advice Centre	Other student support service	Other student support service used
N	Valid	183	183	183	183
	Missing	0	0	0	0

SPSS then displays a separate frequency table for each variable:

Health and Counselling Centre

		Frequency	Percent	Valid Percent	Cumulative Percent
Valid	No	146	79.8	79.8	79.8
	Yes	37	20.2	20.2	100.0
	Total	183	100.0	100.0	

From the first frequency table we can see that 37 students (20.2%) in the Department of Applied Studies visited the Health and Counselling Centre.

Student Advice Centre

		Frequency	Percent	Valid Percent	Cumulative Percent
Valid	No	122	66.7	66.7	66.7
	Yes	61	33.3	33.3	100.0
	Total	183	100.0	100.0	

The second frequency table shows that 61 students (33.3%) – that is, one-third of the students – have used the Student Advice Centre during their first year.

Other student support service

		Frequency	Percent	Valid Percent	Cumulative Percent
Valid	No	169	92.3	92.3	92.3
	Yes	14	7.7	7.7	100.0
	Total	183	100.0	100.0	

Finally, we see that 14 students (or 7.7%) have used another student support service throughout the year. We can look to the following frequency table to see a list of the descriptions of the service they have given, which is the way SPSS displays text data as a frequency table:

Other student support service used

		Frequency	Percent	Valid Percent	Cumulative Percent
Valid		169	92.3	92.3	92.3
	Careers guidance	1	.5	.5	92.9
	Careers office	1	.5	.5	93.4
	Computer people	1	.5	.5	94.0
	Computer service	2	1.1	1.1	95.1
	IT services	5	2.7	2.7	97.8
	Technical services	1	.5	.5	98.4
	The creche	1	.5	.5	98.9
	University creche	2	1.1	1.1	100.0
	Total	183	100.0	100.0	

SPSS has simply listed out the different text descriptions that we input into the dataset as 'string' variables. There are 169 blank entries. As there are only 14 descriptions (and they are quite short) we can easily see what has been given. From this table, it seems that two students used the careers guidance service, 8 students

Notice that 1 is given for a blank value. The majority of students did not specify another service so the string variable is blank for all the participants except the 14 who wrote the name of the other service they used. We can produce a frequency table for this new variable by the **Frequencies** command.

Other student support service used

		Frequency	Percent	Valid Percent	Cumulative Percent
Valid	1	169	92.3	92.3	92.3
	Careers guidance	1	.5	.5	92.9
	Careers office	1	.5	.5	93.4
	Computer people	1	.5	.5	94.0
	Computer service	2	1.1	1.1	95.1
	IT services	5	2.7	2.7	97.8
	Technical services	1	.5	.5	98.4
	The creche	1	.5	.5	98.9
	University creche	2	1.1	1.1	100.0
	Total	183	100.0	100.0	

You might be happy with this, but we are going to tidy this up a bit, as a number of different answers are actually referring to the same service (such as 'Careers guidance' and 'Careers office'). In fact, there are only three categories chosen: 'Careers guidance', 'Computing and IT service' (which includes computers and technical services) and the 'University crèche'.

To change the responses from the nine categories into three categories, we do the following:

■ Select the **Transform** drop-down menu and select the **Recode into Different Variables** option.

Transform	Analyze	Direct Marketing	Graphs
▦ Compute Variable...			
➕ Programmability Transformation...			
▧ Count Values within Cases...			
Shift Values...			
▨ Recode into Same Variables...			
▨ Recode into Different Variables...			
▤ Automatic Recode...			
➕ Create Dummy Variables			

We are going to create a new variable with the three different categories coded and labelled as 1 = 'Careers guidance', 2 = 'Computing and IT service' and 3 = 'University crèche'. In the first dialog box, we give the new variable a **Name** ('Q8_4B') and a **Label** ('Other student suport service used').

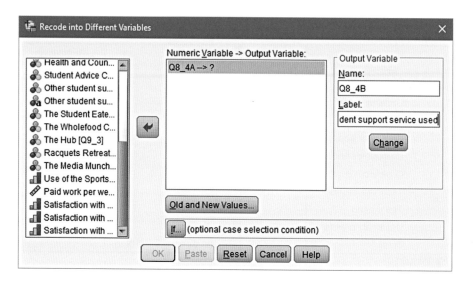

■   We click on **Change**.
■   Now we click on the **Old and New Values** button.

The following dialog box appears.

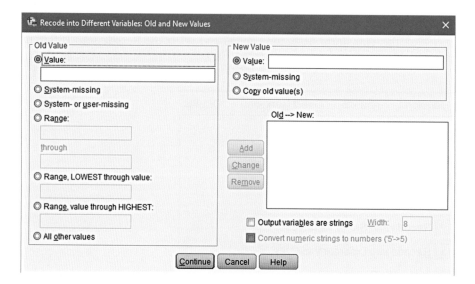

■ In the left-hand side of the window, we ensure that the **Value** radio button is selected and enter in the **Old Value** of 1 which is currently 'blank'. In the **New Value** section, we click on **System-missing** (as these are the people who did not specify another service) and click **Add**.

■ In the **Old Value**, **Value** option we type in the value 2 and in the **New Value** section we type in the number 1 (which we will be labelling 'Careers guidance'), and click **Add**.

■ We type 3 into **Old Value** and 1 in **New Value** (as this is also be careers guidance), and click **Add**.

■ The codes of 4, 5, 6 and 7 all refer to the computing and IT service. In **Old Value**, we click on **Range** and type 4 in the first box and 7 in the second. In **New Value**, we type 2 (which we will be labelling 'Computing and IT service' later). We click **Add**.

■ For **Old Value** 8 we type **New Value** 3 (which we will later label as 'University crèche') and click **Add**.

■ Finally, for the **Old Value** 9 we input a **New Value** of 3 (as this is the crèche as well), and click **Add**.

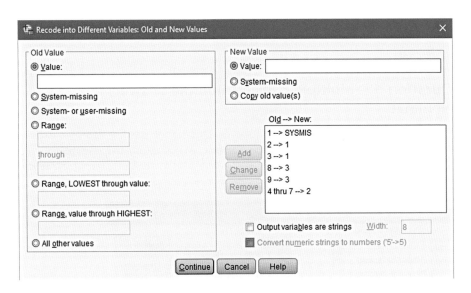

■ Click on **Continue** and then **OK**.

We now have a new variable 'Q8_4B', which has three numeric codes in it. We now switch to **Variable View**, add the value labels for the three codes (1 = 'Careers guidance', 2 = 'Computing and IT service', 3 = 'University crèche') for this variable – and make sure that the rest of the details of the variable are what we want (such as decimal places set to zero).

If we now use the **Frequencies** command to produce a frequency table for this variable, 'Q8_4B' we get the following output.

We now have the data stored in the correct format, in that only 14 people filled in this response so that the other 169 are missing (rather than give a 'blank' response).

Statistics

Other student support service used

N	Valid	14
	Missing	169

Other student support service used

		Frequency	Percent	Valid Percent	Cumulative Percent
Valid	Careers guidance	2	1.1	14.3	14.3
	Computing and IT service	9	4.9	64.3	78.6
	University creche	3	1.6	21.4	100.0
	Total	14	7.7	100.0	
Missing	System	169	92.3		
Total		183	100.0		

We have now converted a set of text responses to categories in a new nominal variable and produced the frequency of the choices of the other support services that students used.

Question 9 – Multiple choice (multiple answer) – Nominal

The question about the campus social spaces, Question 9, has five items, so each of the different spaces is a separate SPSS variable. We send all five variables to the **Variable(s)** box.

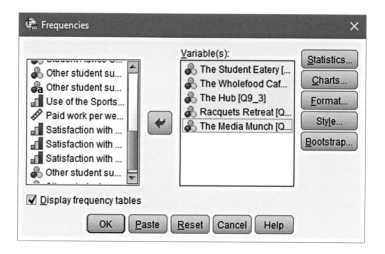

■   We do not choose any options so we just click **OK**.

The first table **Statistics** confirms that there are no missing values for all five of the variables. The frequency tables for the five social spaces follow.

Statistics

		The Student Eatery	The Wholefood Café	The Hub	Racquets Retreat	The Media Munch
N	Valid	183	183	183	183	183
	Missing	0	0	0	0	0

The Student Eatery

		Frequency	Percent	Valid Percent	Cumulative Percent
Valid	No	61	33.3	33.3	33.3
	Yes	122	66.7	66.7	100.0
	Total	183	100.0	100.0	

The Wholefood Café

		Frequency	Percent	Valid Percent	Cumulative Percent
Valid	No	94	51.4	51.4	51.4
	Yes	89	48.6	48.6	100.0
	Total	183	100.0	100.0	

The Hub

		Frequency	Percent	Valid Percent	Cumulative Percent
Valid	No	126	68.9	68.9	68.9
	Yes	57	31.1	31.1	100.0
	Total	183	100.0	100.0	

Racquets Retreat

		Frequency	Percent	Valid Percent	Cumulative Percent
Valid	No	154	84.2	84.2	84.2
	Yes	29	15.8	15.8	100.0
	Total	183	100.0	100.0	

The Media Munch

		Frequency	Percent	Valid Percent	Cumulative Percent
Valid	No	99	54.1	54.1	54.1
	Yes	84	45.9	45.9	100.0
	Total	183	100.0	100.0	

While these tables have some useful data, the key results could be summarised much more simply in a single table. Essentially, the results show that 122 (66.7%, or two-thirds) of the students went to the Student Eatery during the year, 89 (48.6%) to the Wholefood Café, 57 (31.1%) to The Hub, 29 (15.8%) to the Racquets Retreat and 84 (45.9%) to The Media Munch. The Student Eatery was the most popular, with the Racquets Retreat attracting the fewest students. It would be nice to have this information combined into a single simple table. (We will explain how to do this in Chapter 6.)

See Chapter 6

Question 10 – Likert Scale – Ordinal

Question 10, about the use of the Sports and Fitness Centre, is a Likert scale question, so the data is ordinal.

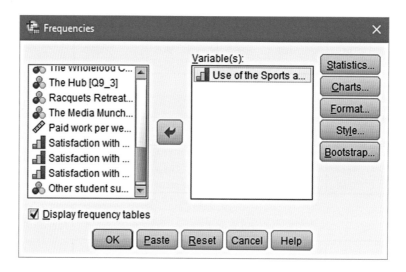

■ We have selected the **Charts** option and asked for a bar chart to be displayed along with the frequency table, to graphically show the frequency of the different categories, and then clicked **OK**.

The first table shows that there are no missing values (and we have not shown this table here). The second table is the frequency table of the Likert scale categories.

Use of the Sports and Fitness Centre

		Frequency	Percent	Valid Percent	Cumulative Percent
Valid	Never	49	26.8	26.8	26.8
	Rarely	31	16.9	16.9	43.7
	Occasionally	25	13.7	13.7	57.4
	Regularly	37	20.2	20.2	77.6
	Often	41	22.4	22.4	100.0
	Total	183	100.0	100.0	

The frequency table shows that 49 (26.8%) of the students – just over one-quarter of them – have never visited the Sports and Fitness Centre. However, 78 students (37 + 41 or 42.6%) visit the centre either 'Regularly' or 'Frequently'. While the students are spread across all the categories (with each category having at least 25 students in it), the two extreme categories have the highest frequency.

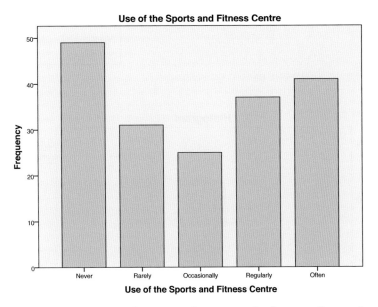

The bar chart shows the frequency data quite clearly. Broadly speaking, the students tend to split into those who 'Never' or 'Rarely' use the centre (80 students or 43.7%) and those who use it 'Regularly' or 'Often' (78 students or 42.6%). (This is an example of an ordinal 'scale' where the idea of an 'average' or typical student does not make sense. It is better to see the students in group terms – possibly a 'not-sporty' group and a 'sporty' group.)

Question 11 – Scale

The final question in the third section of the survey, Question 11, asks the students to specify the number of hours of paid work they undertake on average per week. This is scale data, as number of hours is measured on an interval scale.

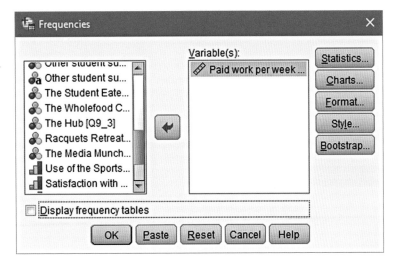

With this question, the mean, median, mode and standard deviation are chosen in the **Statistics** option, and a histogram is selected in the **Charts** option.

The first two row of the **Statistics** table shows that there are no missing values.

This table also shows that the mean, media and mode are very similar values, showing that the distribution of hours worked is fairly symmetrical around a 'middle' postion of about 11 hours or so. The histogram shows this pattern quite clearly.

Statistics

Paid work per week

N	Valid	183
	Missing	0
Mean		11.28
Median		11.00
Mode		11
Std. Deviation		3.861

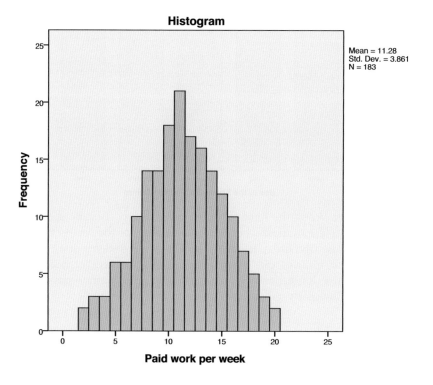

The number of hours worked by the students clusters around the mean of 11.28 hours. The standard deviation of 3.86 also tells us most of the students work between 7.42 hours and 15.14 hours (as these figures indicate 1 standard deviation lower than the mean and 1 standard deviation higher than the mean). However, it might be more interesting to see whether there are any differences in the amount of hours worked per week by breaking this figure down across the different major subjects or comparing men and women. This will be examined in Chapter 7.

See Chapter 7

Question 12 – Likert scale – Ordinal

The final question in the survey comprises three five-point Likert scale items about the students' satisfaction with different aspect of their life, with the response categories ranging from 'very unsatisfied' through to 'very satisfied'. The student response data is ordinal and stored in three variables, so we send all three variables across to the **Variable(s)** box.

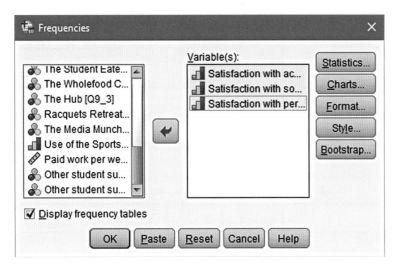

■ We have selected **Bar charts** in the **Charts** option. Then clicked **OK**.

The first table shows that there are no missing values (and we have not shown this table here). The next table shows the frequencies for the 'Satisfaction with academic life' variable. Notice that here the category 'very unsatisfied' is missing from the table. This is because no one selected that category. We can see that all 183 students selected one of the other four categories. The **Frequencies** command leaves out a category from the frequency table if the frequency is 0. (We show in Chapter 6 how to produce a frequency table with all the categories listed, if that is what you prefer to present.)

Satisfaction with academic life

		Frequency	Percent	Valid Percent	Cumulative Percent
Valid	Unsatisfied	17	9.3	9.3	9.3
	Neither unsatisfied nor satisfied	55	30.1	30.1	39.3
	Satisfied	70	38.3	38.3	77.6
	Very satisfied	41	22.4	22.4	100.0
	Total	183	100.0	100.0	

As can be seen, 111 students (70 + 41 or 60.7%) are 'satisfied' or 'very satisfied' with their academic life.

The second table shows the student satisfaction with their social life.

Satisfaction with social life

		Frequency	Percent	Valid Percent	Cumulative Percent
Valid	Very unsatisfied	1	.5	.5	.5
	Unsatisfied	15	8.2	8.2	8.7
	Neither unsatisfied nor satisfied	53	29.0	29.0	37.7
	Satisfied	68	37.2	37.2	74.9
	Very satisfied	46	25.1	25.1	100.0
	Total	183	100.0	100.0	

Here, there is one person 'very unsatisfied' with university social life but 114 (62.3%) are 'satisfied' or 'very satisfied' with it.

The third table shows the results of the 'Satisfaction with personal development' question.

Satisfaction with personal development

		Frequency	Percent	Valid Percent	Cumulative Percent
Valid	Unsatisfied	27	14.8	14.8	14.8
	Neither unsatisfied nor satisfied	43	23.5	23.5	38.3
	Satisfied	67	36.6	36.6	74.9
	Very satisfied	46	25.1	25.1	100.0
	Total	183	100.0	100.0	

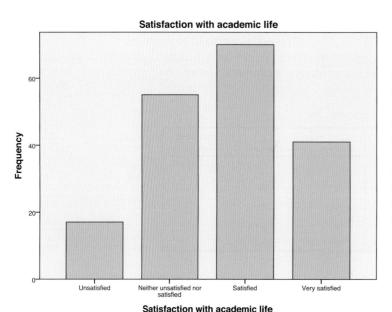

Satisfaction with academic life

Here, again, we see that there are no responses in the 'very unsatisfied' category as this is missing in the table. Generally, the results show that the students are satisfied with these three aspects of their lives.

SPSS has also displayed a bar chart for each of the satisfaction questions, charting the frequency data. Notice again that the 'very unsatisfied' category is absent as no students ticked this category, in the first chart.

It is interesting to note that the results appear to cluster around the mode of 'satisfied' for 'Satisfaction with academic life'. (You may wish to produce a bar chart with all five categories in it. In Chapter 7, we explain how to produce a bar chart from a table with the zero frequency categories included.) The bar chart for 'Satisfaction with social life' does include all the categories as every category was selected by at least one participant.

See Chapter 7

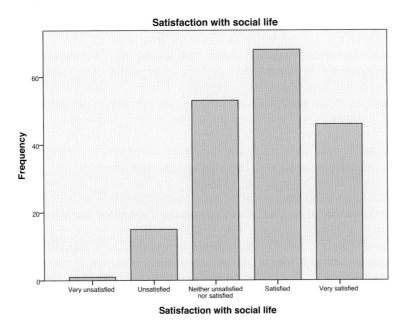

Again we can see that 'satisfied' is also the most popular category with 'Satisfaction with social life' as well.

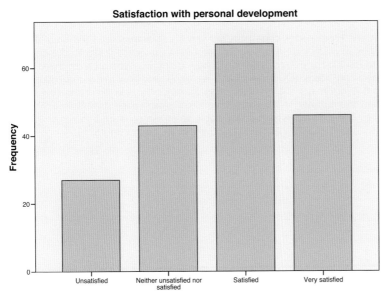

Finally, a similar pattern is found with 'Satisfaction with personal development', which also has 'satisfied' as its most frequent category. This is one way to present these variables; however, you may want to combine the variables together into one table or in the form of a chart or charts, as shown in Chapters 6 and 7.

See Chapters 6 and 7

DESCRIBING THE RESULTS OF A SINGLE VARIABLE

As we have seen in this chapter, the **Frequencies** command allows you to describe the data from a single variable regardless of the level of measurement. A frequency table can be produced with both counts and percentages of the various categories for nominal and ordinal data. However, under the **Statistics** options, a range of different descriptive statistics can be produced, including the mean and the standard deviation, which are normally presented with scale data. You can produce, on the click of a button, a pie chart, bar chart or histogram. SPSS will also create the pie or bar charts for either frequency counts or percentages and the order of the slices or bars in the chart can be in numeric order of the codes or in ascending or descending category frequency. Thus, the **Frequencies** command provides a range of different options for describing a variable – and may be all you need to analyse your data in certain situations. SPSS also provides two other useful commands in the **Descriptive Statistics** list: **Descriptives** and **Explore**. These allow you to go into more detail about the 'shape' and structure of the data produced for a variable. Some people prefer to use the **Descriptives** command rather than the **Frequencies** command to produce means and standard deviation (even though they both give the same result!). The **Explore** command (along with **P-P Plots** and **Q-Q Plots** commands, also listed under the **Descriptive Statistics** menu) can be used to examine more complex aspects of the data, but are beyond the scope of the present book. (Interested readers who wish to learn about these commands are directed to our companion volume *SPSS Explained*.)

While the **Frequencies** command has very nicely summarised the data of a single variable, in many cases we want to combine variables together in the description of the results. For example, we know how many women and men there are in the Sparcote Study (Question 1) and we also know how many students study each the four major subjects (Question 3), but we would like to be able to present the number of female and male students in each subject area. Often we wish to combine more than one variable when we produce a table (or graph). The following chapters explain how this can be done using SPSS.

Creating tables

152 CREATING TABLES IN SPSS

152 CROSS-TABULATING DATA

154 THE CROSSTABS COMMAND

169 INTRODUCTION TO CUSTOM TABLES

Chapter aim: To explain how to create a variety of tables using SPSS

A table enables you to present your data in a concise manner to summarise your findings. As we showed in Chapter 5, the SPSS **Frequencies** command offers an easy way to describe the findings of each of your variables. However, you often want more complex tables than just reporting on how many people responded in a particular way to a question or a single task. You will no doubt be seeking answers to your research questions by combining the results of more than one variable, such as looking to see if certain demographic characteristics of your sample influence the responses they give to other variables. For example, in a study on employee satisfaction in a company, two of the questions asked were: *Do you feel a sense of belonging to this organisation?* and *How long have you worked for this company?* Now, the individual results of these two questions will show, separately, how many people feel a sense of belonging (or not) to the organisation and the how long the different participants have worked for the company. However, people who have been working for a company for a long time may respond differently to the 'belonging' question than people who have only just started working for the company. To explore this, the researchers may wish to combine the results of the two questions in a single table: Examining the 'belonging' results for people who have worked for the company for different lengths of time. In a similar fashion, you may wish to examine your own data to see how the pattern of responses to one question (or task) combines with the responses of other questions (or tasks). Indeed, you may have specific predictions in your research questions that you wish to see if they are supported by the data, such as 'Does a sense of belonging to the organisation increase the longer a person has worked for the company?' This chapter aims to show you how to create a variety of tables in SPSS that combine responses to more than one item, question or task in the same table. Chapter 5 gave us a summary of our findings and Chapter 6 gives us the opportunity produce tables that will help to answer our research questions.

See Chapter 5

CREATING TABLES IN SPSS

We saw in the last chapter that the **Frequencies** command can create basic tables showing the frequency and percentage of responses (or mean and standard deviation) of a single variable. However, there are many cases in which, rather than simple a table showing the summary of a single variable, we want to combine this with another variable, such as the number of men and women who buy a particular product and how many who do not. With the Sparcote Study data, the SPSS **Frequencies** command was able to present a table of descriptive statistics of each variable (or item). However, researchers do not always want to present their results in terms of these single-item tables. The Sparcote researchers want to combine the results of a multi-item question into a single table for that question. For example, Question 9, on which social spaces the students frequented, asked about five different locations. The **Frequencies** command displayed five separate tables. We want to show here how the results of these items can be combined into a single table for Question 9. Furthermore, the researchers want to combine the results of different questions in order to provide answers for their research questions. For example, it is of interest to see whether the experience of the students is different across the four major subjects. Initially, they simply want to know how many women and men there are studying each major subject, which can only be done by combining the findings of the variables 'Gender' and 'Major subject' (written as Gender * Major subject by SPSS). We show how SPSS can do this in the next section.

SPSS has a variety of methods that you can use to produce tables. Three key methods are:

See Chapter 5

■ The **Analyze > Frequencies** command (see Chapter 5).

■ The **Analyze > Crosstabs** command.

■ The **Analyze > Custom Tables > Custom Tables** command.

This chapter examines the two new SPSS commands that enable you to produce tables displaying statistics of one or more variables, such as the frequency counts or the means. We start by discussing **crosstabulation** and show you how to cross-tabulate the data from two or more variables using the **Crosstabs** command. The chapter then examines the use of the **Custom Tables** command to create custom tables, that is, any table you want!

crosstabulation
Frequency data can be represented in a table with the rows as the categories of one variable and the columns as the categories of a second variable. This is a crosstabulation. We can include more variables by adding 'layers' to the crosstabulation in SPSS

categorical variable
A variable measured by nominal or ordinal data

CROSSTABULATING DATA

We can produce a table to show the frequency of counts for two or more **categorical variables** in one table. By tabulating the frequency counts of one variable against the frequency counts of another variable, we create a crosstabulation table. A crosstabulation table (often referred to as a 'contingency table' or simply as 'crosstabs') has rows and columns that display the shared distribution of the variables. The SPSS **Crosstabs** command analyses data that is in categories (nominal and ordinal data) because it produces a table of counts. Normally, the categories are mutually exclusive, that is, they are independent categories and a participant only contributes to the count of a single category. Crosstabulation tables are very useful because they show the number of times that each of the combinations of categories have occurred in the data that you have collected. You can often see at a glance from this table if there is a relationship between the variables.

We are going to consider an example now to illustrate a crosstabulation. The staff at a local sports and fitness club are interested to see if there any gender preferences in the use of their two busiest facilities, the racquets arena and the swimming pool, so they can tailor their provision to meet the needs of their members. Over a set period of time, they collected data on how many men and how many women visited the club, along with where they took part in sports within the club (the racquets arena or the swimming pool). Rather than look at the frequency counts of the two variables independently, by creating a crosstabulation table, the researchers can see the distribution of men and women across the two different sports locations.

They first produce the following frequency tables for the variable 'Gender' and 'Location of activity', using the **Frequencies** command in SPSS (as described in Chapter 5).

See Chapter 5

Gender

		Frequency	Percent	Valid Percent	Cumulative Percent
Valid	Female	381	49.0	49.0	49.0
	Male	397	51.0	51.0	100.0
	Total	778	100.0	100.0	

The first table shows us that, while there were 16 more visits by men than women to the club, a similar number of female (49%) and male (51%) members attended the sports and fitness club over the test period. The second table shows the location of the activity on each visit.

Location of activity

		Frequency	Percent	Valid Percent	Cumulative Percent
Valid	Racquets arena	430	55.3	55.3	55.3
	Swimming pool	348	44.7	44.7	100.0
	Total	778	100.0	100.0	

The racquets arena is generally more popular with the clients than the swimming pool, as it was used by more than half of the sample (55.3%, or 430 visits), compared to the swimming pool, which attracted less than half of the visits (44.7%, or 348) – a difference of 82 visitors.

However, you can't see from these tables the breakdown of males and females using each of these facilities. A crosstabulation table will illustrate the pattern of frequencies combining these two variables, with the results from one variable

dimensions
In a crosstabulation, the dimensions refer to the number of categories in each variable in the table. For example, a crosstabulation of dimensions 2 × 3 is a table with one variable of two categories tabulated against a second variable of three categories

displayed in the rows of the table and the results of the other variable displayed in the columns. The **dimensions** of a crosstabulation table refer to the number categories in the rows and columns in the table (excluding the totals). The following table shows the template of the crosstabulation table (with the dimensions of 2 × 2) of 'Gender' by 'Location of activity'. SPSS can produce this table with the **Crosstabs** command (with the results included!).

		Location of activity		Total
		Racquets arena	Swimming pool	
Gender	Female			
	Male			
Total				

If the sports and fitness club had decided to include another area of activity, such as a gym, then the 'Location of activity' variable would have three categories and when this is tabulated with Gender (Gender * Location of activity) the table would then be a 2 × 3 crosstabulation table.

THE CROSSTABS COMMAND

The **Crosstabs** command enables you to produce crosstabulation tables of two or more variables showing the frequency counts of each of the variables. Within the procedure you can also create clustered bar charts to accompany your table.

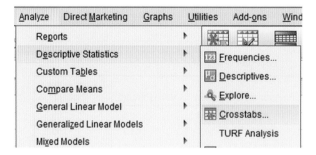

■ The procedure starts with selecting the **Analyze** drop-down menu.

■ Select **Descriptive Statistics** and then **Crosstabs**.

A **Crosstabs** dialog box will appear.

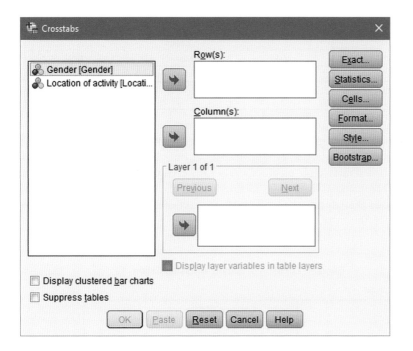

A simple crosstabulation

We are going to examine the data collected at the sports and fitness club to see if there is a relationship between the gender of the clients and the location of the activity when they attended the club:

■ Send 'Gender' across to the **Row(s)** box and 'Location of activity' to the **Column(s)** box.

■ Then press **OK**.

SPSS produces two tables. The first table, the **Case Processing Summary** table, shows how many cases there are in total, in this instance 778. There are no missing values.

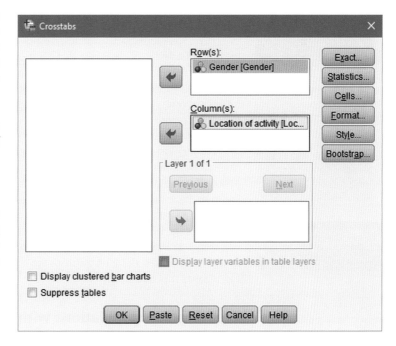

chi-square test
A statistical test of association or independence between categorical variables. It analyses the pattern of observed category frequencies and compares these values to the expected values according to a particular model or pattern of frequencies across the categories

Case Processing Summary

	Cases					
	Valid		Missing		Total	
	N	Percent	N	Percent	N	Percent
Gender * Location of activity	778	100.0%	0	0.0%	778	100.0%

The second table is the crosstabulation table, **Gender*Location of activity Crosstabulation**. The **Total** column shows that there are 16 more male club member visits (397) than female club member visits (381), confirming the results of the **Frequencies** command above on the 'Gender' variable. The **Total** row for 'Location of activity' shows that, during the test period, more clients visited the racquets arena (430) than use the swimming pool (348), again confirming the results of the frequency table for the variable produced by the **Frequencies** command (above).

Gender * Location of activity Crosstabulation

Count

		Location of activity		Total
		Racquets arena	Swimming pool	
Gender	Female	229	152	381
	Male	201	196	397
Total		430	348	778

When there are large differences in the amount of people in each group in a crosstabulation table, it is often useful to include percentages as well as or instead of frequency counts.

For details on undertaking statistical tests, please see Chapter 9

See Chapter 5

The crosstabulation provides details of the relationship between gender and location of activity. We can see that 28 more females visited the racquet arena (229) than male clients (201) and that 44 more males (196) visited the swimming pool than females (152). These findings might help inform the sports and fitness club future activities. For example, follow up research could confirm whether there really is a gender preference for the different locations and, if so, why. Then, depending on the results, this could lead to changes in the club.

The key aspect of a crosstabulation is what the pattern of results implies, for example whether the pattern indicates an association between 'Gender' and 'Location of activity' at the sports and fitness club. In this, case it does look as though women and men have different preferences for the two locations of activity. However, while this appears to be an appropriate implication of these data, the question to be considered is whether this pattern has simply arisen by chance in this study or whether it is implying an underlying association of gender and location of activity in the club. Undertaking an appropriate statistical test, such as the **chi-square test**, can answer this question.

Creating crosstabulations with the Sparcote Study data

We will now use the data from the Sparcote Study to show how the SPSS **Crosstabs** command can be used to examine the relationship between variables, by displaying the joint frequencies of their categories in a crosstabulation. We saw in Chapter 5 that we could produce a separate frequency table for the variables 'Gender' and 'Major subject'. However, it is often more useful to present such demographic information in a crosstabulation, to show how many women and men there are studying each major subject. We will create this crosstabulation of Gender × Major subject in SPSS through the **Crosstabs** command.

■ Select the **Analyze** drop-down menu, **Descriptive Statistics** and then **Crosstabs**.

■ A **Crosstabs** dialog box will appear.

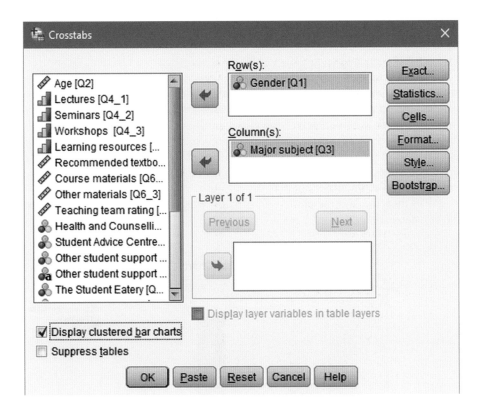

■ Send 'Gender' across to the **Row(s)** box and 'Major subject' to the **Column(s)** box.

■ We would also like to produce a bar chart of the crosstabulation and therefore tick the **Display clustered bar charts** option.

■ Then press **OK**.

If you send one variable to the **Row(s)** box and two variables to the **Column(s)** box, SPSS will produce a separate crosstabulation for the row variable with each of the column variables.

The output window pops up and displays two tables. The first table (not displayed here) the **Case Processing Summary** table shows that all of the 183 participants answered these questions, with no missing values. The second table is a crosstabulation of the two variables under investigation. It shows the breakdown of the frequencies across the two variables.

Gender * Major subject Crosstabulation

Count

		Major subject				Total
		Business	Community Health	Education	Media	
Gender	Female	23	22	27	22	94
	Male	36	11	18	24	89
Total		59	33	45	46	183

By looking at the table, we can see that business (59) is the most popular major subject, followed by media (46), education (45) and then community health (33), which had the fewest students in the department (confirming the results of the **Frequencies** command on the 'Major subject' variable shown in Chapter 5). However, now that these frequencies are broken down by gender, we can see that male students are in the majority in business (13 more male students) and media (although the difference is only two here) and female students are in the majority in community health (11 more female students) and education (nine more female students). Even though there are more or less equal numbers of female and male students overall in the department (shown by the gender totals 94 and 89 – confirming the results of the **Frequencies** command on 'Gender' shown in Chapter 5), these are not evenly distributed across the major subjects.

See Chapter 5

SPSS then displays the clustered bar chart, which is a visual representation of the crosstabulation table.

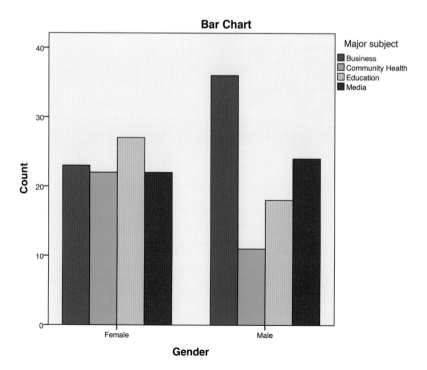

The clustered bar chart illustrates the same data as the crosstabulation table. However, it is easy to see that, while the number of women in each subject is fairly equal (although there are a few more in education) there are larger difference in the number of men in each major subject, with the highest number studying business and the lowest number studying community health. However, you might decide that this clustered bar chart does not present the data as well as one where the clustering was not on gender but on the major subjects. In this way, the female and male bars for each subject would be next to each other (and instead of the label **Gender** at the bottom, on the X-axis, it would be **Major subject**). This can be easily changed by editing the graph, which we will explain in Chapter 8.

For details on editing graphs, please see Chapter 8

Adding percentages to a crosstabulation

Sometimes it is difficult to compare frequencies between categories because the frequency counts across the categories of one variable are very different (such as a lot more women overall than men in a gender variable). At these times, comparing percentages might be more useful than frequency counts. Let's look at the crosstabulation of gender by major subject (above) again, but this time also including percentages as well.

The **Crosstabs** command uses the variable sent to the **Row(s)** for the clusters in the clustered bar chart. If you want the chart to be clustered on the other variable in the crosstabulation, then swap the variables around: Send that variable to the **Row(s)** box (instead of the **Column(s)** box) and the first variable to the **Column(s)** box (instead of the **Row(s)** box).

```
Crosstabs: Cell Display                            ✕

┌─ Counts ──────────┐ ┌─ z-test ──────────────────────┐
│ ☑ Observed        │ │ ☐ Compare column proportions   │
│ ☐ Expected        │ │   ☐ Adjust p-values (Bonferroni method) │
│ ☐ Hide small counts│ │                                │
│   Less than  5    │ │                                │
└───────────────────┘ └────────────────────────────────┘

┌─ Percentages ─────┐ ┌─ Residuals ───────────────────┐
│ ☐ Row             │ │ ☐ Unstandardized               │
│ ☑ Column          │ │ ☐ Standardized                 │
│ ☐ Total           │ │ ☐ Adjusted standardized        │
└───────────────────┘ └────────────────────────────────┘

┌─ Noninteger Weights ──────────────────────────────┐
│ ⦿ Round cell counts    ○ Round case weights        │
│ ○ Truncate cell counts ○ Truncate case weights     │
│ ○ No adjustments                                   │
└────────────────────────────────────────────────────┘

        [ Continue ]  [ Cancel ]  [ Help ]
```

■ While in the **Crosstabs** dialog box, click on the **Cells** option and the **Crosstabs: Cell Display** dialog box appears. You will see that the **Observed** box is already selected as a default. This means that SPSS will always produce frequency counts unless you deselect this option.

■ There are options for selecting percentages: **Row**, **Column** and **Total**. We are going to select the percentages for columns as we wish to see the percentages of females and males in each major subject.

■ Then click on **Continue** and **OK**.

The output table now shows the gender percentage of each major subject alongside the frequency counts.

Gender * Major subject Crosstabulation

			Major subject				Total
			Business	Community Health	Education	Media	
Gender	Female	Count	23	22	27	22	94
		% within Major subject	39.0%	66.7%	60.0%	47.8%	51.4%
	Male	Count	36	11	18	24	89
		% within Major subject	61.0%	33.3%	40.0%	52.2%	48.6%
Total		Count	59	33	45	46	183
		% within Major subject	100.0%	100.0%	100.0%	100.0%	100.0%

As we decided to show percentages in the **Column** option, we can see the breakdown of males and females in percentages for each major subject, with the columns adding up to 100%. The table shows that overall there are 94 female students who accounted for 51.4% of the sample and 89 male students who made up 48.6% of the sample. By examining each major subject in turn, we can see that the gender pattern is different for the different subjects. In business, 61.0% of the students are men and 39.0% women, whereas in community health and education, the majority of students are female (66.7% and 60.0% respectively). The gender balance is more even in media (47.8% female and 52.2% male).

If you wanted to present only the percentages and not the frequency counts in the table, the **Observed** counts would need to be deselected and the **Column** option of **Percentages** would remain ticked.

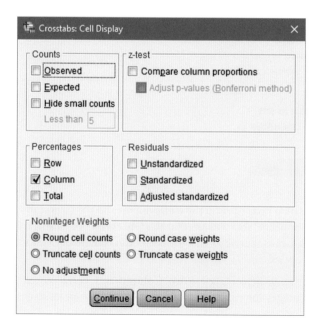

This table is shown below.

Gender * Major subject Crosstabulation

% within Major subject

		Major subject				
		Business	Community Health	Education	Media	Total
Gender	Female	39.0%	66.7%	60.0%	47.8%	51.4%
	Male	61.0%	33.3%	40.0%	52.2%	48.6%
Total		100.0%	100.0%	100.0%	100.0%	100.0%

If you were interested in the row percentages rather than the column percentages, then these can be displayed in the table by the selection of the **Row** box in the **Percentages** section of the **Crosstabs: Cell Display** dialog box.

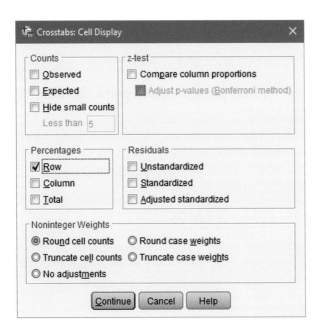

This would produce the following table:

Gender * Major subject Crosstabulation

% within Gender

		Major subject				
		Business	Community Health	Education	Media	Total
Gender	Female	24.5%	23.4%	28.7%	23.4%	100.0%
	Male	40.4%	12.4%	20.2%	27.0%	100.0%
Total		32.2%	18.0%	24.6%	25.1%	100.0%

This table shows that the largest proportion of female students were taking education (28.7%) as their major, followed by business (24.5%) and that community health (23.4%) and media (23.4%) had similar amounts of female students. In terms of the male students, the highest proportion were undertaking a major in business (40.4%), followed by media (27%), then education (20.2%) and, finally, community health (12.4%).

You can select frequency counts and percentages in both rows and columns at the same time by clicking the boxes for row and column counts and percentages. However, we would not recommend this. When looking at the output table with both sets of percentages it can be quite confusing. As we have said throughout this book, you should always have your research questions in mind and therefore ultimately produce a table that helps to answer your research questions. Usually, one percentage (row or column) will be the most relevant to present in the table. For example, in the Sparcote Study, the gender balance in each major subject is the percentage of interest. The column percentages in the gender by major subject crosstabulation mean that the researchers can look across the four major subjects separately and examine the gender balance in each subject. If you are interested in both row and column percentages, it is often clearer to produce two tables: one with the columns percentages and one with the rows percentages.

Creating a new categorical variable from a scale variable

As we have discussed, a crosstabulation is conducted with categorical (nominal or ordinal) data. There are occasions where the data you collect is measured on an interval scale and you would still like to undertake a crosstabulation. At these times, you can transform your scale data into different categories. For example, you may have collected your participants' actual ages but after you have collected the data, you decide that you want to put the ages of the participants into age groups. We are going to illustrate this with the data from the Sparcote Study.

■ Select the **Transform** drop-down menu and select **Recode into Different Variables**. This option allows you to create a new variable and keep the original variable intact.

■ Select the 'Age' variable and send across to the **Numeric Variable -> Output Variable** box.

■ You then need to let SPSS know what you would like to call the new variable.

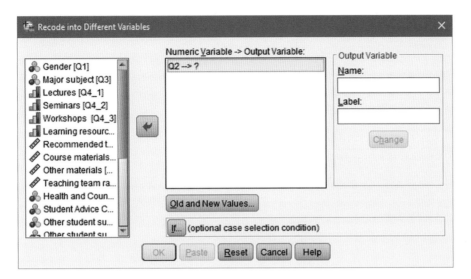

■ Add in the name of the new variable to the **Name** box. We have called ours 'Q2A'. We also add a label for the new variable in the **Label** box. We have given the variable the label 'Age group'.

■ Once you have typed in a name and a label, the **Change** button becomes available. When you select the **Change** button your variable name will appear in the **Numeric Variable -> Output Variable** box.

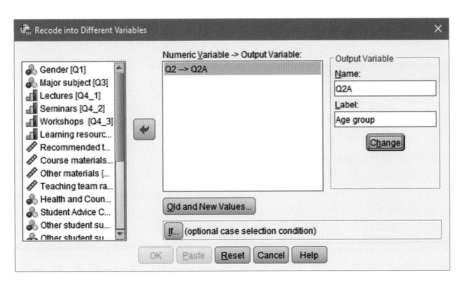

■ Click on **Old and New Values** and a dialog box called **Recode into Different Variables: Old and New Values** appears. Here you will need to tell SPSS what your categories are going to be.

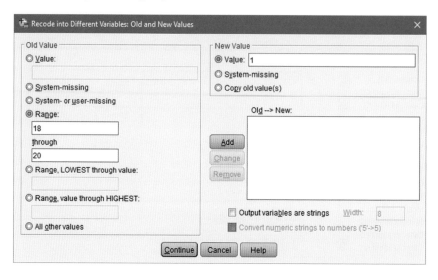

See Chapter 5

■ Generating a frequency table of the Sparcote students' ages showed that they ranged from 18 to 48, with a median age of 22 years (see Chapter 5), so there are quite a lot of younger students in the sample as well as a range of older students. The researchers decide to split the sample into two groups: those under 21 years old and those 21 years and over.

■ As the categories include a range of ages select the **Range** radio button and enter in the youngest age, (the youngest student is aged 18).

■ Then select the oldest age in the range for the first group, in this case 20 years old.

■ The first category is given a numeric value of 1. So, under **New Value**, in the **Value** box, type in 1 and select **Add**.

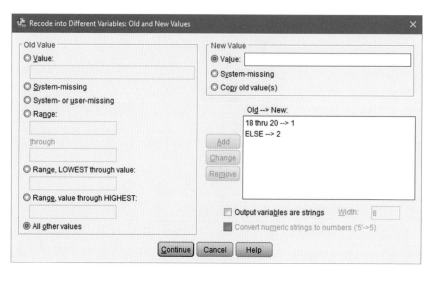

■ The numeric values will then appear in the **Old —> New** box.

■ As all of the other ages will be in the second category, select the **All other values** radio button and these are given the new value of 2 in the **Value** box.

■ Select **Add**, **Continue** and **OK**.

The new variable is then added to the dataset. With a new variable, you can go to the **Variable View** tab and enter in the **Value Labels** for the categories. In this case, we enter the label 'Under 21' for the numeric value 1 and the label '21 and over' for the numeric value 2. We have now constructed a new categorical variable of 'Q2A' from the scale variable 'Q2'. We can now create a crosstabulation of gender by age group, with the SPSS output shown below.

Gender * Age group Crosstabulation

Count

		Age group		Total
		Under 21	21 and over	
Gender	Female	41	53	94
	Male	50	39	89
Total		91	92	183

We can see that there is quite an even split between those aged under 21 years (91) and those 21 and over (92). Also there are only five more females (94) in the department than males (89). Males account for a larger proportion of those under 21 years old (50) than females (41), whereas there are more females (53) than males (39) who are over 21 years old. As there are different frequencies in each category, it can be useful to compare the percentages of participants rather than the frequency counts. We have selected to have percentages for the column variable 'Age group'.

Gender * Age group Crosstabulation

% within Age group

		Age group		Total
		Under 21	21 and over	
Gender	Female	45.1%	57.6%	51.4%
	Male	54.9%	42.4%	48.6%
Total		100.0%	100.0%	100.0%

Displaying the results as percentages makes it a little easier to see that there is a majority of female students in the '21 and over' category and a majority of male students in the 'Under 21' category. (We could undertake a chi-square statistical test to explore this association between 'Gender' and 'Age group' further.)

For details on undertaking statistical tests, please see Chapter 9

Layering in a crosstabulation

Layering enables you to include a third variable (or more) into a crosstabulation table. The crosstabulation of the row and column variables are subdivided by the categories of the layered variable. We are going to produce a crosstabs of 'Major subject' by 'Age group', layered by 'Gender'.

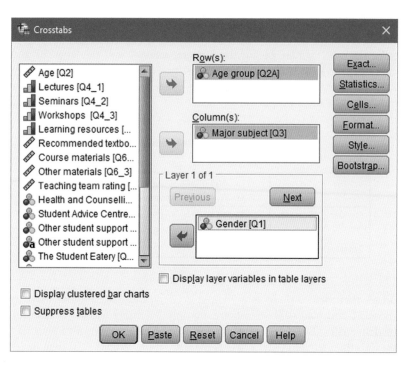

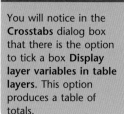

You will notice in the **Crosstabs** dialog box that there is the option to tick a box **Display layer variables in table layers**. This option produces a table of totals.

■ Select the **Analyze** drop-down menu, **Descriptive Statistics** and then **Crosstabs**.

■ Send 'Age group' across to the **Row(s)** box, 'Major subject' to the **Column(s)** box and 'Gender' to the **Layer 1 of 1** box.

■ Press **OK**.

SPSS first produces the **Case Processing Summary** table, showing that there are 183 participants and no missing data. (This table is not shown here.) The next table displays the frequency counts of **Age Group * Major subject * Gender Crosstabulation**.

Age group * Major subject * Gender Crosstabulation

Count

Gender			Major subject				Total
			Business	Community Health	Education	Media	
Female	Age group	Under 21	15	5	10	11	41
		21 and over	8	17	17	11	53
	Total		23	22	27	22	94
Male	Age group	Under 21	18	2	10	20	50
		21 and over	18	9	8	4	39
	Total		36	11	18	24	89
Total	Age group	Under 21	33	7	20	31	91
		21 and over	26	26	25	15	92
	Total		59	33	45	46	183

You can see that once you start adding in more rows and columns, the table can start to become difficult to interpret. You can edit your table in the **IBM SPSS Statistics Viewer** by adding in shading or colours to rows or columns to distinguish between different information. You can also have extra layers by adding more variables, but often it is difficult to understand such a complex table. (Details of how to edit your tables are described in Chapter 8.) We find that a three-variable crosstabulation table such as the one created above is usually the maximum number of variables for clarity of understanding.

For the business major, we can see that nearly twice as many female students are in the younger category (15 students under 21 years) than in the older category (eight students aged 21 and over), but the male students are balanced across the age groups (18 in each group). In community health, the older students (the 21 and over category) are in the majority for both female and male students (with 26 of the 33 students in the older group). In education, there are more mature female students (17 aged 21 and over) than younger (10 aged under 21 years) students, but this is not the case for male students where there are two more in the younger category. Female students of media are evenly balanced between the younger and older categories (11 in each) but for male media students, the majority (20 out of 24) are in the younger category.

Crosstabulating with ordinal data

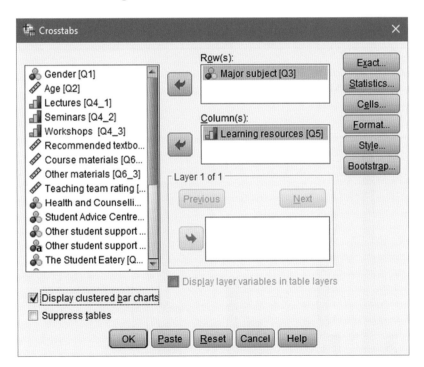

We can also create a crosstabulation including ordinal variables. We will illustrate this with an example from the Sparcote Study. In Question 5, students were asked to respond with their level of agreement with the a statement about the learning resources on their course, measured on a five-point Likert scale, from 'strongly

For details on editing tables, see Chapter 8

As you increase the layers in the table, the counts in the individual categories get smaller and smaller and so may be difficult to interpret. If we are using the data to make predictions then those predictions may be less valid using small samples (in a category) than large samples. Small numbers are not considered to be 'stable' predictors of a general category. For example, nine of the 11 community health males are over 21, which is 82%. However, if next year this only changes by two students to seven out of 11, then the percentage radically changes to 64%. Small numbers are not good predictions of a general pattern in a wider population.

When reporting your results, we advise that you don't detail every finding from your table in prose as well, rather select the most interesting findings (in terms of your research questions) that you want to highlight to the reader from the table.

disagree' to 'strongly agree'. The researchers, however, would like to separate the response to this question in terms of the different major subjects. To do this they undertake a crosstabulation of 'Major subject' by 'Learning resources' as follows:

■ In the **Crosstabs** dialog box 'Major subject' is sent to the **Row(s)** box and 'Learning resources' to the **Column(s)** box.

■ The **Display clustered bar charts** option is ticked to produce a clustered bar chart of the results.

■ **OK** is clicked to run the crosstabulation.

SPSS produces the **Case Processing Summary** table, showing that there are 183 participants and no missing data. (This table is not shown here.) The next table displays the frequency counts of the **Major subject * Learning resources Crosstabulation**.

Major subject * Learning resources Crosstabulation

Count

		Learning resources					Total
		Strongly disagree	Disagree	Neither disagree nor agree	Agree	Strongly agree	
Major subject	Business	4	7	14	20	14	59
	Community Health	7	12	8	5	1	33
	Education	6	8	15	11	5	45
	Media	1	2	9	18	16	46
Total		18	29	46	54	36	183

The **Crosstabs** command has also produced the following clustered bar chart (with the clusters on 'Major subject' as this was the variable sent to the **Row(s)** box).

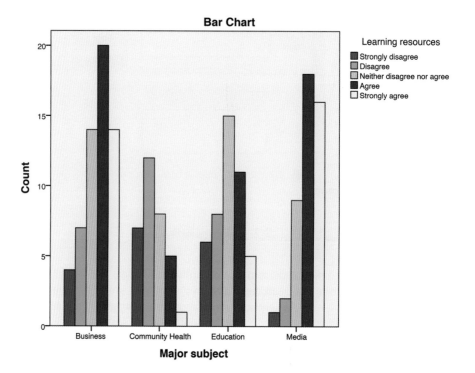

Bar Chart

We can see that the majority of business and media students 'agree' or 'strongly agree' that the learning resources are appropriate for their course. The education students are more neutral in their responses, with their largest frequency is in the 'neither agree nor disagree' category. The community health students are much less positive about the learning resources for their course: Nineteen students (out of 33) have put either 'strongly disagree' or 'disagree' with the adequacy of their learning resources, with only six putting 'agree' or 'strongly agree'. This evidence of low rating of their learning resources by the community health students is likely to be followed up by the course team to explore this issue further (and improve the facilities if they are genuinely found to be inappropriate for this subject).

INTRODUCTION TO CUSTOM TABLES

SPSS produces tables by default in a number of commands (such as in the **Frequencies** command). However, there is also a **Custom Tables** command that allows you to produce a bespoke table with some flexibility in the way in which the table is constructed. Variables can be dragged and dropped into a canvas pane to customise a table that you want to create. This includes the ability to nest, stack or layer multiple variables as well as add sub-totals, totals or additional statistics to the table. For example, sometimes we may wish to display the scores of one variable grouped by a second variable. One way that this can achieved is to use the **Custom Tables** command.

The procedure for producing the custom tables detailed below all start by selecting the **Analyze** drop-down menu, then **Custom Tables** and **Custom Tables**.

>
> **Custom Tables**, like other SPSS commands, displays the variable label rather than the variable name in the procedure. This is one good reason for making sure that you have specified labels and value labels for your variables, and that they are clear and concise, as it can often look clumsy to have a long label (such as a complete question or statement) displayed in **Custom Tables**.

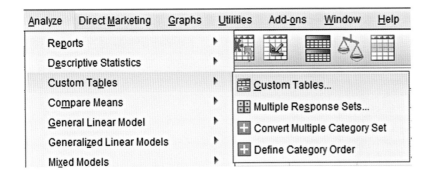

> ✓
>
> In earlier versions of SPSS, the **Analyze** drop-down menu had a **Tables** command rather than **Custom Tables** as the choice in the list. However, when you select **Tables** you can still choose the **Custom Tables** command:
>
>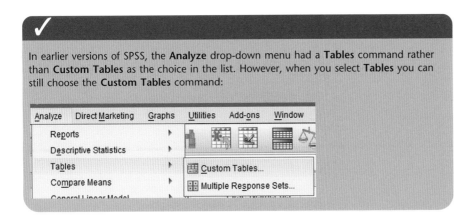

The first time that you use the **Custom Tables** command a dialog box will appear to remind you that you must make sure that your measurement levels are defined correctly. SPSS will only let you produce certain tables with specific levels of measurement. If you would like to make changes to your levels of measurement (or if you have forgotten to define them), select **Define Variable Properties**.

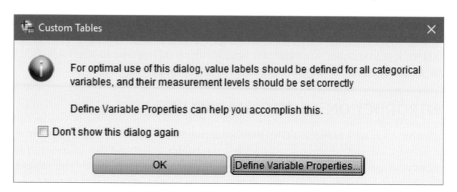

As we shall be using the SPSS dataset for the Sparcote Study, which was set up with value labels and the measurement level specified for all the variables:

■ Click on **OK**. Now, the **Custom Tables** dialog box appears.

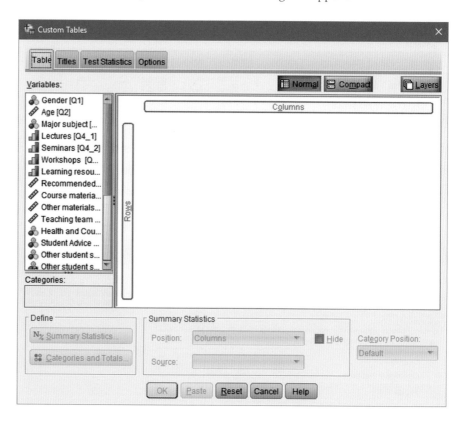

This dialog box displays the variables from your dataset on the left hand side in a **Variables** box. You can see the labels (and names) of each of the variables and next to each one an icon which illustrates how each of them is measured (nominal, ordinal or scale).

In the **Custom Tables** dialog box, there is a large canvas pane, also known as the 'canvas', with **Columns** and **Rows** boxes where you can drag and drop your variables to build the table you require. There are also other tabs and options available to enable you to customise your table or add features such as a title.

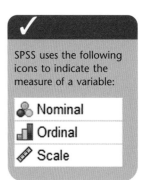

SPSS uses the following icons to indicate the measure of a variable:

   Nominal
   Ordinal
   Scale

Crosstabulation with the Custom Tables command

We have already shown how you can produce a crosstabulation of two or three categorical variables through the **Crosstabs** command. Now we are going to use the Sparcote Study to illustrate how to undertake a crosstabulation (of the 'Age group' variable with the 'Major subject' variable) using the **Custom Tables** command.

■ From the **Analyze** drop-down menu, select **Custom Tables** and then **Custom Tables**.

■ Select 'Major subject' and drag this to the **Columns** box and release.

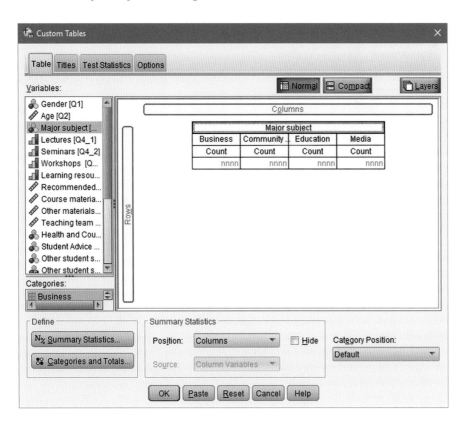

✓

When you drag a variable into a **Columns** or **Rows** box the box outline will change to a red colour.

A black circle with a line through it indicates that you can't drop the variable yet and you will need to move your cursor until the box goes red.

■ A template of the table will then appear in the canvas showing the different categories of your variable. In our example, the labels for the 'Major subject' are shown as columns. As this is a nominal variable, SPSS will produce frequency counts shown by the word **Count** beneath the labels. You can tell when a variable in the canvas is selected as SPSS shades it with a pale yellow colour.

■ Select 'Age group' and drag and drop into the **Rows** box.

■ The table changes to include the age ('Under 21' and '21 and over') as rows. This variable is now highlighted in yellow.

■ Click on **OK**.

✓

SPSS automatically produces counts for data that is measured as nominal or ordinal.

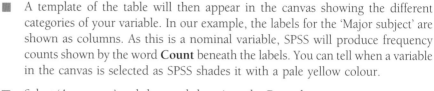

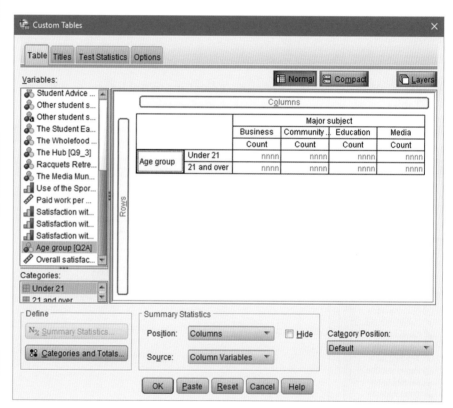

For details on editing tables, see Chapter 8

✓

In academic reports, titles for tables are conventionally placed above the table.

SPSS generates the custom table. The first thing you might notice is that the table does not have a heading. As it is a customised table, SPSS does not presume what you would like to call your table. You can add in a title by clicking the **Titles** tab and typing your title into the **Title** box. (You can always add in a title when editing the table later, or by adding in a title when you have transferred your table to a word processing package.)

	Major subject			
	Business	Community Health	Education	Media
	Count	Count	Count	Count
Age group Under 21	33	7	20	31
21 and over	26	26	25	15

The table shows the crosstabulation of frequency counts between 'Age group' and 'Major subject'. As was noted earlier in this chapter, the highest proportion of students in the '21 and over' category are in community health. It also shows that media has the highest proportion of students in the 'Under 21' category. As this is a custom the table and we did not ask for any total values, they have not been displayed. The **Custom Tables** command only produces the output you ask for.

Adding in totals with a custom table

The **Custom Tables** command allows you to add in subtotals and totals to your table. We are going to add the total for both variables, 'Age group' and 'Major subject'.

■ In the **Custom Tables** dialog window, you can see the variables that you have dragged to the rows and columns. Click on the variable in the canvas pane that you want to show the totals for. This highlights that variable in yellow. Select 'Age group' first.

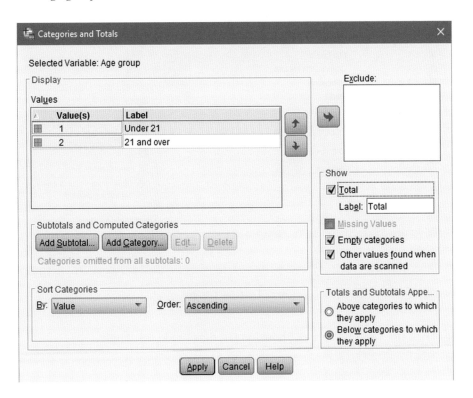

◼ Select the **Categories and Totals** button in the **Custom Tables** dialog box.

◼ As 'Age group' had been highlighted, SPPS will work with the 'Age group' variable.

◼ The **Categories and Totals** dialog box appears, with the categories of the highlighted variable listed on the left.

◼ Tick the **Total** box under **Show** (on the right) and click **Apply**.

◼ Notice that in the canvas pane the word **Total** is listed under the categories for the 'Age group' variable.

We are now going to add in the totals for the 'Major subject' variable in the same way.

◼ Highlight 'Major subject' in the canvas pane.

◼ Select the **Categories and Totals** button.

◼ The **Categories and Totals** dialog box appears, with the categories of the highlighted variable listed on the left.

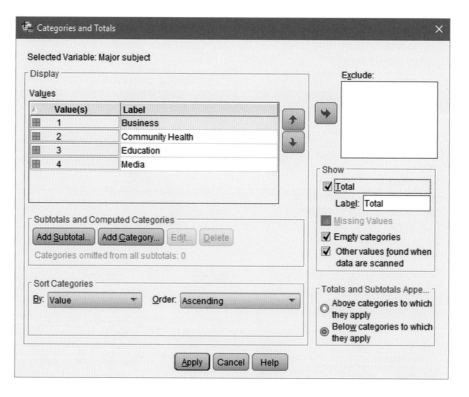

◼ Tick the **Total** box under **Show** (on the right) and click **Apply**.

◼ Now, in the canvas pane, the word **Total** is listed after the categories for the 'Major subject' variable.

This time, when the table is displayed in the **IBM SPSS Statistics Viewer** it also includes the total of the frequencies of the two variables.

		Major subject				
		Business	Community Health	Education	Media	Total
		Count	Count	Count	Count	Count
Age group	Under 21	33	7	20	31	91
	21 and over	26	26	25	15	92
	Total	59	33	45	46	183

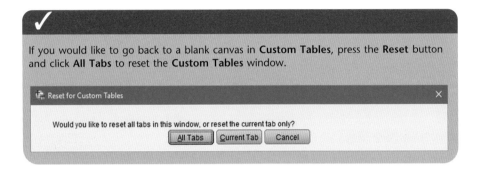

If you would like to go back to a blank canvas in **Custom Tables**, press the **Reset** button and click **All Tabs** to reset the **Custom Tables** window.

Reset for Custom Tables   ×

Would you like to reset all tabs in this window, or reset the current tab only?

[All Tabs] [Current Tab] [Cancel]

Combining the data from more than one variable into a single table

A single frequency table

In Chapters 4 and 5, we saw that a number of questions in the Sparcote survey were multiple item questions; that is, they required more than a single response. To input the data from these questions into SPSS, each item became a separate variable. Using the **Frequencies** command, we are able to produce a frequency table for each variable. However, in many cases, we would like to combine the items into a single frequency table for that question. We will explain here how this is done using **Custom Tables**.

See Chapters 4 and 5

We are going to explore how to combine the results of three variables into one frequency table. In Question 4 of the Sparcote Study, the students ranked three different modes of study (Lectures, Q4_1; Seminars, Q4_2; and Workshops, Q4_3) in terms of their preferred learning experience. They assigned a value of 1 (given a value label of 'First') to their favourite mode of study, 2 (labelled 'Second') to their next favourite and 3 (labelled 'Third') to their least favourite. mode of study, a 2 to their next favourite and 3 to their least favourite. Using the **Custom Tables** command we will show how you can produce one table showing all of the frequencies together.

■ Select the variables to include in the table and drag and drop them to the **Columns** box in the canvas pane.

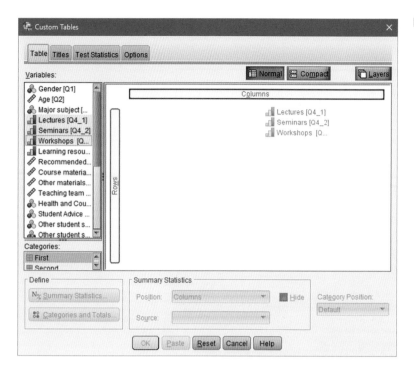

■ Send over 'Lectures', 'Seminars' and 'Workshops' together to the **Columns** box. To do this, select all three variables. Click on one variable with the mouse, so this becomes highlighted. Hold down the control key (ctrl) and click on the other variables with the mouse to select all three. (Alternatively, if the variables are next to each other in the list, press the Shift key and drag the mouse, or use the arrow key to select all three variables.) Drag the variables to the **Columns** box in the canvas pane, which will turn red, and then drop them into the box.

A template of the table of counts will appear in the canvas pane.

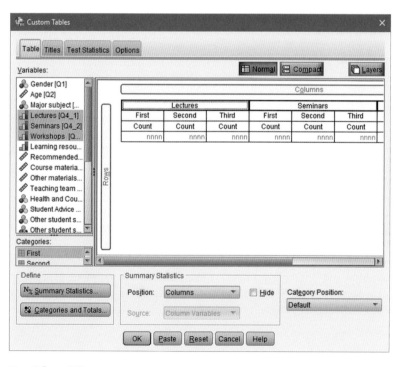

■ Select **OK**.

You will notice that the modes of study are presented as a series of columns in a long row across the top of the table and the choices are shown beneath each mode of study.

Lectures			Seminars			Workshops		
First	Second	Third	First	Second	Third	First	Second	Third
Count	Count	Count	Count	Count	Count	Count	Count	Count
58	64	61	59	65	59	67	56	60

This table includes all three variables in one table. However, it isn't the easiest table to read. We are now going to adjust the table so that the categories (First, Second or Third) are displayed as separate rows in the table. (As we had clicked **OK**, to display the above table we could now select the **Analyze**, drop-down menu, **Custom Tables** and then **Custom Tables**. We would see that the template of the previous table is still in the pane.)

■ Underneath the word **Category Position** select the arrow next to the word **Default** and select **Column Labels in Rows**.

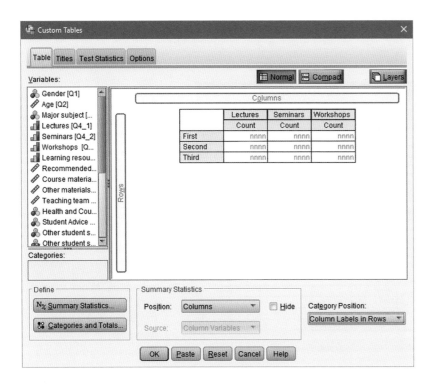

Notice how the categories now form the rows in the table template. We are also going to display the column totals in the table as well:

■ Select the **Categories and Totals** button and tick the **Total** box under **Show** in the **Categories and Totals** dialog box. This will display the column totals. Then select **Apply** and finally click **OK**.

The table on the right is displayed in the **IBM SPSS Statistics Viewer:**

Notice how we have produced a clear table of results for Question 4, despite its being made up of three items in the survey and three variables in SPSS. The custom table shows the three modes of study and students' preferences in a single frequency table. As the preferences for their first, second and third choices are neatly listed in the same column it is easy to compare the preference counts for the three modes of study.

	Lectures	Seminars	Workshops
	Count	Count	Count
First	58	59	67
Second	64	65	56
Third	61	59	60
Total	183	183	183

Overall, there are no strong preferences shown by the students. Each value in the table has been chosen by between 56 and 67 students. There appears to be a tendency for workshops to be slightly preferred (it was the first choice of 67 students), but there is little difference in the pattern of the frequency counts with the lectures and seminars, in particular, producing almost identical results. This is an example where a further breakdown of the data into the different major subjects could reveal differences that are hidden when the data is combined across all the students. We can, therefore, add 'Major subject' to this custom table.

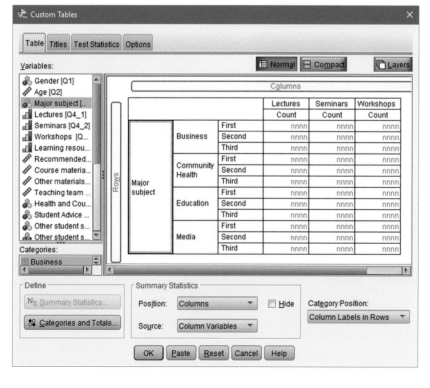

■ Select the **Analyze** drop-down menu, **Custom Tables** and then **Custom Tables** again – you will notice that the template of your table is still in the pane. (If the template is no longer in the canvas pane, follow the instructions above to produce it.)

■ Select the 'Major subject' variable and drag it into the **Rows** box in the canvas pane, to produce the template on the left.

■ Click **OK**.

SPSS displays the following custom table in the **IBM SPSS Statistics Viewer**.

			Lectures	Seminars	Workshops
			Count	Count	Count
Major subject	Business	First	20	20	19
		Second	21	18	20
		Third	18	21	20
	Community Health	First	2	16	15
		Second	11	12	10
		Third	20	5	8
	Education	First	26	17	2
		Second	15	18	14
		Third	4	10	29
	Media	First	10	6	31
		Second	17	17	12
		Third	19	23	3

If this table is not quite what is wanted, then the rows and columns can be adjusted as before, and, as we explain the Chapter 8, you can edit the table to add grid lines and colours to make a larger table easier to read.

See Chapter 8

✓

In Chapter 8, we will explain how to change the style of a table to make it exactly as you would like it. For example, we have edited the above table to produce the following table by using the **TableLooks** command (selecting 'Horizontal' style with no background colour) and adding a title, as explained in Chapter 8:

Table 4: Student preferences for modes of study

			Lectures	Seminars	Workshops
			Count	Count	Count
Major subject	Business	First	20	20	19
		Second	21	18	20
		Third	18	21	20
	Community Health	First	2	16	15
		Second	11	12	10
		Third	20	5	8
	Education	First	26	17	2
		Second	15	18	14
		Third	4	10	29
	Media	First	10	6	31
		Second	17	17	12
		Third	19	23	3

We notice immediately that there is almost no preference for the different modes of study in business. However, it is clear that the community health students like the lectures the least (with only two students putting lectures as their first preference and 20 students placing it third), but have little difference in their preference for seminars or workshops. The education students clearly prefer lectures (with 26 students putting it as their first preference and only four placing it third), with workshops the least preferred (two first preferences and 29 third preferences). Finally, the media students prefer their workshops the best (with 31 first preferences and only three third preferences), with lectures only marginally preferred over seminars. We can now see that, despite there being little difference overall, when broken down into the major subjects, different patterns of preferences emerge.

A single table of means

See Chapter 3

See Chapter 5

In the Sparcote Study, there is a constant sum question – Question 6 (see Chapter 3). The students were asked to portion out 100 (as a percentage) to indicate their relative use of three resources: recommended textbooks, course materials and other materials. In Chapter 5, we showed that you can produce a table of means and standard deviations to summarise the students' responses to the three items using the **Frequencies** command. We can produce a similar table through the **Custom Tables** command. However, via **Custom Tables**, we can also produce these values broken down for the different major subjects as well.

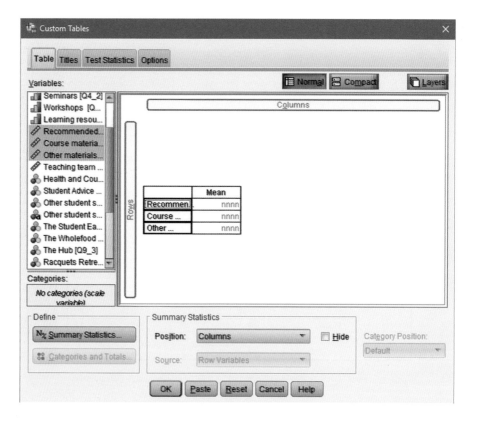

■ Select the three variables ('Recommended textbooks', 'Course materials' and 'Other materials') together and drag and drop them to the **Rows** box. The labels will be highlighted.

■ As these three variables are scale measures, SPSS will automatically produce mean values rather than frequency counts in the table.

■ As a default SPSS does not display any decimal places in **Custom Tables** unless you change them.

■ When the variable labels and **Mean** are highlighted in the canvas pane, the $N_\%$ **Summary Statistics** will be available for you to choose. Click on this button to change the decimal places.

In the **Summary Statistics** dialog box the **Display** window shows that the mean values will be displayed. The decimal places **Format** is defaulted to Auto. Click on the arrow inside the 'Auto' cell and select 'nnnn'. Then click in the **Decimals** cell adjacent and change it to two decimal places.

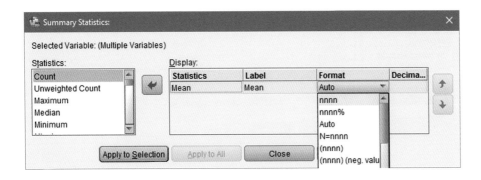

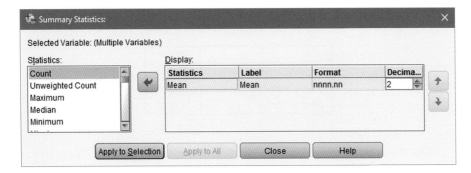

■ The **Format** box now shows 'nnnn.nn'. Then select **Apply to Selection** and **OK**.

■ You will see that the template in the canvas pane will reflect your choice of decimals.

■ Select **OK**.

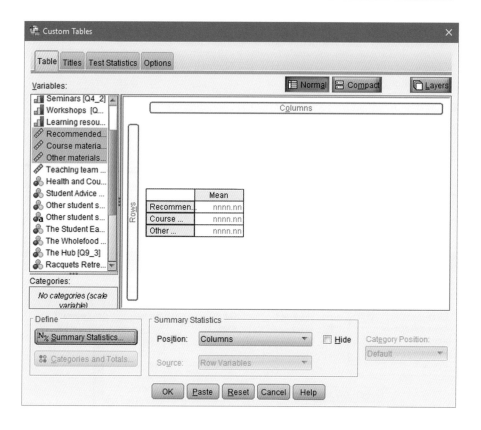

SPSS produces the following custom table in the **IBM SPSS Statistics Viewer.**

	Mean
Recommended textbooks	40.19
Course materials	43.27
Other materials	16.56

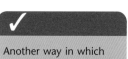

Another way in which we can display the mean values of more than one scale variable in a single table in SPSS is by using the **Compare Means** command. We select the **Analyze** drop-down menu, then **Compare Means**, followed by **Means**. In the **Means** dialog box, we send the variables across to the **Dependent list** box and click **OK**. A table of means (and standard deviations) is displayed in the **IBM SPSS Statistics Viewer.**

This table shows that students in the Department of Applied Studies predominantly use the course materials (43.27%), and the recommended textbooks (40.19%), with 'Other materials' used the least (16.56%).

A crosstabulation of mean values

We will now produce a crosstabulation of means through the **Custom Tables** command between the three constant sum variables ('Recommended textbooks', 'Course materials' and 'Other materials') and the different major subjects. This cannot be achieved using the **Crosstabs** command – which requires categorical variables – due to these three variables being measured as scale variables rather than in categories using frequencies.

- Select the **Analyze** drop-down menu, **Custom Tables** and then **Custom Tables**.

- The three variables are dragged into the **Rows** box and then 'Major subject' is dropped into the **Columns** box.

- Set the decimal places to two, as described above. (If we are building on the previous custom table the decimal places are still set to two decimal places.)

- Click on **OK**.

The following custom table is displayed in the **IBM SPSS Statistics Viewer**.

| | Major subject | | | |
| | Business | Community Health | Education | Media |
	Mean	Mean	Mean	Mean
Recommended textbooks	42.15	26.97	41.87	45.50
Course materials	41.73	56.91	46.64	32.17
Other materials	16.20	16.12	11.24	22.54

Examining the table of means above, we can see that media students use the recommended textbooks the most (45.50%) and the community health students use them the least (26.97%). However, the community health students use the course materials the most (56.91%) and the media students use them the least (32.17%). The media students also use other materials the most (22.54%) and education students use them the least (11.24%). There is some evidence of a different pattern in the use of these resources by students in the different majors.

A table to display multiple choice questions with multiple answers

When you have a multiple choice question with multiple answers the **Custom Tables** command allows you to produce one customised table for the whole question (unlike the **Frequencies** command, which produces a separate table for each item or variable). In Question 8 of the Sparcote Study, students were asked which support services they used and, in Question 9, which social spaces they had visited during the last academic year. As we saw in Chapter 5, the **Frequencies** command will list out the results of each separate variable in a separate table. We show now how to create a custom table to include all the items from one question in the same table.

See Chapter 5

- In both cases select the variables for the question and drag and drop them into the **Rows** box.

- Underneath the word **Category Position**, select the arrow next to the word **Default** and select **Row Labels in Columns** from the drop-down menu.

- Finally press **OK**.

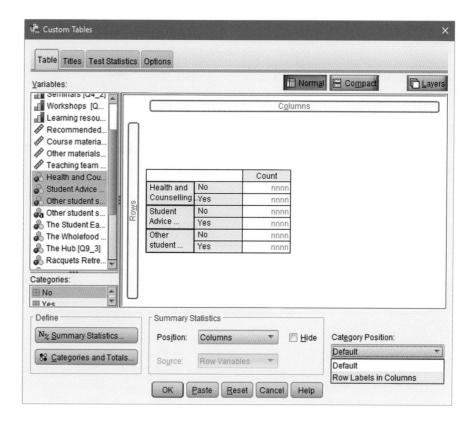

For Question 8, only Q8_1, Q8_2, and Q8_3 have been dragged into the canvas pane. The names of the other student support services used, Q8_4, has not been included in this table. The following custom table is produced.

| | No | Yes |
	Count	Count
Health and Counselling Centre	146	37
Student Advice Centre	122	61
Other student support service	169	14

As we have selected the **Row Labels in Columns** the No and Yes responses move from next to the category labels to above the frequency of responses.

For illustration, we will demonstrate how to include totals for each row, for this example.

■ Select the **Analyze** drop-down menu, **Custom Tables** and then **Custom Tables**.

■ Send the five social spaces to the **Rows** box. The labels will be highlighted.

■ Underneath the word **Category Position**, select the arrow next to the word **Default** and select **Row Labels in Columns**. Tick the **Hide** box.

■ Click on the **Categories and Totals** button to bring up the **Categories and Totals** dialog box.

■ Tick the **Total** box and click **Apply**.

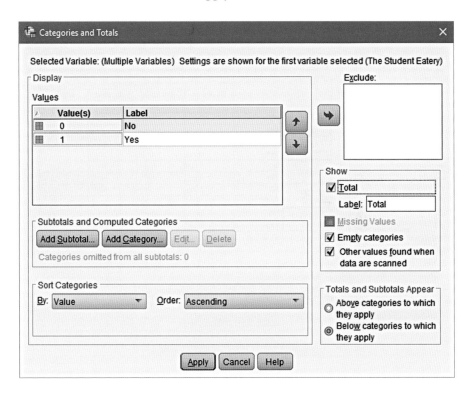

■ Finally, click **OK** in the **Custom Tables** dialog box to create the table.

Now the table is produced with the row totals.

	No	Yes	Total
The Student Eatery	61	122	183
The Wholefood Café	94	89	183
The Hub	126	57	183
Racquets Retreat	154	29	183
The Media Munch	99	84	183

We are now going to combine the information from Question 9 on social spaces, in a crosstabulation with major subject, to examine the use of the different social spaces by the students on the different major subjects. However, we are only going to display the 'Yes' counts in this table.

- Select **Analyze** drop-down menu, **Custom Tables** and then **Custom Tables**.

- Send 'Major subject' to the **Columns** box and the five social spaces to the **Rows** box. The labels will be highlighted. The following template is shown in the canvas pane.

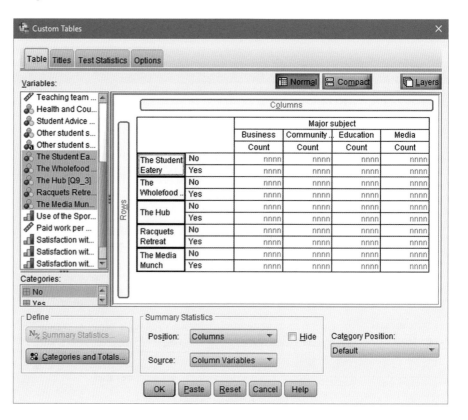

- We only want to include the 'Yes' values in our table. We click on the **Categories and Totals** button. The **Categories and Totals** dialog box appears.

- In the **Values** box, select the 'No' row and send it to the **Exclude** box. A warning message will appear (see next page).

- Click on **OK**, and then select **Apply** and, in the **Custom Tables** dialog box, click **OK**.

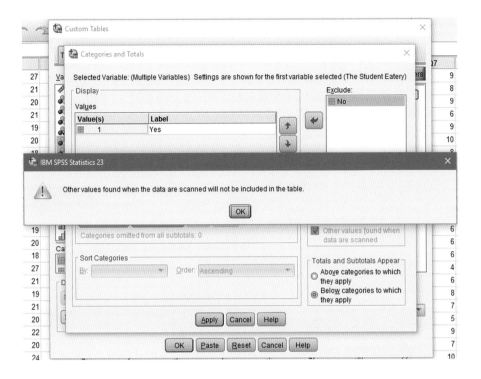

SPSS produces a table showing how many students taking each major subject visited each social space.

		Major subject			
		Business	Community Health	Education	Media
		Count	Count	Count	Count
The Student Eatery	Yes	39	26	26	31
The Wholefood Café	Yes	25	21	29	14
The Hub	Yes	19	10	14	14
Racquets Retreat	Yes	14	3	5	7
The Media Munch	Yes	24	12	14	34

The Student Eatery was generally popular with all student groups (being the most popular for business and community health). The Wholefood Café was also popular (producing the highest count for education students) but not with media students, whose most popular choice was the Media Munch. The Racquets Retreat was the least popular social space with all the major subjects.

A table to display multiple Likert items

In the Sparcote Study the final question, Question 12, asked the students (on the basis of their experience in the last year) to indicate their satisfaction with different aspects of their life (academic, social and personal life). These three responses were recorded on separate five-point Likert scales. We are going to put the results of the three Likert scales into a single custom table.

■ Select the **Analyze** drop-down menu, **Custom Tables** and then **Custom Tables**.

■ We select the three satisfaction variables (Q12_1, Q12_2, and Q12_3) and drag and drop them into the **Rows** box.

■ Underneath the word **Category Position**, select the arrow next to the word **Default** and select **Row Labels in Columns** (so that the table has the three satisfaction scales as the row and the Likert categories as the columns).

■ Click **OK**.

The following table is produced:

	Very unsatisfied	Unsatisfied	Neither unsatisfied nor satisfied	Satisfied	Very satisfied
	Count	Count	Count	Count	Count
Satisfaction with academic life	0	17	55	70	41
Satisfaction with social life	1	15	53	68	46
Satisfaction with personal development	0	27	43	67	46

The table shows that there was only one student who was 'very unsatisfied' with any aspect of their life – and this was with their social life at Sparcote. It is clear that overall the students in the department are satisfied at Sparcote (with the majority of scores ranging from 'neither unsatisfied nor satisfied' through to 'very satisfied' on all three measures of satisfaction). However, it would be useful to know if this pattern in the student satisfaction is the same or different when the results are broken down into the different major subjects. To do this we can create the following custom table.

We follow exactly the same procedure as above to produce the previous table. However, before clicking **OK**, we drag and drop the 'Major subject' variable to the **Rows** box.

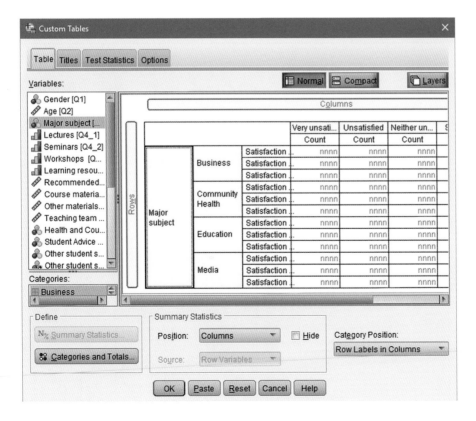

A template of the new table is shown in the canvas pane. Notice that, in the canvas, 'Major subject' is to the left of the satisfaction scales – which are nested within 'Major subject'.

■ Click **OK**.

The following table is displayed.

			Very unsatisfied	Unsatisfied	Neither unsatisfied nor satisfied	Satisfied	Very satisfied
			Count	Count	Count	Count	Count
Major subject	Business	Satisfaction with academic life	0	3	16	25	15
		Satisfaction with social life	0	4	16	28	11
		Satisfaction with personal development	0	8	15	23	13
	Community Health	Satisfaction with academic life	0	7	10	10	6
		Satisfaction with social life	1	3	15	8	6
		Satisfaction with personal development	0	4	7	12	10
	Education	Satisfaction with academic life	0	2	16	18	9
		Satisfaction with social life	0	6	12	17	10
		Satisfaction with personal development	0	0	10	24	11
	Media	Satisfaction with academic life	0	5	13	17	11
		Satisfaction with social life	0	2	10	15	19
		Satisfaction with personal development	0	15	11	8	12

✓

See Chapter 8

We might wish to edit the table in some way so that it easier to read, such as changing the 'look' of the table and adding in colours to highlight the rows, as in the example below (this is explained in Chapter 8).

			Very unsatisfied	Unsatisfied	Neither unsatisfied nor satisfied	Satisfied	Very satisfied
			Count	Count	Count	Count	Count
Major subject	Business	Satisfaction with academic life	0	3	16	25	15
		Satisfaction with social life	0	4	16	28	11
		Satisfaction with personal development	0	8	15	23	13
	Community Health	Satisfaction with academic life	0	7	10	10	6
		Satisfaction with social life	1	3	15	8	6
		Satisfaction with personal development	0	4	7	12	10
	Education	Satisfaction with academic life	0	2	16	18	9
		Satisfaction with social life	0	6	12	17	10
		Satisfaction with personal development	0	0	10	24	11
	Media	Satisfaction with academic life	0	5	13	17	11
		Satisfaction with social life	0	2	10	15	19
		Satisfaction with personal development	0	15	11	8	12

Many researchers would present this data and explain the key findings from it. Essentially, it looks as though the overall levels of satisfaction are repeated in the individual subject majors; however, it does look as though the community health students are somewhat less satisfied than the students on the other majors. Generally, the responses appear to be similar across both the major subjects and the three satisfaction measures.

See Chapter 3

However, as we noted in Chapter 3, some researchers treat data collected on (ordinal) Likert scales as scale data and calculate means for the different groups of responses. We will use this example to illustrate what happens here if the data is treated as if from a scale measure. Rather than producing frequency counts for the categories, as we did above, we will produce the mean values. However, the **Custom Tables** command will not let you generate mean values unless the variable is defined as Scale in the **Measure** box in **Variable View**. The three satisfaction scales in the Sparcote Study are defined as ordinal in **Variable View**, so only counts can be produced for them in **Custom Tables**. To produce mean values, the **Measure** must be changed to scale for each variable. Rather than go back to the **Variable View** screen to change the **Measure**, right click on the variable in the **Variables** box in the **Custom Tables** dialog box and change the measure to Scale.

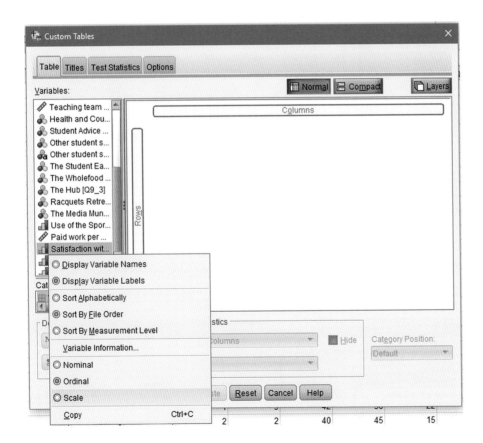

Once we have changed all three satisfaction variables to Scale, we create a new custom table.

■ 'Major subject' is dragged to the **Columns** box of the canvas pane and the three satisfaction scales are dragged to the **Rows** box.

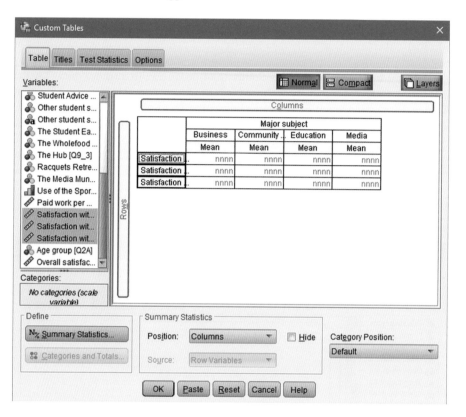

■ Change the decimal places for the means to two decimal places, by highlighting the three satisfaction scales in the canvas pane and double clicking to bring up the **Summary Statistics** box.

■ Change **Format** from Auto to 'nnnn', and then change **Decimals** to '2'.

■ Click on **Apply to All**.

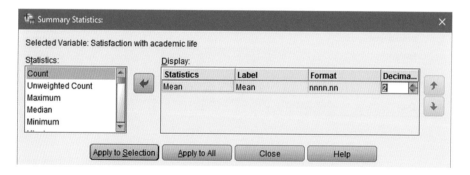

■ Click **OK** in the **Custom Tables** dialog box.

This produces the following table:

	Major subject			
	Business	Community Health	Education	Media
	Mean	Mean	Mean	Mean
Satisfaction with academic life	3.88	3.45	3.76	3.74
Satisfaction with social life	3.78	3.45	3.69	4.11
Satisfaction with personal development	3.69	3.85	4.02	3.37

The table is now a table of means rather than a table of frequencies (but, of course, should only be produced if it is appropriate to do so – see Chapter 3). We can see that, on average, all the students are 'satisfied' with their experiences at Sparcote as the mean values are all greater than 3 (the 'neither unsatisfied nor satisfied' central position on the scale). The business students are most satisfied with their academic life, the community health and education students are most satisfied with their personal development and the media students are most satisfied with their social life. However, there are three mean values a little lower than the rest. The means for community health students on 'Satisfaction with academic life' and 'Satisfaction with social life' are both at 3.45, and the mean for media students 'Satisfaction with personal development' is 3.37. It is possible that these differences have occurred by chance, but given other supporting information in the survey (such as the results on other questions) then this might guide further investigations into the student experience, to examine whether it differs between the major subjects.

See Chapter 3

Creating a new variable with the Compute command

Sometimes you may want to add items or questions together to arrive at one composite score. For example, a study exploring health behaviours may include one question about how much exercise an individual does, and another about their alcohol consumption. The researchers argue that the response scales can be coded from 'unhealthy' to 'healthy', so the responses can be combined to produce an overall health behaviour score.

The research team in the Department of Applied Studies decide to create an 'Overall satisfaction' score which is the sum of the three satisfaction scores in Question 12 (now that they have decided to treat the satisfaction results as scale data). Therefore they need to create a new variable that combines the three different satisfaction scores together. This can be done using the SPSS **Compute** command.

■ Select the **Transform** drop-down menu, and then select **Compute Variable**. The **Compute Variable** dialog box appears.

■ We are going to call the new variable, 'Q12Sum', so we type this name into the **Target Variable** box.

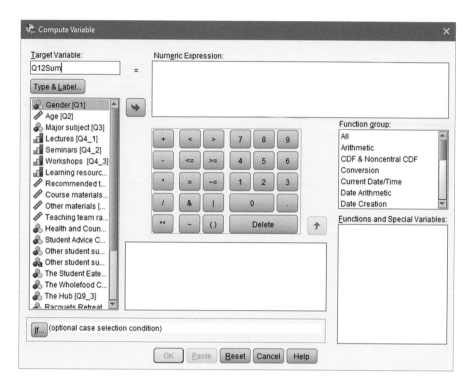

■ Click on the **Type & Label** button to input a label for the new variable. Type the label 'Overall satisfaction' into the **Label** box and click **Continue**.

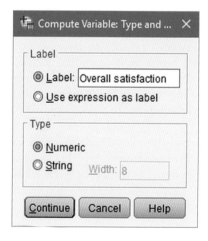

■ In the **Compute Variable** dialog box, select the first variable ('Satisfaction with academic life') and send it to the **Numeric Expression** box, then click on the plus sign (+).

■ Next send the second variable ('Satisfaction with social life') across to the **Numeric Expression** box and click on the plus sign (+).

■ Finally, send the third variable ('Satisfaction with personal development') across to the **Numeric Expression** box.

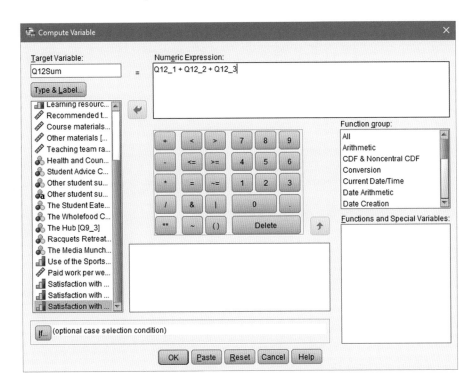

■ Notice that the numeric expression now tells SPSS to add up the results of the three variables, 'Q12_1', 'Q12_2' and 'Q12_3' and to store the result in the new variable 'Q12Sum'. We click on **OK** to compute the new variable. The variable 'Q12Sum' is now added to the dataset. (We do not need to tell SPSS the **Measure** of the new variable if it is the sum of three scale variables, as it will set it to scale automatically. However, if we had summed three ordinal variables we would need to change the **Measure** in **Variable View** if we wanted it to be scale.)

We can now produce a table that shows the overall mean satisfaction for the students on each major subject using the **Custom Tables** command.

■ Send 'Major subject' to the **Columns** box and 'Overall satisfaction' to the **Rows** box of the canvas pane in **Custom Tables**. We set the decimal places to 2.

The following table is produced:

	Major subject			
	Business	Community Health	Education	Media
	Mean	Mean	Mean	Mean
Overall satisfaction	11.36	10.76	11.47	11.22

We can see that three of the major subjects have similar mean overall satisfaction scores with education students being the most satisfied, then business and media, all with mean scores of over 11. The students studying community health are the least satisfied, with an overall mean of 10.76. This, along with other evidence from the survey, indicates that the community health students, although not *unsatisfied*, are not as positive about their first-year experience as the other students.

We have seen how to produce a range of tables using the **Crosstabs** and **Custom Tables** commands. Chapter 7 explores how we can create a variety of graphs and charts in SPSS.

Creating graphs

200 CHOOSING A CHART

209 USING CHART BUILDER

233 CREATE GRAPH – GENERATING GRAPHS FROM OUTPUT TABLES

Chapter aim: To show how to produce a range of graphs in SPSS

Charts, graphs, plots and diagrams all can be used to provide visual representation of research data. They can often be easier to interpret than numerical data written in text or displayed in a table, particularly when you want to convey patterns, trends and comparisons. As discussed in Chapter 2, plots of frequencies, percentages, and means are often referred to as illustrative statistics, as they provide a visual illustration of the summarised data. Communicating research data graphically, in a way that the reader can make sense of the main findings, can make a report both clear and interesting to read. However, it is important to ensure that you do not illustrate the data in a manner that misrepresents your findings. The goal is to create a graph that is simple to understand, providing an accurate representation of the findings and labelled with clarity. The aim of this chapter is to show you how to use SPSS to produce a range of different graphs including a pie chart, bar chart, line graph, scatterplot and a histogram, explaining when each graph is used to illustrate different levels of measurement and different response types.

See Chapter 2

SPSS has a variety of methods that you can use to produce different charts and graphs. The four key methods are:

- The **Analyze > Frequencies** command (see Chapter 5). See Chapter 5

- As part of the output when you perform a procedure using commands such as the **Analyze > Crosstabs** command (see Chapter 6). See Chapter 6

- **Chart Builder** in the **Graphs** drop-down menu.

- From a table in the **IBM SPSS Statistics Viewer**, using the **Create Graph** command.

See Chapters 5 and 6

The terms 'chart' and 'graph' are both used for the visual representation of research data, such as a bar chart or a line graph. A 'chart' can be viewed as a diagram or map (like a pirate's chart), presenting a situation or a state of affairs. The term 'graph' tends to be used to visually represent variation or change – for example, one variable changing along with a second variable, such as sales over time. However, these distinctions are rarely made and the terms chart and graph are usually used interchangeably. SPSS uses both terms through the **Chart Builder** and **Create Graph** commands, where you will find a similar set of charts and graphs.

In Chapter 5 and 6, we discussed how easy it is to use the **Frequencies** and **Crosstabs** commands to generate charts. This chapter provides an overview of a range of different charts and when you might use them. We start by looking at the different charts you can choose and then focus on the use of **Chart Builder**, and **Create Graph**.

CHOOSING A CHART

When considering how to summarise your data for presentation, you need to consider first whether you actually need to present a chart. If you have only had a few numerical values that you have discussed adequately in prose then a chart might provide no extra help to the reader to understand your research study. Similarly, you may have produced a clear summary table of your results and a chart might not add any additional information or further clarify the findings presented in that table. However, you may decide you want to include a chart as an alternative to a table or to illustrate relationships not so clearly shown in a table. But which chart? There are a range of different charts (which are often used with different levels of measurement), but there is also some flexibility in which to use so you may have a choice of alternative formats when deciding to present your data visually. Descriptions of the most popular types of chart are shown below with general rules of thumb to indicate when you would choose each type of chart.

Pie charts

Pie charts are circular graphs which illustrate part-to-whole relationships. Each segment or slice of the pie represents a proportion of the total or whole pie. Often researchers convert their data to percentages before plotting their results in a pie chart, so the whole pie represents 100% and each slice is the percentage contribution of a particular category of the whole. Pie charts are visually appealing, especially where segments vary in size. However, they are not universally approved of by researchers, as it is argued that the size of the slices is not always clear and any comparison between them is quite hard to make, so the detractors recommend using bar charts instead. Some of the reasons why pie charts are criticised is that a report cluttered with numerous pie charts can confuse the main findings. Also, producing a pie chart with only two slices is probably superfluous and one with too many slices might be difficult to interpret in terms of what each slice represents (in terms of its relative contribution). Therefore, we recommend that a pie chart works best when there are between three to seven slices. Pie charts are also not very good when you want to compare two variables (rather than the components of one) so it is a good idea to think about using a bar or line chart when the point being illustrated is a comparison. However, the occasional pie chart might present a very clear visual representation of specific data in certain circumstances, such as illustrating the set of items in a category.

We show here an example of a pie chart illustrating the staffing within a company. A company administrator wants to present the makeup of the company staff to a meeting, to illustrate the number of people involved in the different activities within the organisation. The total number of people in the company is 415 but these are broken down by the administrator into six groups: Manufacturing (227 people), sales (52), IT (12), research and development (24), management (36) and administration (64). This information can be presented visually in the pie chart below.

For details on editing graphs and charts, please see Chapter 8

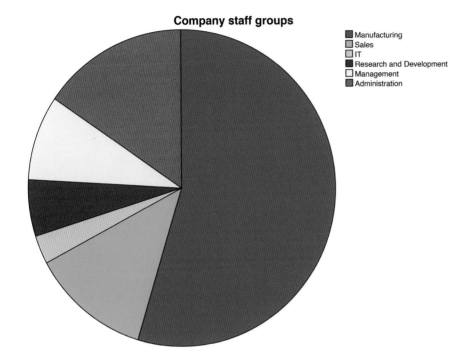

Company staff groups

- Manufacturing
- Sales
- IT
- Research and Development
- Management
- Administration

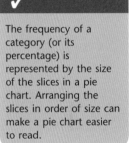

The frequency of a category (or its percentage) is represented by the size of the slices in a pie chart. Arranging the slices in order of size can make a pie chart easier to read.

Bar charts

Bar charts are versatile visual representations of data that are easy to create and interpret.

Discrete categories of data are presented as separate and spaced bars with each bar representing a summary statistic, such as frequencies, percentages, means or medians. The bars can be displayed as either vertical columns or horizontal bars. In a vertical bar chart, the height of the bars represents the value of the summary statistic for the different categories. The widths of each bar in the chart are the same size, which allows you to be able to make meaningful comparisons between each bar.

The following example shows how data can be displayed as a bar chart. A social care community organisation offered four parenting programmes to young parents in their community to promote positive relationships within families and ultimately the well-being of their children. Four different programmes were run: promoting positive behaviours (which 47 attended), child development (attended by 45 people), managing relationships (42 attendees) and building resilience (attended by 60 people). The following bar chart was produced of the attendance at the classes.

Arranging the bars in a specific order can make a bar chart easier to read. For example, the chart can be ordered by the relative size of the bar or by the name of the categories that the bars represent.

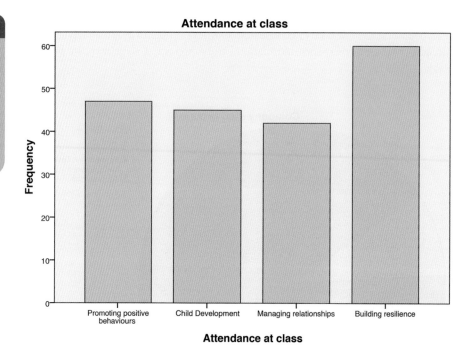

Researchers usually start the scale of the Y axis at zero as this helps the reader to compare the height of the bars in the bar chart. If you start the scale with an arbitrary number then the differences between the bars can be exaggerated, making it harder for the reader to work out if differences in the lengths of the bars are meaningful.

Clustered bar chart

Clustered bar charts enable you to add another variable to the chart so that further comparisons can be made. The bars comprising the categories of one variable are clustered together (or grouped) within each category of a second variable. The bars should again be presented in a way that the reader can make clear comparisons such as having the bars of data from the same variable in the same position in each of the different clusters. Researchers often present the actual counts in the bars, to illustrate the number in each category. However, using percentages rather than counts may allow more meaningful comparisons if the overall frequencies vary across the categories.

Using the parenting programmes example, a researcher is interested in comparing the attendance at the four different programmes by gender. Breaking down the above findings into gender we get: promoting positive behaviours (attended by 24 females and 23 males), child development (attended by 18 females and 27 males), managing relationships (attended by 26 females and 16 males) and building resilience (attended by 30 females and 30 males). The following clustered bar chart shows the differences between the female and male attendance at the classes.

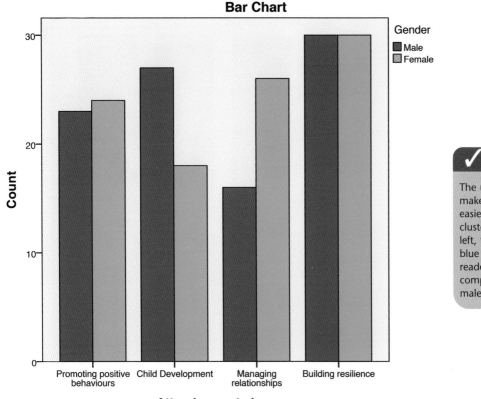

The use of colour can make a complex chart easier to read. In the clustered bar chart to the left, the use of green and blue means that the reader can easily compare the female and male bars in the chart.

By observing the clustered bar chart, we can see that one more female than males attended the classes on promoting positive behaviours. The child development sessions were attended by more males than females and females attended more classes on managing relationships than males. We can also see that the course on building resilience was the most popular parenting programme and had the same number of male and female attendees.

Stacked bar chart

Stacked bar charts, like clustered bar charts, are used when a second variable is added to a bar chart. Rather than including additional bars to a chart in a cluster, stacked bar charts stack the additional bars on top of each other, so that the results of one variable are summarised within categories of another variable. It is important that when different values are stacked together that the values are meaningful. Some researchers prefer to report stacked bar charts in percentages so that each of the bars have equal heights representative of 100%. The data displayed in the clustered bar chart above is displayed in terms of percentages as a stacked bar chart, as follows.

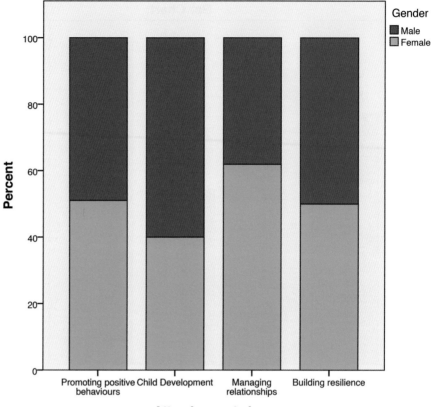

When a clustered or stacked bar chart is converted from counts to percentages, it does lose some information, so we can no longer see the overall pattern of course attendance. In this stacked bar chart managing relationships was the least well attended and building resilience the most popular. However, this chart shows the gender breakdown across the different programmes very clearly. The managing relationships course had the largest proportion of female attendees, while the child development course had the largest proportion of male attendees.

✓

For some researchers bar charts are always better than pie charts. The separate bars are easier to see and compare, with the labels on the two axes facilitating reading the values the bars represent. As a result a number of academic journals will feature bar charts but not pie charts. However, there are cases were comparisons are the not main purpose of presenting the chart, which is used to simply represent proportions of a whole, so a pie chart is often easy to understand for a range of readers (who may not be an academic audience). In these cases a clear and simple pie chart can serve a useful illustrative purpose.

Line graphs

Line graphs are particularly effective when you want to show a sequence of values such as changes in values over time. They can also be used when showing how changes in one variable effect changes in another variable. Line graphs can be used in a similar way to bar charts (particularly clustered bar charts) in that they can be used to show differences between the categories of data on one variable in terms of the categories of a second variable.

Line graphs showing trends

It is possible to represent trends, such as changes over time, with a bar chart; however, in many cases a line graph can be superior in that the data points are connected together (by a line) and so the trend is easier to appreciate visually. Furthermore, a line graph can be a clearer illustration of a trend when there are many data points, rather than as a large number of bars. For example, a new song was released for sale by a popular singer and the number of downloads of the song were recorded weekly by the record company. The line graph below shows that the trend in the song downloads over a period of 20 weeks.

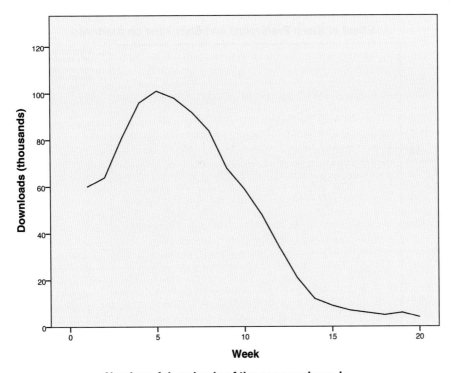

Number of downloads of the song each week

It can be seen from the line graph that the sales rose within the first five weeks of the song being released and then went down over the next 15 weeks.

Line graphs for plotting relationships between means

When researchers are looking for an effect of one or more variables on an outcome measure they will often use a line graph, rather than a clustered bar chart, to plot the mean values. For example, a group of paramedics were asked to rate themselves as 'morning' or 'evening' people in terms of their sleep and waking preferences. Ten 'morning' and 10 'evening' paramedics were carefully selected (and matched so that they did not differ on other factors such as age or gender) and measured on their alertness at the end of an early morning shift and at the end of a late evening shift. The researchers were examining the effect of the two nominal variables 'person type' and 'time of shift' on the alertness scores (measured on an interval scale). The mean alertness values for the four categories of the two variables (morning-early-shift, morning-late-shift, evening-early-shift, evening-late-shift) could be displayed as a clustered bar chart but often researchers prefer the line plot below, as it shows the relationship between the variables very clearly – the 'time of the shift' interacts with the 'person type' in the alertness results. This pattern of alertness would not have been shown if the alertness scores had been displayed for the two variables separately, but when examined together it can be seen that the morning people are more alert after a morning shift and the evening people are more alert after an evening shift.

✓

A heading or caption and axis labels on a table or graph can be written with all the key words starting with a capital letter, as we have done with the figure on this page. Alternatively, the heading or caption can be written with only the first word starting with a capital, as on the figure on the following page. There are different guidelines for different organisations and you need to check what is required for your report. We explain how to add a title and edit labels in Chapter 8.

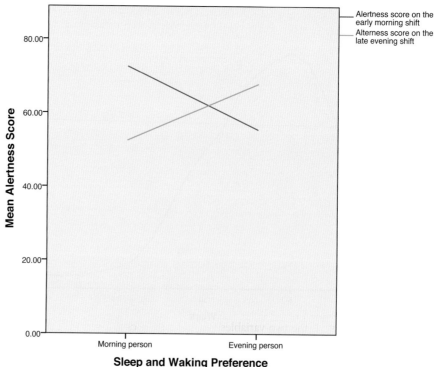

Effect of Sleep Preference and Shift Time on Alertness

Alertness score on the early morning shift
Alterness score on the late evening shift

Scatterplots

Scatterplots, also known as scattergrams, present the data from two variables plotted on a graph where the values of one variable are measured on the X axis and the values of the other on the Y axis. In scatterplots, the data points are not connected together. The aim is to show any relationship between the two variables by the way in which the points are scattered on the graph. For example, researchers have recorded the performance on a mathematics test and a reading test by a group of 20 8-year-old children. They plot the results on an X–Y plot with the X axis as the reading test score and the Y axis as the mathematics test scores. Each dot represents a particular child's position on the graph.

This graph shows a linear relationship between the mathematics scores and reading scores. The two variables are said to correlate, that is they co-relate – as the score on one variable changes then the score on the other variable changes accordingly. It does not tell us what has caused this relationship to occur – only that it has been found. In Chapter 8, we look further at how we can add a straight line that 'best fits' the points to the scatterplot then, in Chapter 9, we examine statistically how 'good' a correlation it is (that is, how close the points are to the straight line).

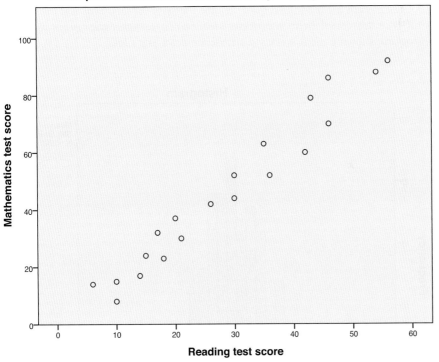

Scatterplot of mathematics test scores by reading test scores

correlate
Two variables are said to correlate if their values vary together (i.e. they 'co-relate'). See also **negative correlation**; **positive correlation**

Even though the mathematics test was scored out of 100 and the reading test scored out of 60, we can see there is a clear relationship between the two sets of scores. There is a narrow band of the graph within which all the scores lie. Furthermore, this band appears to be following a straight line. This indicates that the relationship between the two variables (the mathematics test scores and reading test scores) is **linear**.

linear
Following a straight line. In a scatterplot, researchers are interested in whether the relationship between two variables is linear, that is, the points fall (roughly) along a straight line

Histograms

Histograms are used to show the distribution of data measured on a continuous scale. Unlike a bar chart, there are no gaps between the bars as a histogram is plotted on a continuous scale. The histogram is one of the best ways of illustrating the pattern of frequencies of scores. This is important as a number of inferential statistics (see Chapter 9) make assumptions about the distribution of the data and often these assumptions can be checked by plotting the data on a histogram. A histogram can also show two key aspects of the data. First, does the distribution of scores form a single cluster (rather than form separate groups of scores)? Second, is the distribution symmetrical about a 'middle' point? If both these conditions are met then the mean and standard deviation are likely to provide a good summary of the results. For example, a doctor's surgery is interested in finding out the actual patient waiting times at the surgery. As a preliminary investigation, during the busiest surgery time, 200 patient visits are monitored from the time they register their arrival at the surgery until they are called in to the doctor's office. These figures are recorded on a histogram, showing the following distribution of waiting times.

See Chapter 9

Notice the graph has a symmetrical appearance with the results clustering around a middle point – the mean of 14.85 minutes – and then gradually spreading out as the times are lower or higher than this figure.

USING CHART BUILDER

Chart Builder is a flexible graph creating module in SPSS. Essentially, it provides you with a list of chart and graph types to choose from, and then allows you to build the structure of the specific graph that you need using a drag-and-drop method.

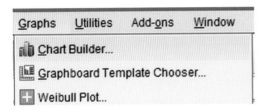

The procedure for the graphs detailed below start with selecting the **Graphs** drop-down menu and then selecting the **Chart Builder** command.

You will notice that the first time you use **Chart Builder** a warning appears reminding you to make sure that you have set the correct measurement level for your variables. If you decide that you want to treat ordinal data as scale then you would need to ensure that you have changed the measurement level as SPSS will not let you create certain graphs without doing this. If you don't want to see this box again tick the **Don't show this dialog again**. Then click **OK**.

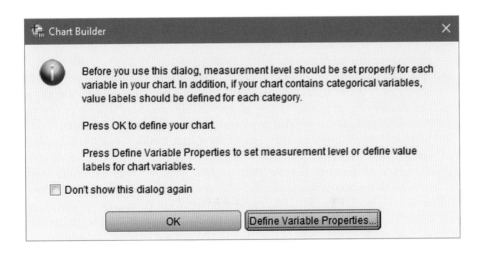

The **Chart Builder** dialog box appears, with a separate **Element Properties** window.

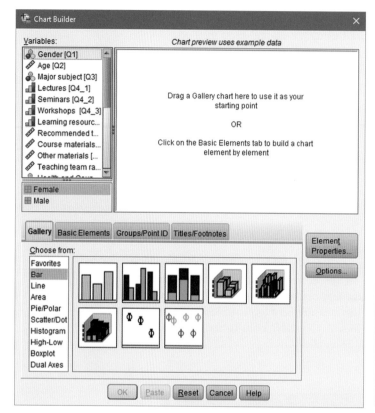

The **Chart Builder** dialog box is similar to the **Custom Table** dialog box in that it contains a list of the variables from your dataset on the left-hand side in a **Variables** box. You can see the labels and names of the variables and next to each one is an icon that identifies how the variable is measured (nominal, ordinal or scale).

There is a large 'canvas' on the right of the **Chart Builder** dialog box headed by **Chart preview uses example data**, which allows you to preview your chart. We will refer to this as the canvas or the 'chart preview window'. Blue text in the chart preview window indicates that a variable still needs to be added to it. The **Chart Builder** dialog box also includes other tabs and options to permit you to customise your chart. The **Element Properties** window enables you to adjust different aspects of your chart such as the scale of the axes or the statistic you are presenting (for example, changing from frequency counts to percentages).

You first click on the **Gallery** tab to select the type of chart you want, from the list under **Choose from**. This then displays a range of predefined charts of this type as icons in the box in the lower centre of the dialog box. You then select one of these charts by double clicking on it or dragging it into the chart preview window. Once you have selected which chart you want to build, the canvas displays an **X-Axis** and **Y-Axis** and, depending on the type of chart you have chosen, it shows

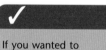

If you wanted to temporarily change the **Measure** of one of the variables, then right click on the name of the variable in the **Variables** box and change the **Measure** from the right-click menu.

other boxes where you can drag and drop your variables to build the chart you require. Every chart requires you to drag a variable into the **X-Axis**.

We are going to discuss the following commonly used charts: Pie, bar, line, histogram and scatterplot, which we will illustrate using the data from the Sparcote Study.

Pie charts

Students who completed the survey in the Sparcote Study were asked, in Question 3, to indicate which major subject they were studying. We are going to produce a pie chart to chart their responses to this question.

▦ Select **Pie/Polar** from the **Choose from** list in the **Gallery** tab.

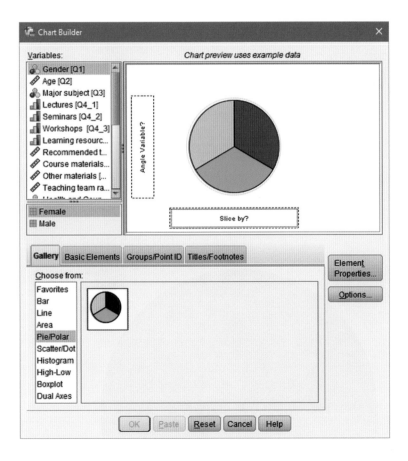

▦ Drag the pie chart icon (or double click on the icon) from the lower box to the chart preview window where a template pie chart will now become visible.

▦ Next, drag the variable 'Major subject' to the **Slice by?** box. The box now has the variable name in it and a title appears.

▦ Click on **OK**.

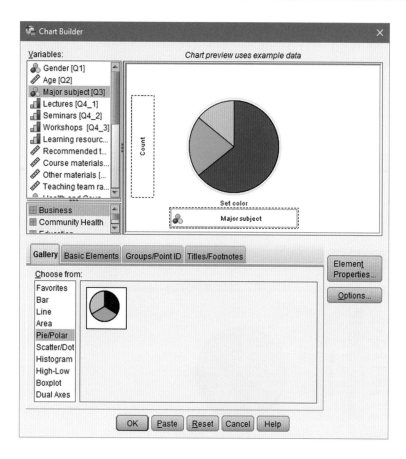

The pie chart generated by SPSS is then shown in the **IBM SPSS Statistics Viewer.**

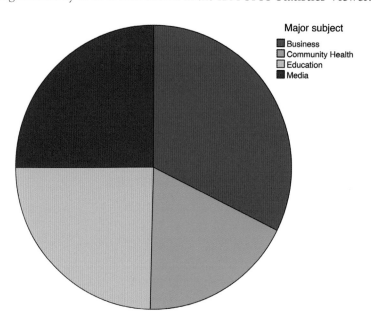

We can see that the largest slice of the pie shows the number of students who are taking business and the smallest slice is for community health. The chart would need to be edited to display the actual values or percentages on it and a title should be added before the chart is ready to present in a report.

For details on editing charts, see Chapter 8

SPSS does allow you to produce a pie chart with patterns instead of colour. Once your variable is in the **Slice by?** box in the chart preview window, then double click on the box and a **Grouping Zone** dialog box appears.

▓ Click on the drop-down menu of **Distinguish Groups by** and select **Pattern**.

▓ Then click on **OK** and, to generate the chart, click **OK** in the **Chart Builder** window.

The pie chart with patterned monochrome slices produced by SPSS can be seen below.

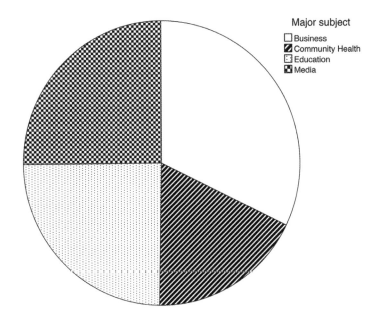

For details on editing charts, see Chapter 8

Comparing this pie chart with the coloured pie chart above, it can be seen that monochrome does distinguish the slides but it is not as visually strong as the colour slices. However, a chart with patterns rather than colours is useful if you are printing in black and white.

Bar charts

Chart Builder in SPSS offers a variety of bar charts, giving eight different choices of format. We are going to discuss the three most popular types of bar chart here: a basic bar chart, a clustered bar chart and a stacked bar chart.

Simple bar chart

Using the Sparcote Study we are going to produce a bar chart to explore participants' use of the sports and fitness centre over the previous year. This is Question 10 of the survey and the students could choose from one of the five categories: 'Often', 'Regularly', 'Occasionally', 'Rarely' or 'Never'.

■   Select **Bar** from the chart options in the **Gallery**.

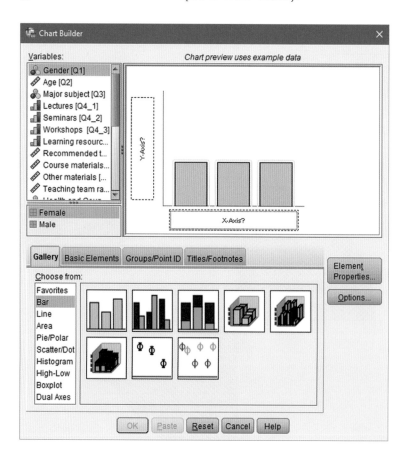

■ Eight different bar chart options appear in the **Gallery** dialog box. Select the first icon, **Simple Bar**, and drag and drop this into the chart preview window.

■ Drag 'Use of the Sport and Fitness Centre' to the **X-Axis** box. This will ensure that the five categories are shown on the **X-Axis** (so there will be five bars in the chart).

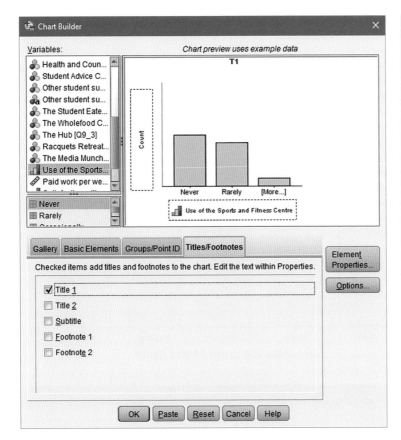
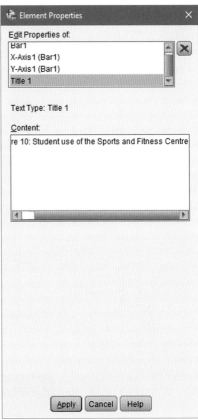

The **Statistic** in the **Element Properties** window is listed as **Count**, so the bar chart will produce bars of frequencies for each of the categories of the variable.

■ You can add a title to the chart in the **Chart Builder**. Select the **Titles/Footnotes** tab and tick the **Title 1** box below it.

■ The chart preview window will now be headed by **T1**, and the **Elements Properties** window provides a space for you to type in the title of the chart. This chart is given the title 'Figure 10: Student Use of the Sports and Fitness Centre'.

■ Click on **Apply** in the **Elements Properties** window.

■ Click on **OK**.

SPSS displays the bar chart in the **IBM SPSS Statistics Viewer** window. We can see that that there seems to be two groups of students, those who never (or rarely) use the sports facilities and those who use it regularly or often. The smallest group of students is in the 'middle' category, the students who occasionally use the sports facilities. The title is shown at the top of the chart.

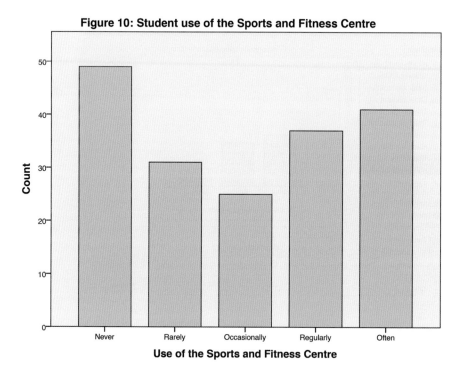

Figure 10: Student use of the Sports and Fitness Centre

SPSS places the title above the chart. However, many academic journals require the title to be placed underneath a chart or graph. (This is viewed as good practice as charts are usually read from the bottom to the top.) Charts, graph or diagrams are also called 'figures' in academic journals. SPSS does not provide an option to place the title at the bottom of the chart. However, instead of ticking the **Title 1** box in the **Titles/Footnote** tab of **Chart Builder** you can tick the **Footnote 1** box. If you type your title here, then it will be displayed below the chart. (You may wish to increase the size of the footnote and make it bold when you want it to be the title. You can do by editing the chart, as explained in Chapter 8.)

See Chapter 8

Clustered bar chart

We are going to use Question 5 on learning resources from the Sparcote Study to illustrate the procedure for generating a clustered bar chart with **Chart Builder**. Students were asked to state their level of agreement (ranging from 1 – 'strongly disagree' to 5 – 'strongly agree') with a statement on whether they thought the learning resources were appropriate to support their course. This question is measured on an ordinal scale. We are going to produce a clustered bar chart to illustrate any differences between students of the different major subjects on their responses to this question.

■ Select **Bar** from the bar options in the **Gallery** tab.

■ Select the second icon, **Clustered Bar** and drag and drop it into the chart preview window.

■ Select 'Major subject' and drag it to the **X-Axis** box. This will ensure that the four major subjects will appear on the **X-Axis**.

■ Select 'Learning resources' and drag it to the **Cluster on X:set color** box.

■ Click **OK**.

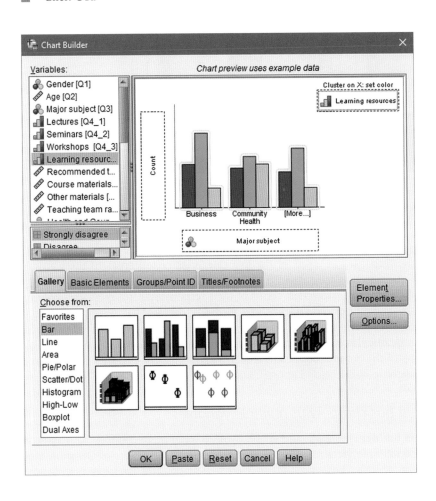

The following clustered bar chart is produced and displayed in the **IBM SPSS Statistics Viewer**.

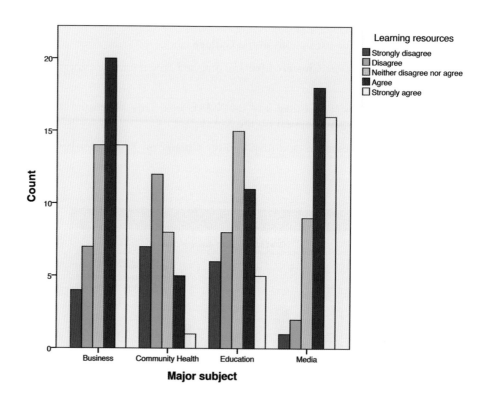

SPSS has generated a bar chart that separates the four different subjects and clusters the responses in terms of the five categories of responses to the learning resources question for each subject. This is a useful chart for comparing the students on the different major subjects in terms of their responses to this question. We can see that the majority of the business and media students either agreed or strongly agreed that the learning resources were appropriate of their course. Education students are rather less positive about the appropriateness of their learning resources. The results of the community health students show that the majority do not agree that the learning resources are appropriate for their course.

Clustered bar charts with multiple variables

The **Chart Builder** command also enables you to build more complex bar charts to summarise multiple variables. We are going to explore the results of Question 6 of the Sparcote Study, where the students were asked about their relative use of three different resources in their studies. This is an example of a constant sum question, with three items or three separate SPSS variables (see Chapter 3). These are scale variables so **Chart Builder** will automatically produce a chart of mean values and not frequency counts. We are going to also separate these results in terms of the four

> ✓
>
> **Chart Builder** will leave the previous chart in the canvas when you return to it. To remove this chart and start a new one, click on the **Reset** button at the bottom of the **Chart Builder** dialog box.

See Chapter 3

major subjects (Question 3), so we can examine the different use of these resources by the different student groups.

- Select **Bar** from the chart options in the **Gallery**.

- Select the second icon, the **Clustered Bar** chart and drag and drop it into the chart preview window.

- Drag 'Major subject' to the **X-Axis** box.

- Drag 'Recommended textbooks' to the **Y-Axis** box.

- Then drag 'Course materials' and 'Other materials' to the top section of the **Y-Axis box.** You see a small box with a red plus sign appear at the top of the **Y-Axis** box. It is here where you need to drop the two variables.

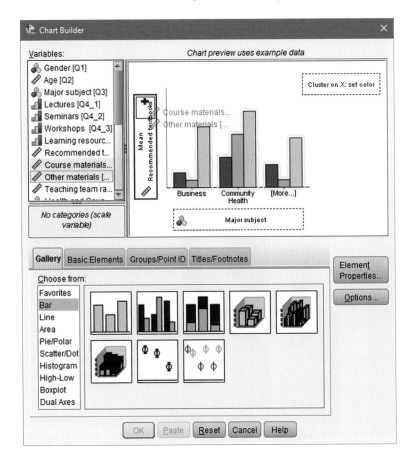

- A **Create Summary Group** window appears. This shows you the variables that you have dragged to **Y-Axis** which will be summarised (see next page).

- Press **OK** on the **Create Summary Group** window.

- The chart has now been set up so we press **OK** in the **Chart Builder** dialog box to generate the chart.

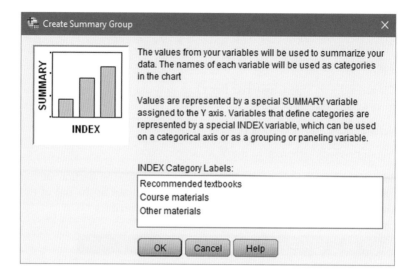

The following chart is displayed in the **IBM SPSS Statistics Viewer**.

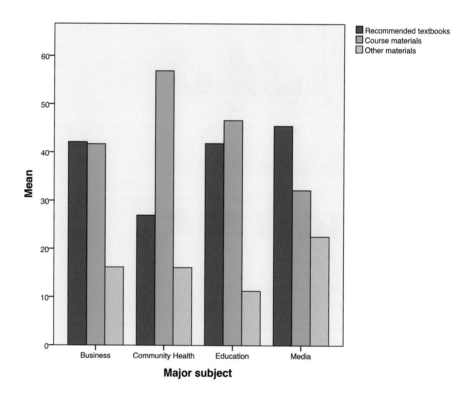

We can see that, while the business, education and media students' relative use of the textbooks is over 40%, it is under 30% for the community health students, who use the course materials in their studies more than any other group (nearly 60%). Media students use their textbooks the most but also use 'Other materials' relatively more than the other groups (over 20% of their usage).

Stacked bar chart

A stacked bar chart is similar to a clustered bar chart but the 'cluster' is shown within a single bar. To illustrate this we are going to use the Sparcote Study data to create a stacked bar chart of the number of female and male students in the different subject majors.

■ Select **Bar** from the chart options in the **Gallery**.

■ Select the third icon, the **Stacked Bar Chart** and drag and drop it into the chart preview window.

■ Drag 'Major subject' to the **X-Axis** box.

■ Drag 'Gender' to the **Stack: set color** box.

■ Click on **OK**.

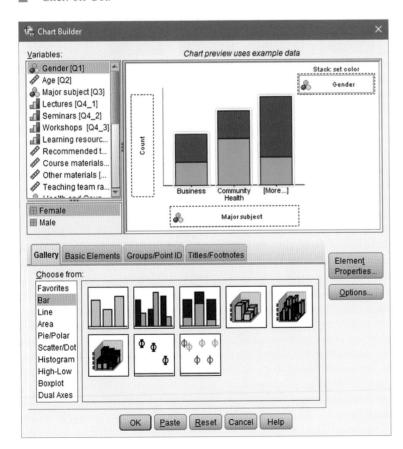

The following stacked bar chart is displayed in the **IBM SPSS Statistics Viewer**.

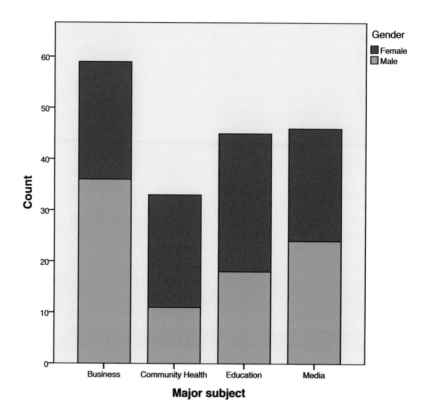

The stacked bar chart shows that the highest number of students is in the business major. The nice feature of the stacked bar chart is that this bar – of the number of students in the major – is colour coded in terms of gender, so we can see how the total is broken up into males and females. It is clear from the chart that there are more male students than female students studying the business major. Community health had the lowest total number of students, but the majority are female. The relatively larger blue section also shows that the majority of students in education were female. Finally, the chart shows a relatively even balance of male and female students studying the media major.

✓

If you wanted to show the stacked bar charts in percentages with each bar representing 100%, the following changes will produce this.

- In the **Element Properties** window change the **Statistic** to **Percentage ()** and then click on the **Set Parameters** button.
- Change the **Denominator for Computing Percentage:** to **Total for Each X-Axis Category.**
- Click on **Apply** in the **Element Properties window.**
- Click on **OK** in the **Chart Builder** dialog box.

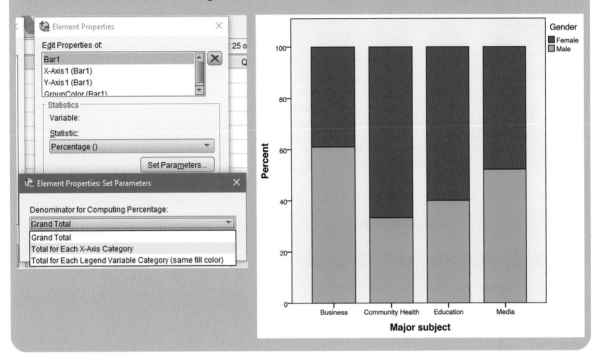

Line graphs

Simple line graph

Line graphs illustrate trends or the relationship between variables. We are going to produce a line graph to show the relationship between 'Major subject' and 'Teaching team rating' (Questions 3 and 7 of the Sparcote Study). The students were asked to rate of the teaching team on their course on a 10-point scale in terms of their overall teaching quality (1 – low quality, 10 – high quality). It was assumed that this data was scale rather than treated as ordinal in the study.

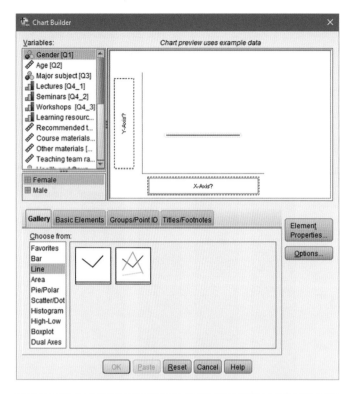

- In the **Chart Builder** dialog box, select **Line** from the chart options in the **Gallery**.

- Two different line chart options are shown as icons. Select the first icon, **Simple Line** and double click on it or drag and drop it to the chart preview window.

- Drag 'Major subject' to the **X-Axis** box.

- Drag 'Teaching team rating' into the **Y-Axis** box.

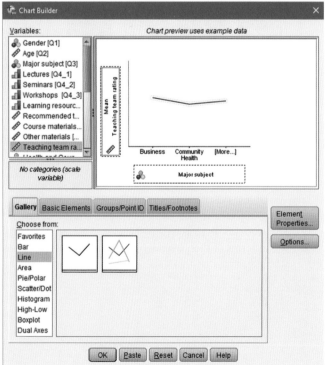

SPSS displays a template of the line graph in the chart preview window. Notice that, as 'Teacher team rating' is measured as a scale variable, SPSS automatically chooses **Mean** to display on the **Y-Axis** of the graph.

- Select **OK**.

The line graph is displayed in the **IBM SPSS Statistics Viewer**. The major subject categories are displayed on the **X-Axis** and the mean of the teaching team ratings is presented on the **Y-Axis**.

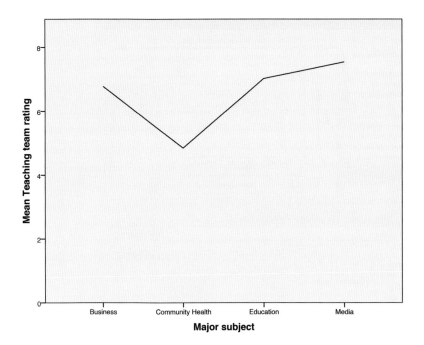

When presenting these findings in a report you could also include a table of mean values with the graph to show exactly what the mean values are. Alternatively, you can display the mean values on the chart. We discuss how to edit a graph in Chapter 8.

Media students rate their teaching team highest, followed by education and business, but the differences between these groups appear small from the graph. All three groups rate their teaching teams higher than 6 on the 10-point scale, indicating a positive view of the teaching quality. We can see that the students studying community health were least happy with their teaching team, with a mean value just under 5.

Multiple line graph

We can also create a multiple line graph with **Chart Builder**. Using the Sparcote Study data, we are going to illustrate how to produce a multiple line graph to see if gender (Question 1) has an influence on the ratings of the teaching teams (Question 7) in the different major subjects (Question 3). We want the major subjects to be on the X axis and there to be a separate line for female students' teacher team ratings and for male students' teacher team ratings.

■ Select **Line** from the graph options in the **Gallery**.

■ Select the second icon, **Multiple Line** and either double click on it or drag and drop it into the chart preview window.

■ Drag 'Major subject' to the **X-Axis** box.

■ Drag 'Teaching team rating' to the **Y-Axis** axis. As this variable is defined as scale, SPSS automatically selects the mean values to be plotted.

■ Drag 'Gender' to the **Set color** box. This is the variable that will be used for the lines in the multiple line graph.

■ Click **OK**.

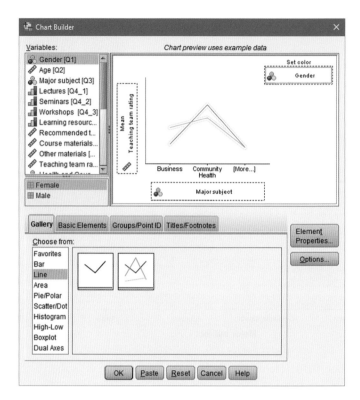

The following multiple line graph is displayed in the **IBM SPSS Statistics Viewer**.

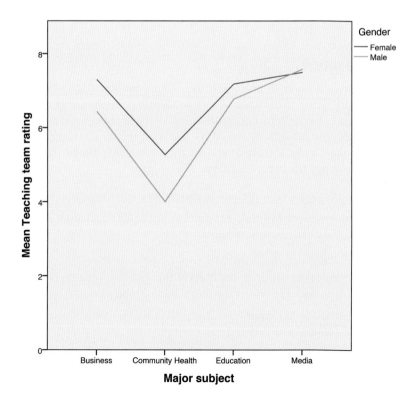

The multiple line graph shows that the females generally rated their teaching team higher than the males (as the blue female line is above the green male line for three subjects), except for media, where males rated their teaching team just slightly higher than the females on average. Males studying community health rated their teaching team the lowest.

Histogram

There are four different options that can be chosen to produce a histogram in **Chart Builder**. The most popular of these is the **Simple Histogram**, which we will illustrate here. We are going to produce a histogram from the Sparcote Study that illustrates the number of hours of paid work per week that the students undertook (Question 11). The responses of this question are measured on a scale, which is required for a histogram.

- Choose **Histogram** from the list of available charts in the **Gallery**.

- Select the first icon for a **Simple Histogram** and double click or drag and drop the selected chart into the chart preview window.

- Select the 'Paid work per week' and drag it to the **X-Axis** box.

- Click **OK** and the histogram is displayed in the **IBM SPSS Statistics Viewer**.

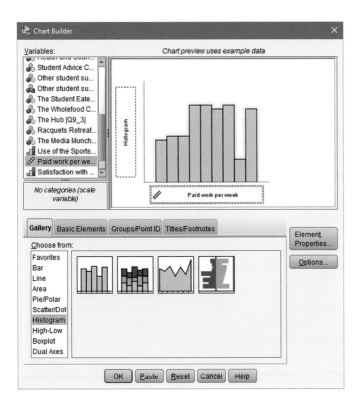

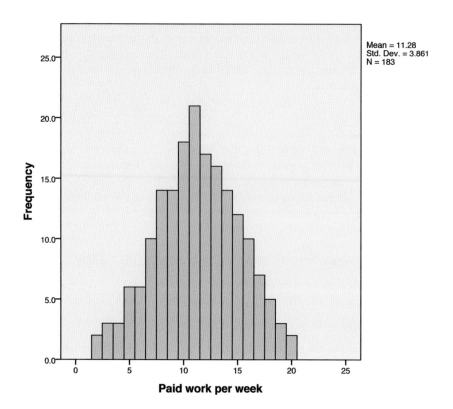

For details on editing charts and graphs, please see Chapter 8

SPSS displays the mean, standard deviation, and number of participants (**N**) alongside the histogram. By looking at the histogram above, we can see that the bars cluster around a 'middle' position. As the distribution is also fairly symmetrical, the mean provides a good summary description of the results. Students in the Department of Applied Studies (N = 183) undertake paid work alongside their studies (with a mean of 11.28 hours, and a standard deviation of 3.86).

✓

SPSS automatically decides on the width of the bars of the histogram. In this case, it has simply (and sensibly) chosen a width of one hour per bar. In other cases, you may find that it is does not produce the bar size that you want. To make sure that the histogram has the width of bar that you want, you can click on the **Set Parameters** button in the **Element Properties** dialog box. Then choose **Custom** under **Bin Sizes** in the **Element Properties: Set Parameters** box. Here, we can choose the width of interval that we want – in this case the interval width is set to 1.

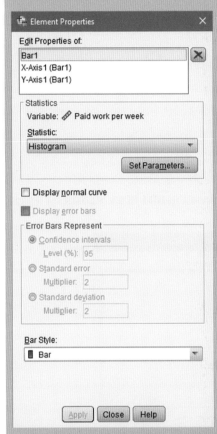 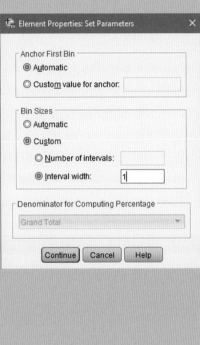

(Notice that you can also change other parameters if you wish to, such as the number of bars in the histogram rather than their width.)

• Click the **Continue** button in **Element Properties: Set Parameters** box.
• Click the **Apply** button in the **Element Properties** dialog box and you will return to the **Chart Builder** window.

Scatterplots

Scatterplots enable you to illustrate relationships between two variables. The two variables are usually measured on a scale. In the Sparcote Study, an overall satisfaction score was calculated for the students by adding up the results of the three different satisfaction scales in Question 12 (see Chapter 6 for an explanation of how we did this). The researchers decide that it would be interesting to see if there is a relationship between the ratings of the teaching team (Question 7) and this overall measure of satisfaction.

See Chapter 6

We are going to illustrate this with a scatterplot of the two variables: 'Teacher team rating' and 'Overall satisfaction'.

- ■ Choose **Scatter/Dot** from the list of available graphs in the **Gallery**.

- ■ Select the first icon for a **Simple Scatter**.

- ■ Double click on the icon or drag the selected chart into the chart preview window.

- ■ Drag 'Teaching team rating' to the **X-Axis** box.

- ■ Drag 'Overall satisfaction' to the **Y-Axis** box.

- ■ Click **OK** and the scatterplot will appear in the **IBM SPSS Statistics Viewer**.

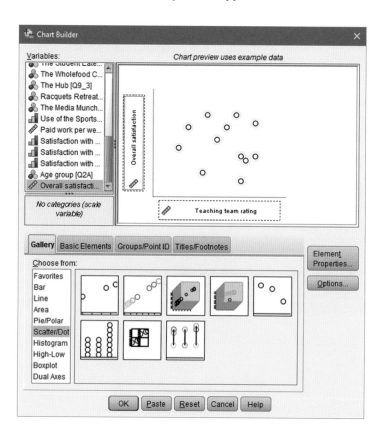

We can see a pattern of dots in the graph. Notice that when SPSS plots two or more results in the same place it indicates this by making the small circle marking the position darker.

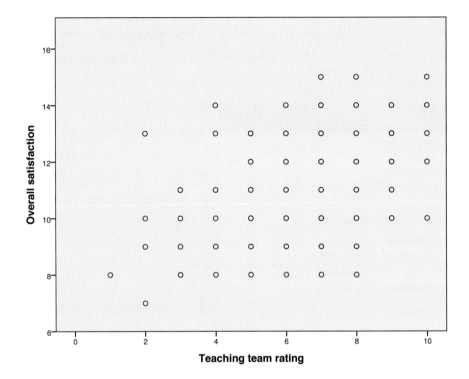

If you wish to change the marker from circles to another marker (such as a cross), this can changed in **Chart Editor** (explained in Chapter 8).

While not particularly easy to see, there does appear to be a tendency for those students who rated their teaching team highly to also rate their overall satisfaction highly (with a low score on one variable to be related to low score on the other). While this is not obvious from the graph (although we can see the results roughly lie within a broad band), we can analyse this relationship statistically to see the extent to which the variables do, in fact, correlate in the study (see Chapter 9). This finding (if the variables do actually correlate) could provoke further research into the relationship between student satisfaction with their teaching team and their overall satisfaction with their studies.

For details on undertaking statistical tests, please see Chapter 9

Notice that SPSS has automatically adjusted the length of the axes. While the X axis has been set from 0 to 10 (for 'Teaching team rating'), the Y axis is set from 6 to 16 (for 'Overall satisfaction'). It has done the latter as there are no 'Overall satisfaction' values below 6 in the data. However, if you wanted to change the axes to the actual range of possible scores, we would reset the X axis as 1 to 10 (as these as the possible values for 'Teaching team rating') and the Y axis as 3 to 15 (as the lowest overall possible 'Overall satisfaction' score is 3 and the highest is 15). You can set specific minimum and maximum values for the axes in the **Element Properties** dialog box. Often researchers want the axis to start at 0. We show here how to change the Y axis to start from 0.

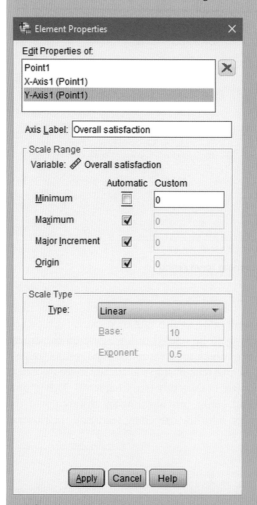

- Select the axis you wish to change – we have chosen the Y axis.
- Unclick the **Automatic** box. We have done this for **Minimum**.
- Now set the value you want in the **Custom** box. We have entered zero.

Now SPSS will display the scatterplot with the Y axis ranging from 0 to 16 and not 6 to 16. You can always change these values to reset the graph in **Chart Editor** (explained in Chapter 8).

See Chapter 8

As a scatterplot examines the co-relationship (or correlation) between two variables, it does not matter which variable is chosen for the X axis or the Y axis. However, it is common practice, if you consider one variable to have an effect on another variable, to put the influencing variable on the X axis (in this case, the researchers were interested in the influence of 'Teacher team rating') and the variable that may be influenced ('Overall satisfaction') on Y axis. We discuss this further in Chapter 8.

See Chapter 8

CREATE GRAPH – GENERATING GRAPHS FROM OUTPUT TABLES

The **Create Graph** command is a feature of the **IBM SPSS Statistics Viewer**, so rather than creating a graph through the **Analyze** or **Graphs** drop-down menus, this is a command that is undertaken after some output has already been produced.

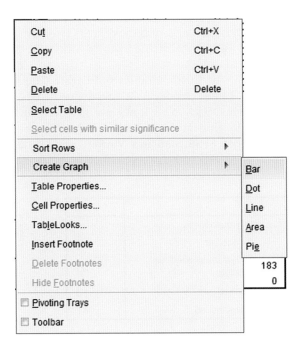

You may not always know that you want to produce a graph when you have created some output, but this method allows you to create a graph from a table that you have already produced. By double clicking on a table in the **IBM SPSS Statistics Viewer**, this activates the editing options for the table enabling you to do additional things through a menu of options. (These are discussed further in Chapter 8.) One of these choices is to create a graph. If you right click anywhere on the activated table, a menu appears, with the option **Create Graph** in the middle of the list. When you select this **Create Graph** option, there are five choices of graphs: bar, dot (a line graph without the lines – just dots), line, area (area under the line graph) and pie.

See Chapter 8

A key point with the **Create Graph** command is that we can highlight the cells in the table we wish to make into a graph first, then when we right click to bring up the **Create Graph** command it knows which cells to use for the graph. If we do not select the cells we are interested in first, then **Create Graph** makes a chart or graph using all the cells in the table.

See Chapter 5

We have seen that a number of charts can be produced by the **Frequencies** command and by **Chart Builder**. However, occasionally, these methods may not produce the chart that you want. Sometimes, **Create Graph** can be used to produce just that chart you wish to display.

We are going to demonstrate the creation of bar charts and line charts through this method.

Bar

Bar chart (to include zero categories)

In Chapter 5, presenting the first set of results of the Sparcote Study, we produced a table and bar chart of Question 12, item 1, showing the student 'Satisfaction with academic life', using the **Frequencies** command. This was measured on a five-point Likert scale. However, as none of the students ticked the 'very unsatisfied' category, the **Frequencies** command only produced four entries in the frequencies table and four bars in the bar chart for 'unsatisfied', 'neither unsatisfied nor satisfied', 'satisfied' and 'very satisfied'. The **Frequencies** command did not allocate a cell in the table or a bar in the bar chart for the 'very unsatisfied' category as the count is zero. Some researchers find this frustrating as they want the table and chart to include 'zero categories' as well.

We can get round this problem using the **Custom Tables** and **Create Graph** commands. We first select the **Custom Tables** command. We send Question 12, item 1 (Q12_1) – 'Satisfaction with academic life' – to the **Rows** box (and click **OK**) to produce a table of frequency counts for this variable. We can see that the table generated by **Custom Tables** in the **IBM SPSS Statistics Viewer** includes the category 'very unsatisfied' in the frequency table with the count of 0.

		Count
Satisfaction with academic life	Very unsatisfied	0
	Unsatisfied	17
	Neither unsatisfied nor satisfied	55
	Satisfied	70
	Very satisfied	41

Now all we need to do is to create a bar chart from this table. We double click on the table to activate it. We then click on the first cell we want in the chart (the 0). The cell is highlighted in black. Holding down the left click on the mouse, we drag it down the column so that all the figures are highlighted in black; then we right click to bring up the editing menu and select **Create Graph** and then **Bar**.

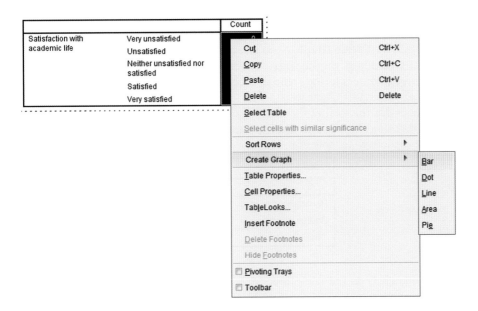

The following bar chart is now displayed in the **IBM SPSS Statistics Viewer**.

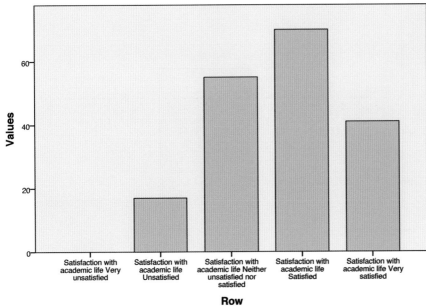

We can see that the bar chart has all five categories listed, with the space allocated for the 'very unsatisfied' category, indicating a 'zero bar' showing that there were no counts in this category.

Bar chart (with scale data)

You can also use **Create Graph** to produce a bar chart with scale data. In the Sparcote Study, in Question 6, the students were asked to give an estimate of their relative use of three resources in their studies ('recommended textbooks', 'course materials' and 'other materials'). They were asked to place a percentage figure against each resource so that the total of the three figures adds up to 100% (as a constant sum question). Using the **Custom Tables** command we showed in Chapter 6 how to produce the following table of mean values, for the three variables.

For details on creating tables, see Chapter 6

	Mean
Recommended textbooks	40.19
Course materials	43.27
Other materials	16.56

We double click on the table to activate it. We then select the first data cell by clicking on it – which highlights it in black. We then highlight all the means value cells (by holding down the left click and dragging the mouse). We right click anywhere in the highlighted area and the editing menu pops up. We select **Create Graph** and then **Bar** to produce the following chart.

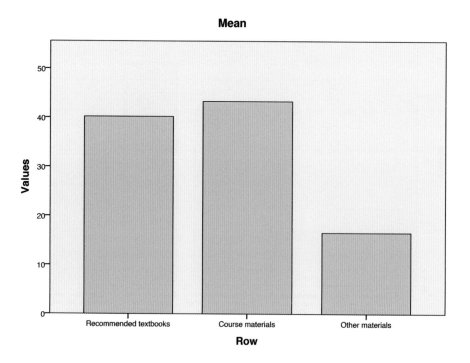

The chart shows that that most students use the course materials and the recommended textbooks, with the use of other materials being less than 20%.

Bar chart (combining variables)

We saw in Chapter 5 that with a multi-item question, the **Frequencies** command will produce a separate table of frequencies for each variable (item). In the Sparcote Study, we demonstrated this with Question 9, examining which of the five on-campus social spaces the students had visited. The **Frequencies** command produced five separate tables. We saw, in Chapter 6, that we could create a single table with all the items combined using the **Custom Tables** command. This is shown again here.

	No	Yes
	Count	Count
The Student Eatery	61	122
The Wholefood Café	94	89
The Hub	126	57
Racquets Retreat	154	29
The Media Munch	99	84

However, unlike the **Frequencies** command, **Custom Tables** cannot produce a chart. This is where **Create Graph** can be used. In the **IBM SPSS Statistics Viewer**, we double click on the table to activate it. We only want a chart of the 'Yes' responses (as it is obvious the other students did not go to the social space), so we highlight the first cell in the 'Yes' column in the table by clicking on it (and the cell turns black). Holding down the left click we drag the mouse down the column to highlight all the cells. Then we right click to bring up the edit menu and select **Create Graph** and **Bar**.

See Chapters 5 and 6

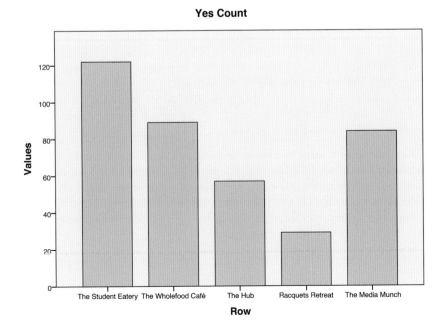

The following bar chart is produced and displayed in the **IBM SPSS Statistics Viewer**.

The bar chart shows the number of students who had visited the different social spaces. The Student Eatery is the most popular venue, followed by the Wholefood Café, The Media Munch and The Hub, with Racquets Retreat the least popular social space for the students in applied studies.

Clustered bar chart (with two categorical variables, where one is multi-item)

You can also create a clustered bar chart with two variables using **Custom Tables** followed by **Create Graph**. In this example, we are going to combine two questions from the Sparcote Study to produce a clustered bar chart. We are going to look at the number of students visiting three different student services – the Health and Counselling Centre, the Student Advice Centre and 'other' (Question 8), which requires us to combine three variables (but not the fourth, which is a text response to which other service they visited). We are also going to break down these results into the students on the different major subjects (Question 3). We cannot use the **Crosstabs** command in this case to produce the clustered bar chart as Question 8 is a multi-item question. We produce the following table using the **Custom Tables** command, by sending 'Major subject' to the **Columns** box and the three Question 8 student service variables to the **Rows** box.

		Major subject			
		Business	Community Health	Education	Media
		Count	Count	Count	Count
Health and Counselling Centre	No	46	23	34	43
	Yes	13	10	11	3
Student Advice Centre	No	39	22	29	32
	Yes	20	11	16	14
Other student support service	No	55	30	42	42
	Yes	4	3	3	4

We only want to create a table of the 'Yes' responses (as it is obvious that the other students did not visit the service). This makes it quite tricky (but possible) to select the cells we want from the table in the **IBM SPSS Statistics Viewer**.

■ Double click on the table to activate it.

■ Select the cells in the 'Yes' rows of the table. To do this, select the first cell and click on it to highlight it (the cell will turn black) and then hold down the Ctrl key and left click on each of the cells you would like to include. You should then end up with only the 'Yes' rows highlighted. (You will find that this is sometimes quite tricky as some cells annoyingly become unhighlighted as you are trying to do it – but it can be done!)

■ Right click on the highlighted area and the editing menu pops up.

■ Select **Create Graph** followed by **Bar**.

			Major subject								
		Business	Community Health	Education	M
		Count	Count	Count	C
Health and Counselling Centre	No	46	23	34	
	Yes	13	10	11	
Student Advice Centre	No	39	22	29	
	Yes	20	11	16	
Other student support service	No	55	30	42	
	Yes	4	3	3	

Select Table
Select cells with similar significance
Sort Rows ▶
Create Graph ▶   Bar
Table Properties...   Dot
Cell Properties...   Line
TableLooks...   Area
Insert Footnote   Pie

The following clustered bar chart is produced and displayed in the **IBM SPSS Statistics Viewer**.

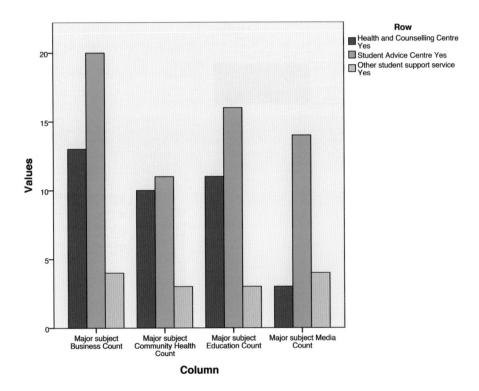

The graph shows that the student advice centre was the most popular service for all student groups. Also, that there was low frequency of media students attending the Health and Counselling Centre compared to the other students in the department. This information might be useful for the course team to follow up in terms of the amount of use of these facilities by the applied studies students compared to other students across the university. It is also intriguing to examine whether the media students are actually more healthy that the other applied studies students or are simply choosing not to visit the Health and Counselling Centre.

✓

The **Create Graph** command also allows you to produce clustered bar charts with three nominal variables. This table shows the breakdown of students who took part in the Sparcote Study, in each demographic sub-group; age group, gender and major subject.

				Major subject			
				Business	Community Health	Education	Media
				Count	Count	Count	Count
Age group	Under 21	Gender	Female	15	5	10	11
			Male	18	2	10	20
	21 and over	Gender	Female	8	17	17	11
			Male	18	9	8	4

Using the same procedure as above the following clustered bar chart is produced.

				Major subject				Select cells with similar significance	
				Business	Community Health	E		Sort Rows ▶	
				Count	Count			Create Graph ▶	Bar
Age group	Under 21	Gender	Female	15	5			Table Properties...	Dot
			Male	18	2			Cell Properties...	Line
	21 and over	Gender	Female	8	17			TableLooks...	Area
			Male	18	9			Insert Footnote	Pie
								Delete Footnotes	

You will notice that once you have lots of variables or subcategories the bar chart may become difficult to interpret unless there are very distinctive findings.

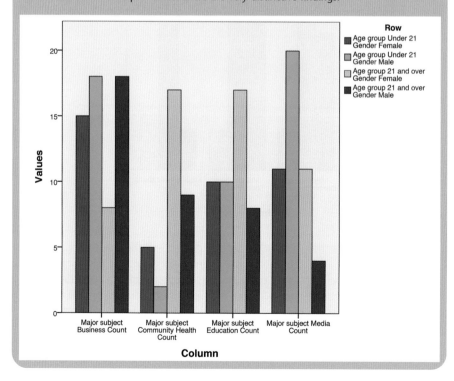

Line graph (combining categorical and scale data)

We can also produce a line graph use the **Create Graph** command. In the Sparcote Study, the researchers would like to produce a plot of the mean number of hours of paid work per week undertaken by the students, broken down by both gender and major subject. Using the **Custom Tables** command, 'Paid work per week' was sent to the **Rows** box and 'Major subject' to the **Columns** box. (The variable in the **Columns** box will be on the **X-axis** of the line graph.) This produces a table of mean hours paid work for each major subject. Now the variable 'Gender' is dragged to the left of 'Paid work per week' in the canvas pane, which produces a row for 'Female' and a row for 'Male' The table comprises two nominal levels of data (major subject and gender) and also one variable with a scale measure for the data (the number of paid hours worked per week). Due to the presence of the scale variable **Custom Tables** presents the summary statistic as mean values. We have changed the number of decimal places to two. The following custom table is produced.

			Major subject			
			Business	Community Health	Education	Media
			Mean	Mean	Mean	Mean
Gender	Female	Paid work per week	12.22	14.55	10.37	10.73
	Male	Paid work per week	11.39	13.55	9.83	8.79

To plot this table graphically with lines representing 'Female' line and a 'Male' line, we do the following:

- Double click on the table to activate it.
- Highlight all of the cells in the table by clicking on the first cell, holding down the left click and dragging the mouse to highlight all the cells.
- Right click anywhere in highlighted area and the editing menu pops up.
- Select **Create Graph** and select **Line**.

SPSS generates the following line graph.

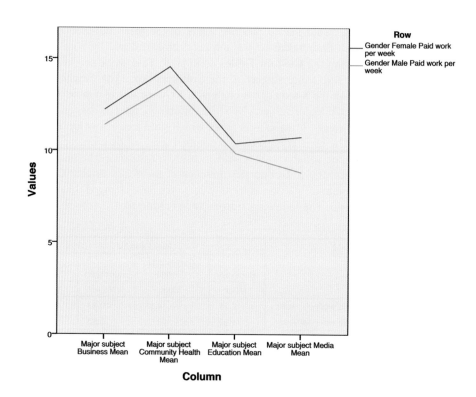

The line graph provides a clear illustration of the data. We can see that there is a similar pattern of paid work between the major subjects for both male and female students with males working less on average than females in every student group. The community health students (both male and female) work the most per week. For students majoring in education, the difference between males and females in the hours that they worked was the smallest, whereas the greatest difference in hours worked between males and females was for the students studying media.

For details on editing graphs and charts, please see Chapter 8

We have shown how to produce a range of graphs using different SPSS commands. However, SPSS allows you to edit graphs as well, such as changing the chart and background colours, the axes or the labels and title. Chapter 8 explains how to edit tables and graphs in SPSS.

Editing tables and graphs for presentation

8

243 EDITING A TABLE
– PIVOT TABLE

268 EDITING A CHART
– CHART EDITOR

303 EXPORTING
TABLES AND
GRAPHS TO
OTHER
APPLICATIONS

Chapter aim: To demonstrate how to edit your tables and graphs to make them look professional and easy to understand

All of the results of your SPSS analysis are stored in the **IBM SPSS Statistics Viewer**. This can be saved as a file to open and edit with SPSS later, with a file type of .spv (such as the SPSS output from the Sparcote Study saved as 'Applied Studies Student Survey.spv'). While this output file contains a record of what you have done in SPSS, it is also the place where you can make changes to the tables and graphs you have produced. The tables and graphs that SPSS generates are often exactly what you want. However, they may not be in the format that is appropriate for your final report. You may wish to change the title and labels of your tables and graphs. The rows and columns of a table might not be the way round that you prefer or you may want to change the look of table, such as changing the style, colours or font. SPSS has flexible editing options and there are a number of different ways in which the editing can be achieved. This chapter explains how to edit tables and charts, and how to export them to other applications such as Microsoft Word.

EDITING A TABLE – PIVOT TABLE

Once you have generated a table, it is displayed in the **IBM SPSS Statistics Viewer**. To make any changes in this viewer to the table, you need to **activate** it, to bring up the editing options. The activated table is sometimes known as a **pivot table**. That is a table that can be manipulated in some way, such as swapping the rows and the columns.

Activation can be achieved in three different ways:

- Double click on the table (with the left mouse button), which will allow you to edit the table in the **IBM SPSS Statistics Viewer**.

activate
Before a table or a chart in the **IBM SPSS Statistics Viewer** can be edited, it has to be activated, by double clicking on it. Right clicking on the table or chart and selecting **Edit Content** from the menu also activates it for editing

pivot table
A pivot table is an advanced form of spreadsheet that allows for more complex operations on the data within the table than simply displaying it in the form of rows and columns, such as producing summaries, totals and other statistics. SPSS has the facility for complex editing of tables in the **IBM SPSS Statistics Viewer** and this editing takes place in the **Pivot Table** window

■ Right click on the table to bring up a right-click menu and select the **Edit Content** command: **Edit Content ▶ In viewer**. This will allow you to edit the table in the **IBM SPSS Statistics Viewer**. (This command achieves the same result as double clicking the table to activate it.)

■ Right click on the table to bring up the menu and select the **Edit Content** command: **Edit Content ▶ In Separate Window**. This option allows you to edit the table in a separate window.

So, essentially, you either edit a table in the **IBM SPSS Statistics Viewer** or **In Separate Window**. We will discuss both of these functions.

Editing a table in the IBM SPSS Statistics Viewer

You can edit your table in the **IBM SPSS Statistics Viewer** by either double clicking on the table or if you right click on the table to produce the following menu, select **Edit Content ▶ In viewer**.

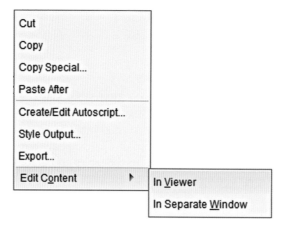

You will notice in both cases that the first row of the table is highlighted in black and there is a dotted line around the table and a red arrow to the left of the table. This shows that the table is activated and you can make changes to it.

Gender * Major subject Crosstabulation						
Statistics **Count**						
			Major subject			
		Business	Community Health	Education	Media	Total
Gender	Female	23	22	27	22	94
	Male	36	11	18	24	89
Total		59	33	45	46	183

Depending on where you right click on the table, a different menu of options will appear.

Right clicking on the highlighted bar brings up the menu shown on the right.

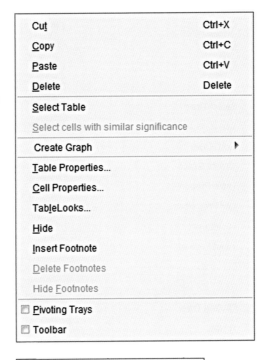

Cut	Ctrl+X
Copy	Ctrl+C
Paste	Ctrl+V
Delete	Delete
Select Table	
Select cells with similar significance	
Create Graph	▶
Table Properties...	
Cell Properties...	
TableLooks...	
Hide	
Insert Footnote	
Delete Footnotes	
Hide Footnotes	
▢ Pivoting Trays	
▢ Toolbar	

Right clicking on a label for a row or a column brings up a more complete menu, allowing you to edit the labels and sort the rows too.

What's This?	
Cut	Ctrl+X
Copy	Ctrl+C
Paste	Ctrl+V
Delete	Delete
Select	▶
Show Dimension Label	
Hide Category	
Show All Categories	
Group	
Ungroup	
Sort Rows	▶
Create Graph	▶
Table Properties...	
Cell Properties...	
TableLooks...	
Insert Footnote	
Delete Footnotes	
Hide Footnotes	
▢ Pivoting Trays	
▢ Toolbar	

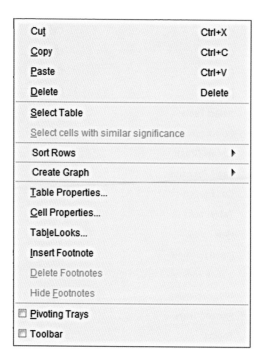

If you right click on a numeric cell in the table it brings up a slightly different menu without the label commands but with the command to sort the rows.

Working with your activated table

See Chapter 5

Once you have activated a table, you can edit any cell entry by double clicking on the cell in the table that you would like to edit and then typing over the content to replace it. In Chapter 5, we produced a frequency table for the Sparcote Study showing the number of students taking each major subject (Question 3), using the **Frequencies** command. We are going to make some changes to the 'activated' frequency table.

Major subject

		Frequency	Percent	Valid Percent	Cumulative Percent
Valid	Business	59	32.2	32.2	32.2
	Community Health	33	18.0	18.0	50.3
	Education	45	24.6	24.6	74.9
	Media	46	25.1	25.1	100.0
	Total	183	100.0	100.0	

The frequency table is headed by the name of the variable – in this case **Major subject**. The table uses the labels **Valid** and **Missing** to group the rows of the table. In this example, there are no missing values so the only 'grouping' label is **Valid** for the rows of the major subjects in this table. The **Frequencies** command does this as it is important to know how many missing values there are in the dataset.

Other commands will put the variable label in place of the word **Valid** in the table (as these other tables are produced with only the valid data).

However, in this case, there are no missing values and the table can be edited before it is presented in a report. We would like to remove the **Valid** label in the left column and head up the column with the major subject category names with the label 'Major subject' (that is, put it in the empty cell in the top left of the table).

There are two ways that we can include the label in the top left column. First, in the activated table, double click on the (empty) first cell of the major subject column (in the left corner – SPSS calls this 'corner text') and you will see that inside of the cell a yellow text box appears.

Major subject

		Frequency	Percent	Valid Percent	Cumulative Percent
Valid	Business	59	32.2	32.2	32.2
	Community Health	33	18.0	18.0	50.3
	Education	45	24.6	24.6	74.9
	Media	46	25.1	25.1	100.0
	Total	183	100.0	100.0	

We can then type in the name of the column 'Major subject' and press return. The cell turns black until you have clicked somewhere else outside of the activated table. The new label is now shown. This is the technique that is used for changing any of the values in a cell in a table. If you want to delete the contents of a cell just click on the cell and remove the data, by pressing the delete key on your keyboard. (You can also right click on a cell to highlight it and bring up the edit menu, selecting **Delete** will delete the contents of the cell – but not remove the cell from the table.)

Major subject

Major subject		Frequency	Percent	Valid Percent	Cumulative Percent
Valid	Business	59	32.2	32.2	32.2
	Community Health	33	18.0	18.0	50.3
	Education	45	24.6	24.6	74.9
	Media	46	25.1	25.1	100.0
	Total	183	100.0	100.0	

A second, alternative method in this frequency table is to:

■ Click on the empty cell where the column title will appear until it goes black and right click.

■ From the menu select **Show Dimension Label**.

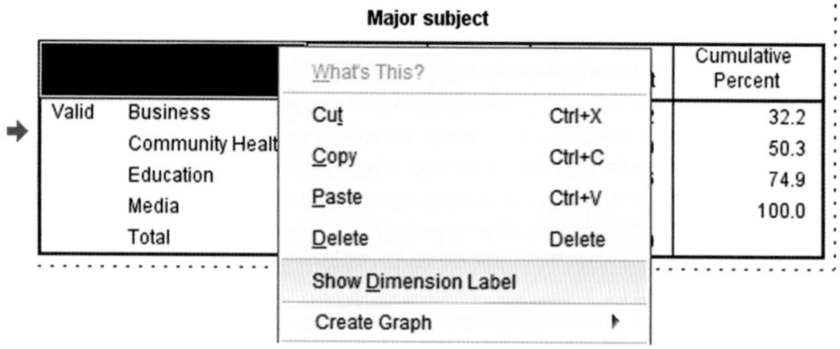

Major subject

		What's This?			Cumulative Percent
Valid	Business	Cut	Ctrl+X		32.2
	Community Healt	Copy	Ctrl+C		50.3
	Education				74.9
	Media	Paste	Ctrl+V		100.0
	Total	Delete	Delete		
		Show Dimension Label			
		Create Graph	▶		

The variable label will now be included as the column heading as previously shown.

In our case, we no longer want the cell with the label **Valid** in it (as all the values in the table are valid). The alignment of the heading of the first column and the category labels could also be neater. To remove the cell with **Valid** in it:

▊ Highlight the cell (and it will turn black).

▊ Right click to bring up the menu and select the **Ungroup** command.

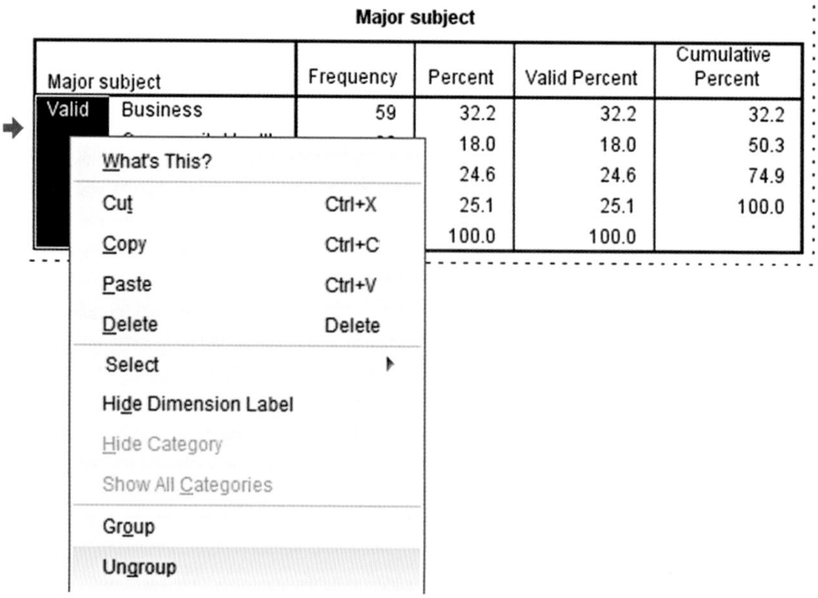

Major subject

Major subject		Frequency	Percent	Valid Percent	Cumulative Percent
Valid	Business	59	32.2	32.2	32.2
	What's This?		18.0	18.0	50.3
			24.6	24.6	74.9
	Cut	Ctrl+X	25.1	25.1	100.0
	Copy	Ctrl+C	100.0	100.0	
	Paste	Ctrl+V			
	Delete	Delete			
	Select	▶			
	Hide Dimension Label				
	Hide Category				
	Show All Categories				
	Group				
	Ungroup				

This 'ungroups' the major subject categories from their group label of **Valid**, which (to translate into English!) simply means it removes the cell with the **Valid** label in it, to produce the following table:

Major subject

Major subject	Frequency	Percent	Valid Percent	Cumulative Percent
Business	59	32.2	32.2	32.2
Community Health	33	18.0	18.0	50.3
Education	45	24.6	24.6	74.9
Media	46	25.1	25.1	100.0
Total	183	100.0	100.0	

The table now includes the left-hand column with the variable label at the top of the column and the category labels aligned below it.

Moving rows in a table

In our table, we can see that the major subjects are arranged in rows by their category numeric codes. (The **Frequencies** command lists them out in numeric code order as we labelled them alphabetically, with 1 = Business and so on.) Business is in the first row, followed by Community Health, Education and Media.

Major subject

Major subject	Frequency	Percent	Valid Percent	Cumulative Percent
Business	59	32.2	32.2	32.2
Community Health	33	18.0	18.0	50.3
Education	45	24.6	24.6	74.9
Media	46	25.1	25.1	100.0
Total	183	100.0	100.0	

Sometimes it is more useful if the rows are in ascending or descending order of frequency. We are going to change the order so that the major subjects are shown in ascending order of frequency (the number of students taking this major). While the table is activated:

▓ Click on the first value in the **Frequencies** column which, in this example, is 59.

▓ Right click and select **Sort Rows ▶** followed by **Ascending**.

Major subject

Major subject	Frequency	Percent	Valid Percent	Cumulative Percent	
Business	59	32.2	32.2	32.2	
Community Health		Cut		Ctrl+X	
Education		Copy		Ctrl+C	
Media		Paste		Ctrl+V	
Total	1	Delete		Delete	

Select Table

Select cells with similar significance

Sort Rows	▶	Ascending
Create Graph	▶	Descending

Table Properties

The rows are now ordered by frequency in ascending order.

Major subject

Major subject	Frequency	Percent	Valid Percent	Cumulative Percent
Community Health	33	18.0	18.0	50.3
Education	45	24.6	24.6	74.9
Media	46	25.1	25.1	100.0
Business	59	32.2	32.2	32.2
Total	183	100.0	100.0	

However, you will notice that the **Cumulative Percent** column no longer makes any sense. You can either alter these amounts manually to reflect your changes or just delete this whole column. As the **Valid Percent** column is the same as the **Percent** column, you might want to delete this column as well. You can highlight the columns (so that they are shown in black) and use the delete key (or right click and select the **Delete** option from the menu).

Major subject

Major subject	Frequency	Percent	Valid Percent	Cumulative Percent
Community Health	33	18.0	18.0	50.3
Education	45	24.6		
Media	46	25.1		
Business	59	32.2		
Total	183	100.0		

Cut	Ctrl+X
Copy	Ctrl+C
Paste	Ctrl+V
Delete	Delete
Select Table	

These columns have now been removed from the table.

Major subject

Major subject	Frequency	Percent
Community Health	33	18.0
Education	45	24.6
Media	46	25.1
Business	59	32.2
Total	183	100.0

This table is now easier to understand than the original table as there are headings for each column and we have removed columns that are not necessarily important to us. However, the percentage of students studying each major doesn't necessarily need to show the decimal places, so these can be altered to zero decimal places.

Changing the decimal places

You can change the decimal places displayed for the numbers in your table. You can either do this for individual cells, a highlighted column or, indeed, for the whole table.

We are going to change the **Percent** column to 0 decimal places.

■ Highlight the values in the **Percent** column, right click and select **Cell Properties** from the menu.

■ In the **Cell Properties** window, select the **Format Value** tab.

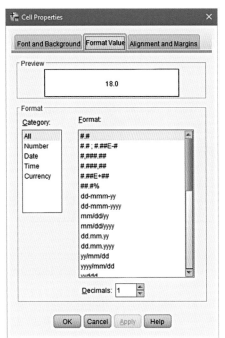 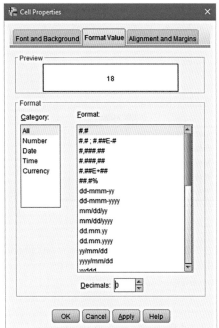

■ Select the number of decimal places that you want by using the arrows in the **Decimals** box or type the number in the box. We have decided not to have any decimal places, so set the value to 0 in the box.

■ Click on **Apply** and **OK**.

Major subject

Major subject	Frequency	Percent
Community Health	33	18
Education	45	25
Media	46	25
Business	59	32
Total	183	100

We can now see that the table has no decimal points for the **Percent** column. From just this simple editing we have changed the original table produced by **Frequencies** in SPSS to a simpler one that we might use in our report. However, there are a variety of other editing options we can use in SPSS.

Adding or changing a title

SPSS includes a title automatically for each table it produces, but it may not necessarily be the title that you want. Different SPSS commands produce different headings. The **Frequencies** command heads up the table with the variable name and **Crosstabs** provides a heading of the name of the crosstabulation. These can be changed by editing, such as in the frequency table we are considering here. We are going to call our table: 'Table 3: Number of students studying each major subject'. Activate the table in the **IBM SPSS Statistics Viewer** and then double click on the current heading to bring up the outline yellow box. Type the new title inside the yellow box.

Table 3 : Number of students studying each major subject		
Community Health	33	18
Education	45	25
Media	46	25
Business	59	32
Total	183	100

Table 3 : Number of students studying each major subject		
Major subject	Frequency	Percent
Community Health	33	18
Education	45	25
Media	46	25
Business	59	32
Total	183	100

The title is automatically centrally aligned. You can change the alignment of the title by selecting **Cell Properties** then, in the **Alignment and Margins** tab, choosing the alignment that you want.

You can see that you quite easily transform your table so that it contains the information you want for your report. As we show below you can also change the style of the table with **TableLooks**.

> ✓
>
> In academic reports, titles for tables are conventionally placed above the table as shown in the example here.

Editing a table in a separate window

> *See Chapter 5*

As well as editing within the **IBM SPSS Statistics Viewer** window, there is an option to edit a table in a separate window. We are going to edit a table that we produced in Chapter 5 using the **Frequencies** command, which showed how many students in the Sparcote Study visited the Health and Counselling Centre (Question 8 item 1 of the survey: Q8_1).

Cut

Copy

Copy Special...

Paste After

Create/Edit Autoscript...

Style Output...

Export...

Edit Content ▶

In Viewer

In Separate Window

■ Right click on the table to bring up the following menu and select **Edit Content**
▶ **In Separate Window**.

The new window is headed **Pivot Table** and then the label of the variable, so, in
this case, that is: **Pivot Table Health and Counselling Centre**.

Some SPSS users find editing in a separate window preferable to editing an activated table in the **IBM SPSS Statistics Viewer** as the editing options are available as drop-down menus from a toolbar at the top of the editing window.

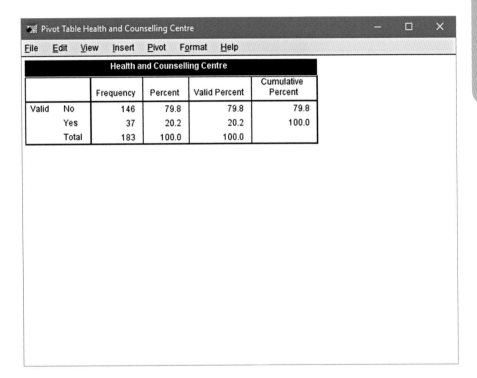

Transposing rows and columns

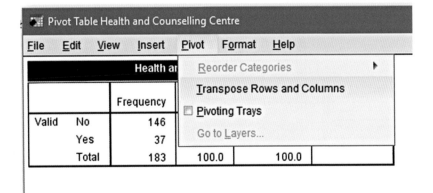

■ To transpose the rows and columns of your table so that the rows and columns swap with each other, click on the **Pivot** drop-down menu and select the **Transpose Rows and Columns** command.

Pivot Table Health and Counselling Centre

File   Edit   View   Insert   Pivot   Format   Help

Health and Counselling Centre

	Valid		
	No	Yes	Total
Frequency	146	37	183
Percent	79.8	20.2	100.0
Valid Percent	79.8	20.2	100.0
Cumulative Percent	79.8	100.0	

You can then see that the different response types are now shown in columns with the frequencies and percent values shown in rows.

Pivoting Trays

Any SPSS table presents statistics in it, in this case the statistics are frequency, percent and cumulative percent shown in the columns therefore the columns in this table are labelled as **Statistics**.

An alternative method of transposing the rows and columns is with the **Pivot** drop-down menu, **Pivoting Trays** command. The **Pivoting Trays** command allows you to change the structure of your table. The variable names are shown in the **ROW**, **COLUMN** and **LAYER** boxes with a 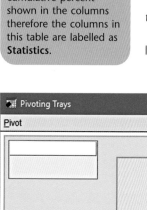 icon. Using the mouse, these icons and variable names can be clicked and dragged to an alternate row, column or layer.

From the original table produced by the **Frequencies** command, we are going to transpose the rows and columns.

■ Drag the 'Health and Counselling Centre' variable to the **COLUMN** box and then drag **Statistics** to the **ROW** box.

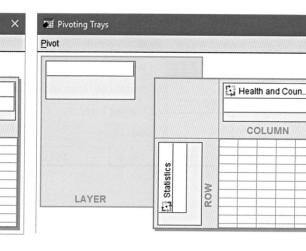

When you close the **Pivoting Trays** window, you will see that the rows and columns have been transposed.

■ Close the **Pivot Table** window and the table shows the responses in columns and the frequencies and percentages in rows.

Health and Counselling Centre

	Valid		
	No	Yes	Total
Frequency	146	37	183
Percent	79.8	20.2	100.0
Valid Percent	79.8	20.2	100.0
Cumulative Percent	79.8	100.0	

✓

The **Pivoting Trays** command is particularly useful for when you have layered crosstabulations. In Chapter 6, we saw the output of a crosstabulation between age group*major subject*gender.

See Chapter 6

Age group * Major subject * Gender Crosstabulation

Count

Gender			Major subject				Total
			Business	Community Health	Education	Media	
Female	Age group	Under 21	15	5	10	11	41
		21 and over	8	17	17	11	53
	Total		23	22	27	22	94
Male	Age group	Under 21	18	2	10	20	50
		21 and over	18	9	8	4	39
	Total		36	11	18	24	89
Total	Age group	Under 21	33	7	20	31	91
		21 and over	26	26	25	15	92
	Total		59	33	45	46	183

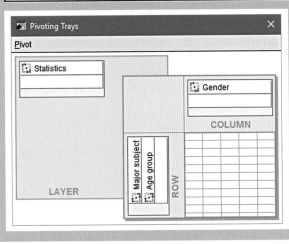

In the **Pivoting Trays** command, if you drag 'Gender' to the **COLUMN** box and 'Major subject' to the **ROW** box, it produces the following output table. (Notice that we have 'Age group' nested within 'Major subject' in the rows, as the 'Major subject' is to the left of 'Age group' in the **ROW** box.)

Age group * Major subject * Gender Crosstabulation

Count

				Gender		
				Female	Male	Total
Major subject	Business	Age group	Under 21	15	18	33
			21 and over	8	18	26
		Total		23	36	59
	Community Health	Age group	Under 21	5	2	7
			21 and over	17	9	26
		Total		22	11	33
	Education	Age group	Under 21	10	10	20
			21 and over	17	8	25
		Total		27	18	45
	Media	Age group	Under 21	11	20	31
			21 and over	11	4	15
		Total		22	24	46
Total		Age group	Under 21	41	50	91
			21 and over	53	39	92
		Total		94	89	183

You need to consider what you are interested in conveying to the reader. This transposed table highlights differences between the females and males at different ages taking the four major subjects.

Rotating the column labels

While in the **Pivot Table** window, you can also amend the direction of the writing of your labels. We will demonstrate this using the 'Health and Counselling Centre' frequency table.

■ Click anywhere on the row for the labels (ours are 'No' and 'Yes') and then select the **Format** drop-down menu and **Rotate Inner Column Labels**.

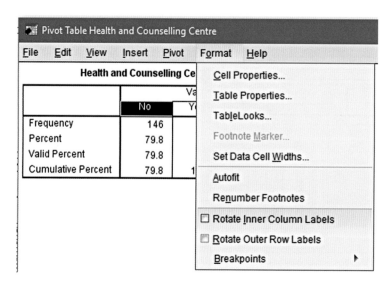

You will notice that your table instantly rotates the column labels.

Health and Counselling Centre

	Valid		
	No	Yes	Total
Frequency	146	37	183
Percent	79.8	20.2	100.0
Valid Percent	79.8	20.2	100.0
Cumulative Percent	79.8	100.0	

■ Close the **Pivot Table** window.

We can now see our column labels have been rotated.

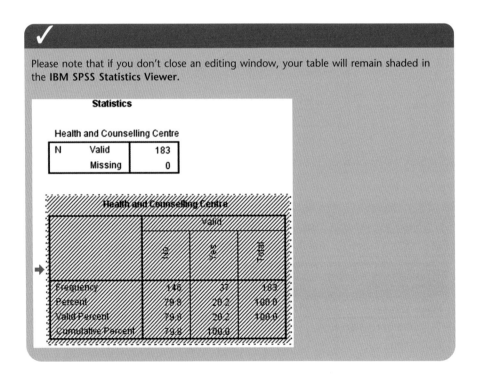

✓

Please note that if you don't close an editing window, your table will remain shaded in the **IBM SPSS Statistics Viewer.**

Changing the style of your table: TableLooks

After you have produced your table you may want to change the style of the table to fit formatting guidelines for your institution, organisation or publication (for example, a number of academic journals follow the American Psychological Association (APA) guidelines). SPSS provides a wide range of table styles in the **TableLooks** command. This command can be accessed, to edit your table, from the right click menu in the **Viewer**, or from the drop-down menu in the **Format** command when editing in the separate pivot table window. In the following section we will demonstrate how to use the **TableLooks** command in a separate pivot table window.

TableLooks: The Academic style

We are going to change the look of the 'Major subject' frequency table from the Sparcote Study that we produced earlier to the **Academic** style using **TableLooks**.

Table 3: Number of students studying each major subject

Major subject	Frequency	Percent
Community Health	33	18
Education	45	25
Media	46	25
Business	59	32
Total	183	100

■ From the **Format** drop-down menu select **TableLooks**.

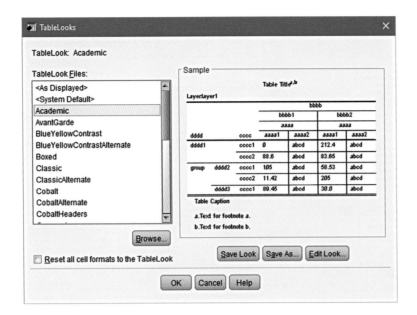

■ We want to change the look of our table and decide to select **Academic** in the **TableLook Files** box.

■ Click **OK**.

The table shown on the right is produced in an academic style:

Table 3: Number of students studying each major subject

Major subject	Frequency	Percent
Community Health	33	18
Education	45	25
Media	46	25
Business	59	32
Total	183	100

Even though you may have chosen a particular table style, you can still edit the various features of the table. We are going to change the text in our table to Times New Roman font at 10 point and remove bold from the title. There are a number of ways that this can be done.

We find it easier to make changes to fonts in a whole table using **Cell Properties** (although you can make the changes using **Cell Formats** in the **Edit Look** option of **TableLooks**). We have made these changes.

Now we are going to change the double horizontal line borders in the table to single lines. This can be done by accessing **Table Properties** (found by right clicking on activated table or in the **Format** option of Pivot Table window):

• In the **Table Properties** window, select the **Borders** tab.

You can change each of the borders to produce the style of border that you would like. As we have selected **Academic** style, this table only has horizontal borders, but no vertical borders. We are changing the horizontal borders from a double line to a single line:

• From the **Border** list, select the frame that you wish to change.
• Select the chosen style of border from the **Style** list.

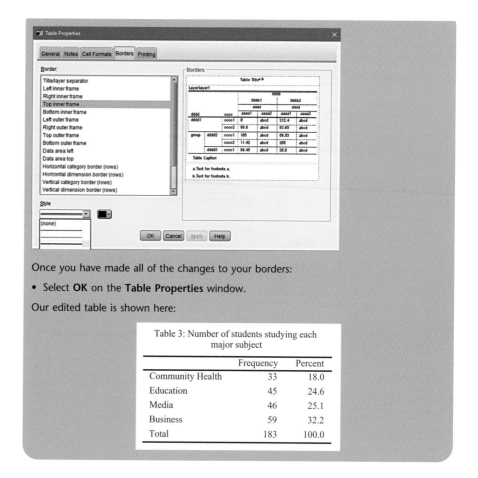

Once you have made all of the changes to your borders:

• Select **OK** on the **Table Properties** window.

Our edited table is shown here:

Table 3: Number of students studying each major subject

	Frequency	Percent
Community Health	33	18.0
Education	45	24.6
Media	46	25.1
Business	59	32.2
Total	183	100.0

TableLooks: The Horizontal style

See Chapter 6

In Chapter 6, we produced a custom table showing how students taking part in the Sparcote Study ranked their lectures, seminars and workshops (Question 4 in the survey).

			Lectures	Seminars	Workshops
			Count	Count	Count
Major subject	Business	First	20	20	19
		Second	21	18	20
		Third	18	21	20
	Community Health	First	2	16	15
		Second	11	12	10
		Third	20	5	8
	Education	First	26	17	2
		Second	15	18	14
		Third	4	10	29
	Media	First	10	6	31
		Second	17	17	12
		Third	19	23	3

This table does not have a title. We are going to add a title and change the style of this table.

- Right click on the table and select the **Edit Content ▶ In Separate Window**.

- From the **Format** drop-down menu select the **TableLooks** command and then the **Horizontal** style.

- To add a title from the **Insert** drop-down menu select the **Title** command and insert the title.

Pivot Table Table 1						

File	Edit	View	Insert	Pivot	Format	Help

		Title		Lectures	Seminars	Workshops
		Caption		Count	Count	Count
Major subject	Busi	**Footnote**	First	20	20	19
			Second	21	18	20
		Row ▶	Third	18	21	20
	Com	Column ▶	First	2	16	15
			Second	11	12	10
			Third	20	5	8
	Education		First	26	17	2
			Second	15	18	14
			Third	4	10	29
	Media		First	10	6	31
			Second	17	17	12
			Third	19	23	3

SPSS automatically enters the word 'Table 1' and so all you need to edit this text to produce your own title. We have called ours: 'Table 4: Student preferences for the different modes of study'.

- Press the return key on the keyboard and your title is positioned at the top of the table.

In this example, we are going to left align the title.

- From the **Format** drop-down menu select **Cell Properties**. In the **Alignment and Margins** tab, choose the alignment for the title that you would like (we have selected left alignment and bottom of the cell for the title position).

- Click **Apply** and **OK** and close the **Pivot Table** window.

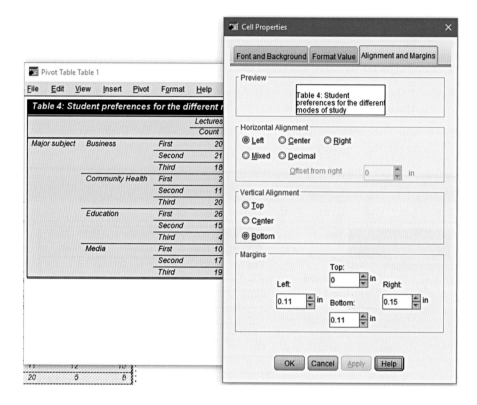

The new table is different to the original table as there are no longer any internal vertical lines and the font is now all in italics with a title of our choice.

Table 4: Student preferences for the different modes of study

			Lectures	Seminars	Workshops
			Count	Count	Count
Major subject	Business	First	20	20	19
		Second	21	18	20
		Third	18	21	20
	Community Health	First	2	16	15
		Second	11	12	10
		Third	20	5	8
	Education	First	26	17	2
		Second	15	18	14
		Third	4	10	29
	Media	First	10	6	31
		Second	17	17	12
		Third	19	23	3

However, we would like to remove the grey background colour.

▤ Double click to activate the table and highlight all the cells with the grey background.

▤ Right click and select **Cell Properties** and **Font and Background**.

▤ Click on the **Background** box, which is coloured grey.

▤ Click on the colour you want on from the palette on the right. The **Background** box changes to this colour. (We have selected white.)

▤ Click **Apply** and **OK**.

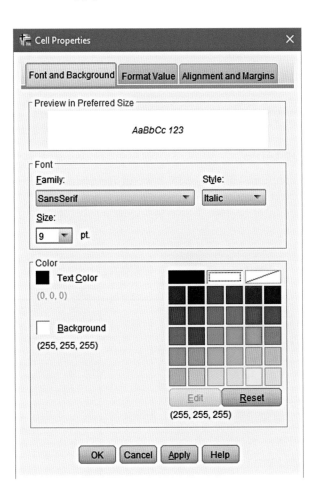

The table is now displayed with the grey background removed.

Table 4: Student preferences for the different modes of study

			Lectures Count	Seminars Count	Workshops Count
Major subject	Business	First	20	20	19
		Second	21	18	20
		Third	18	21	20
	Community Health	First	2	16	15
		Second	11	12	10
		Third	20	5	8
	Education	First	26	17	2
		Second	15	18	14
		Third	4	10	29
	Media	First	10	6	31
		Second	17	17	12
		Third	19	23	3

Adding colour to your table

See Chapter 6

In Chapter 6, we produced a custom table to show how, in the Sparcote Study, students in the four major subjects were satisfied with different aspects of their life (academic, social and personal life) at Sparcote University (Question 12). This table is shown below.

			Very unsatisfied Count	Unsatisfied Count	Neither unsatisfied nor satisfied Count	Satisfied Count	Very satisfied Count
Major subject	Business	Satisfaction with academic life	0	3	16	25	15
		Satisfaction with social life	0	4	16	28	11
		Satisfaction with personal development	0	8	15	23	13
	Community Health	Satisfaction with academic life	0	7	10	10	6
		Satisfaction with social life	1	3	15	8	6
		Satisfaction with personal development	0	4	7	12	10
	Education	Satisfaction with academic life	0	2	16	18	9
		Satisfaction with social life	0	6	12	17	10
		Satisfaction with personal development	0	0	10	24	11
	Media	Satisfaction with academic life	0	5	13	17	11
		Satisfaction with social life	0	2	10	15	19
		Satisfaction with personal development	0	15	11	8	12

We would like to edit the table so that it is easier to see the difference between the categories more clearly by adding colours to the background.

■ Right click on the table and select the **Edit Content** command: **Edit Content ▶ In Separate Window**.

■ Highlight the area that you would like to change the background colour. We have selected the whole table.

■ Select the **Format** drop-down menu and select **Cell Properties**.

■ Put the cursor in the **Background** box and select the new colour by clicking on it in the palette.

■ Click on **Apply** and **OK**.

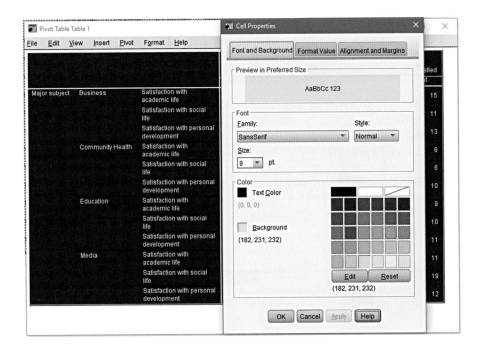

The table now looks like this.

Major subject			Very unsatisfied Count	Unsatisfied Count	Neither unsatisfied nor satisfied Count	Satisfied Count	Very satisfied Count
Major subject	Business	Satisfaction with academic life	0	3	16	25	15
		Satisfaction with social life	0	4	16	28	11
		Satisfaction with personal development	0	8	15	23	13
	Community Health	Satisfaction with academic life	0	7	10	10	6
		Satisfaction with social life	1	3	15	8	6
		Satisfaction with personal development	0	4	7	12	10
	Education	Satisfaction with academic life	0	2	16	18	9
		Satisfaction with social life	0	6	12	17	10
		Satisfaction with personal development	0	0	10	24	11
	Media	Satisfaction with academic life	0	5	13	17	11
		Satisfaction with social life	0	2	10	15	19
		Satisfaction with personal development	0	15	11	8	12

Next, highlight the rows that you want to change to a new background colour. We are going to change the 'Satisfaction with academic life' rows to light purple. We can either make this change one row at a time or (using the Ctrl key) select the four 'Satisfaction with academic life' rows.

- ▦ Select the **Format** drop-down menu and select **Cell Properties**. (In this window, you can change the colour of the text or the colour of the background.)

- ▦ Put your cursor in the **Background** box and change the colour.

- ▦ Click on **Apply** and **OK**.

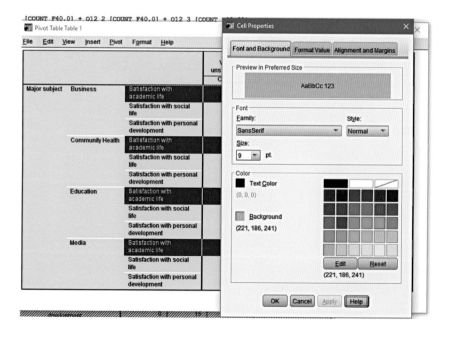

The table now includes the 'Satisfaction with academic life' rows in a light purple colour.

			Very unsatisfied	Unsatisfied	Neither unsatisfied nor satisfied	Satisfied	Very satisfied
			Count	Count	Count	Count	Count
Major subject	Business	Satisfaction with academic life	0	3	16	25	15
		Satisfaction with social life	0	4	16	28	11
		Satisfaction with personal development	0	8	15	23	13
	Community Health	Satisfaction with academic life	0	7	10	10	6
		Satisfaction with social life	1	3	15	8	6
		Satisfaction with personal development	0	4	7	12	10
	Education	Satisfaction with academic life	0	2	16	18	9
		Satisfaction with social life	0	6	12	17	10
		Satisfaction with personal development	0	0	10	24	11
	Media	Satisfaction with academic life	0	5	13	17	11
		Satisfaction with social life	0	2	10	15	19
		Satisfaction with personal development	0	15	11	8	12

We follow the same procedure to change the 'Satisfaction with social life' rows to light green and the 'Satisfaction with personal life' to light yellow. This produces the following coloured table.

			Very unsatisfied	Unsatisfied	Neither unsatisfied nor satisfied	Satisfied	Very satisfied
			Count	Count	Count	Count	Count
Major subject	Business	Satisfaction with academic life	0	3	16	25	15
		Satisfaction with social life	0	4	16	28	11
		Satisfaction with personal development	0	8	15	23	13
	Community Health	Satisfaction with academic life	0	7	10	10	6
		Satisfaction with social life	1	3	15	8	6
		Satisfaction with personal development	0	4	7	12	10
	Education	Satisfaction with academic life	0	2	16	18	9
		Satisfaction with social life	0	6	12	17	10
		Satisfaction with personal development	0	0	10	24	11
	Media	Satisfaction with academic life	0	5	13	17	11
		Satisfaction with social life	0	2	10	15	19
		Satisfaction with personal development	0	15	11	8	12

When there a lot of rows in a large table, alternating colours can help the reader pick out which row a cell belongs to. In this table, we have three different types of row (the three satisfaction measures), so colouring them in different backgrounds makes it easier for the reader to compare the same satisfaction item for the four major subjects, for example, the purple rows all show the results for 'Satisfaction with academic life'.

EDITING A CHART – CHART EDITOR

Editing a chart or a graph, like editing a table, is fairly straightforward. Just like editing tables, a graph or chart needs to be 'activated' before you can work on it to make the changes that you want. If you hover the mouse over a chart in the **IBM SPSS Statistics Viewer**, a yellow box appears with the words **Double-click to activate** in it, as in this example chart.

If you right click on some text output (such as the information SPSS lists in the **IBM SPSS Viewer** file, or a heading) and choose **Edit Content ▶ In Separate Window** then the new window is headed **Text Output**, and you can edit the text. If you do this with a graph, the new window is called **Chart Editor** and you have a wide variety of options to edit the graph, as explained below.

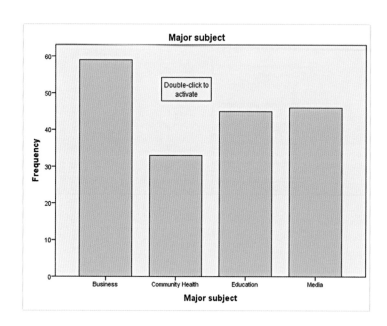

Alternatively, right click on the chart and select the **Edit Content ▶** followed by **In Separate Window** will activate the chart.

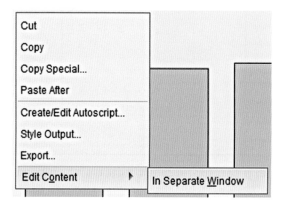

In both cases, the **Chart Editor** window appears.

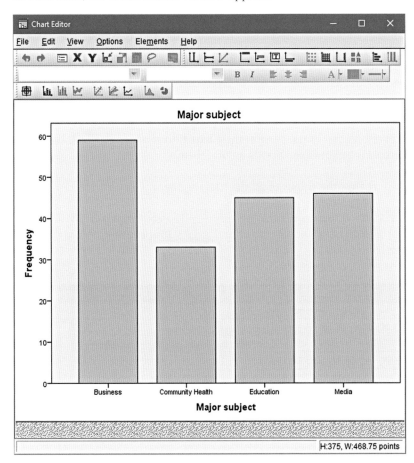

The **Chart Editor** window (similar to the **Pivot Table** window for a table) presents a range of drop-down menus with options to enable you to manipulate your chart, such as adding a title to the chart or changing the axes. Alternatively, if you right click on an element of a chart, the options appear as a menu, which provides a list of the available editing features. This menu will be slightly different dependent on where you right click on the chart.

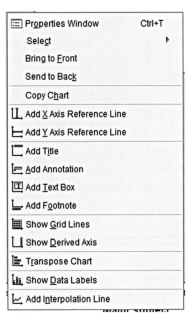

Changing colours in a chart

When SPSS produces a basic frequency bar chart, you will notice that all of the bars are the same tan colour. A clustered bar chart created with **Crosstabs**, or a pie chart created by the **Frequencies** command, are presented more colourfully. Changing the colour of your chart can potentially enhance the presentation of your data. Here, we explain how to change the colours of a bar chart.

■ Activate the **Chart Editor**.

■ Click once on a bar of the chart in the **Chart Editor** window, which highlights all the bars (a yellow line appears around them).

First, we will change the colour of all the bars together.

■ Right click to bring up the editing menu and select **Properties Window** (or select the **Edit** drop-down menu and select **Properties**) to bring up the **Properties** window.

Just as right clicking on a chart will bring up a slightly different editing menu depending on where in the chart you click, the options available in the **Properties** window will depend on what you have selected to edit. In some cases, the **Properties** window will have only three tabs but at other times it will have six.

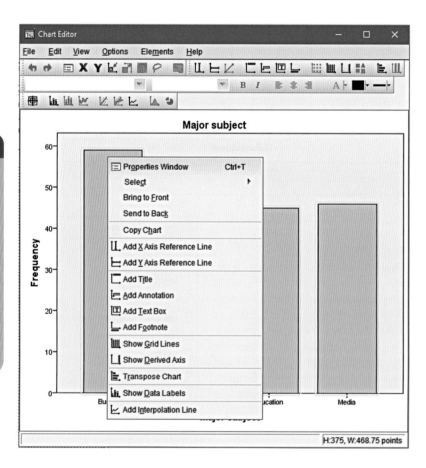

- Select the **Fill & Border** tab in the **Properties** window. You can now choose a colour from the palette for your bars.

- Click on the **Color** box next to **Fill**, to indicate that you wish to change the colour of the bar.

- Select the colour for the bars by clicking on a colour choice from the palette on the right – we have chosen green. (Double click on any colour to bring up the full palette to choose from.)

- Click **Apply**.

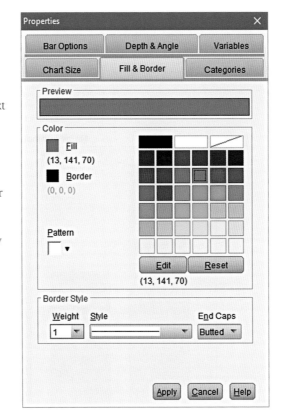

The following change to the chart has now been made.

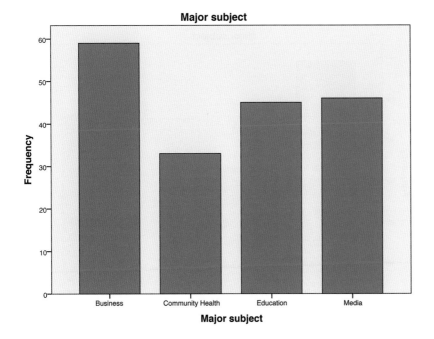

We can change each individual bar in a bar chart to a different colour as well. To do this, in **Chart Editor**, we click once to highlight all the bars, but if we click a second time on a bar it highlights just that one bar (shown by the yellow outline) so that you can change the colour of only that bar. Using the same procedure as described above we can change the colour of the first bar in the bar chart to blue, as shown below.

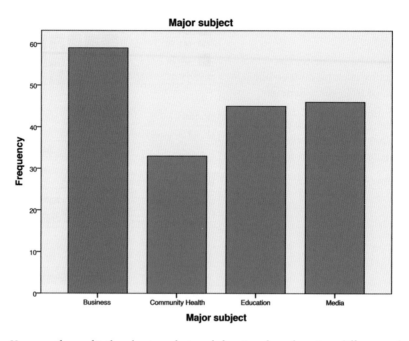

You can then edit the chart so that each bar in a bar chart is a different colour. For example:

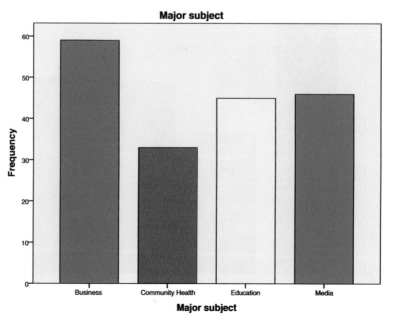

The background colour used by default in SPSS is not to everyone's choice. You can change the colour of the background of your charts as described below. Also, you can use colour in a number of different ways to emphasise aspects of your charts. For example, you may wish to use changes in colour to show a graded sequence, as in an ordinal scale such as a Likert scale. We are going to illustrate this using an example from the Sparcote Study. Question 10 asked the students about their use of the sports and fitness centre, with the five choices ranging from 'Never' to 'Often'. When we select a bar chart in the **Frequencies** command for this variable (described in Chapter 5) we produce the following chart in SPSS.

See Chapter 5

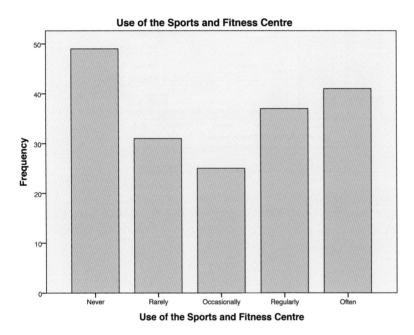

We are first going to change the background colour.

■ Activate the chart (by double clicking on it) to bring up the **Chart Editor** window.

■ Place the mouse on the background of your chart. Right click to bring up the editing menu.

■ Select the **Properties Window**.

■ In the **Properties** window, click on the **Fill** box and then select the colour from the palette and click on the chosen colour – we have chosen light yellow. The colour choice appears in the **Preview** box as well as the **Fill** box.

■ Click **Apply**.

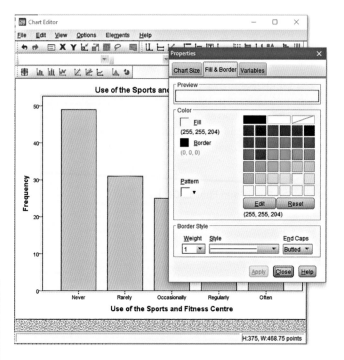

Following the procedure described above, we change the colour of each of the bars in the bar chart. However, this time we decide to use dark green for 'Often' and change the shades of green as the attendance at the sports and fitness centre goes down, with the lightest green bar being the 'Never' category. The edited chart is now shown below.

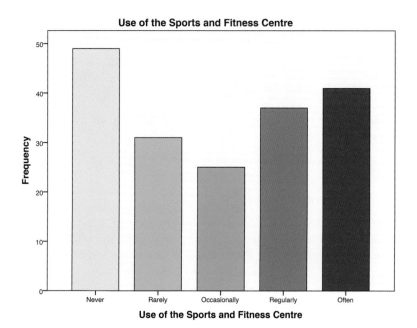

When changing the colour of graphs, it is a good idea to make sure that the colours serve a illustrative purpose. There are occasions when a researcher wants to group certain categories together but not combine their results. For example, on a five-point scale of 'strongly disagree' to 'strong agree', the central (neutral) position may be given a neutral colour, and the two 'agree' categories given the same colour (such as green to indicate a 'positive' response) and the two 'disagree' colours the same colour (such as red to indicate a 'negative' response), as in the example below, from the Sparcote Study. The results from Question 5 (asking the students whether they agree that the learning resources are appropriate to support their course) are shown on a bar chart created by using the **Frequencies** command (see Chapter 5). However, here the bars have been edited to colour code the two 'disagree' categories in red and the two 'agree' categories in green.

See Chapter 5

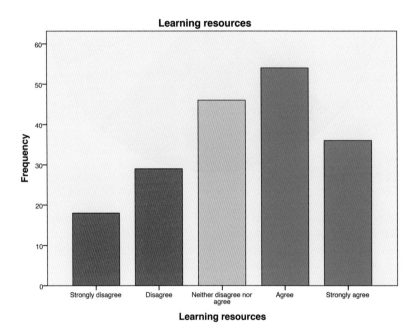

The reader of the chart can easily compare the results in terms of how many student disagree with the statement that the learning resources are appropriate for their course (coloured red) and those who agree that the learning resources are appropriate for their course (green).

Separating the slices of a pie chart

The **Chart Editor** window provides a range of options to make changes to the structure of the charts produced with the SPSS commands. In Chapter 5, we introduced you to the example of a group of 76 10-year-old children who were asked to select their favourite future occupation from a list of six different choices: doctor, scientist, teacher, vet, athlete, and musician. We showed there how to use the **Frequencies** command to produce a pie chart for these data. We have reproduced that pie chart here.

See Chapter 5

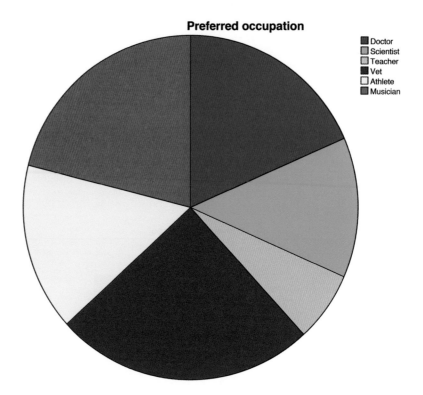

For details on creating a
pie chart, see Chapters 5
and 7

If there is a particular category that is of importance in a set of data, then only
this slice can be exploded to emphasise it against the others. For example, if the
study on the children was specifically concerned with the question of how many
children of this age wanted to be scientists then only the 'Scientist' slice might be
exploded from the pie chart.

■ In the **Chart Editor** window, click on the slices to highlight them. A single click
  highlights all the slices with a yellow outline. A second click on a slice highlights
  just that one slice. We click twice on the green slice for the 'Scientist' category.

■ Click on the **Explode Slice** icon 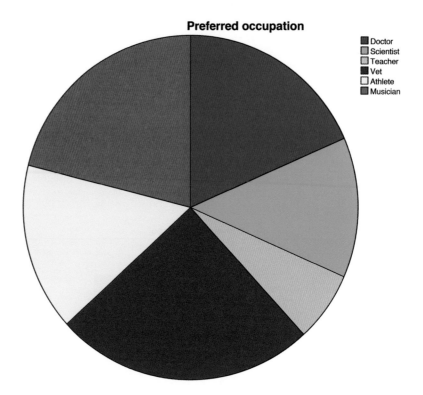 – the ninth icon on the bottom toolbar.
  (You can also select **Explode Slice** from the **Elements** drop-down menu and
  right clicking on the slice and selecting **Explode Slice** from the menu.)

■ Close the **Chart Editor** window.

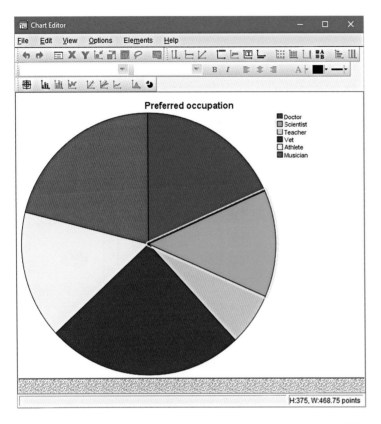

The following edited pie chart is now displayed in the **IBM SPSS Statistics Viewer** with the slice of the pie separated.

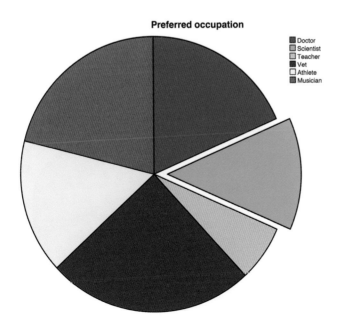

You may decide that you also want to show the value of the slices on the pie chart. You can do this by clicking the **Show Data Labels** icon – explained below.

Creating a 3-D pie chart

You can also change a pie chart to a three-dimensional chart instead of the usual two-dimensional chart.

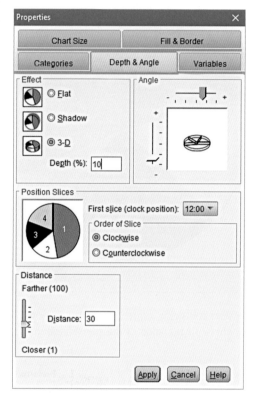

- In the **Chart Editor** window, either select the **Edit** drop-down menu followed by **Properties**, or right click on the chart and select the **Properties Window** from the editing menu.

- Click on the **Depth & Angle** tab in the **Properties** window and select the **3-D** radio button.

- If you want to increase the depth of your slices, the **Depth** is shown as a percentage of the inner frame. We have changed the depth value from the default 5% to 10%. Click on **Apply**.

- Close the **Properties** and **Chart Editor** windows.

The transformed pie chart is shown below.

✓

SPSS automatically starts the first slice at the 12 o'clock position in a pie chart. You can change the position of a slice in the **Depth & Angle** tab (but it is good practice to start at 12 o'clock).

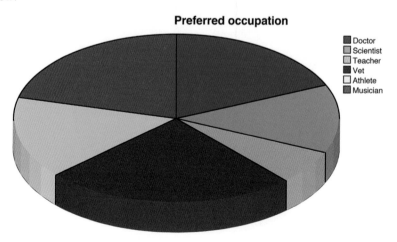

Preferred occupation

- ■ Doctor
- ■ Scientist
- □ Teacher
- ■ Vet
- □ Athlete
- ■ Musician

However, while it might look interesting (to show a chart in 3-D), it is more difficult to see exactly how many children have selected each occupation. Therefore we would advise that you add in frequencies or percentage values. It may also not be a wise choice to present the pie chart in 3-D if it adds nothing to the clarity of the chart for the reader.

Changing the order of the slices in a pie chart

SPSS allows you to choose the order of the slides in a pie chart. We are now going to change the order of the slices by size of slice.

■ Select the **Categories** tab in the **Properties** window. Notice that you can manually move the categories around to create any order. However, we have decided to set **Sort by** to **Statistic** (which, in this case, is frequencies) and **Direction** to descending. We have chosen descending as it is often relevant to the research question to have the largest frequencies first (as these are often the most important).

■ Click on **Apply** and close the windows.

We have sorted slices of the 2-D pie chart so that it now shows the preferences of occupation in descending order.

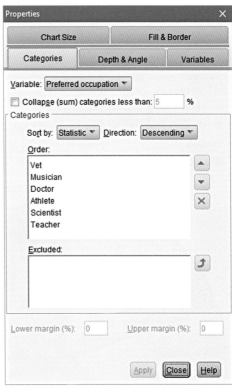

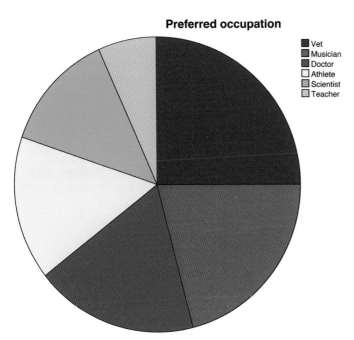

Preferred occupation

- Vet
- Musician
- Doctor
- Athlete
- Scientist
- Teacher

✓

In the **Frequencies** command (described in Chapter 5), you can use the **Format** option to order categories in your results. In the **Format** option, if you select **Order by** as **Descending counts** you will produce the same pie chart as shown here.

Adding data labels to a chart, to display the category counts

We can add data labels (such has the frequency or percentage) to each slice of the pie chart (or to the bars of a bar chart, or to any other chart).

■   Click on the pie chart in the **Chart Editor** window and then select the **Show Data Labels** icon from the toolbar. (Alternatively select the **Elements** drop-down menu and select **Show Data Labels**.)

The frequency counts will then be shown on the pie chart.

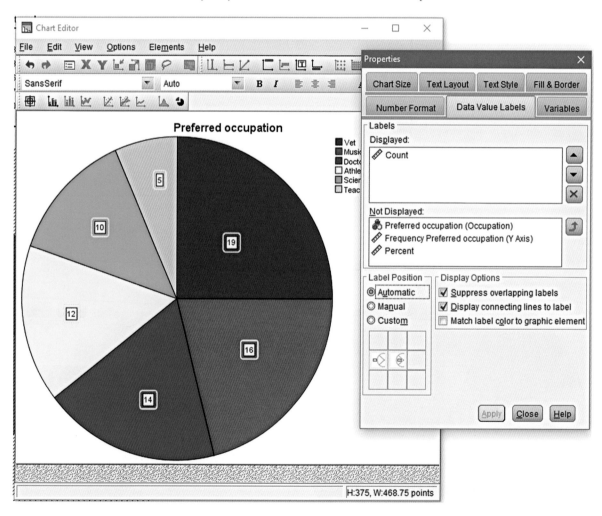

Close the **Chart Editor** to see your amended pie chart.

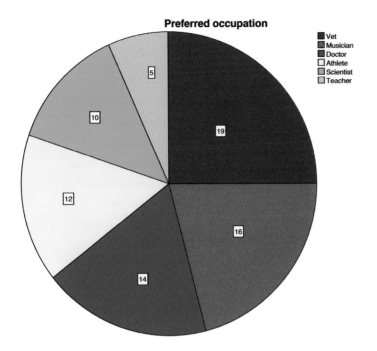

Adding data labels to a chart to show the category percentages

This time we are going to display the percentages on the chart rather than the frequencies.

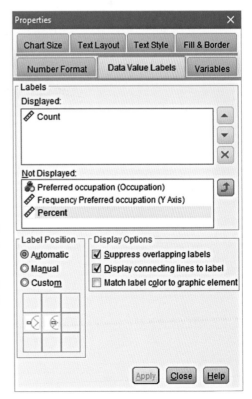

■ First, we make sure that the data labels icon is clicked.

■ We open the **Properties** window in **Chart Editor**. (The **Properties** window now has the **Data Value Labels** tab.)

■ Click in the **Data Value Labels** tab.

■ Click on **Percent** in the **Not Displayed** box and click in the green arrow to the right of the box. This sends **Percent** to the **Displayed** box.

■ Now click on **Count** in the **Displayed** box and click on the the red cross (✗) to the right of the box to remove the counts from the chart.

■ Click **Apply**. Now only percentages will be displayed.

■ Finally, we have chosen to round the results to the nearest percentage. Click on the **Number Format** tab and change **Decimal Places** to 0.

■ Click **Apply**, and close the **Chart Editor** window.

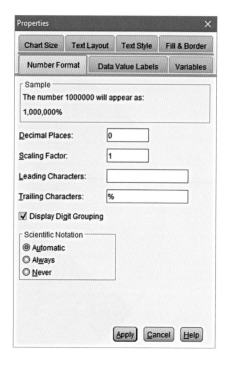

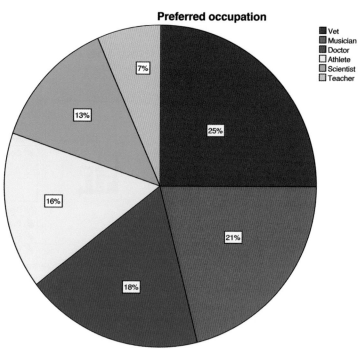

Now we can see that the pie chart has the percentage value displayed on each of the slices so, for example, we can see that 25% of the children wanted to be a veterinarian and only 13% a scientist.

Changing the type of chart

SPSS allows you to change the type of chart using **Chart Editor**. It has the option to switch to specific alternative charts (depending on the level of the data). However, it can be a useful option if, say, you had a number of pie charts that you wished to convert to bar charts. This is the example (from a pie chart to a bar chart) that we will demonstrate here with the children's preferred occupation ordered pie chart.

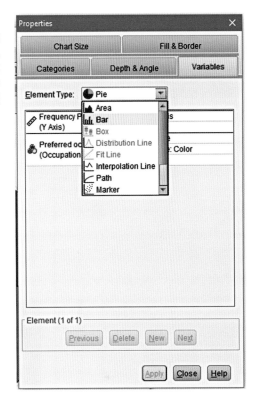

- ▦ Open up the **Properties** window and select the **Variables** tab.

- ▦ From the **Element Type** drop-down menu select **Bar**.

- ▦ Click **Apply** and close **Chart Editor**.

The pie chart of the children's occupation choices has now been converted into the following bar chart.

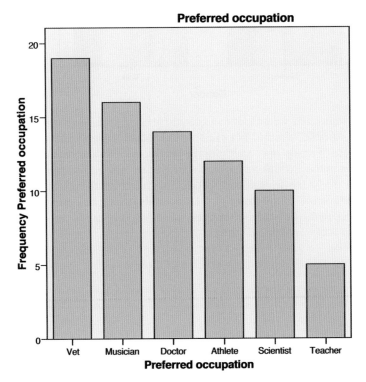

Remember that we ordered the pie chart by frequency, so the bar chart is also ordered by frequency. We can add the data labels to a bar chart in exactly the same way as we described with a pie chart.

Changing the clusters in a clustered bar chart

See Chapter 6

In Chapter 6, we showed an example from the Sparcote Study of a crosstabulation of gender by major subject. We also clicked on the box in the **Crosstabs** dialog box to produce a clustered bar chart. The following chart was displayed.

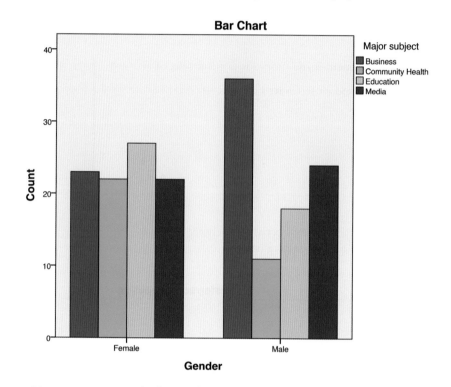

Now, sometimes we look at a clustered bar chart and see that the clustering is not on the variable we want. For example, the 'Major subject' bars are clustered on 'Gender' here ('Female' and 'Male' are the labels on the X axis as 'Gender' was sent to the **Rows** in the crosstabulation). Imagine that we wanted the categories of 'Major subject' on the X axis instead and 'Gender' to cluster on them. One solution is to send 'Major subject' to the **Rows** in the **Crosstabs** dialog box rather than 'Gender' (and 'Gender' to the **Columns**). However, we will show how you can edit the original bar chart to achieve the same solution.

For details of how to produce a clustered bar chart, see Chapters 6 and 7

■ Open the **Properties** window in **Chart Editor** and select the **Variables** tab.

■ Change the menu choice next to 'Gender' from **X Axis** to **X Cluster**. Notice that SPSS automatically changes 'Major subject' from **X Cluster** to **X Axis**. (If not, we change it to this.)

■ Click **Apply** and close the **Chart Editor**.

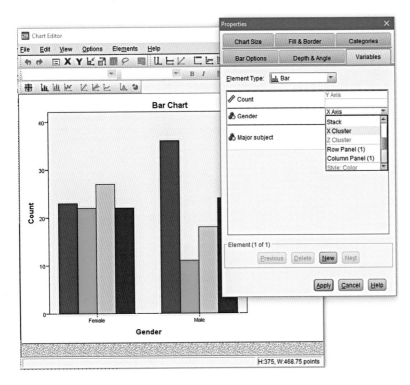

Now the bar chart shows four clusters for the major subjects and not two clusters for the gender categories.

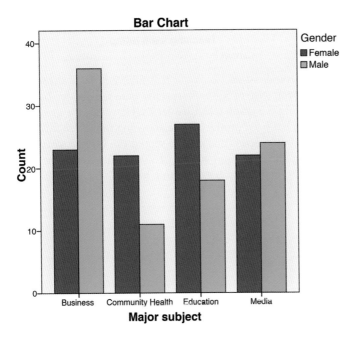

Changing the range of values on an axis on a graph

SPSS will automatically select the range of the values on the axis of a graph. For example using **Chart Builder**, SPSS produced the following scatterplot for 'Overall satisfaction' and 'Teaching team rating' from the Sparcote Study (produced in Chapter 7).

See Chapter 7

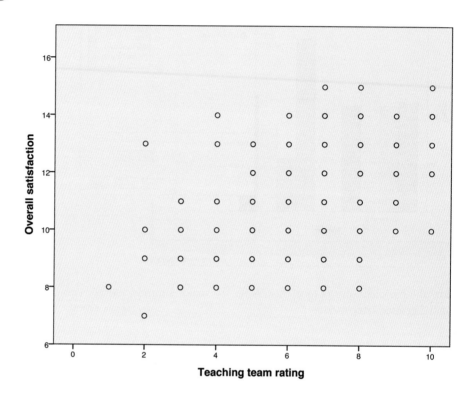

As the lowest 'Overall satisfaction' value is 7, SPSS automatically set the minimum of the Y axis at 6. If you wish SPSS to use specific values, these can be input in **Chart Builder** when creating the graph (see Chapter 7). However, the graph can be edited to alter them after it has been produced. We are going to replace this minimum with 3 as this is the minimum score that can be scored on 'Overall satisfaction'. We are also going to change the maximum value to 15. We will also set the 'Teaching team rating' to a minimum of 1 and a maximum of 15.

See Chapter 7

■ Right click on the label on the Y axis ('Overall satisfaction') to open up the **Properties** window.

■ In the **Minimum** row, unclick the **Auto** box and put 3 in the **Custom** box.

■ In the **Maximum** row, unclick the **Auto** box and put 15 in the **Custom** box.

■ Click **Apply** then **Close**.

■ Close the **Chart Editor**.

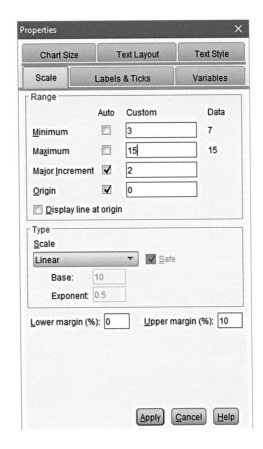

We now have the following scatterplot displayed.

SPSS sets the axis increments and labels automatically, but these can also be changed in **Chart Editor**, if you wish to do so.

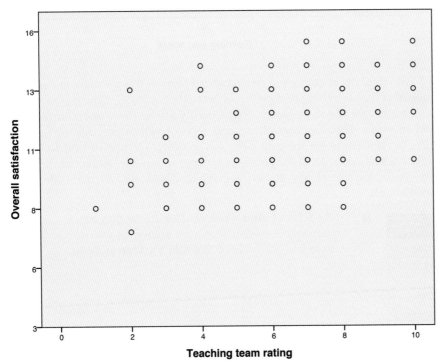

Adding a line of best fit on a scatterplot

See Chapter 7

In Chapter 7, we used the example of children's reading scores and their mathematics scores to see whether there was a relationship between them by displaying the results on a scatterplot. We saw that the points on the scatterplot all lay within a narrow band in the graph, which appeared to follow a straight line – indicating a linear relationship.

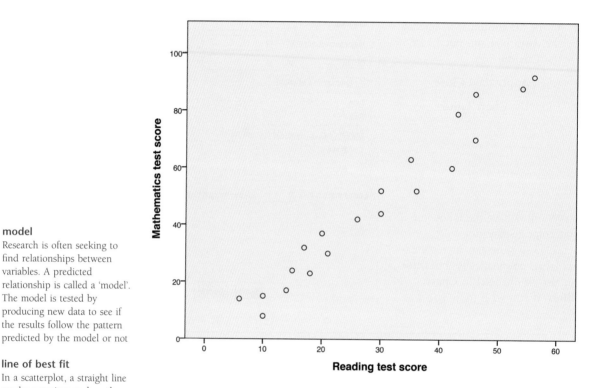

model

Research is often seeking to find relationships between variables. A predicted relationship is called a 'model'. The model is tested by producing new data to see if the results follow the pattern predicted by the model or not

line of best fit

In a scatterplot, a straight line can be superimposed on the points, where this line has been mathematically calculated to be the 'best fit' or closer to the data points than any other straight line. This is also called the linear regression. See also **regression**

With this type of example, a researcher can propose that a straight line provides a **model** of the underlying relationship between the variables. Using this model it is assumed that the reason the points do not exactly line on this straight line is due to random errors. The researcher often wants to know which particular straight line offers the best model for the data. SPSS can work out the **line of best fit**, that is, the line that is closest to all the points (or to put it technically, minimises the error). SPSS places the line of best fit on the graph and also provides the mathematical formula for it.

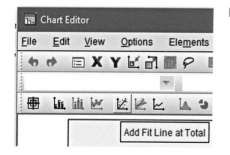

■ In the **Chart Editor** window, click on the fifth icon on the bottom toolbar showing a scatterplot with a straight line on it. This is the **Add Fit Line at Total** icon.

■ The **Properties** window opens automatically and the **Fit Line** tab is automatically selected. The **Fit Method** is also automatically set to **Linear**. These default options are correct ones for a 'best fit' straight line.

■ Click **Close**.

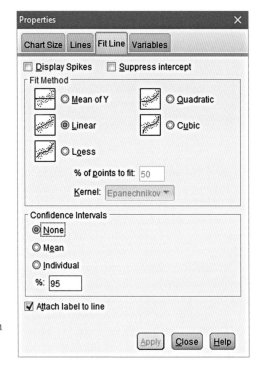

The line of best fit then appears on the plot.

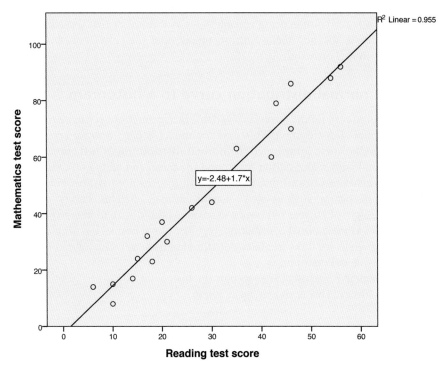

We can see, in this case, that all the points on the graph lie very close to this straight line, telling us that a straight line is a good model of the data.

regression
If two variables are related in some way (for instance, they are *correlated*) then this relationship can be used to predict the values of one variable from the values of the other. This prediction, or regression, of one variable by another is usually expressed as a mathematical formula. If the relationship between the variables is linear, then the regression is a linear regression

See Chapter 9

For details on correlations and statistical tests, see Chapter 9

We are taught at school that the mathematical formula for a straight line can be expressed as $Y = a + bX$, where 'a' is the point where the line crosses the Y axis (at $X = 0$) and 'b' is the slope of the line. SPSS provides the formula for the best fit straight line, also called the regression line. This allows the researcher to use the formula to predict a child's mathematics score from their reading score. Using this straight line model for the data predicts a mathematics score to be $-2.48 + (1.7 \times \text{reading score})$.

To see if this linear model is a good predictor of the relationship between the variables (or is simply a chance effect), a statistical test called a correlation can be conducted (discussed in Chapter 9).

As a scatterplot examines the co-relationship (or correlation) between two variables, it does not matter which variable is chosen for the X axis or the Y axis. However, it is common practice (and useful when you are working out a linear model to predict the effect of one variable on another – called a regression) to put the variable you are *predicting from* on the X axis (also called the independent variable) and the variable you are *predicting to* on the Y axis (also called the dependent variable). In the case of the Sparcote Study, the question is the possible effect of 'Teaching team rating' on 'Overall Satisfaction'. That is why 'Teacher team rating' was put on the X axis and 'Overall satisfaction' on the Y axis. (We should always remember that correlations do not show causation, so if any correlation is found in a study, it requires further research to decide on the specific reason it has arisen. It could be that variable X is really influencing variable Y, or vice versa, or that something else, a third variable is affecting them both or, finally, that the correlation is simply a chance effect in this one study.)

Adding a normal distribution curve to a histogram

normal distribution
A bell-shaped frequency distribution that appears to underlie many human variables. The normal distribution can be worked out mathematically using the mean and standard deviation

See Chapter 7

A histogram produced for the results of a variable in a research study can be compared to a specific model distribution. This time the model is not linear (a straight line) but a very specific curved line called the **normal distribution** or bell curve – like a symmetrical hill with scores clustering around the mean and tailing off to the sides. Many human characteristics are distributed according to the normal distribution when plotted on a histogram, such as men's heights, women's heights, babies' gestation periods, the weight of 10-year-old boys and so on. As this distribution is so common, it is referred to as the 'normal distribution'. We can plot a normal distribution curve on to a histogram to see if the frequency distribution from our data follows the same pattern as this model distribution.

From Chapter 7, we used SPSS to plot the histogram of patients' waiting times in a doctor's survey. This is shown again below.

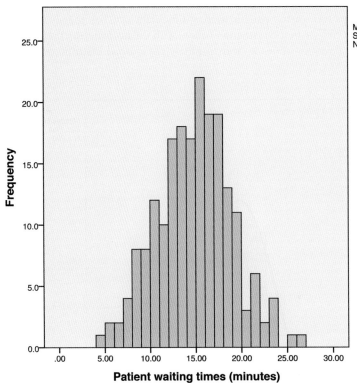

We activate the chart by double clicking on it to bring up the **Chart Editor** window.

■ In the **Chart Editor** window, we select the eighth icon on the bottom toolbar – **Show Distribution Curve**.

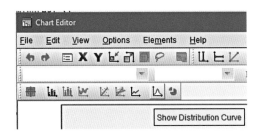

■ The **Properties** window appears showing the **Distribution Curve** tab selected. **Curves** is already selected as **Normal** by default, so we only need to click on **Close** and close the **Chart Editor**.

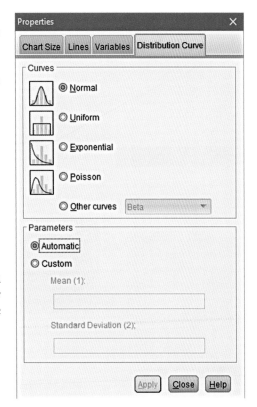

Now the normal distribution curve is superimposed on the histogram to show how closely the pattern of the patient waiting time data matches the shape of the bell curve. As you can see in the histogram below, with the normal distribution curve added, the patient waiting times appear to follow the normal distribution pattern quite closely.

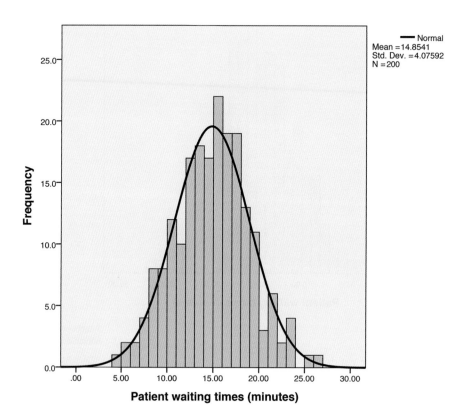

This bell-shaped distribution is typical of many continuous, interval scale variables, particularly when measuring human characteristics as noted above. This distribution is also important for statistical inference tests (explained in Chapter 9), many of which assume that the data is normally distributed within the population.

See Chapter 9

✓

We can ask SPSS to plot a normal distribution curve onto any histogram to show how close to the normal distribution it is, in a number of commands in SPSS. In the **Frequencies command**, and in the **Chart Builder** command, when choosing a histogram, a box can be ticked to show the normal distribution as well.

Creating special charts using Chart Editor

SPSS has such a range of editing features that it is not possible to describe them all in a book of this size. However, to give you a flavour of the variety of charts you can create, we are going to demonstrate with one example the sort of changes that can be made to a basic chart with the editing facilities of SPSS. You always have to bear in mind when creating charts that their key point is to illustrate your findings to a reader. Usually, the more complex the graph, the more difficult it is to understand and the less effective it is as a way of communicating information. Clear and simple charts are often the best way to present data visually. Adding a range of features to a chart, simply for the sake of it, such as garish colours and complex images, can simply irritate and confuse the reader. However, if by editing a chart, it makes the information easier to appreciate then it is worth considering how this can be achieved. Rather than being a question of knowing about SPSS, it is often more about chart design – essentially what looks good and communicates the information well. Usually this means looking at the charts and graphs that other researchers in your field produce and deciding which ones are most effective.

To demonstrate the various editing features of SPSS, we are going to start with a basic clustered bar chart showing the results of the three satisfaction scales from the Sparcote Study (Question 12). We are then going to edit this chart so that it becomes three horizontal bar stacked bar charts showing the percentage of students choosing each category for the three satisfaction scales. It is up to you to decide if you prefer the clustered bar chart or the horizontal stacked bar chart. Hopefully, it will get you thinking about what makes a good chart to communicate research findings – and also demonstrate the capability of the SPSS editing features.

A multiple horizontal stacked bar chart of percentages for three Likert scales

In this example, we will create a chart for Question 12 of the Sparcote Study. This question has three satisfaction Likert scale items, so the results are stored in three SPSS variables. The **Frequencies** command can display the results for each variable separately and produce a simple bar chart of the results of each variable. However, we are going to create a horizontal stacked bar chart including each of the three scales in the question, to demonstrate the capabilities of SPSS **Chart Editor**. The final chart is clear and easy to interpret (which is what we want from a chart) but does involve a number of steps to produce it. However, these will illustrate a number of **Chart Editor** features.

First, we will use the **Custom Tables** command to create a single table that shows all three students' satisfaction variables, with their categories represented as percentages.

■ Drag all three satisfaction scales (Q12_1, Q12_2, Q12_3) to the **Columns** in the **Custom Tables** canvas.

■ Change **Position** to **Rows**.

■ Select **Category position** as **Column Labels in Rows**.

▨ Click the **Summary Statistics** button and in the **Summary Statistics** dialog box, remove **Count** from the **Display** box and send **Column N %** to the **Display** box.

▨ Click the **Apply to Selection** button.

▨ In the **Custom Tables** dialog box, click **OK**.

This produces the following table.

		Satisfaction with academic life	Satisfaction with social life	Satisfaction with personal development
Very unsatisfied	Column N %	0.0%	0.5%	0.0%
Unsatisfied	Column N %	9.3%	8.2%	14.8%
Neither unsatisfied nor satisfied	Column N %	30.1%	29.0%	23.5%
Satisfied	Column N %	38.3%	37.2%	36.6%
Very satisfied	Column N %	22.4%	25.1%	25.1%

▨ In the **IBM SPSS Statistics Viewer**, double click on the table to edit it, highlight the table contents, right click and select **Create Graph** ▶, then **Bar** to create a bar chart.

		Satisfaction with academic life	Satisfaction with social life	Satisfaction with personal development		
Very unsatisfied	Column N %	0.0%	0.5%	0.0%		
Unsatisfied	Column N %	9.3%	8.2%	Cut		Ctrl+X
Neither unsatisfied nor satisfied	Column N %	30.1%	29.0%	Copy		Ctrl+C
Satisfied	Column N %	38.3%	37.2%	Paste		Ctrl+V
Very satisfied	Column N %	22.4%	25.1%	Delete		Delete
				Select Table		
				Select cells with similar significance		
				Sort Rows	▶	
				Create Graph	▶	Bar
				Table Properties...		Dot

We have created a clustered bar chart of the percentages for each of the three satisfaction scales, in the table below.

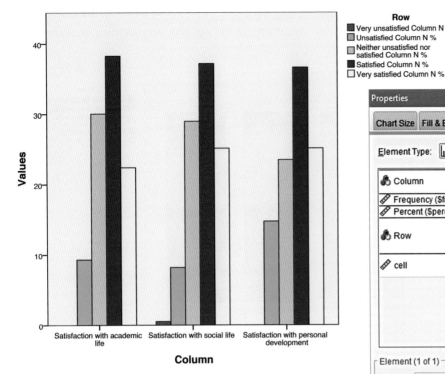

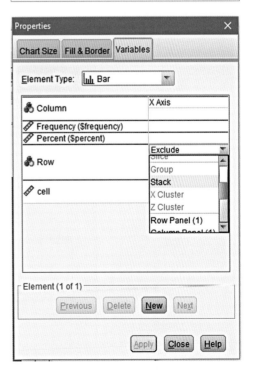

At a first glance, this looks quite good. We can see that the pattern of results is quite similar for the three satisfaction scales, with a little more dissatisfaction with 'personal development' than the other two scales (the long green 'unsatisfied' bar). However, some basic editing can change the format of the chart. We are now going to change the chart from a clustered bar chart to a stacked bar chart.

- Double click on the chart to 'activate' it and open **Chart Editor**.

- Double click on the chart to bring up the **Properties** window. (Remember that where you click on the chart determines how many tabs appear in the **Properties** window.)

- Select the **Variables** tab.

- Click on the right-hand end of the box containing the words **X Cluster** in the **Row** section. This brings up a drop-down menu.

- Change **X Cluster** to **Stack**.

- Click **Apply** and **Close**.

Unfortunately, we can see that the stacked bar chart has the categories displayed in reverse order with 'very unsatisfied' at the top and 'very satisfied' at the bottom of the stack. We need to reverse this order.

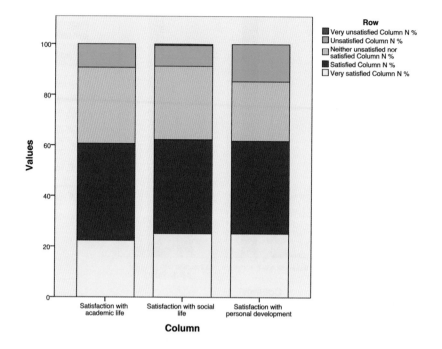

- We open **Chart Editor** and right click on one of the bars and select **Properties Window**. (We right click on the bar to make sure the **Categories** tab appears in the Properties window.)

- In the **Properties** window, select the **Categories** tab and change the **Sort By Value** from **Ascending** to **Descending**.

- Click **Apply** and **Close** the **Properties** window.

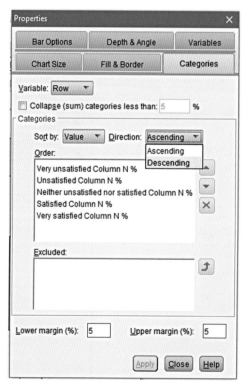

We now have a stacked bar chart with 'very satisfied' at the top of the bars.

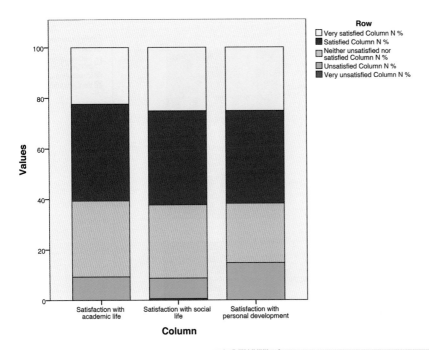

Again, if you like this stacked bar chart you can stop here and simply use this chart. However, we are going to change it to a horizontal bar chart.

■ In the **Chart Editor**, click **Options** followed by **Transpose Chart**.

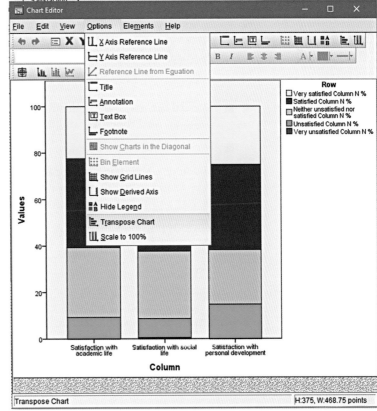

This produces the following horizontal stacked bar chart.

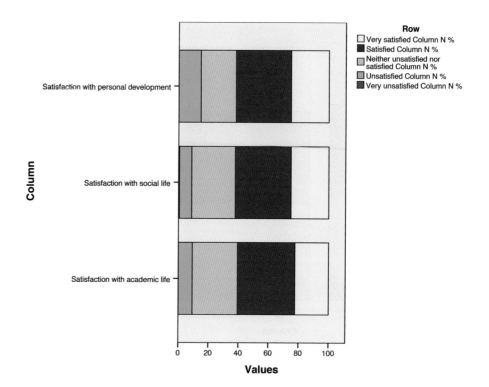

Aesthetically, the chart looks rather narrow, with the bars rather short for their width, so we adjust the size of the chart.

■ We activate the chart again and, in **Chart Editor**, double click on the chart to bring up the **Properties** window.

■ We select the **Chart Size** tab.

■ We untick **Maintain aspect ratio** in the **Chart Size** option and try out a few sizes until we find the one we like. (We selected a height of 300 and a width of 700.)

■ Click **Apply** and **Close** in the **Properties** window.

Finally, we have produced a horizontal stacked bar chart of the three satisfaction scales displayed together. With the stacks all the same size the different pattern of responses can be observed. In this case, the differences are small, but in other cases these horizontal bar charts will clearly show any differences in the pattern of percentages across the different items.

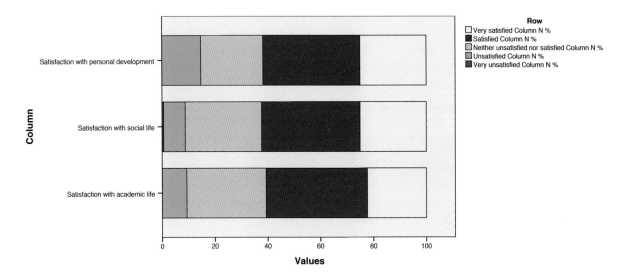

Finally, now that we are happy with the chart, we add a title and edit the labels. In **Chart Editor**, we will add the title 'Figure 18: Student satisfaction with their first-year experience' first. In **Chart Editor**:

▨   Select **Title** from the **Options** drop-down menu.

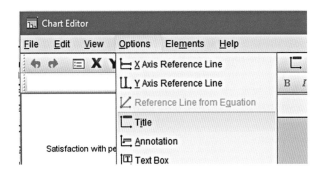

The word **Title** appears at the top of the chart. This is highlighted by a yellow line around it and we can simple type in the text of our chosen title. The **Text Style** tab of the **Properties** window also appears – so we can change any details of the font here.

We now change the labels on the chart. We will change the labels of the X axis and Y axis to 'Percentages' and 'Satisfaction ratings'.

▨   Click on the X axis label so that it can be changed. We change **Values** to **Percentage** as the label on the X axis.

▨   Click on the Y axis label at the side of the chart and it then has a yellow line around it, e.g. **Column** . We change the text to 'Satisfaction ratings'.

Finally, we change the key to the chart to what we want.

■ Click on the key (headed by the word **Row**). The text now has a yellow outline and we can change it directly from the keyboard. We change **Row** to **Key** as the header of the colour codes, and remove **Column N%** from the key labels.

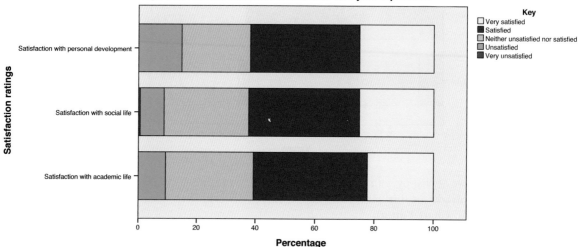

Figure 18: Student satisfaction with their first-year experience

Changing the position of the title on a chart

Some researchers prefer to have the title for a chart at the bottom rather than the top. SPSS will always put the title at the top of a table or a chart or graph. However, there is a way to place a title to the bottom of the chart. (If you have already put a title at the top of your chart, highlight it, so it is surrounded by a yellow line and delete it by pressing delete on your keyboard.) In **Chart Editor**:

■ Select **Footnote** from the **Options** drop-down menu.

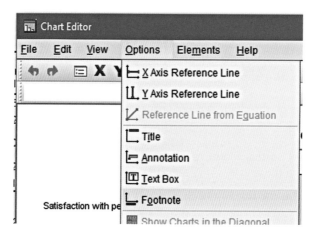

- Type your title into the footnote box. However, this is automatically set to font size 10 and not bold (as SPSS thinks it is a footnote not a title).

- If the **Properties** window is not already shown, right click on the footnote to display the **Properties** window.

- Select the **Text Style** tab and change **Preferred Size** to 12 and **Style** to bold.

- Click **Apply** and **Close**. Now the 'footnote' will be a title.

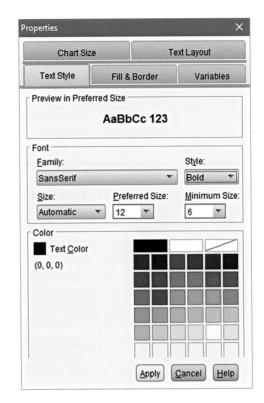

Here is the horizontal bar chart with the title at the bottom.

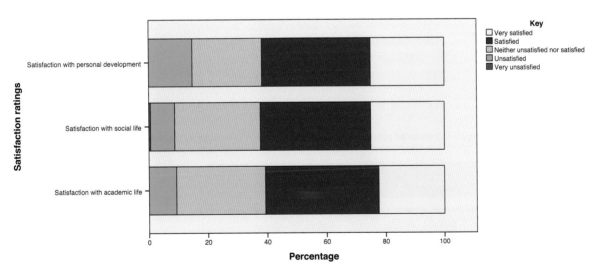

Figure 18: Student satisfaction with their first-year experience

Other examples of horizontal bar charts

We have produced two other examples of horizontal stacked bar charts. In this next example, we have colour coded the categories as red and pink (to indicate disagreement) and light and darker green (to indicate agreement). The following horizontal stacked bar chart, from the Sparcote Study, shows the responses of the students on the different 'Major subject' categories (Question 3) to the question asking about the appropriateness of their learning resources (Question 5).

Figure 10: Student agreement with the appropriateness of their learning resources by major subject

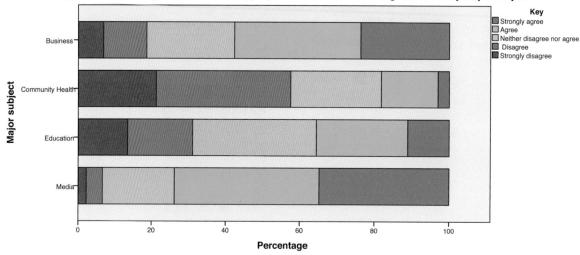

Notice that in this chart we can see easily that a greater percentage of community health students regard their resources as less appropriate to their course than the other students, by the length of the red and pink sections of the chart.

In this second example of a horizontal bar chart from the Sparcote Study, we have displayed the relative use of textbooks, course materials and other materials (Question 6) for the four major subjects (Question 3). We have also displayed the percentage mean values on the bars to show the use of the different resources.

Figure 8: Estimated percentage use of three different resources by major subject

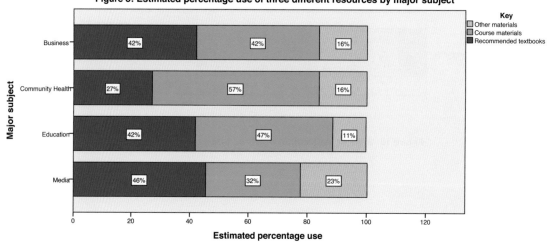

Again, this chart is easy to read, in that we can see that proportionally the community health students use 'Recommended textbooks' (the blue bar) the least and 'Course materials' (the green bar) the most. The media students proportionally use 'Other materials' (the tan bar) more than the other student groups.

Despite the fact that we have had to give a range of editing instructions to SPSS, we have ended up with clean-looking charts that are able to illustrate the key findings of the study in a clear and simple way. We cannot emphasise enough that the value of a table or graph is only in the information it is able to communicate to an interested reader – but SPSS can be used to produce exactly the chart you want.

EXPORTING TABLES AND GRAPHS TO OTHER APPLICATIONS

SPSS allows the whole of the output file (the **IBM SPSS Statistics Viewer**) to be saved (as a .spv file) that can be opened later in SPSS whenever you wish to view or edit it. Individual outputs, such as a graph or a table, can be saved separately, and in different formats (as jpgs, or a pdf file). Many researchers wish to produce high-quality tables for publication and this can be achieved in SPSS by exporting the tables in the portable document format (or pdf). We will explain now how to export your output to other software here.

SPSS, as many modern applications do, allows you to copy and paste in a way that is familiar to all users of programs such as Microsoft Office. In the **IBM SPSS Statistics Viewer**, with the mouse cursor over an output, such as a table or graph, and right click to bring up the following menu.

Major subject				
		Frequency	Percent	Valid
Valid	Business	59	32.2	
	Community Health	33	18.0	
	Education	45	24.6	
	Media	46	25.1	
	Total	183	100.0	

Cut
Copy
Copy Special...
Paste After
Create/Edit Autoscript...
Style Output...
Export...
Edit Content ▶

The table or graph can simply be copied (by the **Copy** command) and then pasted into another open application (such as Microsoft Word or other application). The advantage of this is that a table in SPSS becomes a table in Microsoft Word and can be manipulated in the word-processing application. Sometimes, however, users prefer to copy SPSS tables as images and this can be achieved through the **Copy Special** command – the next command below **Copy** in the right click menu.

Clicking **Copy Special** brings up the following dialog box.

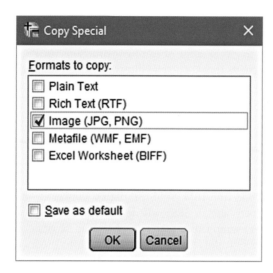

Rather than copying a table as a table, it can now be copied as plain text or an image. Notice that it can also be copied as an Excel Worksheet and pasted directly into Excel. In this case, we have selected the **Image** format.

While **Copy** and **Copy Special** may be all that is required in most cases, they may not save the material with a high enough resolution for authors who wish their work to be published. So there is an alternative way of saving an output and this is via the **Export** command on the right click menu.

Major subject				
		Frequency	Percent	Valid
Valid	Business	59	32.2	
	Community Health	33	18.0	
	Education	45	24.6	
	Media	46	25.1	
	Total	183	100.0	

Cut
Copy
Copy Special...
Paste After
Create/Edit Autoscript...
Style Output...
Export...
Edit Content ▶

This brings up the **Export Output** window.

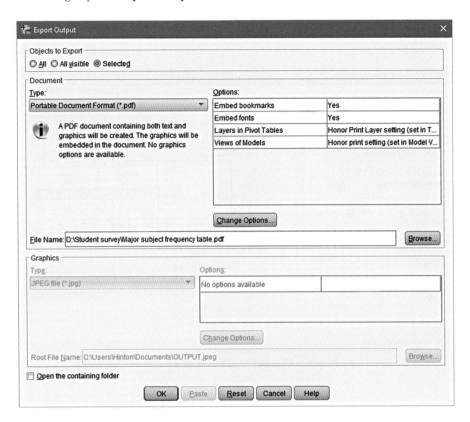

There are a number of different formats in which you can save the output. These are listed under **Type** (such as Microsoft Excel, Powerpoint or Word formats). Notice in the example above we have selected **Portable Document Format (*.pdf)**. Exporting as a pdf means that the output can be increased to any size and, by using the **Take a Snapshot** option in Adobe Reader, a very large image can be created of the output. However, particularly if you have a large table, before you export the output to another file type (.pdf or .doc) you have to ensure that the table fits on a single page, otherwise when you open up Adobe Reader or Microsoft Word you will find the table broken up into sections to fit on a page in the new application.

To make sure a table in the **IBM SPSS Statistics Viewer** will fit on an A4 page when exported to another application we must do the following:

- Double click on the table to activate it.

- Right click to bring up the editing menu and then select the **Table Properties** option.

- Select the **Printing** tab in the **Table Properties** window.

We have not selected the **Change Options** button as we have accepted the default options for exporting the output. The default choices work well in most cases. However, if you wish to export a range of documents in a particular format then it is worth exploring the choices in **Change Options** to produce the exported output in the form that you wish.

■ There are two boxes on the left of the window: **Rescale wide tables to fit page** and **Rescale long tables to fit page**. Both can be ticked for a very large table but here we have simply ticked **Rescale wide table to fit page** as generally we have found tables are often too wide for an A4 page and rarely too long.

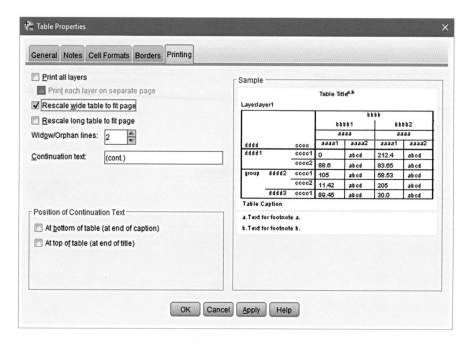

When the table is now exported to a different format by SPSS, such as a pdf, the table will be rescaled to keep the table together, without being broken up over a number of pages. The pdf file can be manipulated in Adobe Reader or other pdf viewing program to produce a high-quality image.

For many readers, producing their tables and graphs will be enough information to present the results of their research. However, some researchers may wish to statistically analyse their data to see if it supports a particular prediction or not. Chapter 9 provides an introduction to inferential statistics that can be used to statistically analyse the data for possible relationships between variables.

An introduction to statistical tests in SPSS

309 WHY PERFORM A STATISTICAL TEST?

312 UNDERTAKING STATISTICAL TESTS WITH SPSS

312 LOOKING FOR RELATIONSHIPS BETWEEN VARIABLES

314 THE CHI-SQUARE TEST OF AN ASSOCIATION BETWEEN CATEGORICAL VAIRABLES

319 THE PEARSON TEST OF A LINEAR RELATIONSHIP BETWEEN SCALE VARIABLES

355 THE *t* TEST FOR COMPARING TWO CATEGORIES ON A SCALE MEASURE

Chapter aim: To explain the purpose of interferential statistics and illustrate their use in SPSS

For many researchers, presenting a summary of their findings in the form of descriptive statistics in tables and charts gives a clear account of their results, which provides answers to their research questions. They can start to draw some conclusions from their study and put forward recommendations from their findings, and suggestions for theory, practice or follow-up research. For other researchers, however, there is more analysis to do. This is particularly the case for researchers who are interested (in terms of their research questions) in examining differences, relationships and comparisons in their data, in order to generalise their findings to a wider group of people.

If a specific prediction has been made then researchers will want to make a decision about whether that prediction has been supported, or not, by the results. Consider this example. A retail outlet wants to know which cola drink to stock out of Brand A or Brand B. The researchers compare Brand A and Brand B, predicting that one will be preferred over the other. After a carefully planned test, with 30 participants randomly allocated to the two different tasting conditions and all the cola drinks presented in identical unmarked cups, the results show that more people prefer Brand A over Brand B. Is it enough for the researchers to simply present *any* difference and say the prediction is supported? Unfortunately not. Imagine that the results showed that 16 people preferred Brand A and 14 preferred Brand B. On the basis of this result, would you bet money that people *in general* prefer Brand A over Brand B? The retail outlet is unlikely to feel confident that Brand A is generally favoured, based on this data. It is not a very big difference and could have occurred by chance – if only one person who stated a preference for Brand A changes his mind then the results are even. The evidence for a preference is very slim. Now imagine how you would view the situation if the result showed that 26 people preferred Brand A and only 4 preferred Brand B. Here the result indicates a more

effect

In quantitative research, differences in numerical outcomes are examined to see if there is an effect of one variable on another – such as a difference, an association or a correlation

probability

The chance of a specific event occurring from a set of possible events, expressed as a proportion. For example, if there were four women and six men in a room, the probability of meeting a woman first on entering the room is 4/10 or 0.4 as there are four women out of 10 people in the room. A probability of 0 indicates an event will never occur and a probability of 1 that it will always occur. In a room containing only men and there are 10 of them, there is a probability of 0 (0/10) of meeting a woman first and a probability of 1 (10/10) of meeting a man

reliable difference, with it being much less likely that it could have arisen by chance – so there probably *is* a general preference for Brand A. This evidence of a preference for Brand A is strong and, from this result, the retail outlet might be happy to choose Brand A for their stock. This raises the question: How big does a difference in a study have to be for a researcher to generalise the difference to a wider group of people? Or, to put it another way: When do we infer that a difference, a relationship or an association found in a study with samples can be generalised to populations? This is where statistical tests come in. These tests work out, on the basis of the research data, an answer to the question: Is this **effect**, found in the study, big enough to *infer* its more general applicability? This is why statistical tests are often called 'inferential statistics'.

Research questions can range from very specific predictions to more general questions, such as the Sparcote researchers looking to see if the students on the different major subjects view aspects of their experience differently. In many cases, the results show evidence of relationships, differences or associations relevant to the research questions. However, before the researchers waste a lot of effort, time and money following up these **effects**, they will usually check whether the results are indicating a general effect or whether these results could have simply occurred by chance. For example, the researcher in the cola study does not want to tell the retail outlet that there 'really' is a preference for Brand A when the result in the study could be simply explained by random factors. Statistical tests cannot give a definitive answer but they can, on the basis of **probability**, provide a decision point to decide that an effect found in a study has probably not occurred by chance and, hence, can be generalised to the wider population.

This chapter briefly explains the key concepts used in statistical inference testing, so that the basic principles of statistical inference and statistical tests can be understood. One of the major strengths of SPSS is that it is able to perform a large range of statistical tests on a variety of types of data. However, in this chapter, we will focus on three popular statistical tests and explain how to perform them on your research data using SPSS.

✓

Researchers who examine the whole population do not need to perform any statistical tests because this is the only group they are interested in – the sample and the population are one – so there is no need to infer from sample data to a population. For example, in the Sparcote Study, the researchers have a small population – the first-year students on the applied studies program – who are all available and willing to complete the survey. If the 183 student who filled in the survey comprise the whole population – i.e. every student filled in the survey – then this would have been one of the very rare cases of the whole population being tested. Let us assume, for sake of argument, that 12 students did not complete the survey for one reason or other (five were ill, one was at a funeral and six absent for other reasons). Now the sample of 183 out of 195 students is 94% of the whole population, still a very large sample of the population. For illustration purposes, will be performing statistical tests on the Sparcote Study data (below).

WHY PERFORM A STATISTICAL TEST?

What do statistical tests do?

It may appear odd at first to see researchers undertaking research about large populations by examining small samples. The reason that they are able to do this is because statisticians have developed some clever statistical tests that – assuming certain assumptions are met – can make a judgement about whether effects found with samples are '**significant**' or not – where a 'significant difference' is a difference (found in a study) that is generalisable from the samples (in the study) to the populations (of interest). For example, a researcher is interested in the effect of a classical piece of music on people solving a crossword puzzle. The researcher is not sure if the music will help concentration or be a distraction – but the prediction is that it will have an effect: there will be a difference in the crossword solution times for people listening to the classical music piece compared to people with no music. Forty volunteers are randomly assigned to the two conditions – 20 people to each. The researcher also arranges things so that all other aspects of the task are controlled (the participants all do the same puzzle in the same small room on their own). The results show that the 'music group' solve the puzzle in 26.5 minutes on average (mean = 26.50, Standard Deviation = 1.85) and the 'no music group' solve the puzzle in 28 minutes on average (mean = 28.00, Standard Deviation = 2.18). There is a mean difference between the groups – of a minute and a half – in favour of the music group. Does this indicate that the prediction has been supported? Well, not quite yet. The researcher does not rush off at this point claiming that the classical music piece improves crossword-solving times. The problem is whether a difference of 1.5 minutes (on average) could simply be explained by chance or whether it is big enough to infer that this effect is generalisable to other people.

Statistical inference tests are used to make the choice between these two possibilities. From the result of the test the researcher makes a judgement of whether the effect (found in the research) is significant – indicating it is (probably) generalisable to the population – or '**not significant**' – indicating that they should (probably) not rule out chance factors producing the effect in the study. These statistical inference tests go under the name of **null hypothesis significance testing** (NHST). There are a number of different tests used for different types of data, but they follow the same logic. They are constructed on the assumption that there is *no* underlying difference between the populations on the outcome measure, so any difference found between the samples is due to chance. This assumption is called the **null hypothesis**. A statistical test makes further assumptions about the underlying pattern or distribution of the population data, which allows it to calculate a value of an inferential statistic based on the research data. Finally, it then works out how probable such a calculated value of the statistic is, given the assumption of the null hypothesis. Probability ranges from 1 (certainly) down to 0 (certainly not), so a probability of 0.5 is equivalent to a 50% or a 50:50 chance. If the probability is high (when the null hypothesis is assumed) then this indicates that even though a difference was found between the samples, it is not big enough to reject the null hypothesis and we conclude that the difference in samples has probably arisen by chance.

However, when this probability is very low, it challenges the null hypothesis assumption, as the low probability implies that the difference between the samples

significant
A statistical term used in null hypothesis significance testing. An effect (such as a difference between samples or a correlation between variables) is only described as 'significant' if, after the data has been subject to a statistical test, the effect is shown to occur with a probability of the significance level (normally 0.05) or lower (assuming the null hypothesis). As a result, the null hypothesis is rejected and the effect found in the study is inferred to be generalisable to a wider population

not significant
In null hypothesis significance testing, a statistical test is used to work out the probability of the effect found in the research arising from the assumption of the null hypothesis. If the calculated probability is not as small as (or smaller) than the significance level, the result is said to be not significant (often abbreviated to 'ns') and the null hypothesis is not rejected

null hypothesis significance testing
A statistical method for making a decision about whether an effect found in a research study (such as a difference or a correlation) can be generalised to a wider population. The null hypothesis is assumed and a probability worked out for the effect found in the study. The effect is only inferred to generalise more widely if the probability is as small as or smaller than the significance level

null hypothesis
A prediction that there is no effect or relationship in the wider population corresponding to the one under investigation in the research study.

significance level

Statistical tests are undertaken to make a decision as to whether an effect (such has a difference or a correlation) found in the study using samples should be attributed to chance or can be generalised to a wider population. The test produces a probability of the effect found in the study occurring by chance (when the null hypothesis is assumed). The decision is then made whether to reject (or not reject) the null hypothesis based on this probability value. If the probability is as small as or smaller than a set criterion, called the significance level (or α), then the null hypothesis is rejected and it is inferred that the effect can be generalised to a wider population. Conventionally, it has been agreed to set the significance level at a probability of 0.05

alpha

Alpha (α) is another term for the significance level in a statistical test. Usually, the significance level, or alpha, is set to a probability of 0.05

p value

This is the probability of the calculated value of an inferential statistic in a statistical test (assuming the null hypothesis). If this value is equal to, or smaller than, the significance level then the effect under test is said to be 'significant' and the null hypothesis assumption is rejected

has probably not arisen by chance. Here the difference in the samples indicates that we should probably reject the null hypothesis and infer that there is a difference in the populations. (Making this inference is why these statistical tests are called statistical inference tests.)

The decision point for making this judgement is called the **significance level** (also referred to as **alpha**, α). Conventionally, it has been agreed that if the probability of the inferential statistic (also called the **p value**) is 0.05 or less, then the null hypothesis is rejected and a difference in the populations is inferred. However, if the probability is greater than 0.05 then the null hypothesis is not rejected. A probability of 0.05 is the same as a 5% or a 1 in 20 chance. The choice of a probability of 0.05 as the significance level means that the null hypothesis will only be rejected when there is a only a 5% or less risk that the difference found in the research could have arisen by chance. This has been agreed as an appropriate probability level to use by researchers for this inferential decision-making.

✓

Researchers sometimes use a significance level of 0.01 – a more conservative level with a lower risk of accepting a chance effect as a difference in populations. However, using this more conservative value all the time increases the risk of inferring that sample differences have (probably) arisen by chance when they may in fact indicate a difference in the populations. The key point about inferring from samples to populations is that we can never be certain that the data from the former will accurately predict the latter. As a result, we have to make an informed gamble based on probability values, which is what null hypothesis significance tests seek to do.

Now let us return to the example of the classical music piece and the crossword-solving times. The null hypothesis here is: *The classical music piece does not affect the crossword solving times* or *There is no difference in the crossword solution times for people listening to the classical music piece compared to people who are not*. Combined with certain assumptions about the data, statisticians have been able to construct statistical tests to apply to a set of data that work out the probability of getting a specific result in a study (assuming the null hypothesis). What is the probability of finding a difference of 1.5 minutes in the crossword puzzle-solving times when the null hypothesis is assumed? To produce this answer, we run the appropriate test on the data (in this case it is called a '*t* test', and is explained below). From performing the test with SPSS, we discover that with the probability of finding a 1.5 minute mean difference in the samples is 0.024. This is very unlikely, indicating that this difference only occurs 2.4% of the time when we assume the null hypothesis. It is also less than the significance level of 0.05. So, according to statistical convention, the researcher rejects the null hypothesis and claims that the crossword-solution times are shorter when listening to the piece of classical music compared to no music.

Why researchers use statistical tests

Statistical inference tests provide tools for testing effects found in research data. Like any other tool they can be used and misused. The key point to remember is that statistical tests only provide a rule for deciding that an effect (found in a study) is probably not due to chance. The statistical test cannot and does not tell you what caused the effect (if you have found one).

If the researcher has carefully planned her research, undertaken appropriate sampling and included the proper controls in her research then any effects found might well be for the reasons proposed by the researcher. Just because a difference has (probably) not occurred by chance, it *might* have occurred for the reasons predicted by the researcher but there is always the possibility that it could have occurred for other reasons – which is why many researchers spend so much time carefully planning their research, seeking to control for (i.e. rule out) some of the alternative possibilities.

However, in many cases, the research questions do not make specific predictions and the study does not have the complex controls of an experiment. This should not be viewed negatively as, in many instances, excellent research is undertaken using methods outside the laboratory and without the controls of an experiment. This does mean that interesting effects can still be found. It is just that we will not know (from this particular study) what has caused them.

One exciting aspect of research is producing data that indicates a number of interesting effects that are pertinent to the research questions, but were not specifically predicted. For example, the Sparcote researchers were interested in the differences between students studying the different major subjects, but had not expected that the community health students would regard their learning resources as less appropriate than the students on any other subject major. However, before the researchers set up a plan of action to follow up the effect they have found in their research, it is often a good idea to check, with a statistical test, that this finding is probably not due to chance. When undertaking studies with small samples, there is always the risk that the results of one or two people will distort the overall results. Statistical tests can provide a degree of reassurance that the effect under investigation is an effect worth following up rather than a random 'one-off' feature of the present study.

It is important, however, to bear one thing in mind when considering using statistical tests. It is not advisable to analyse every potential effect in your data using statistical tests (even though it is easy to do using SPSS). You should be guided by your research questions to examine the relevant effects rather than 'throwing everything into the pot'. The reason why this can be an issue is that analysing the same data in many different ways is likely to produce 'significant' findings simply by chance alone. It is important to note that significance testing is based on a 1 in 20 chance. For a single test, a 'significant' result is unlikely to be due to chance – but there is still a probability of 0.05 or a 1 in 20 chance that it had occurred by chance. Every time you do another test on the same data the probability of a chance result being 'significant' goes up. If you do lots of tests on the same data then the risks multiply of finding a 'significant' effect simply by chance alone. Too much data snooping and a difference is bound to pop up somewhere. Essentially, effects discovered in data snooping – rather than being guided by the research questions – should always be taken as tentative and hinting at possible effects rather than viewed as evidence for anything important – yet. We sum this view up as follows: 'This is an interesting finding. I make no specific claim about it here, as I did not include it in my research questions, but it certainly looks worth following up in future research.'

Serendipity is often the spur for advances in knowledge. A researcher looks for one thing but finds a completely unrelated effect. For example in testing a new drug to reduce high blood pressure (which was not successful) it was serendipitously observed that it produced penile erections and now Viagra is one of the best-selling drugs of all time – not for reducing blood pressure, but for maintaining sexual potency. We should not forget that the unexpected finding is often the most interesting.

In confirmatory research, there is sometimes a much greater chance of getting your research published in an academic journal if the predictions are supported by 'significant' results. This has led some academics to be concerned about the way some researchers are 'snooping' in their data looking for significant findings (even though their main prediction has not been supported), in order to get them published. The reason for their concern is that it is quite likely – on the basis of the 1 in 20 effect – that, if the data is 'tortured' enough, eventually a significant finding will be found – which might lead to a publication, even though it could easily have arisen from chance factors alone. This approach is characterised by the following reasoning: 'I set out to test one prediction – which was not supported by the data: yet this other interesting result has appeared, so I'll pretend I was really predicting that all along.' This reasoning is playing fast and loose with probability – and is not a good thing for research, as meaningless effects (arising from chance) are being published. However, a simple change of logic and the situation can be improved: 'I set out to test one prediction – which was not supported by the data: yet this other interesting result has appeared, so I'll follow this up in my next research study.' The reason that this is fine is that the same data is not being used to both devise the prediction and test it (which is statistically dubious at best) but an unexpected finding in one study is used stimulate a prediction for the next piece of research (using a different dataset). The more times an effect is repeated (or replicated) with different data the more confident we can be that it is a genuine effect (and not a quirk of a single study).

UNDERTAKING STATISTICAL TESTS WITH SPSS

SPSS is an exceptionally good program for a variety of statistical analyses. Indeed, SPSS can perform a wide range of complex statistical analyses on numerical data collected from a number of different research methods. In this chapter, we will show you a number of NHST statistical tests that can easily be undertaken on research data using SPSS. In these analyses, we will show how a particular test can be applied to different types of data to examine whether a difference between samples is (probably) due to chance or whether a genuine underlying difference can be inferred.

Readers who would like further information about inferential statistics are recommended to look at Hinton, P.R. (2014) *Statistics Explained*, also published by Routledge.

LOOKING FOR RELATIONSHIPS BETWEEN VARIABLES

In a lot of research, we are looking for a relationship between two (or more) variables. There are many different relationships that can be examined and there are many different statistical tests that can be applied to different types of data. SPSS can perform an extremely comprehensive set of tests of research data. However, we are going to concentrate on only a few of these in this chapter. Here, we will be considering three examples, each one illustrating a different type of relationship.

Different patterns of frequency

In the first example, a researcher is interested in whether there is a preference for locally based soap operas by viewers. Two popular television soap operas are examined: *Northern Streets*, based in the north of the country, and *Southern Town*, based in the south of the country. Participants are asked to give their preference for either one or the other soap opera. (A third choice is included for participants who have no preference or have not watched either soap opera.) One group of 100 participants is selected (randomly if possible) from the north of the country and a second group of 100 participants is selected (randomly too) from the south of the country. The researcher is looking for an association between the categorical variables 'participant location' and 'soap opera preference'. If this is the case, we would expect the frequency of responses to have a different pattern for the two participant groups – there will a higher frequency count for the northern participants in the *Northern Streets* category than the *Southern Town* category and a higher frequency count for the southern participants in the *Southern Town* category than the *Northern Streets* category. If there were no association between these two variables, then the preference for one soap opera over the other would be independent of where the person lived, so the pattern of frequencies would not differ between the northern and southern participants. When the nominal data is collected, the results are examined to see if the soap opera preferences of the people from the two locations are similar or different. The statistical inference test that is used to examine this association is called the chi-square test.

A correlation

In a second example, a researcher is interested in the relationship between two scale variables: ice cream sales and daytime temperature. Over a specific period of time (the months of July to September) an ice cream vendor in a holiday resort is asked to record the number of ice creams sold each day and also to record the peak temperature during that day. The results for the 92-day period are plotted on a scatterplot with the ice cream sales on the Y axis and the temperature on the X axis. The researcher is interested in whether the two variables, rather than presenting a random pattern on the graph, vary together (correlate) linearly (following a straight line), so that – in this case – it is suggested that when one goes up the other also goes up and when one goes down the other goes down. The statistical inference test used to examine the correlation between two scale variables is the **Pearson correlation**.

Pearson correlation
An inferential statistical test to determine the linear relationship between two variables

A difference between groups on an outcome measure

In the third example, a researcher wants to test whether experienced drivers drive more safely than novice drivers. In testing this hypothesis, there are two variables: 'driving experience' and 'driver safety'. 'Driving experience' is the independent variable that the researcher 'manipulates', that is, operationally defines. For example, novice drivers might be defined (for the purposes of the study) as 'drivers within the first year of passing their driving test' and experienced drivers might be defined as 'five or more years since passing their driving test'. The researcher then selects (randomly if they can) a sample of drivers from the two categories, such as 20 novice drivers and 20 experienced drivers. Notice that the researcher has to decide how to select the sample and how many participants to test. The researcher then decides to test these drivers on a driving simulator that detects and records driving errors. The error scores are used as a measure of 'driver safety' with a low error score viewed as safer than a higher error score. The researcher does not know what the two groups will score on the simulator, as this is the point of the research. 'Driver safety' is the dependent variable as the prediction of the researcher is that driver safety will differ with driver experience. As it is measured by the number of errors on the simulator, this data is from a scale measure. The statistical inference test for comparing two groups on a scale measure is called a t test.

THE CHI-SQUARE TEST OF AN ASSOCIATION BETWEEN CATEGORICAL VARIABLES

The chi-square test looks at the pattern of the results in the various categories of nominal or ordinal data to compare the frequencies with what we would expect according to a particular known pattern. Consider tossing a coin. If it is a 'fair' coin then we expect heads and tails with equal frequency. We are not surprised if it is not exactly 50% heads and 50% tails over a series of tosses as we know that we are not likely to get exactly equal numbers of heads and tails due to chance factors – but we do expect them to more or less even out over time. If we found that over a large number of tosses we were getting 80% heads and 20% tails we might begin to suspect that the coin was not fair. The chi-square test allows us to make a judgement about whether the frequencies in the categories follow an expected pattern (in this case, equal numbers of heads and tails) or a different pattern (such as mostly heads).

See Chapter 6

Consider the sports centre example from Chapter 6. The results show the use of the racquets arena and swimming pool by the men and women clients. We want to know whether the men and women use these facilities with different frequencies. To answer this question the chi-square test considers what the frequencies would be if the men and women used the two locations equally (like the fair coin above). This is a bit more difficult than the coin toss as we have two variables: location and gender. However, chi-square works out the expected pattern by looking at the totals.

Gender * Location of activity Crosstabulation

Count

		Location of activity		Total
		Racquets arena	Swimming pool	
Gender	Female	229	152	381
	Male	201	196	397
Total		430	348	778

We notice that the 778 visits to the centre is divided into 381 by women and 397 by men, so just 16 more visits by men overall. Looking at location, we see that the 778 visits are divided into 430 to the racquets arena and 348 to the swimming pool, so the racquets arena is more popular overall. From these figures, the chi-square works out what would be expected if this pattern of usage (shown by the totals) was the same for the men and the women. In the following table, the **Observed Count** shows the frequencies actually found in the study and the **Expected Count** shows what chi-square would expect if there was no difference in the pattern of female and male visits across the two locations (they simply followed the same pattern as the totals).

Gender * Location of activity Crosstabulation

| | | | Location of activity | | Total |
			Racquets arena	Swimming pool	
Gender	Female	Count	229	152	381
		Expected Count	210.6	170.4	381.0
	Male	Count	201	196	397
		Expected Count	219.4	177.6	397.0
Total		Count	430	348	778
		Expected Count	430.0	348.0	778.0

We can see that the women are visiting the racquets arena more often and the swimming pool less often, than expected. Also the men are visiting the racquets arena less often and the swimming pool more often, than expected. It doesn't seem as if the men and the women are visiting the facilities with the same frequency patterns.

The chi-square test uses the observed and expected values to create a statistic called the Pearson chi-square statistic. A small value means that the observed frequencies are not very different to the expected frequencies and a large value indicates that they are different. In this case the chi-square value is calculated as 7.06, which is quite large for a chi-square statistic. Associated with this value is a probability, 0.008. This is the probability of getting these results simply by chance – assuming that pattern of frequencies for men and women really is the same (the null hypothesis). Notice that this probability (called p) is very tiny. As this calculated probability is less than 0.05 (the significance level), the result is very unlikely to have occurred by chance and it is concluded that that the pattern of frequencies for men and women are 'significantly' different: the women visit the racquets arena more often than the men, and the women visit the swimming pool less often that the men.

Performing a chi-square test in SPSS is very easy as it simply involves ticking a box in the **Crosstabs** command or the **Custom Tables** command. We are going to look at an example from the Sparcote Study, the crosstabulation of gender and major subject (which was described in Chapter 6). We can see the frequency table displayed by SPSS below.

Gender * Major subject Crosstabulation

Count

| | | Major subject | | | | Total |
		Business	Community Health	Education	Media	
Gender	Female	23	22	27	22	94
	Male	36	11	18	24	89
Total		59	33	45	46	183

The first thing to note is that the gender totals (in the final column) show similar number of female and male students in the department (only five more women out of 183 students). However, this pattern of (more or less) equal numbers is not matched across all the major subjects. While media has similar numbers of men and women (only two more men), community health has twice as many female students than male students. Education has more women than men (27 out of 45 equals 60% of the group) and business has more men than women (36 out of 59 equals 61% of the group). It looks as if the variables 'Gender' and 'Major subject' are not independent of one another but are associated. The pattern of female and male students in the individual subject majors looks different to the general pattern of the totals. We can test out whether this is a 'significant' difference by performing a chi-square test.

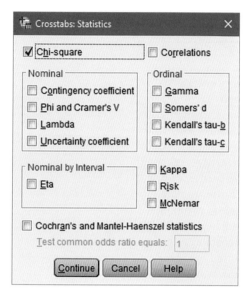

- In SPSS, select the **Analyze** drop-down menu.

- Select the **Descriptive Statistics** and **Crosstabs** commands.

- Send 'Gender' to the **Row(s)** box and 'Major subject' to the **Column(s)** box. This time, however, we select the **Statistics** option, and tick the **Chi-square** box.

- Click on the **Cells** option and the **Crosstabs: Cell Display** window pops up and we see that **Observed** is already ticked. Just for interest, we are going to tick the **Expected** box as well – to see what the data is expected to look like (if there is no association between the variables and the pattern of males and females was the same for each major subject).

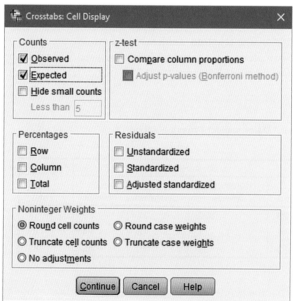

- Click **Continue** and **OK** in the **Crosstabs** dialog box.

The first table SPSS displays is the **Case Processing Summary** table which shows that all the data is valid without any missing values.

Case Processing Summary

	Cases					
	Valid		Missing		Total	
	N	Percent	N	Percent	N	Percent
Gender * Major subject	183	100.0%	0	0.0%	183	100.0%

The second table is a crosstabulated frequency table for 'Gender' and 'Major subject'. This includes the expected frequencies as well as the observed frequencies.

Gender * Major subject Crosstabulation

			Major subject				Total
			Business	Community Health	Education	Media	
Gender	Female	Count	23	22	27	22	94
		Expected Count	30.3	17.0	23.1	23.6	94.0
	Male	Count	36	11	18	24	89
		Expected Count	28.7	16.0	21.9	22.4	89.0
Total		Count	59	33	45	46	183
		Expected Count	59.0	33.0	45.0	46.0	183.0

Notice that if the pattern of frequency in each major subject were the same as the overall pattern, we would expect, for example, 17 female and 16 male students in community health. In fact, the observed values (the actual frequencies) are 22 female and 11 male students. The calculated chi-square statistic is shown in the third and final table, the **Chi-Square Tests** table.

Chi-Square Tests

	Value	df	Asymptotic Significance (2-sided)
Pearson Chi-Square	8.288[a]	3	.040
Likelihood Ratio	8.388	3	.039
Linear-by-Linear Association	.984	1	.321
N of Valid Cases	183		

a. 0 cells (0.0%) have expected count less than 5. The minimum expected count is 16.05.

We are only usually interested in the first row of this table. The probability value (p) is given in the column headed **Asymptotic Significance (2-sided)**. For the gender by major subject crosstabulation, the chi-square statistic has a value of 8.288 with a p value (probability) of 0.040. As this p value of 0.04 is less that the significance level of 0.05, it is concluded that the observed data are 'significantly' different from the expected pattern. It is concluded that the pattern of frequencies of female and male students is associated with the major subjects.

degrees of freedom

When calculating a statistic, we use information from the data (such as the mean or total) in the calculation. The degrees of freedom is the number of scores we need to know before we can work out the rest using the information we already have. For example, if nine friends were coming to your house for dinner (total of 10 people at the table) and you politely let them sit down first, you would not have a choice of where to sit as there is only one seat left. Here, the degrees of freedom is nine, rather than 10 (as nine people have a choice of where to sit and only one does not). Statistical tests use the degrees of freedom in their analysis to work out the probability (p value)

When we undertake a statistical test there are three important calculations. First, the value of the inferential statistic. In this case, the statistic is chi-square (reported using the Greek letter χ^2) and the calculated value is 8.288 (shown in the column headlined **Value** in the above table). Second, the degrees of freedom, which is presented in the above table in the column headed **df**, with a value of 3. This is related to the number of categories in our chi-square test and is used in the test to work out the probability value. Finally, we have the probability value p listed in the column headed **Asymptotic Significance (2-sided)**.

When we report the results of the test we would report these three values to two decimal places:

$$\chi^2 = 8.29, df = 3, p = 0.04$$

Some academic organisations ask for the actual probability value to be reported but others prefer to report the probability in terms of the significance level, as either $p < 0.05$ or $p < 0.01$ to show significance or 'ns' to show the result is not significant. So the result could be reported alternatively as:

$$\chi^2 = 8.29, df = 3, p < 0.05$$

You need to know how your institution or publication requires you to report the results to decide which to use.

A chi-square statistical test can also be conducted using the **Custom Tables** command.

- In the **Custom Tables** window, after you have dragged the two variables to the **Rows** and **Columns** boxes ('Gender' to the rows and 'Major subject' to columns, in our example), select the **Test Statistics** tab.
- Tick the **Tests of independence (Chi-square)** box. Notice that SPSS has already selected **Alpha** as 0.05 (the conventional significance level as 0.05).
- Click **OK**.

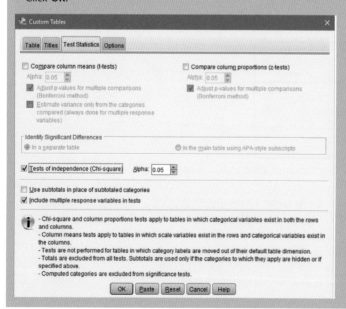

The output shows the observed counts for how many males and females are studying each major subject. If you would like to include the totals for the rows and columns, this is discussed in Chapter 6.

See Chapter 6

		Major subject			
		Business	Community Health	Education	Media
		Count	Count	Count	Count
Gender	Female	23	22	27	22
	Male	36	11	18	24

SPSS also produces a short table which shows the **chi-square** statistic of 8.288, with a p (probability) value of 0.040. As the p value of 0.04 is less that the significance level of 0.05, it is concluded that there is a relationship between gender and the major subjects.

Pearson Chi-Square Tests

		Major subject
Gender	Chi-square	8.288
	df	3
	Sig.	.040*

Results are based on non-empty rows and columns in each innermost subtable.

• The chi-square statistic is significant at the .05 level.

THE PEARSON TEST OF A LINEAR RELATIONSHIP BETWEEN SCALE VARIABLES

In Chapter 7, we saw the example of 20 8-year-old children taking a reading test and a mathematics test (both measured on an interval scale). These results are plotted onto a scatterplot as shown below.

See Chapter 7

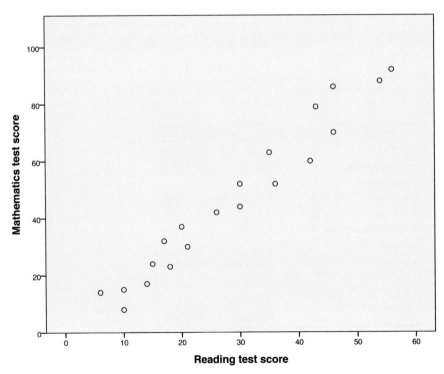

positive correlation

Two variables correlate if they co-relate or vary together. If the second variable increases and decreases as the first variable increases and decreases the correlation is said to be positive. An example of a positive correlation is that between the number of hours studied and a student's grade

negative correlation

Two variables correlate if they co-relate or vary together. However, if, as the first variable increases, the second variable decreases, then the correlation is said to be negative. An example of a negative correlation is that between a person's spending and her savings. As spending goes up then savings go down

Notice that the scores are not randomly scattered around the chart. There appears to be a relationship between the two sets of scores as they all lie within a fairly narrow band of the chart. First, the relationship looks to be linear – it follows a straight line (the pattern of scores is not curved and does not change direction). The relationship of these two variables is that they vary together – they correlate – roughly along a straight line. This is called a linear correlation. Second, the scores going from the bottom left to the top right of the chart indicate that a low score on one measure is associated with a low score on the other measure and, likewise, that the high scores are associated. This is called a **positive correlation**. If one score goes up and the other goes down – like the relationship between smoking and health – then it is called a **negative correlation**.

The tricky question is: how close to a line do the scores have to be for us to agree that there is a linear correlation and how spread out do they have to be to reject the view that they are linearly correlated? Judging the scatterplot by eye is quite a useful test but a more formal test we can apply is the Pearson test for scale variables. This test calculates a statistic called the Pearson correlation coefficient. This value will be 0 if there is no correlation between the variables at all (they are randomly scattered around the chart), +1 if there is a perfect positive correlation (all the points lie exactly along a straight line) and –1 for a perfect negative correlation (all the points lie exactly along a straight line). The method it uses is to work out which straight line fits the data the best. It then works out how far the points are from this line – how good a fit it actually is. If the points are close to the line then the probability is that the correlation is 'significant', and they are genuinely related in this way. If the points are far from the line then the correlation is probably not 'significant'; that is, the two variables are probably not be related in this way.

Let us assume that the researchers in this study predicted, in advance of carrying out the study, that there would be a positive correlation between the children's' mathematics cores and their reading scores. To carry out the Pearson test, we undertake the following procedure.

■   Select the **Analyze** drop-down menu, and then **Correlate** and **Bivariate**.

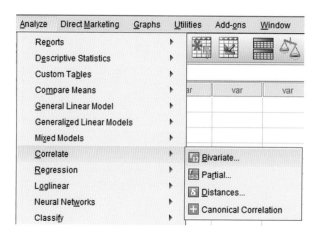

The **Bivariate Correlations** dialog box appears.

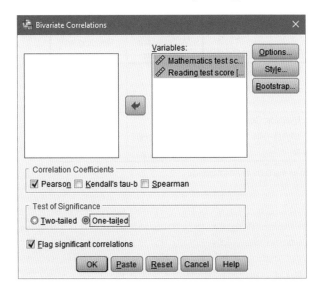

- Send the two variables 'Mathematics test score' and 'Reading test score' to the **Variables** box.

With certain statistical tests, like the Pearson correlation test (but not the chi-square test), SPSS gives you a choice of **Two-tailed** or **One-tailed** as a **Test of Significance**. If you are simply predicting a correlation but do not specifically predict whether the correlation is positive (the values of both variables go up and down together) or negative (as the values of one variable go up the values on the other variable go down) then you choose the two-tailed test of significance. If a specific prediction is being made that the correlation is positive (or negative) then the one-tailed test of significance is chosen. Predicting simply that the mathematics and reading scores are correlated is a two-tailed prediction. Here predicting a positive correlation (their values will go up and down together) is a one-tailed test of significance.

- There is already a tick in the **Pearson** box under **Correlation Coefficients**, so we leave this default value. The researchers change the selection of the **Test of Significance** from **Two-tailed** to **One-tailed**, as they are specifically predicting a positive correlation.

- Click **OK**.

If we double click on the table and highlight the cell with .000, then SPSS displays 6.598E-14 which is a shorthand way of writing the number .00000000000006598. This is simply very small, so the probability of this correlation occurring by chance is definitely less than 0.05. Notice at the bottom of the table SPSS is very helpful in saying that the correlation is significant at 0.01, an even stricter level than 0.05.

When reporting the findings of a Pearson correlation, we would include three figures (to two decimal places): the value of r, the number of participants (or data points in the correlation) labelled N in the above table and the probability value. The calculated probability value here is extremely small and difficult to express easily, so we simply report that it is lower than the stricter significance level of 0.01, as follows:

$r = 0.98$, N = 20, $p < 0.01$

See Chapter 6

The **Correlations** table is displayed in the **IBM SPSS Statistics Viewer**.

Correlations

		Mathematics test score	Reading test score
Mathematics test score	Pearson Correlation	1	.977**
	Sig. (1-tailed)		.000
	N	20	20
Reading test score	Pearson Correlation	.977**	1
	Sig. (1-tailed)	.000	
	N	20	20

**. Correlation is significant at the 0.01 level (1-tailed).

The table presents the correlations of each of the variables with each other. The first row of the tables refers to the mathematics test scores. The first cell of the table shows the correlation of the mathematics scores with the mathematics scores. Not surprisingly, this is a perfect correlation – as they are the same scores! The second cell is the one we are interested in, the correlation of the 'Mathematics test scores' with the 'Reading test scores' variables. We can see that this is an extremely high correlation, with a **Pearson Correlation** value (known as r) of 0.977. The probability value p is shown directly below this (on the **Sig. (1-tailed)** row). It looks like 0 (as it is displayed as .000), but is actually such a small number that SPSS cannot show in a space allocated only three decimal places.

The researchers can see that the correlation between the mathematics test scores and the reading test scores is highly 'significant'. They can therefore conclude that there is a positive linear correlation between the mathematics test scores and the reading test scores (in support of their prediction).

(The second row of the table refers to the reading test scores. However, the first cell repeats what we already know – the reading test scores are correlated with the mathematics test scores, and it gives the same Pearson Correlation and p value. Finally, the second cell states the reading test scores are perfectly correlated with the reading test scores, which is as it should be.)

This correlation example – constructed for illustration – produced an extremely high correlation coefficient that we are unlikely to find in our research. A more typical example is shown below from the Sparcote Study.

The researchers were interested in the correlation between the students' teaching team ratings (which were assumed to be measured on an interval scale) and their overall satisfaction with the year. We saw in Chapter 6 that an overall satisfaction measure was constructed by adding together the three items in Question 12: satisfaction with academic life, with social life and with personal development. Even though these were individually measured on a Likert scale, the researchers decided to treat the overall satisfaction measure as an interval scale. Now the relationship of the teaching team ratings and the overall satisfaction scores can be plotted on a scatterplot.

Figure 20: Scatterplot of Overall satisfaction by Teaching team rating

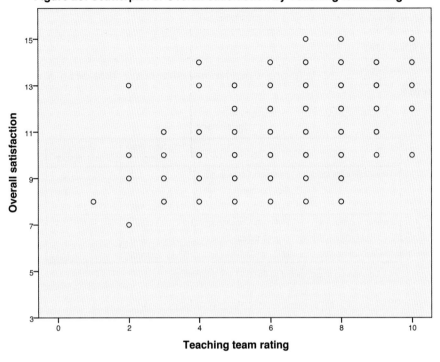

We have added a title to the chart and changed the default axes to show both scales in full. The 'Teacher team ratings' range from 1 to 10 and the 'Overall satisfaction scores' range from 3 (the lowest possible score) to 15. The points are darker to indicate where there is more than one point in the same location. There is some indication that the scores lie within a linear strip – but it is nothing like the previous example. The data here is much more spread out.

Now the Sparcote researchers have made no specific prediction in their research questions about this correlation. When they perform a statistical test it is to really see if there is something of interest to follow up. Therefore, in this case the statistical test is a two-tailed test, not a one-tailed test, as they have not made a specific prediction about the relationship between these variables. To examine this correlation we undertake the following procedure.

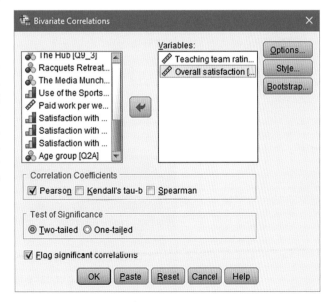

- Select the **Analyze** drop-down menu.

- Select the **Correlate > Bivariate** command.

- Send the two variables to the **Variables** box.

We can leave all the options as the default values, as the **Pearson** box is already ticked under the **Correlation Coefficients** and **Two-tailed** is selected in the **Test of Significance**.

■ Click **OK**.

SPSS displays the following **Correlations** table in the **IBM SPSS Statistics Viewer**.

Correlations

		Teaching team rating	Overall satisfaction
Teaching team rating	Pearson Correlation	1	.453[**]
	Sig. (2-tailed)		.000
	N	183	183
Overall satisfaction	Pearson Correlation	.453[**]	1
	Sig. (2-tailed)	.000	
	N	183	183

**. Correlation is significant at the 0.01 level (2-tailed).

The table shows the variables correlated with themselves (which will always give a Pearson correlation of 1) and with each other – which is what we are interested in. The data from 'Teaching team rating' and 'Overall satisfaction' produces a **Pearson Correlation** value of .453. The probability value, p, of .000, is given on the row headed **Sig. (2-tailed)**. This probability value is not actually 0, which we can show by double clicking the table and highlighting the cell. SPSS displays 1.2152E-10, which is a shorthand way of writing .00000000012152. The probability of the Pearson value of .453 occurring by chance is extremely small indeed and much smaller than the significance level of 0.05. Notice at the bottom of the table SPSS helpfully tells us that the correlation is significant at the stricter significance level of 0.01. The conclusion is that the data does show a 'significant' positive correlation between 'Teaching team rating' and 'Overall satisfaction'. We report this like this:

$r = 0.45$, N = 183, $p < 0.01$

This is definitely something that might be followed up in future research as this indicates a link between student satisfaction and the quality of the teaching.

✓

It is possible to correlate data measured on two ordinal scales rather than two interval scale variables. In this case the **Spearman** correlation coefficient is chosen rather than the **Pearson** in the **Bivariate Correlations** dialog box.

┌─ Correlation Coefficients ─────────────────────
☑ Pearso<u>n</u> ☐ <u>K</u>endall's tau-b ☑ Spearman

THE *t* TEST FOR COMPARING TWO CATEGORIES ON A SCALE MEASURE

The chi-square test examines the association between categorical variables by examining the patterns of frequencies between the different categories. The Pearson correlation coefficient examines the co-relationship of two scale variables by examining how close the points lie along a straight line in a scatterplot. However, in many examples of research a categorical variable is used to create different groups. For example, 'morning' and afternoon' can be defined as two categories of a variable called 'Time of day'. This is then combined with a second (usually scale) variable to test a particular hypothesis. For example, do participants perform better on a particular task in the morning compared to the afternoon? Are men or women safer drivers? Do participants read more accurately with text displayed in blue or red? Does being told the first letter result in shorter anagram solution times than not being given the first letter? All these research questions are predicting the effect of one categorical variable on a second scale variable. If a researcher makes a prediction that people will perform better on a task in the morning compared to the afternoon, this prediction is stating that one variable ('time of day') – the independent variable – will effect a second variable (scores on the test of performance) – the dependent variable (or outcome measure). In this case, the researcher is making a specific prediction as to the direction of the difference: morning will produce the better performance scores. If we test a group of people in the morning on a test and find their mean score we can then compare this value with the mean score of a second group of participants' scores on the same task in the afternoon (assuming the researcher has undertaken the proper controls to avoid sampling). The comparison of the mean values can be used indicate whether there is a difference between the performance on the task between the two groups in support of the researcher's prediction. At a simple level, we could argue that large differences are more likely to indicate genuine differences between the group and small differences might be explainable by chance alone. The question is: how can we formally make this judgement? The answer comes in the form of the *t* test. The *t* statistic has been set up specifically to answer the question of when a difference of means is large enough to be 'significant' or is simply not large enough to reject the explanation of a chance effect.

The *t* test compares the difference in means between the two groups with an estimate of the variation that could result by chance alone. This second calculation is like a measure of background 'noise'. If the difference in means stands out 'loud and clear' against the background noise then it is likely to indicate a genuine underlying difference in the performance of the two populations that the samples have been selected from. However, if the difference in means is 'drowned out' by the background noise then the difference is not likely to indicate any genuine differences between the groups. If we perform a *t* test and the *t* statistic comes out as 1, with a particular set of data, then it simply means the difference in means is no different to the background noise. As it gets bigger – twice as big, three times as big as the background noise – we get more confident it represents a genuine difference. Again, we use the probability or *p* value to determine when the *t* statistic is big enough to indicate a 'significant' difference in the means. When *p* is less than the significance level of 0.05 then the difference is judged as 'significant', and difference between the means is taken to indicate a difference in the performance of the two groups.

independent samples
***t* test**
A statistical test to examine the difference in sample means obtained from two unrelated or independent samples

paired samples *t* test
A statistical test to examine the difference in sample means obtained from two related samples

A breakfast cereal manufacturer decides to run a special offer on one of its products but before it rolls out the offer across the country it decides to trial it in 10 designated supermarkets, which, during the test period, run the special offer for half the time and sell the product at the usual price for rest of the time, with the sales being recorded. The manufacturer is interested in seeing if the special offer has an effect on sales at the 10 supermarkets. (The breakfast cereal company decides to be cautious in its prediction. It hopes that the special offer will increase sales but it is keeping an open mind and is not excluding the possibility that it will result in lower sales. Its prediction is therefore that the special offer will simply have an effect on the sales. This is a two-tailed prediction.)

This is an example of a comparison that can be undertaken with a *t* test. There are two forms of the *t* test and we must choose the right one before analysing the data with SPSS. When there are different participants in the two groups we undertake the **independent-samples *t* test** and when the same participants take part in both groups then we undertake the **paired-samples *t* test**. As each supermarket provided figures for both sales conditions, there are the same participants in the two groups (each supermarket is a 'participant') so we undertake a paired-samples *t* test.

■   In SPSS, we select the **Analyze** drop-down menu, followed by **Compare Means** and then **Paired-Samples T Test**.

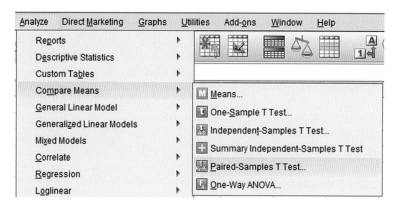

The **Paired-Samples T Test** dialog box appears.

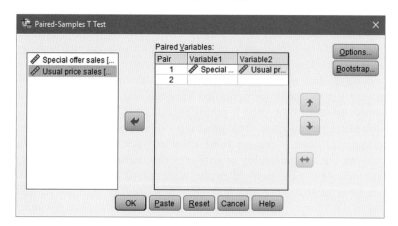

■ Send 'Special offer sales' to **Variable 1** and 'Usual price sales' to **Variable 2** in the **Paired Variables** box.

■ We do not need to change any options, so simply click on **OK**.

SPSS displays three tables for the paired-samples *t* test. The first is the **Paired Samples Statistics** table.

Paired Samples Statistics

		Mean	N	Std. Deviation	Std. Error Mean
Pair 1	Special offer sales	3230.40	20	274.890	61.467
	Usual price sales	3072.35	20	242.837	54.300

This table shows the mean sales for the two categories 'Special offer sales' and 'Usual price sales'. There definitely are more sales during the special offer.

The next table is the **Paired Samples Correlations** table and is not normally reported.

Paired Samples Correlations

		N	Correlation	Sig.
Pair 1	Special offer sales & Usual price sales	20	.371	.108

> The **Paired Samples Correlations** table shows the correlation between the two variables, and is not normally reported with the *t* test. Out of interest, it tells us whether the supermarkets selling the most (or least) under one condition are also the supermarkets selling the most (or the least) under the other condition. We can see that there is a tendency for a positive correlation here but the *p* value (in the **Sig.** column) of 0.108 is not less than 0.05 so we would not claim that this correlation is 'significant'.

The final table is the **Paired Samples Test** table.

Paired Samples Test

		Paired Differences							
					95% Confidence Interval of the Difference				
		Mean	Std. Deviation	Std. Error Mean	Lower	Upper	t	df	Sig. (2-tailed)
Pair 1	Special offer sales - Usual price sales	158.050	291.604	65.205	21.575	294.525	2.424	19	.026

This table provides the results of the *t* test. The first thing to note is the first column (headed **Mean**) that shows the mean difference in sales is on average **158.05** more for the special offer compared to the usual price. Now we need to decide if this difference is a chance effect or 'significant', implying a genuine difference. The table includes various pieces of statistical information but if we look at the column headed **t**, we can see that the *t* statistic is calculated as 2.424 (over twice as large as we would expect from chance factors alone). We can also see the *p* value of .026 in the column headed **Sig (2-tailed)**. As this is less than the significance level of 0.05, the difference in means is 'significant' and it is concluded that the special offer does have an effect on sales, and we can see from the means of the two groups that this effect is an increase in sales.

When we report the results of a *t* test, we report three values from the above table. First, the *t* statistic value (to two decimal places), the degrees of freedom (based on the number of participants in the samples) shown in the column headed **df**, and the probability value from the column headed **Sig (2-tailed)**:

$t = 2.42$, df = 19, $p < 0.05$

Here we are not reporting the actual *p* value (0.026) but that it is less than the significance level (0.05).

See Chapter 6

We shall show a second example of a *t* test, to demonstrate an independent-samples *t* test in SPSS. This example comes from the Sparcote Study. Here, we are going to examine the amount of paid work (Question 11) undertaken by the younger (under 21 year) students compared to the older (21 and over) students. We computed this second variable 'Q2A' with the label 'Age group' in Chapter 6. There are different participants in the two groups, so to analyse the differences between them we perform an independent-samples *t* test. No specific prediction was made in advance about this comparison so it is a two-tailed test.

■ In SPSS, select the **Analyze** drop-down menu, followed by **Compare Means** and then **Independent-Samples T Test**.

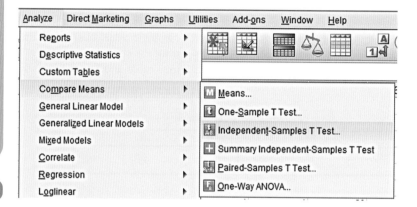

The **Independent-Samples T test** dialog box appears.

■ Send the scale variable we are interested in ('Paid work per week') to the **Test Variable(s)** box and the categorical variable ('Age group') to the **Grouping Variable** box. (SPSS shows the variable's name in the **Grouping Variable** box rather than the label.)

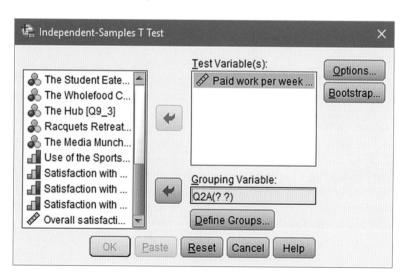

Notice that there are two question marks after 'Q2A' (the name of the 'Age group' variable) in the **Grouping Variables** box. This is because we need to tell SPSS which are the two groups we want to compare.

■ Click on the **Define Groups** button, which brings up the **Define Groups** box. We have to type in the numeric code for the two groups rather than the label here.

■ The first group, the under 21-year-old students, has the numeric code of 1, so we type that in to the **Group 1** box.

■ The second group, the 21 years and older students, has the code of 2, so we type that into the **Group 2** box.

■ Press **Continue** and return to the **Independent-Samples T Test** dialog box.

■ No options need to be selected so simply press **OK** to run the test.

Group Statistics

	Age group	N	Mean	Std. Deviation	Std. Error Mean
Paid work per week	Under 21	91	10.70	3.863	.405
	21 and over	92	11.85	3.794	.396

We can see here that the mean number of hours worked by the under 21-year-old students is 10.70 hours and 11.85 hours for the 21 and older students, so the older students are working 1.15 hours more on average than the younger students. (0.15 of an hour converts to 9 minutes.) We now need to see if this difference is large enough to claim a 'significant' difference between the students. The second table, the **Independent Samples Test** table provides all the information about the *t* test.

Independent Samples Test

		Levene's Test for Equality of Variances		t-test for Equality of Means					95% Confidence Interval of the Difference	
		F	Sig.	t	df	Sig. (2-tailed)	Mean Difference	Std. Error Difference	Lower	Upper
Paid work per week	Equal variances assumed	.329	.567	-2.022	181	.045	-1.145	.566	-2.261	-.028
	Equal variances not assumed			-2.022	180.848	.045	-1.145	.566	-2.261	-.028

There is a lot of detail about the test here that is beyond this book. We will focus on the key results. Notice the two rows have very similar figures in them, but normally researchers will select the figures from the first row labelled **Equal variances assumed**. We now examine the column headed **t**. This is the value of the t statistic. The minus sign simply indicates that the first group (the younger students) has the lower mean value, but the size of the t statistic is the crucial information. A t value of 2.022 shows that the difference in the means is twice that we would expect by chance factors alone, so we now check the p value to see if it is significant. If we look at the column headed **Sig. (2-tailed)** we can see that the p value for this t statistic is 0.045, which is smaller than the significance level of 0.05, so the difference is 'significant'. This can be reported as follows:

$t = -2.02$, df = 181, $p < 0.05$

The Sparcote researchers can conclude that the older students are undertaking more paid work each week than the younger students.

parametric tests

Statistical tests that make assumptions about the data (that it is measured on a scale and comes from a normally distributed population) in order to make statistical inferences from samples to populations.

nonparametric tests

Not all data satisfies the assumptions of a parametric test and so a different set of statistical tests – the nonparametric tests – have been devised to make statistical inferences when this is the case.

The t test is called a **parametric test** as it makes certain assumptions about the data (such as being measured on a scale and from a normally distributed population). There are other parametric tests, such as the analysis of variance (ANOVA), which can test for differences between more than two samples. Also, there are a range of other statistical tests you can use when your data does not meet the assumptions of a parametric test – called **nonparametric tests**. These can all be found in the SPSS **Analyze** drop-down menu.

Further explanation of all of these statistical tests and how to undertake them using SPSS can be found in our more advanced companion volume: Hinton, P.R., McMurray, I. and Brownlow, C. (2014) *SPSS Explained*, also published by Routledge.

Glossary

activate   Before a table or a chart in the **IBM SPSS Statistics Viewer** can be edited, it has to be activated, by double clicking on it. Right clicking on the table or chart and selecting **Edit Content** from the menu also activates it for editing.

alpha   Alpha (α) is another term for the significance level in a statistical test. Usually, the significance level, or alpha, is set to a probability of 0.05.

categorical data   Data can be measured at different levels: nominal, ordinal or scale. Nominal and ordinal data are recorded by a response being allocated to a category, so the term 'categorical data' is used to refer to either nominal data or ordinal data or both.

categorical variable   A variable measured by nominal or ordinal data.

chi-square test   A statistical test of association or independence between categorical variables. It analyses the pattern of observed category frequencies and compares these values to the expected values according to a particular model or pattern of frequencies across the categories.

codebook   In any one particular research study, there may be a number of categorical variables that require coding for analysis. Writing down the codes for each variable in a single document – called a codebook – avoids potential mistakes of different researchers using different codes in recording and analysing the results.

coding   In research using categorical variables, responses are placed in a category (such as 'day' or 'night'). These labels are given a numeric code (such as 1 for 'day' and 2 for 'night') so that they can be analysed by statistical software. Coding is the process of allocating codes to categorical responses in a study.

confirmatory research   The aim of this type of research is to confirm (or otherwise) a prediction (also called a hypothesis) made at the beginning of the study.

constant sum   A technique used to determine the relative contribution of elements to a 'whole' or specific total in research (such as a survey), where it is required that the value given to the elements must always add up to the same amount.

For example, a person could be asked to give the number of hours per day they worked (by allocating a specific number of hours to the category 'work'), slept ('sleep') and did other things ('the rest of my time'). However, every participant is required to make sure that the total number of hours adds up to the constant sum of 24 hours.

convenience sampling   A method of choosing a sample for research where the participants are selected from the people who happen to be available at the time, rather than seeking a representative or random sample.

correlate   Two variables are said to correlate if their values vary together (i.e. they 'co-relate'). See also **negative correlation**; **positive correlation**.

crosstabulation   Frequency data can be represented in a table with the rows as the categories of one variable and the columns as the categories of a second variable. This is a crosstabulation. We can include more variables by adding 'layers' to the crosstabulation in SPSS.

cumulative percentage   When data are allocated to categories, the frequency values in each category can be converted to their percentage of the total. The percentage values of the categories can be can be added together to produce a cumulative percentage for the categories chosen. When all categories are selected the cumulative percentage will be 100%.

Data View   The Data View window in the SPSS Data Editor presents a spreadsheet style format for entering the data.

dataset   A collection (or set) of data, usually comprising all the results of a particular study.

degrees of freedom   When calculating a statistic, we use information from the data (such as the mean or total) in the calculation. The degrees of freedom is the number of scores we need to know before we can work out the rest using the information we already have. For example, if nine friends were coming to your house for dinner (total of 10 people at the table) and you politely let them sit down first, you would not have a choice of where to sit as there is only one seat left. Here, the degrees of freedom is nine, rather than 10 (as nine people have a choice of where to sit and only one does not). Statistical tests use the degrees of freedom in their analysis to work out the probability (p value).

demographic   In research involving human participants, the relevant characteristics of the sample are called the demographics. Details of these characteristics (often age, gender and other qualities, such as relevant group membership) and their frequency are included in the research report.

dependent variable   The variable measured by the researcher and predicted to be influenced by (that is, depend on) the independent variable. A dependent variable is an outcome measure.

descriptive research   Research that sets out to describe the situation under investigation.

descriptive statistics   Usually, researchers wish to describe and summarise their research data to report the findings of a study. Descriptive statistics such as frequency counts, totals, percentages, the mean and standard deviation enable a researcher to summarise a dataset.

dialog box   A type of window in SPSS in which options can be selected, choices made and information input, in order to carry out a command.

dichotomous response   In certain research situations (such as a particular question in a survey), a participant has to make a choice between only two options (such as yes or no): this is a dichotomous response.

dimensions   In a crosstabulation, the dimensions refer to the number of categories in each variable in the table. For example, a crosstabulation of dimensions 2 × 3 is a table with one variable of two categories tabulated against a second variable of three categories.

effect   In quantitative research, differences in numerical outcomes are examined to see if there is an effect of one variable on another – such as a difference, an association or a correlation.

ethics   All researchers should behave morally in carrying out their research. In particular, when using human participants, they should make sure that they do not inadvertently cause any harm. Academic research, whether carried out by students or academic staff, is scrutinised by ethics committees, which may require changes before the research is allowed to proceed.

exploratory research   The research question or questions do not have any specific preconceptions or predictions about what answers to expect from the research, but aims to explore what is going on in a specific situation.

forced choice   In some research situations, participants are required to make a choice from the available options (such as yes or no) rather than being given an option *not* to make a specific choice (which is possible when categories such as 'sometimes' or 'maybe' are included in the choices).

frequency   Another name for 'count', indicating the number in a particular category.

frequency table   A table listing out the frequencies of the different categories of a variable (or variables), often used to show the results of a research study.

hypothesis   A predicted relationship between variables. For example: 'As the attendance at safety workshops increases so the number of accidents at work will decrease' or 'Experienced drivers make fewer driving errors than drivers who have recently passed the driving test'.

illustrative statistics   Illustrative statistics are the visual representation of data, often in the form of a chart or a graph. It may be easier to understand a graphical representation of data than the same information in the form of a table or written description.

independent samples *t* test   A statistical test to examine the difference in sample means obtained from unrelated or independent samples.

independent variable   A variable chosen by the researcher, who selects the categories of the variable to study, which is predicted to influence the dependent Variable (an outcome measure).

inferential statistics   Statistics that can be used to make inferences about the data collected from samples to wider groups or populations: Whether, on the basis of probability, data showing a difference in samples can be used to infer a difference in populations or not.

instructions   In any research study involving human participants, they need to be given precise details of what to do – written or verbal instructions – in their role as participant.

interpretivism   An opposing philosophical perspective to positivism that suggests that there is not one objective truth but instead that knowledge itself is of a subjective nature.

item   A part or whole of a question in a survey.

labels   Variables are often given short names for the convenience of researchers. However, they can also be given more meaningful labels that can be used in reports. SPSS allows variables to have both a name and a label.

levels of measurement   (also known as level of data). Not all data is produced by using numbers in the same way. Sometimes we associate numbers with categories (nominal), we place items in an order (ordinal), or we use a measuring scale with equal intervals (scale or interval scale).

Likert-type scale   A measuring scale in which participants are asked to indicate their level of disagreement or agreement to a particular statement on, typically, a 5- or 7-point scale (from strongly disagree to strongly agree), named after psychologist Rensis Likert.

line of best fit   In a scatterplot, a straight line can be superimposed on the points, where this line has been mathematically calculated to be the 'best fit' or closer to the data points than any other straight line. This is also called the linear regression. See also **regression**.

linear   Following a straight line. In a scatterplot, researchers are interested in whether the relationship between two variables is linear, that is, the points fall (roughly) along a straight line.

mean   A measure of the 'average' score in a set of data. The mean is found by adding up all the scores and dividing by the number of scores.

measure of central tendency   In describing a set of results from a single variable, researchers often wish to summarise the data by presenting a typical or 'middle' value to represent the results. There are different ways of calculating a 'middle' position or measure of central tendency. The mean is the most popular for scale data, but the median and the mode may also be chosen.

median   If we order a set of data from lowest to highest, the median is the point that divides the scores into two, with half the scores below and half above the median.

missing values   A missing value indicates that a person did not answer a question.

mode   The most frequently occurring category or score in a set of data.

model   Research is often seeking to find relationships between variables. A predicted relationship is called a 'model'. The model is tested by producing new data to see if the results follow the pattern predicted by the model or not.

negative correlation Two variables correlate if they co-relate or vary together. However, if, as the first variable increases, the second variable decreases, then the correlation is said to be negative. An example of a negative correlation is that between a person's spending and her savings. As spending goes up then savings go down.

negative skew When a frequency distribution is plotted in a histogram, it can be seen whether the distribution is symmetrical or not. Often the pattern of data looks like a hill or a bell shape with the most frequent scores in the centre and the frequencies tailing off in both directions. However, if most of the scores pile to the right of the distribution with a long tail to the left then the distribution is said to be negatively skewed.

nominal Nominal refers to the term 'name'. In research terms, nominal data is data collected in named categories for a variable, such as the variable 'home location' with the categories 'north', 'midlands', 'south'. A person gives the location of his home by selecting one of these three categories.

nonparametric tests Not all data satisfies the assumptions of a parametric test and so a different set of statistical tests – the nonparametric tests – have been devised to make statistical inferences when this is the case.

normal distribution A bell-shaped frequency distribution that appears to underlie many human variables. The normal distribution can be worked out mathematically using the mean and standard deviation.

not significant In null hypothesis significance testing (see entry), a statistical test is used to work out the probability of the effect found in the research arising from assumption of the null hypothesis. If the calculated probability is not as small as (or smaller) than the significance level, the result is said to be not significant (often abbreviated to 'ns') and the null hypothesis is not rejected.

null hypothesis A prediction that there no effect or relationship in the wider population corresponding to the one under investigation in the research study.

null hypothesis significance testing A statistical method for making a decision about whether an effect found in a research study (such as a difference or a correlation) can be generalised to a wider population. The null hypothesis is assumed and a probability worked out for the effect found in the study. The effect is only inferred to generalise more widely if the probability is as small as or smaller than the significance level.

operationalisation Redefining a concept so that it can be studied. Concepts such as intelligence or happiness are often difficult to define. However, in order to study such ideas, researchers operationalise them in terms of measurable outcomes. For example, 'intelligence' has been studied by operationalising the term as 'the quality measured by an intelligence quotient (IQ) test'; 'happiness' may be defined in terms of the responses to certain items in a questionnaire. It is important to specify in a research report how such terms have been operationalised so that other researchers are aware of how the concept has been defined.

opportunity sampling   Another name for convenience sampling. The members of a sample are selected from a population simply on the basis that there is an opportunity to select them, rather than selecting sample members randomly or representatively.

ordinal   Ordinal comes from the word 'order'. In research, when items are ordered or people are asked to make rating or ranking judgements, it cannot be assumed that they are making these judgements using a measurement scale of equal intervals, so the data are referred as ordinal rather than scale.

outcome measures   In all quantitative research, data is collected to answer research questions. However, these data are obtained by using outcome measures, recording category frequencies, such as how many people select each of a set of choices in a survey, or scores on a performance measure, such as the number of correct answers in a test. The researcher devises the appropriate outcome measure (or measures) to obtain data relevant to the research question(s).

Output Navigator   An SPSS navigation and editing system in an outline view in the left-hand column of the output window. This enables the user to hide or show output or to move items within the output screen.

p value   This is the probability of the calculated value of an inferential statistic in a statistical test (assuming the null hypothesis). If this value is equal to, or smaller than, the significance level then the effect under test is said to be 'significant' and the null hypothesis assumption is rejected.

paired samples t test   A statistical test to examine the difference in sample means obtained from two related samples.

parametric tests   Statistical tests that make assumptions about the data (that it is measured on a scale and comes from a normally distributed population) in order to make statistical inferences from samples to populations.

Pearson correlation   An inferential statistical test to determine the linear relationship between two variables.

percentage   A proportion of a whole, expressed out of a total of 100. To turn a frequency or count into a percentage for a category, the category count is divided by the total for all the categories and multiplied by 100.

pivot table   A pivot table is an advanced form of spreadsheet that allows for more complex operations on the data within the table than simply displaying it in the form of rows and columns, such as producing summaries, totals and other statistics. SPSS has the facility for complex editing of tables in the **IBM SPSS Statistics Viewer** and this editing takes place in the **Pivot Table** window.

population   A complete set of items or events. In statistics, this usually refers to the complete set of participants or scores we are interested in, from which we have drawn a sample.

positive correlation   Two variables correlate if they co-relate or vary together. If the second variable increases and decreases as the first variable increases and decreases the correlation is said to be positive. An example of a positive correlation is that between the number of hours studied and a student's grade.

positive skew   When a frequency distribution is plotted in a histogram, it can be seen whether the distribution is symmetrical or not. Often the pattern of data looks like a hill or a bell shape with the most frequent scores in the centre and the frequencies tailing off in both directions. However, if most of the scores pile to the left of the distribution with a long tail to the right then the distribution is said to be positively skewed.

positivism   The approach that historically has predominated in the sciences and assumes that knowledge is based on the experiences of our senses and can be measured with value-free quantitative measures (such as observations and experiments).

prediction   A testable statement or hypothesis.

probability   The chance of a specific event occurring from a set of possible events, expressed as a proportion. For example, if there were four women and six men in a room, the probability of meeting a woman first on entering the room is 4/10 or 0.4 as there are four women out of 10 people in the room. A probability of 0 indicates an event will never occur and a probability of 1 that it will always occur. In a room containing only men and there are 10 of them, there is a probability of 0 (0/10) of meeting a woman first and a probability of 1 (10/10) of meeting a man.

purposeful sampling   This is a sampling method that relies on the judgement of the researcher for the selection of the sample. While this is clearly not going to produce a random or representative sample, it can be very useful in certain circumstances. For example, a researcher exploring the treatment of workers in a company may choose certain people who he believes to be particularly of interest (such as those who are viewed by the researcher as potentially vulnerable to exploitation or discrimination).

qualitative   Pertaining to 'qualities'. Qualitative research is about obtaining insight of a situation or position; it seeks to produce a depth of understanding or explores the subjective interpretation of events (rather than breadth typical of quantitative methods).

quantitative   Pertaining to 'quantities'. Quantitative research is undertaken where numerical outcomes (quantities) are produced to answer research questions. Quantitative research is often about sampling, control and prediction, along statistical analysis to test predictions and make generalisations.

random sampling   To avoid bias in sample selection, a research may engage in random sampling, in which each member of a sample is randomly selected from a larger group (or population).

range   The difference between the lowest score and the highest score in a set of results.

rank order   When a set of data is ordered from lowest to highest, the rank of a score is its position in this order.

rating scale   Human participants are often asked in research to make a rating on a rating scale, such as a teacher asked to judge the politeness of the children in the class on a 1 to 10 scale. Rating scales often provide a way of measuring a difficult to define concept, such as politeness. The data from a rating scale should normally be treated as ordinal as the raters may not be using it like an interval scale. However, in a number of subject areas, researcher do (for various reasons) choose to treat rating data as if it were measured on an interval scale.

regression   If two variables are related in some way (for instance, they are *correlated*) then this relationship can be used to predict the values of one variable from the values of the other. This prediction, or regression, of one variable by another is usually expressed as a mathematical formula. If the relationship between the variables is linear, then the regression is a linear regression.

replicate   The findings of a single research study, however well carried out and analysed, may still be subject to chance effects. Repeating the study to see if the same findings reoccur is a way of demonstrating that the effect did not arise by chance. If the same results do reoccur in further studies, it provides further support that the findings are not 'one-off' or chance effects. The ability to replicate (repeat) a finding is a crucial aspect of knowledge development in a field of study.

sample   A subset of a set of items, usually a group of participants that are all members of a larger group (or population).

sampling   Researchers want to use the results of their studies to make claims about populations but (normally) they can only test a sample rather than the whole population. Therefore, they engage in sampling; that is, undertake a process to select their samples to represent the populations under investigation.

scale   A measurement scale with equal intervals (like centimetres on a tape measure), and the data collected by using it.

semantic differential   This is a rating scale employed in research where a point has to be chosen between two opposing adjectives, such as good–bad, or happy–sad. These semantic differential scales are often used to gauge a person's attitudes or feelings about a particular action, activity or situation.

significance level   Statistical tests are undertaken to make a decision as to whether an effect (such has a difference or a correlation) found in the study using samples should be attributed to chance or can be generalised to a wider population. The test produces a probability of the effect found in the study occurring by chance (when the null hypothesis is assumed). The decision is then made whether to reject (or not reject) the null hypothesis based on this probability value. If the probability is as small as or smaller than a set criterion, called the significance level (or α), then the null hypothesis is rejected and it is inferred that the effect can be generalised to a wider population. Conventionally, it has been agreed to set the significance level at a probability of 0.05.

significant   A statistical term used in null hypothesis significance testing. An effect (such as a difference between samples or a correlation between variables) is only described as 'significant' if, after the data has been subject to a statistical test, the effect is shown to occur with a probability of the significance level (normally 0.05) or lower (assuming the null hypothesis). As a result, the null hypothesis is rejected and the effect found in the study is inferred to be generalisable to a wider population.

skew When scale data is plotted on a frequency distribution, it can be observed whether the distribution is symmetrical about a 'middle' position or not. If the distribution is not symmetrical, it is said to be 'skewed'. See also **negative skew**; **positive skew**.

snowballing sampling Selecting a sample where one participant leads to the recruitment of further participants by her connections associated to the topic of the research.

standard deviation A measure of the standard ('average') difference (deviation) of a score from the mean in a set of scores.

statistics Characteristics of a sample, such as the total or the sample mean. A set of data can be summarised by descriptive statistics, such as describing the results of a scale variable by the mean and standard deviation. Statistical tests calculate the value of an inferential statistic using the data from the study (assuming the null hypothesis is true). If the probability of producing the value of the statistic (the p value) is equal to or less than the significance level (α), then the null hypothesis is rejected and the effect under study is inferred to have general applicability (to the population under investigation).

stratified sampling One way of selecting a representative sample from a population is to match key strata within the sample. For example, the population of people who visited a dentist's surgery in the last year included 50% male and 50% female, and 40% under 18 years, 35% between 18 and 64 years and 25% of 65 years and older. The population is, in this example, stratified by gender and age. A researcher selecting a sample of patients for a research project may choose to use stratified sample selection, by making sure that the sample contains the same proportions of male and female patients and the same proportions of the different age groups as in the population.

t test A statistical test to examine the difference in means obtained from two samples, to see if the difference in the samples can be generalised to the populations under investigation.

total The 'total' is a statistic – it describes a characteristic of the sample, fundamentally – how many there are.

valid percentage In any study, there a possibility that there will be missing data, for various reasons. For example, a participant in a survey may miss a question or choose not to answer it. In analysing the data, it is important to know both the number of valid responses (where a result was present) and the number of missing responses. The valid percent is the number of valid responses in a category divided by the total number of valid responses, and then multiplied by 100.

value label The categories of a nominal or an ordinal variable are given numeric codes (such as 1 for men and 2 for women) so that the data collected on these categories can be analysed by statistical software (such as SPSS). However, these numeric codes are not informative about the category itself, so SPSS allows a value label to be included with the numeric code to identify the category, for example, the value label 'men' for the numeric code 1 and the value label 'women' for the numeric code 2. Then when SPSS displays the results of the study, it uses the (meaningful) value labels rather than the numeric codes to label the results.

Variable View   The Variable View window within the SPSS Data Editor is where the characteristics of the variables are assigned.

variables   Variables are something that are not fixed but that can change or vary. There would be no point in quantitative researchers studying situations, activities or behaviour that remains constant. Indeed, the aim of the research is to study factors that vary and seek to find explanations for why they vary. This is why quantitative research is all about the study of the relationship between variables, such as gender, age or time of day, and other variables, or outcome measures, such as the performance on a task or the responses to certain questions in a survey.

Index

activate tables and graphs
    tables 233–238, 241, 243–244,
    246–247, 249; graphs 268, 273, 291,
    295, 298

bar charts 120–122, 157–159, 201–204,
    214–223, 234–240, 268–275,
    293–302
        clustered bar chart 157–159, 168–169,
        202–203, 216–221, 238–240,
        284–285, 294–295; stacked bar chart
        203–204, 221–223, 293–303

categorical data 46, 49, 55
categorical variable 40, 55, 152, 156,
    162–165, 171, 238–240, 313–314
charts see graphs
Chart Builder 209–233
Chart Editor 268–303
chi-square 156, 165, 313–318
codebook 62–63, 94–95
coding 39–40, 51, 55–61, 71–72, 74–83,
    90, 92, 94–95, 98, 105–106, 137–142
comma separated values (.csv) file 98–105
Compute 195–197
confirmatory research 12, 16, 19, 312
constant sum 58, 132–33, 180–82,
    218–221, 236
copying and pasting between applications
    110, 115, 303–304
correlation 16, 207, 313, 233
        Pearson correlation coefficient 313,
        320–324; scatterplot 207, 230–233,
        286–290, 313, 319, 323; Spearman

correlation coefficient 234
Create Graph 233–242
Crosstabs 154–162, 165–169
crosstabulation 34, 152–169, 171–175,
    182–183, 188–189, 255–256, 314–319
cumulative percentage 42, 47, 246–257
Custom Tables 169–198, 293–294, 318

Data Editor see IBM SPSS Statistics Data
    Editor
data entry 73–106
Data View 71–72, 74
dataset 71–73 see also SPSS dataset (.sav) file
        an example of 74–106
demographics 24, 107
dependent variable 16
descriptive research 12–13, 16
descriptive statistics 31, 40–48
Descriptives 150
dialog box 79
dichotomous response 50
dimensions 154

editing graphs 268–303
editing tables 243–267
ethics 18, 20–22
Excel 69–70, 95–98, 304–305
exploratory research 11–13, 19
Explore 150
exporting tables and graphs 303–306

forced choice 50
Frequencies 111–150
frequency table 40–42

Go to Case 88
Go to Variable 88
graphs (charts)
changing axis range; 286–287; changing colours 270–275; creating graphs 111–150, 199–242; editing graphs 268–303

histogram 117–119, 126–127, 133–134, 145–146, 208, 227–229
    add in normal distribution curve 290–292
hypothesis 12, 17, 23, 309–310

IBM SPSS Statistics Data Editor 71–73
IBM SPSS Statistics Viewer 73
importing data 89–106
independent-samples *t* test *see t* test
independent variable 16
inferential statistics 31, 308–330
Insert Cases 88
Insert Variable 88
item 51

label 39–40, 72
levels of measurement 39–48, 170
    nominal 39–42; ordinal; 45–48; scale 42–45
line graphs 205–206, 223–227, 241–242
Likert-type scale 53–54

mean 30–31, 43–45,
median 44–45, 48
missing values 86–87, 114
mode 42–45, 113
multiple choice
    single answer 49–50, 56; multiple answer 51, 59–60

nominal 39–42
normal distribution 290–292
null hypothesis significance testing (NHST) 309–310

operationalisation 38
ordinal 45–48
outcome measures 23, 37–39, 48–55
Output Navigator 73

paired-samples *t* test *see t* test
Pearson correlation coefficient 313, 320–324

percentage 41–42, 58, 113, 159–162, 203–204, 223, 281–282, 293–300
    cumulative percentage 42; valid percentage 41
population 18–20, 308–310
pie chart 113–116, 200–201, 204, 211–214, 275–283
    adding in data labels and percentages 281; changing the order of the slices 279; separating the slices 275–277; 3-D pie chart 278–279
Pivot Table 243–244, 253–267
probability 308–312
    probability value (*p* value) 310

qualitative methods 15
quantitative methods 16–17
question types 48–55

range 45
rank order 45–46, 52
rating scale 47–48, 53
recoding data 92–93, 137–142, 162–164
research
piloting research 29; research methods 14–18; research proposal 22; research questions 9–11, 23; research stages 10

saving your data 78–79, 85
saving your output 122–123, 304
sample 18–22, 308–312
sampling 18–20
    convenience sampling 19; opportunity sampling 19; purposeful sampling 19; random sampling 19–20; snowballing sampling 19; stratified sampling 19–20
semantic differential 53
scale variable 162, 182, 197–198, 319–322
scatterplot 207, 230–33, 286–90, 313, 319, 323 *see also* correlation
    line of best fit 288–290 scale 42–45
significance testing *see* null hypothesis significance testing
Spearman correlation coefficient 324
SPSS dataset (.sav) file 69; 78–79, 89–90, 107–109
SPSS output (.spv) file 110, 122–124
standard deviation 45, 47–48, 117–118
statistics 30–31, 40–48, 308–330
    descriptive statistics 31, 40–48; inferential statistics 31, 308–330

statistical tests 156, 165, 307–330
    alpha (α) 310; analysis of variance
    (ANOVA) 330; assumptions underlying
    statistical tests 309–310; 330; chi-
    square 156, 165, 313–318; degrees of
    freedom 318, 328; p value 310; Pearson
    correlation coefficient 313, 320–324; t
    test 325–330; statistical significance
    309–310
Statistics Viewer *see* IBM SPSS Statistics
    Viewer
string *see* text variable

t test 325–330
tables
    adding colour 264–267; changing the
    decimal places 252–252; changing the
    style 258–264; creating tables
    111–150, 151–198; editing tables
    243–267; moving rows 249–250;
    rotating labels 256–257

text variable 54–55, 59–60,81–82
title
    adding to table 172, 252, 261–262
    adding to a graph 215–216, 299,
    changing the title position on a chart
    301
total 31
transposing rows and columns in a table
    253–255
transposing axes on a graph 297

valid percentage 41–42
Value Labels 75–76
variable 16
    categorical variable 40, 55, 152, 156,
    162–165, 171, 238–240, 313–314;
    dependent variable 16; independent
    variable 16; scale variable 162, 182,
    197–198, 319–322; SPSS variables 73;
    text variable 54–55, 59–60, 81–82
Variable View 71–72, 74

Taylor & Francis eBooks

Helping you to choose the right eBooks for your Library

Add Routledge titles to your library's digital collection today. Taylor and Francis ebooks contains over 50,000 titles in the Humanities, Social Sciences, Behavioural Sciences, Built Environment and Law.

Choose from a range of subject packages or create your own!

Benefits for you

» Free MARC records
» COUNTER-compliant usage statistics
» Flexible purchase and pricing options
» All titles DRM-free.

Benefits for your user

» Off-site, anytime access via Athens or referring URL
» Print or copy pages or chapters
» Full content search
» Bookmark, highlight and annotate text
» Access to thousands of pages of quality research at the click of a button.

eCollections – Choose from over 30 subject eCollections, including:

Archaeology	Language Learning
Architecture	Law
Asian Studies	Literature
Business & Management	Media & Communication
Classical Studies	Middle East Studies
Construction	Music
Creative & Media Arts	Philosophy
Criminology & Criminal Justice	Planning
Economics	Politics
Education	Psychology & Mental Health
Energy	Religion
Engineering	Security
English Language & Linguistics	Social Work
Environment & Sustainability	Sociology
Geography	Sport
Health Studies	Theatre & Performance
History	Tourism, Hospitality & Events

For more information, pricing enquiries or to order a free trial, please contact your local sales team:
www.tandfebooks.com/page/sales

 Routledge Taylor & Francis Group | The home of Routledge books | **www.tandfebooks.com**